CRITICAL THINKING

———◆———

AN INTRODUCTION TO
ANALYTICAL READING AND REASONING

Larry Wright
University of California, Riverside

New York • Oxford
OXFORD UNIVERSITY PRESS
2001

Oxford University Press

Oxford   New York
Athens   Auckland   Bangkok   Bogotá   Buenos Aires   Calcutta
Cape Town   Chennai   Dar es Salaam   Delhi   Florence   Hong Kong   Istanbul
Karachi   Kuala Lumpur   Madrid   Melbourne   Mexico City   Mumbai
Nairobi   Paris   São Paulo   Shanghai   Singapore   Taipei   Tokyo   Toronto   Warsaw

and associated companies in
Berlin   Ibadan

Published by Oxford University Press, Inc.
198 Madison Avenue, New York, New York 10016
http://www.oup-usa.org

Oxford is a trademark of Oxford University Press

Library of Congress Cataloging-in-Publication Data

Wright, Larry, 1937–
    Critical thinking: an introduction to analytical reading and reasoning / Larry Wright.
        p. cm.
    Includes bibliographical references and index.
    ISBN-13: 978-0-19-513033-1

    1. Critical thinking. I. Title.

B809.2.W75 2001
160—dc21   00-051500

Printing number: 9 8

Printed in the United States of America
on acid-free paper

CONTENTS

For my wife

PREFACE

We often reason inarticulately, that is, think things through without saying anything. When I think about tomorrow's errands, I let various possibilities come to mind, imagine tasks in different combinations, and finally make a list of things to do in a certain order. I may then feel quite satisfied that I have adequately thought the matter through, even though I have said nothing at all, and the only words involved in the whole process might be those that end up on the list. The thinking will have been silent and mostly nonverbal.

On the other hand, when we *give reasons* for holding a view or reaching a conclusion, the process is intrinsically articulate. Giving reasons requires language, concepts, and skill with words, not just a simple ability to talk. For two (or more) people to *share* their reasoning requires a kind of reflective articulateness, an ability to express reasoning in a way that is intelligible to a particular audience. This is because our perceptions and judgments about things vary greatly according to our different interests and personal histories. We can bridge these gaps with *words* only if we are aware of them, and if we have some sense of the required structure.

Reasoning is interesting—and worthy of a whole book—only because of the hazards lurking in this endeavor. We often do not see what gap needs bridging, or how big a gap it is, or what sort of bridge will do. That is why so much of this text is devoted to developing our *articulation skills*. Before we can evaluate reasons we must understand them. Before we can give reasons we must know what needs to be said. In both of these tasks, our competence tapers off dramatically as we get away from familiar matters and congenial perceptions. A major task of this text, therefore, will be to raise the reader's level of reflective articulateness, to expand the range within which he or she can give, grasp, and evaluate reasons.

What we call "argument" here is meant to capture everything we make explicit when we give reasons for a view or proposition. So giving and evaluating arguments deeply involve our articulateness. Much of the difficulty we have in reasoning together comes from simply not understanding each other's arguments—from not understanding the significance of the words used to express reasons and the views they support. From the point of view of a reasoning course, this shows up most dramatically in examining examples of reasoning we come across in our reading. We tend naturally to impose our own values—*our* sense of what is important—on the passages we read, and consequently understand only those with whom we sympathize.

This sharply limits the value of public reasoning, but the tendency is very hard to avoid, much harder than you might expect. For understanding what others say always involves fitting it into your general perception of things, and reasoning is no exception. But if we are to expand our ability to reason with others, or to increase the value of reasoning for ourselves, we must learn how to grasp and evaluate arguments we initially find obscure, perverse, and even loathsome. The only resources we have to exploit in this endeavor are a certain level of articulateness (skill with language) and our general understanding of how the world works.

So the project of this text will be to *increase our articulateness* about reasoning and to do so in a way that helps us *bring our understanding to bear* on it. Having this pair of goals, however, requires starting off in what may be a surprising place: with an intense study of reading in general. The first two chapters are devoted completely to sharpening our understanding of the descriptive or expository writing that we read, only some of which has anything directly to do with reasoning. This is both more difficult and more important than you might think. It is difficult because it requires developing a slightly technical vocabulary for talking about our reading and a method for systematically representing its content. It is important because mastering the basic distinctions developed in this way make articulating our reasoning far easier than it otherwise would be. It does this in part by generally enhancing our articulateness about expository writing: giving us the concepts and distinctions required to see that it has a complex structure and to describe it in a useful way. More important, it gives us an easy way to *distinguish reasoning from other kinds of expository relationships* and allows us to see the complex ways those other connections can bear on our reasoning.

The text is divided into two parts. Part 1 contains the two chapters on reading and concludes with a third in which we use our new expository sensitivity to carefully pull the reasoning out of passages and represent it in clear, schematic form. Part 2 concerns the analysis and evaluation of the reasoning thus schematized. Chapter 4 develops a picture of the internal structure of schematized arguments, at first without any attempt to evaluate or criticize them. In analysis, too, we need to practice setting aside our interests and sympathies. For the rest of the text, however, articulation and evaluation will go hand in hand. The concepts we have developed to articulate reasoning will also show how our understanding may be brought to bear in evaluating it. In the end, we should be better equipped to recognize, understand, and talk about arguments. This, in turn, should improve our judgments about them.

ACKNOWLEDGMENTS

This text owes its existence to a long list of teaching assistants who have helped generate the basic reasoning course at UC Riverside. Special mention should go to Jerry Burke, Chris Campolo, Scott Christensen, Zack Fish, and Dale Turner. I am indebted to Maurice Finnocchiaro and Kurt Nutting for thoughtful comments on the entire manuscript.

PART ONE

• • •

PARAPHRASING

CHAPTER 1

THE BARE-BONES PARAPHRASE

················
OVERVIEW
················
In this chapter we develop a technique for summarizing expository passages. Writing out brief paraphrases will help you think about and demonstrate your understanding of what you read. It will also deepen that understanding.

INTRODUCTION

This is primarily a reasoning text. But we will devote the first two chapters simply to paraphrasing various kinds of familiar expository writing. We do this because we will need to look at many examples of reasoning to find out what it is supposed to accomplish, and what makes it better or worse. And the best examples of reasoning to examine are ones people have taken the trouble to write down in articles, columns, letters to the editor, and the like. So our first goal will be to become reflective readers, which is harder than it sounds.

A second, related goal will be to develop a particular way of talking about what we read. It may surprise you, but expressing your understanding of a passage is also very difficult, even for relatively simple passages. Experience has shown that intelligent people will describe in remarkably different ways something they have all read, and they must struggle to reach an agreement about what was said. This is largely due to the way we choose vocabulary to express our understanding. It naturally springs from, and is thus infected with, our own interests and preoccupations on the matter in question. We won't see the point of someone else's description until we grasp their often very different perception of it. So, part of our aim will be to minimize the way our different interests affect the way we describe what's going on in a passage.

Developing a technique for paraphrasing will accomplish both of these goals. It will give us a common vocabulary and some apparatus for communicating our understanding of a passage to each other; *and* it will force us to become more re-

3

flective about what we read. This is why the first two chapters are devoted to developing a way of talking about our reading.

THE CONCEPT OF PARAPHRASE

To paraphrase something is, roughly, to say the same thing in different words. We do this all the time, for example, when somebody fails to understand what we've said. Suppose my phone rings in its peculiar high-tech way while I am searching for a book. I say to the person sitting near the phone, "Would you get that for me?" Not familiar with my phone, or my office, he responds, "Huh?" So I try again: "That's the phone. Could you answer it for me?" I make the same request, in different words, hoping different words will express it more clearly. Because human conversation frequently requires restatement such as this, we all develop rudimentary paraphrasing skills as we become mature users of language.

A more intricate case will begin to raise the issues we need to examine.

CHRIS: "Sure is a good thing I didn't wash the car!"

KAREN: "What do you mean? You never wash your car."

CHRIS: "Of course, that wasn't the point. I was just trying to say it looks like rain."

Here Chris offers "It looks like rain" as a paraphrase of "It's a good thing I didn't wash the car"; that is, he tried to make the same observation using different words. What happened is pretty obvious. He tried to draw Karen's attention to the threatening weather in a cute way, but it didn't work: she missed the point. So he gave up on cute and said it more directly. This example helps us see how deep and subtle our paraphrasing skill is. To understand that Chris said essentially the same thing twice, we must know more than just words and sentences: we must know both something about people and what motivates normal conversation. Ordinary paraphrasing such as this reveals the wide range of social and perceptual skills at work in our use of language. These are the skills we need to think about to make our reading more reflective and our discussing of it more articulate.

Exercise 1.1

would you like a paper or plastic bag for your groceries?

Suppose you're a cashier at a supermarket that offers its customers the choice of paper or plastic bags for their groceries. As you start to bag a customer's groceries you ask, "Paper or plastic?" The customer replies, "Huh?" What paraphrase might you offer in response? (Answer on p. 31.)

Context

Much of our ability to read and paraphrase comes from our sense of context. To understand the conversation in the previous paragraph, for example, we must imagine a setting in which "It's a good thing I didn't wash the car!" might plausibly mean the same thing as "It looks a lot like rain." No problem: Chris might be looking at a menacingly gray sky or perhaps listening to a weather forecast, and the context will make that clear. Obviously, however, those two sentences will not *always* mean the same thing everywhere they are found. Sometimes, "It's a good thing I didn't wash the car" will have nothing at all to do with rain. What words and sentences mean is deeply connected with the circumstances in which they occur. Hence, paraphrases will be delicately sensitive to those circumstances too.

We are normally so good at taking context into account that we scarcely notice our dependence on it. But to develop paraphrasing techniques we will want to pay particular attention to this aspect of our skill. So let us begin by briefly noting two very general features of the way context affects our understanding. First, even though it is always crucial, the role of context is more obvious in some cases than in others. If I said, without explanation,

It needs a twist to the right, next to that greenish space,

you would not have the faintest idea what I was talking about. To understand this sentence, something in the circumstances would have to make clear what a twist was, and what it might accomplish, and how a greenish space could locate it, and perhaps much else as well. The importance of context is plain in a case such as this. But now suppose I said

The cat is on the mat.

This seems perfectly clear without anything further. But that is not because it doesn't need a context. It is just that in this case, unlike the first sentence, we know enough about the subject matter to provide a context on our own. We naturally think of a pet, perhaps curled up on the floor; but we do this only because such domestic settings are a routine part of our lives. With a little effort, however, we can think of ourselves in a different context, say, at a construction site. Here *cat* may mean *bulldozer* so this very same sentence could describe a bulldozer parked on a blasting mat, not a pet curled up on a rug. The setting in which you find it matters to any sentence. It is just easier to see that in some cases than in others.

Second, one of the most general, constantly important features of context is that it provides words with a *motivation*. If we understand what somebody would *want* to say—what would be interesting in the circumstances, or urgent—that will do much to give their words meaning. And sometimes simply following the conversation will be adequate to provide this guidance. Suppose, for example, we have just discovered that the person scheduled to give a talk next week is having major surgery, and someone says,

We'll have to get a new speaker.

We can be pretty sure the sentence concerns the victim of the surgery and the fate of our lecture. So a good paraphrase would be:

We'll have to find somebody else to give the talk.

But think of a different setting. Suppose I'm investigating why the bass sounds so ratty when I turn up the stereo. Here the *very same sentence* will mean something completely different. Perhaps:

> We need to buy another 4-ohm woofer.

In this way very general features of the environment, things we can hardly miss, govern our understanding of what we read and hear. The very same sentence will read one way in a textbook and quite another in a friendly letter; it may have one interpretation in a business meeting, and another in casual conversation, a military briefing, an advertisement, or a subpoena. In our effort to read carefully we will need to reflect constantly on the source and nature of our reading skill; and the most general source is our grasp of context.

Exercise 1.2
....

five what?, five min?

Think of how the following sentences might vary in significance from context to context: "Take five." "Put that on the board." "He made the connection." Give two different paraphrases for each. (Answers on p. 31.)

Exposition

Our work with paraphrasing will confine itself exclusively to expository writing. This is writing designed to describe, explain, illustrate, interpret, or evaluate something. Exposition comprises much of our everyday reading, from textbooks and journalism to instruction manuals and warning labels. But it excludes a lot too. Much of creative writing and poetry, for instance, is not simply descriptive or explanatory. One reason to focus on exposition is that the point of expository writing is usually obvious and mundane (unlike fiction and poetry), and this will allow us to develop specific rules and techniques more easily. It will also serve to direct our thinking toward the upcoming chapters on reasoning, for reasoning is one form exposition can take. The skills and apparatus you acquire here will, with a little work, often be useful in treating more exotic and artistic passages too. But our primary aim will be the treatment of more practical writing, and especially practical reasoning.

READING AND PARAPHRASE

One way to paraphrase a passage is simply to say everything in it over again differently, reproducing every detail in a different way. This will always be possible, given the resources and flexibility of natural language. And it can actually be a valuable thing to do if what you need is intimate familiarity with the passage. Because your work in this course will require this sort of familiarity, let us begin with full-scale paraphrases. Consider the following short newspaper article, which appeared in 1992.

A San Francisco man suffering from cholera apparently caught the disease in the city, the first such locally acquired case since 1970, health officials said. Cholera, which is generally carried through inadequate sewage systems, has resurfaced as a serious public health problem in South America, but locally acquired cases are rare in the United States.

The unidentified man was treated last week and was reportedly recovering at a private hospital. Laboratory tests confirmed that the man's disease was caused by the bacteria *Vibrio cholera*, said Ronald Roberto, an epidemiologist with the California Department of Health.

(The Associated Press)

The content of this article obviously may be expressed in many different ways. The dispatch writer doubtless wrote these sentences because they say what needs to be said about as clearly as possible within the constraints of a short piece. But once we understand it, we can, with a little effort, make up a different article that says the very same thing using different sentences. Simply changing the order of presentation, for instance, and altering the vocabulary would yield something like this:

Laboratory tests confirmed last week that a man from San Francisco was infected with the bacterium *Vibrio cholera*, according to epidemiologist Ronald Roberto of the California Department of Health. The man, whose name was not released, was apparently exposed to the microbe somewhere in the city, making it the first locally acquired case of cholera in 22 years. He is currently recovering in a private hospital.

Cholera, which is rare in the United States, has once again become a public health problem in South America due to deficient sewage management.

To produce a paraphrase like this requires you to check back and forth between the two versions to make sure the second contains everything in the first. At the end of the process you will always have an intimate familiarity with details of the piece that you did not have before. You will be able to answer more detailed questions—such as What sort of hospital is the patient recovering in? or How long ago was the case treated?—about even simple articles such as this one than you would have on first reading. Writing out paraphrases such as this one requires reading a passage with unusually intense attention to its content. We will call this **Type II Reading** to distinguish it from the more casual kind of reading we normally do (which we might call *type I reading*). Type II reading is slow and exhausting, so we will want to do it only when it is called for. The exercises in this book will always call for it.

Exercise 1.3

Choose a passage (suggestion: a paragraph from this text or an exercise passage) that you do not understand well and rewrite it in your own words as we did with the cholera article. Note what you learned about the passage.

The Bare Bones

Type II reading does not always require writing out full-scale paraphrases, although some readers may find it useful at the beginning. Writing much shorter summaries will usually be adequate to encourage deep understanding, and they will be far more valuable to us. We will want our paraphrases to do jobs such as these:

1. To help us think about the issues contained in a passage.
2. To compare our reading of it with that of others.
3. To help us examine its internal structure.
4. To display our understanding of it to an instructor.

And for such purposes we will not want to reproduce every detail of a passage but rather to select the central items of substance and ignore less important details. To do this will still require understanding everything in a passage, but it will not require writing it all down. Short summaries of essential content we will call **Bare-Bones Paraphrases.** The rest of this chapter is devoted to showing how to construct them and use them in talking about what we read.

Our ability to distill the essential content from a passage relies primarily on our reading comprehension. So we can begin to see how it is done by looking at the cholera article, which we should understand pretty well by now. Since the context is journalism, and order of presentation tips off what is important, the bare bones of the article would look something like this.

The first locally acquired case of cholera in 22 years has been reported in San Francisco.

This is the article's main point in simplest terms. Everything else in the article hangs on this spine. With a few abbreviations, it would make a decent headline. So let us adopt this as the basic test for a "shortest possible paraphrase": *would it make a decent headline* for the piece? The procedure would be something like this: think of the piece you are trying to summarize as a newspaper article, and write a brief headline for it. Pare away all sorts of interesting detail to reveal the central kernel of substance:

Rare cholera case reported.

Then, to turn this into a bare-bones paraphrase, you would add whatever detail is required to fashion a grammatical sentence such as the longer one with which we began. That will be your first attempt at a bare-bones paraphrase. It will always be a good beginning, and sometimes your first attempt will be good enough for the task at hand.

Even here you will have some discretion of course. The exact formulation, even of a bare-bones summary, will depend on details of the context: on just what you want the paraphrase to do. Are you explaining the passage to someone who does not understand it, trying to see if you understand it yourself, sketching reminders for future use, displaying your understanding to your instructor, or some combination of these perhaps? Each of these contexts requires a paraphrase that clearly expresses your understanding of a piece. But each will usually require different expression and different words, and will highlight different aspects. A reminder for yourself could be cryptic shorthand, using jargon only you might understand.

SF resident locally infected by b. *Vibrio cholera* (v. rare).

By contrast, a reformulation designed to help somebody baffled by the passage would doubtless be less abbreviated and in plainer words.

It's newsworthy that somebody picked up the cholera bug in San Francisco because it is so rare in the United States.

Exercise 1.4
....

Background: Electricians are working on your neighbor's burglar alarm and the neighbor has apologized in advance for its occasional blaring this morning while they sort out a problem in its circuitry. The alarm goes off, disturbing your conversation with someone. You say, "Try to ignore that; they're doing some repairs on the alarm." Rephrase this for the following audiences: (a) someone who has never heard a burglar alarm; (b) someone you know feels terrible because they once ignored a neighbor's burglar alarm while irreplaceable valuables were stolen; (c) a member of your household for whom this is the sixth time the same troublesome alarm has blared recently during repair work. (Answers on p. 31.)

This text presents a very special context, of course. Recall that our work on paraphrase has two clear motivations: to make our reading more reflective, and to develop a clear way to express our understanding of it. The second of these always entails careful attention to the requirements of your audience; and your audience here is the instructor in this course. You will always want to design your paraphrases to *display your understanding of a passage* to your instructor. The rest of this chapter is devoted to providing some guidance in doing this.

TECHNIQUE AND VOCABULARY

The first thing we need is a handy way to talk about the parts of a passage we omit from a bare-bones summary of it. That is, we will want descriptive names for the kind of detail that can be left out of its paraphrase once we understand it. In the cholera article, for instance, the paraphrase we gave above does not mention the higher incidence of the disease in South America or the conditions of its propagation. What might we call these things? "Useful background" sounds right. These items help us see why the case is comparatively rare; but the point of the article is mainly to report the rare case, so they will be relegated to background

and not included. This is also true of the place of occurrence and physician responsible for the diagnosis: these are details of the context in which the passage
is set but not part of its substance.

Padding

Let us then begin the list of things to suppress in writing bare-bones paraphrases
with categories such as "background" and "setting." These may at first be hard
to distinguish. That won't matter. These terms are just to guide your eye in spot-
ting things to omit, so the category is secondary. Distinguishing among various
kinds of "padding" will become more natural as we examine more cases. Another
example will help us add to the list.

> Climatologists say early signs of El Niño, an ocean warming condition that could
> spawn tremendous storms, have all but disappeared. "At this point, it looks rather
> unlikely that we'll get anything this year," said Eugene Rasmusson of the federal
> Climate Analysis Center in Maryland. "It's not out of the question," he said, "but
> unusually dramatic changes in the ocean would have to take place this month for
> an El Niño to occur this year."
>   An El Niño is an abnormal temperature pattern in the pacific ocean that oc-
> curs every few years. Its effects last about two years.

To develop a paraphrase, let us try the headline trick again. Read the piece, then
look away for a few seconds, thinking about what it said, and finally blurt out a
brief headline. Something like "No El Niño" sounds right. Flesh it out into a sentence and you get a bare-bones paraphrase:

El Niño is unlikely this year.

Let us take this as the paraphrase and look through the article to see what we've
left out. First, much of the article consists of direct quotations from a federal cli-
matologist; but since we merely want a summary of *what* was said, not how or
by whom, we do not use the quotations and we omit their source.[1] Second, the
main point is stated three times, in slightly different terms, in the first three sentences. We merely want the point, so we omit the repetition. Third, the next to
last sentence essentially defines the term *El Niño*; and because we merely want to
express our understanding, not say *how* we reached it, helpful additions such as
this will be omitted from a bare-bones paraphrase as well. Finally, as we did in
the cholera article, we omit useful background such as that offered in the last sentence and the middle part of the first sentence. These help us understand why El
Niño's likelihood might be of interest, but the point of the piece is simply the
(low) likelihood. So we can add to our list of categories descriptive terms such as
repetition, illustration, and *definition.*

---

1. Sometimes speakers will appear in paraphrases, but that requires special circumstances. We will shortly examine a case in which the author talks about himself; so he becomes part of the topic. But normally an author is not part of the substance of a passage.

Exercise 1.5

Give (i) a headline and (ii) a bare-bones paraphrase for the following two articles. (Answers on p. 31.)

a. NEW YORK—Astronomers have found an unprecedented collection of stars that emit very fast bursts of energy, a discovery that may help in studying the formation of galaxies. Researchers said they found 10 "millisecond pulsars" in a single cluster of other stars, almost doubling the known number of the objects.

Pulsars are dense stars that appear to emit energy in very regularly spaced bursts. In fact, they are thought to send out the energy in a constant beam that sweeps across the sky as the star rotates, like light from a light-house. An Earth-bound observer detects a burst every time a beam crosses Earth. Millisecond pulsars appear to "blink" at intervals measured in thousandths of a second.

The 10 new millisecond pulsars, which emit radio waves, were found in a star cluster called 47 Tucanae. A single millisecond pulsar had been detected in this cluster before, scientists from Australia, Britain, and Italy said.

(The Associated Press)

b. PARIS—The French say that the art of eating and drinking is their nation's greatest achievement—above even the TGV, a high-speed train, which comes second. New York businessmen may be content to shovel down a burger and slurp up some frozen yoghurt. In London they may wash down a ploughman's with a pint or two. But in Paris, a decent business lunch has always been a sort of gustatory *tricolore* requiring three courses, three sorts of alcohol, and three hours.

No longer. There are disturbing signs of moderation in Paris. According to Bernard Boutboul, head of Gira Sic Conseil, a Paris-based consultancy specialising in the restaurant trade, the number of business meals at restaurants fell from around 48m in 1980 to 19m in 1995. The French now spend three times as much on hamburgers as they do in the smart businessmen's establishments honored with one or more stars by the compilers of Michelin's famous guide.

With the decline in number has come a decline in splendour. The average bill for a business lunch as fallen by 15-20% in real terms since 1985 to a mere FFr250 ($45) per person. Managers these days are mindful of their waists, and tend to have only two courses. Meat drenched in rich sauces is giving way to grilled fish. Gone are the aperitif and liqueur. Lunch partners eye each other guiltily before ordering half a bottle of wine camouflaged by a couple of bottles of mineral water. Stripped of its finery, the Parisian business lunch is now almost rushed, over in a mere hour and three-quarters.

Why the change? Business people say that they are worried about appearing too ostentatious. Lunching a client in style might create a spendthrift impression, as well as irritating subordinates chained to their desks. Many managers have been told by budget-conscious bosses to keep the restaurant bills down.

Some businessmen, moreover, are worried that too many good meals might attract the beady eye of the magistrate. Some of France's most famous managers, including Pierre Suard, former head of Alcatel Alsthom, a telecoms company, have been investigated for charging personal benefits to the company. Nowadays, even in Paris, there is no such thing as a free *déjeuner*.

(From *The Economist* of London)

Let us adopt the word *padding* to stand for all these things we omit from a proper bare-bones paraphrase. Calling something *padding* does not mean it is unimportant to the passage. Background, definitions, and repetition can be indispensable in our understanding a piece well enough to paraphrase it. Such things are omitted only as unnecessary to *expressing* that understanding, once it is understood. (For convenience "bare-bones" will usually be dropped from the phrase "bare-bones paraphrase" in what follows. From now on, when we speak of paraphrases, we will mean bare-bones paraphrases.)

A letter to *The Economist* illustrates several kinds of padding.

Sir—

In your April 13 issue you published an article called "Coquilles St Jacques". Mentioning the possible visit of President Jacques Chirac to the Académie Française, you say: "It was the first time a French president would have honoured a new member since Mr Mitterrand celebrated the induction of Marguerite Yourcenar as the academy's first female 'immortal' in 1981." I am sorry to have to correct this "coquille". Mme Yourcenar was introduced on March 6th 1980. I was then president of France, and I attended, with great pleasure, her inauguration speech.

V. Giscard d'Estaing
Paris

This letter too has a single point: to correct an earlier story that slighted the letter's writer. The bare bones would look something like this.

The French president who attended Mme. Yourcenar's induction into the French Academy was d'Estaing, not Mitterrand, as claimed in *The Economist*.

As letters to editors often do, this one begins with some background that allows the reader to appreciate the significance of the substantive points to follow. Without it we would not understand why d'Estaing had roused himself to write the letter. But it is just background, so we omit it from the paraphrase. Other background helps with the substance itself: that the writer was president of France at the time of Mme. Yourcenar's induction. All of this is padding of a familiar sort. But two other items omitted from the paraphrase do not fit any of our categories. One is the date of the event. This is actually part of the substance, but counts as excessive detail for a bare-bones paraphrase. Let us call it *dispensable detail*. In more complicated passages we will always leave out some of the substance when it goes past a certain level of detail, so this will be a constantly useful category. And, finally, we need another heading to cover the "I am sorry . . ." sentence, and the "with great pleasure" gesture. Let us call them *frills*. Polite asides such as this, together with humor and sarcasm, will decorate much public writing. We will group them all under the category of *frills*.

All this may be summarized in the following list of seven padding categories (with key terms emphasized). The first three categories might be thought of as different kinds of background and the rest as different kinds of detail to omit. We split them into seven specific types simply to help you recognize them.

Categories of Padding
1. **Setting:** story location, source, and so on (when these are incidental, not part of point)
2. *Substantive **Background** (things the reader may not know about the substance of the passage that aid in understanding it or its significance)
3. **Definition** of terms (linguistic background)
4. ***Dispensable Detail** (details of substance beyond what is needed in a bare-bones paraphrase)
5. **Restatement** of substance
6. **Illustration** (a variation on restatement) *examples*
7. **Frills** (humor, polite asides, and so on)[2]

The point of these categories is simply to help you identify things to be left out of a paraphrase when the substance is not simply obvious. By guiding your eye in this way they will help you identify the parts of a passage that go in the paraphrase, eliminating other parts from consideration. Do not think of these categories as strict or absolute. Some padding will fall on a borderline between categories, and other sorts will fall easily into more than one. In such cases you will have identified padding—something to omit from the paraphrase—even though its classification will be difficult. These headings are meant to be rough-and-ready practical tools. Use them in that spirit. The following passages illustrate several of the headings. See if you can identify the padding before reading the discussion below each passage.

Background

From an environmental perspective, our problems became acute only within the last 150 years—a geological wink of an eye. They began during the industrial revolution, when business harnessed the earth's resources and improved the quality of our lives. Now, as the damage is spiraling out of control, the same force responsible for the damage, business, is the only social force powerful enough to undo the harm.

(*Vegetarian Times*, 9.96)

The bare-bones paraphrase of this article will concern the role of business in creating and cleaning up pollution. The historical observations in the first sentence and most of the second will not be part of that paraphrase. They will be omitted as background.

---

2. The two asterisked categories will be heavily dependent on context: how much detail to put in the paraphrase will depend on immediate needs and purposes (typically the audience's needs and the paraphraser's purposes). Guidance in handling the more difficult cases will be provided as we go.

Exercise 1.6

(a) Identify the background padding in the French Business Lunch article of Exercise 1.5 (b) Identify the background padding in the following article. (Answers on p. 31.)

> Although they broke when the high water surged, nearly all of the Central Valley levees that collapsed in recent floods had been given consistently high marks by state inspectors, the San Francisco Examiner reported Saturday. According to state inspection reports, only 10 levees in California's 6,000-mile network of dikes and levees were described as poorly maintained in 1994, the last year for which reports were available. Of those problematic levee systems, only one, near the Tehama County town of Vina, failed.
>
> Many of the state's levees are made of sand and dirt. Under prolonged contact with high water, even the best-built and best-maintained dirt levees can become saturated and give way, said Jason Fanselau, spokesman for the U.S. Army Corps of Engineers.
>
> (*The Associated Press*)

Illustration

Most birds of the foothills are omnivores. It is a disadvantage to be too specialized, because favored food is not always abundant. For example, acorns are not available year-round, nor are they common every year. When the acorn store has been exhausted, as in the summer, animals turn to other forms of food—particularly insects, which are the most abundant animals in the foothills.

(Schoenherr, *A Natural History of California*)

In this passage, the substance is all found at the beginning. As soon as you see the words "for example" at the start of the third sentence you should suspect that what follows will fall in the padding category "Illustration." And so it does: nothing about acorns or insects will be part of the bare-bones paraphrase.

Exercise 1.7

Describe the illustration padding in the assault gun article on p. 71. (Answer on p. 31.)

Background and Setting

Estrogen replacement therapy is known to reduce the risk of death by heart attack in post-menopausal women by about 50 percent, but scientists were puzzled about how estrogen produced this dramatic protective effect. Reporting in the medical journal *Circulation*, a team of Johns Hopkins University researchers said they found the answer: Estrogen increases blood flow to the heart, including diseased hearts. A study of post-menopausal women showed that almost all of them had an average 23 percent increase of blood to the heart after receiving an intravenous dose of estrogen, said Dr. Stemen Reis. Estrogen also appeared to increase blood flow through the arteries that were already partly narrowed from heart disease, he said.

(The Associated Press)

In this article the main substance is to be found about halfway through the paragraph. The opening sentence provides helpful background, raising the question to be addressed by the study motivating the article. But we would also omit from a paraphrase the names of the journal, the university, and the researcher involved. These would not fall in the category "background," but rather "setting."

Exercise 1.8

(a) What kind of padding is the bacterium omitted from the paraphrase of the cholera article? (b) Identify and characterize all the padding in the millisecond pulsar article in Exercise 1.5. (Answers on p. 31.)

Describing the Bare Bones

Next we must decide how to express the paraphrase itself. That is, we must work out how to describe the main substance of a passage after we find and eliminate the padding. This may sound easy: just write down what's left. But what is left are the author's words, stripped of their context (padding, surroundings) and put to a different use (summary and display). Given what we already know about context, you can be reasonably sure those words will not be the best choice to express what you want to say. They may even say something else entirely in the context of a paraphrase. We usually need new words, and this raises a host of problems.

Again you might say: "New words? No problem. Just look at the examples we've paraphrased so far. They use new words, and they're easy!" But experience in courses such as this demonstrates over and over that it is much harder than it looks. What tricks us is that we all have some paraphrasing skill, an ability to rephrase things. But that ability, which we develop naturally in everyday living, is almost exclusively in paraphrasing *ourselves* ("Would you get that for me?"), not what others say. To paraphrase somebody else requires you to become as familiar with what they are trying to say as you would be with something of your own ("That's the phone. Would you answer it for me?"). That means getting inside a point of view that is not your own, that you may not care about, and may even despise. This is what turns out to take effort. And it benefits from guidance and practice.

Exercise 1.9

Suppose someone said to you, "You don't want to come in here; we've had a little accident." Give a paraphrase of "we've had a little accident" in each of several different contexts in which it would be cautioning you against different things. (Answer on p. 32.)

HUMAN UNDERSTANDING

The Point of Paraphrase: Recovering a Perception

When someone asks you to tell them about a passage they will of course not always want a simple summary of it. Instead of a paraphrase, they may want a criticism of it or of the way it is written, or an implication you might draw about its author. They may wish to know whether you grasp its significance for some larger issue outside the passage, or a subtle irony in its vocabulary. But this is not what we care about here. Our aim will simply be to uncover the author's intent as best we can, to find out what he or she was trying to convey.[3] So it will be useful to have a model of how to think of a passage in the right sort of way, to get us to try as hard as possible to uncover the author's perception. And for this we need a context in which the reader's motivation to do this is high. So perhaps the best example would be something like bomb-dismantling instructions.

Suppose you have the job of dismantling an old 500-pound bomb that a French farmer has found under his milking stall. You have a set of instructions that has been successfully used on this kind of bomb for the past 50 years. As you work your way into the detonating mechanism, you read:

> In removing the lead from terminal e, be careful not to ground it against the case.

Your obvious interest is to find the intended interpretation *exactly* before proceeding. For instance, does "lead" refer to a piece of wire (pronounced leed) or a glop of soft metal (pronounced led); and just what counts as grounding? The proper understanding might be expressed in a paraphrase: "In disconnecting this little green wire from its post, you must avoid contact between its exposed metal end and the outside of the bomb." But this would be the right paraphrase only if it accurately rendered the intent of the passage. You will proceed only after you are confident that you have shared the author's perception of the proper procedure.

Much of our expository reading is similar to this, though with lower stakes. When we study the instructions that came with the VCR or the label on a bottle of medicine, our motive is education, to find something out. And if we do find it out, it is because we came to share the author's thought. It works this way simply because most articles, textbooks, warning labels, manuals, and the like are written in a sincere and largely competent attempt to provide us a thought to share.

Empathy: The Human Roots of Reading

Recall that when we first discussed context, the most important thing we learned from it was an author's motivation. This was just a hint of a much larger point.

---

3. Obviously we will not always be able to figure out what the author had in mind. And sometimes a piece will have been composed by several people, or over a period of time, and we will have to think in terms of a composite author or a virtual author. None of these possibilities raises special problems in the everyday examples we will examine.

When we read (or listen to conversation), our understanding of what is said always rests heavily on our ability to appreciate the author as a human being, with human perceptions and interests. It is not that he or she cannot have unusual interests or special perceptions, but our sense of normalcy is the point of departure, what we must take for granted unless we are tipped off to something exotic. When we understand "The cat is on the mat" one way at home and another at a construction site, it is not because we cannot talk of bulldozers in the living room and pets at work. We can, of course, but we would have to alert our audience to what was going on. We read the same words differently in different settings in large part because what people care about changes with the circumstances.

To appreciate how deeply our sense of human interest penetrates our reading, consider the following simple observation:

> The sunset was beautiful this evening.

We naturally understand that these words concern the colors on the western horizon, in one way or another. And we do this because we understand the sort of thing people find entertaining in an evening sky. We do not for a moment think the author might instead be talking about the particular angle the horizon forms with the sun's axis of rotation.

> What a lovely angle!

We do not give this a moment's thought simply because we know people do not tend to notice this angle, and would not naturally think of it as attractive or ugly if they did. Another kind of creature with different perceptions and preoccupations might well be fascinated by the seasonal variations of this angle. But we humans are not, so we naturally do not read the words this way.

We may of course imagine circumstances in which ordinary earthlings might naturally think the angle of the solar axis was the most beautiful thing about a particular sunset. Some astronomers have been waiting days for a special alignment, say, and are immensely relieved when it finally arrives: "What a beautiful sunset!" But this *is* a special circumstance, and it must be spelled out if we are to see that the words have this unusual significance. Visitors from another galaxy, on the other hand, may be naturally attuned to the angle of the sun's axis but not even notice cloud colors. They would require special directions—perhaps special instruments—to understand the sentence the way we do.

To this extent, reading and writing are *social* skills. To have any idea how their words will be understood, writers must know quite a lot about the perceptions and expectations of their audience. Likewise, to find the intended interpretation a reader must grasp the writer's perception of many things, including context and audience. Understanding depends on mutual empathy, on reader and writer appreciating each other's task. Such empathy is a complicated and subtle skill that develops gradually, as we mature, through our social interactions. But we all do develop it to some degree, and it is what allows communication to be effortless, when it is effortless. It also helps when the going gets rough: to interpret an obscure passage we can "put ourselves in the author's shoes" and ask "What might somebody have had in mind here?"[4]

Exercise 1.10
....

Rewrite the following two passages to eliminate the slightly scandalous ambiguity. Note how much understanding of people—especially writers—you must use to do this.

a. (Charity announcement:) The ladies of the church have cast off clothes of every kind and they can be seen in the church basement on Friday afternoon.

b. (Drama summary:) The plot is less than the sum of its parts. It concerns an unconventional family—a free-spirited mother and her three young-adult children—that visits an English seaside resort. There they meet a young dentist, who falls in love with the older daughter, his grumpy landlord, the mother's nervous solicitor, the friendly waiter and a stuffy barrister.

(Suggestions on p. 32)

A little empathy will allow us to begin analyzing passages of greater complexity.

> Editor,
> The recent flap about speed limits raises again the whole problem of traffic control on our neighborhood streets. Kirby Dekalb mentioned the traffic on Walnut (letters, August 6), but a greater problem exists on Richmond avenue at First street.
> Richmond is a major route for youngsters on their way to Hamilton Elementary School, and since the mall opened the traffic on First has gotten very heavy. It is now simply too dangerous to allow children to cross either street on their own. A four-way stop is clearly called for. I have counted as many as one hundred twenty cars passing that intersection in a fifteen minute period.
> It's an accident waiting to happen; it would be inexcusable to wait for a tragedy before doing something about this.
>
> Cathleen Barney
> New Bethany

What we know about human concerns tells us that the point of this letter is to reveal the existence of a dangerous condition, and make a recommendation to deal with it. This is just the sort of thing that would motivate somebody to write a letter in such a context. The dangerous condition concerns cars and kids, and the recommendation is a stop sign, so the simplest summary of the bare bones would be something like this:

---

4. When we know something about the author, as we often do from other parts of the passage, this device is even more powerful. For we may then ask "What would somebody like *this* have had in mind here?"

We should make First and Richmond a four-way stop because the heavy traffic is a danger to children crossing there on the way to school.

Exercise 1.11
....

Describe three different kinds of padding omitted from the paraphrase of this letter. (Answer on p. 32.)

SUBTLER ISSUES

Filling in Blanks: Understanding More Than Is Said

In addition to an understanding of people and their interests, reading also requires a lot of knowledge about the world. Sentences about an unfamiliar subject might as well be written in a foreign language ("It needs a twist to the right next to that greenish space"). But when the topic is commonplace, or something with which we are particularly familiar, we may understand more than is actually put into words.

A useful illustration of this can be found in the humorous fillers scattered throughout *The New Yorker* magazine to use up space at the end of articles. In these fillers the editors will sometimes print butchered passages verbatim from other publications and then pretend to take them seriously. Our normal reading skill and familiarity with the world make the pretense obvious, and that provides the humor, such as it is. The following piece, for instance, was found in the *Schenectady Gazette*.

> Several types of fences and other barriers surround the exterior of the building. Guards are on duty at all times, bark loudly to warn people to move away from a fence and fire warning shots if the first command is disobeyed.

The editors then added that shots might also be fired if the barking guards elicited giggles.

The humor rests on our understanding that the guards' dogs were somehow omitted in editing, inadvertently making the guards themselves look silly (and perhaps dangerously capricious). But notice how much the editors take for granted in thinking we will understand this. For instance, we would have to have the concept of a guard dog, which requires that we know some basic facts about dogs (size, sounds, behavior, etc.), as well as how people react to them in various circumstances (fear, reasonable concern for safety); we would have to understand our occasional interest in isolating property from general public access, and how guards and fences might do this. They also assume we know that people as a rule do not bark, and, if they did, it is the sort of thing we would naturally find amusing. Were the world very different in any of these respects—if people never cared what others did with anything, for instance, or if nobody ever disturbed things left out in the open, or if, on the other hand, spies and vandals developed overnight from spores wafting about in the atmosphere—talk of guards and fences and dogs would not make any sense, or, at least, would make very different sense than it does here. The communication, and the humor, work only because we may be relied on to understand all these things.

Our paraphrases constantly depend on our grasp of things such as this. Sometimes it just allows us to reveal obvious implications, as in the following case.

Editor—

If you think Proposition 14 on the June ballot is the answer to school overcrowding, you simply don't understand our state bureaucracy. Prop. 14 contains no guarantee whatever that the funds it generates will be used to reduce class size; the money will just go into a general fund and disappear without a trace, like so many of our tax dollars.

Cal Scepti
Orange

This is pretty clearly an argument against Proposition 14: a reason to think it should be defeated. But this much is so obvious the author felt no need to actually say "So Proposition 14 is a bad idea," or "Don't vote for it," even though that's the point. In writing out the bare bones of a passage such as this, however, we must say explicitly what an author can simply imply when it is part of the main point. So the paraphrase would be something like this:

We should not enact proposition 14 because it does not specifically target its funds for the reduction of class size.

Exercise 1.12

The main point of the following passage seems to be a recommendation that is never explicitly stated in the passage. What is it? (Answer on p. 32.)

We tend to patronize the poor by preaching to them about birth control: though poverty-stricken parents with four, five, or six children are the most publicized aspect of population growth, they are by no means the most important numerical aspect of the problem. As a matter of simple arithmetic, the four-fifths of the nation's families who earn more than the poverty-line income and who can afford two, three, or four children, produce a greater total of children than the one poor couple out of five who may have six youngsters.
[From Lilienthal, D., "300,000,000 Americans Would Be Wrong," in *Man and Environment*, A. H. Hawley, ed. (New York: New Directions, 1975)]

But the effect of our general understanding of things will sometimes be more subtle than this.

Editor—

Peter Lippe complains about your editorials in the Sunday letters section. He should visit Russia. If we continue the way we are going, we will have the same problems they do, only worse. The media should be less neutral, not more so.

Albert Ross
Paltz

If we try to paraphrase this, without any further context, about the best we could do would be something like this:

> America looks set to have the same kind of difficulties lately encountered by Russia, and journalists might help avoid them if they were just more courageous.

The problem is that we can be pretty sure this does not capture what the author thought he was saying. Why is that? Because of what we know about people and the world. For one thing, anybody concerned enough to write a letter to a newspaper would have to be alarmed about something more exciting than the bland abstraction we came up with in this paraphrase. All sorts of parallels may be found in the problems of two large countries. Ross must have something particular in mind, and something he takes to be urgent. But what it is cannot be found in what he wrote, at least not by the average reader. Another thing we know is that people can get so wrapped up in their concerns that they think all sensible people must share at least their basic picture of what's going on in the world; so they think they can be understood without having to spell things out that are absolutely obvious to them. And we know that different people find very different things obvious. Many things such as this go into our realization that we have not yet shared this author's perception.

So if asked to paraphrase this letter, without knowing any more than we do, we might simply say we can't do it. We know enough to know that we don't yet get the point. We need more words or more context. If forced to paraphrase (if the instructor says to do the best you can, for instance), we could offer the vague summary given above. But it would be worth adding that the writer surely meant to say more than this, and evidently thought his particular concerns would be more obvious than they are.

When writing is clear and sensitive to its audience, the work done by a reader's background knowledge seldom draws any attention. For the talent of a good writer is to exploit a reader's understanding *effortlessly*, so that the toil of reading does not distract us from the point of the passage itself. Only when there is something wrong with the writing or the editing—or when we try reading something that is over our heads—do we become acutely aware of how dependent our ability to read is on what we know. This also is why you as an author must always think about your audience in order to be understood.

Presupposition: What Goes without Saying

In each of the two examples just examined, the author of a passage was taking for granted something that was part of its paraphrase. In the first case (Prop. 14) it was a clear implication, which we could dig out and express; in the second (Russia) it was something we needed for the paraphrase, but had inadequate context to find. Most of what an author takes for granted is not like this, however. Most is simply background we need to follow the words, not anything that we would actually write down in a paraphrase. To understand *The New Yorker* piece, for instance, we had to know an enormous amount about dogs and guards and property and people's interests and much else, only a tiny fraction of which would we mention in explaining the humor. Most of it is simply *presupposed*. We don't mention it because we don't have to, of course. But it's worth noting that communication would be impossible if we had to mention it all, because there's an unlimited amount of it. For reading to be possible at all, most of what a writer takes for granted must go without saying.

Part of this silent background is what changes when context changes. Our skill in following this change is one of the secrets of successful communication, and it is important to keep in mind as we paraphrase. Consider a familiar sentence such as "You may withdraw money from this account at any time." Suppose you are talking with a bank officer about depositing money in a savings account. The officer tells you the bank will give you especially good interest rates if you agree to leave your money on deposit for a certain time, so the bank may use it without worrying about your needing it. The longer you agree to leave it, the higher the rate; but if you want the money early, you will sacrifice interest. The bank also has regular savings accounts, with no such condition, however. And then the officer adds, "You may withdraw money from this account at any time." In this context the sentence quoted may be paraphrased "In a regular savings account, you do not have to keep your money on deposit for a certain length of time to avoid a penalty." Look for a moment at the sorts of things you may be quite properly taking for granted in understanding this sentence. You understand perfectly well that to withdraw funds you must have money in the account, and you must wait your turn in line, and the bank must be open for business, and a nuclear war can't have obliterated the planet. These things, and much else, go without saying.

If we change the circumstances slightly, however, we can substantially change the sense of the sentence, and, as a result, change the list of things that go without saying. Suppose you are discussing checking rather than savings, and the topic is not interest rates but rather overdraft protection and remote access. Then the very same sentence ("You may withdraw money from this account at any time") will mean something else (Paraphrase: "This account is accessible at ATMs, and overdrafts will be treated as a loan"). Here what goes without saying is significantly different. Unlike the previous case, you do not have to have money in the account and the bank does not have to be open. But now things taken for granted include that you know how to use an ATM, that you remember your identification number, and that the machine is not broken or out of cash. Only if all this holds can you get your money at any time. What goes without saying will sometimes vary not only from one paragraph to another but also from one part of a paragraph to another.

We normally follow these changes effortlessly in familiar contexts. But when we paraphrase we have to think about things we normally do automatically. And this involves an unsuspected hazard. Our skill is so subtle and difficult to describe that in struggling to think about it, we may lose our confidence in it. We may come to think we *can't* be doing anything so complicated. Then we are in danger of actually damaging the skill itself.[5] The important thing for us to real-ize is simply that we do have this complex skill, and to try to hold onto it as we analyze what it does. Being alive to the difficulty should help.

Exercise 1.13
....

Which of the following is presupposed in the levee article in Exercise 1.6? (a) California's levees are inspected every year. (b) California should replace its dirt and sand levees with stronger ones. (c) Several levees failed in a recent flood. (d) Only one levee with low marks failed. (e) California's levee inspec-tion is lax. (Answer on p. 32.)

TWO PRINCIPLES OF PARAPHRASING

Implied Significance: Understanding Connections

Let us return to the most important theme of this chapter: that our reading, and hence our paraphrasing, is guided by human considerations, by our understand-ing of people. One way to express this guidance is to always look for significance. Never be satisfied with a trivial paraphrase when one of some human significance is available. We understand what we read by fitting the pieces of a passage into a significant pattern. Writers always count on our doing this, and sometimes we can understand a poorly constructed passage by doing it consciously.

Editor—
Your letters (Open Forum, September 20) on an airport in Moreno Valley are for the birds—I am with Judy Sanchez and Bill Churry.
We do not need it. We have had our homes in Sunnymead since 1959. We always knew this would happen. We already have too many homes and apartments. Let's put a stop to it. And do it now!

Mrs. Adam Holtz

This letter might at first appear to be a collection of very loosely connected sen-tences, united only in unfocused hysteria. But if we try to fit them into a pattern of human concern, we can see that the "it" that we "do not need" and to which Mrs.

---

5. Losing a skill as a result of thinking about it too much is sometimes called the "cen-tipede effect." The story is that a centipede was walking along one day, minding its own business, when it happened on a philosopher, who expressed puzzlement over how it was able to coordinate all those legs and walk in such an orderly and efficient manner. In par-ticular, the philosopher wondered how the myriapod knew which leg to start with: was it the same one each time, or was it the one that would have been next when it last was walk-ing, or did it choose in some other way? The centipede found it could answer none of these questions, and became so puzzled by them that, when he next tried to walk, he could not do it, and remained paralyzed for the rest of his considerably shortened life.

Holtz is trying to "put a stop" is clearly the airport mentioned at the beginning. And as soon as we see this, the significance of mentioning "too many homes and apartments" becomes clear too. An airport might well encourage local development, so pointing out that we have too many homes already would be a way to *object* to building or expanding an airport. So the point of the letter might be simply:

> An airport in the Moreno Valley is a bad idea because it would lead to overdevelopment.

And if we look back at the letter, this is a pretty reasonable guess at what Mrs. Holtz was trying to say. But we had to "put ourselves in her place" and empathize with her concerns to see this.

This case illustrates the way our understanding and use of language is dominated by the **Principle of Implied Significance.** Put generally, the principle holds that whenever we say something we inevitably imply that it is significant, that it has been selected *for some reason* from among the infinitude of things we might have said. We earlier saw that understanding a sentence might depend on surmising a speaker's motive from the context. This principle serves to remind us that we always do this to some extent. It is no accident that we talk of the *meaning* of what somebody says: "meaning" is just another word for significance.

The presumption of significance is part of the mutual empathy that allows communication among us; it is part of taking an author seriously. If you say "the cabinet is heavy" we naturally look to the context for an indication of the sort of weight you might be talking about here: Too much to lift? Enough to hold down the rug? Would it hurt if dropped on your foot? Enough to be a weapon? In different circumstances, different weights would count as heavy. And we would normally not even consider the possibility that you meant to say the cabinet merely *had some weight or other*, because that goes without saying. We would not insult you by reading it that way.

One kind of humor derives from pointedly violating the presumption of significance, and what amuses us is the misbegotten implication. A famous story goes as follows:

> After overlooking his deck officer's misbehavior for some time a ship's captain finally decided to make a formal record of it and entered into the ship's log, "The first mate was drunk last night." Next day, the mate, offended at finding his drinking made public in this way, settled on devious retaliation. He made his own entry in the log: "The Captain was sober last night."

This can be retaliation only if the entry is taken to be significant, that is, if we conclude that the captain's sobriety does not go without saying. The humor lies in our suspicion that the entry is not significant, and that the mate would defend it on the fraudulent ground that mere truth is good enough reason to say something.

Let us apply all this to our reading of a difficult passage.

> El Monte—Vandalism caused the derailment early yesterday of part of a mile-long freight train causing injuries to the engineer and brakeman, a Southern Pacific spokesman said. "The information that we have right now is that the cause of the accident was vandalism," spokesman Tony Adams said. "Our investiga-

tion found what is called a fair, a rail anchor, wedged into the switch mechanism
. . . It didn't get there naturally."

The westbound diesel, the "Memphis Blue Streak," was hauling 81 cars from Ten-
nessee to Los Angeles when it derailed around 3:37 a.m. just east of Santa Anita
Avenue, causing damage "well in excess of $1 million," Adams said. The engi-
neer and the brakeman were in the lead engine that was 80 percent destroyed in
the derailment 15 miles east of downtown Los Angeles. Both men were hospitalized. "The engine cab itself was crushed," Adams said, noting that the men had
to be cut out of the cab.

(The Associated Press)

If we did not have all this context, the spokesman's saying that the fair "didn't get
there naturally" would not be very informative: we would not know just how to
take it. Nature does funny things. But the context makes it clear that he is contrasting "naturally" with "vandalism," as a way the fair could have gotten in the switch.
Someone might have put it there, or . . . what? The "natural" possibility in the circumstances is of course that it got there as a *result* of the wreck: flying bits of roadbed
are characteristic of trainwrecks. So we can see that he is saying something quite
definite, that in his judgment, getting the fair in the switch required human inter-
vention. It could not have just fallen there in the chaos of the event. So the vandalism is being *inferred* and the substance of the passage will include the reasoning:

> A trainwreck near Los Angeles yesterday, which injured 2 crew members,
> was likely due to vandals, because a rail anchor was found suspiciously
> wedged in the switch that derailed it.

Saying that the fair was "suspiciously" wedged efficiently captures the spokesman's judgment.

SUMMARY

When we read for content, we always look for aspects of the context that make
what is said *significant*.

Exercise 1.14

Suppose a friend says, "You just paid more for that engine repair than the whole
car is worth!" On the surface, this looks like a simple arithmetic fact: it's true if
the book value of the car is less than the bill I just paid. However, the significance of your friend's saying this is certainly more than just this subtraction.
Paraphrase the sentence to display its likely significance. (Answer on p. 32.)

The Principle of Charity

A powerful tool is always a hazard to the unwary. Unless we keep our wits about
us the social perception that makes communication work so well *most* of the time
can also betray us. For on difficult or controversial topics, different people's sense

of what is significant will differ markedly. A reader's view of a subject may then be so different from an author's view that comprehension is nearly impossible. The social component of communication plays havoc with our understanding in areas of great controversy or uncommon subtlety. Which is to say that a failure of empathy haunts all the most valuable texts and contexts. Understanding is most difficult and least likely in just those cases in which reading has the most to offer. The question for us, then, is how we as readers can recognize and compensate for this difficulty—to develop the perception necessary to follow a text when the going gets rough.

The underlying principle is, as always, to find the most plausible reading. But when we despise a text, or find it contemptible, or otherwise lack sympathy with it, we naturally express our feeling about it by making the piece sound silly in paraphrase. And paraphrases that make fun of a piece usually ignore or misrepresent its substance, so a plausible rendering requires special effort. We call it **Charity**. An effort to be charitable is required not just when we hate the opinion being offered in a passage, but also when we feel the author is making the point unnecessarily hard to understand or we feel that the writing itself is sloppy or offensive. But the task is just to remind ourselves of what we do automatically, when our emotions don't get in the way. In the right mood we fill in gaps, correct for slips, follow strange dialects, all by simply making the most plausible sense of the words. Barking guards are implausible, so we hunt for something to make sense of the reference. We know that guards sometimes come with guard dogs, and they seem natural in the context, so we fill them in automatically. This principle governs our reading skill. We use our grasp of context and familiarity with human interests to maximize plausibility.

Exercise 1.15

(a) Suppose a headline in a school newspaper reads, "HONOR SOCIETY INDICTS 26." How should it read? (b) A story about a basketball team reads, "For the last two seasons the Redmen were sent off to the National Collegiate Athletic Association tournament with bond fires and pep rallies." How should it read? (Answers on p. 32.)

Obviously we will sometimes want to make fun of something somebody said: parody and caricature have a place in our lives. But not in the project of this chapter. Our single purpose here is to paraphrase for understanding: to capture the content of a passage as well as we can. This provides the discipline required for type II reading. Furthermore, even when we do want to reject an expressed opinion, even make fun of it, we should try to understand it first. This is why we must learn to recognize when contempt and loathing threaten our understanding and adopt a strategy to surmount them. The strategy is to read generously, especially when you don't feel like it.

Public opinion pages in local newspapers provide inexhaustible exercises for charitable reading. Letters to editors are often hasty and ill tempered, filled with more heat than light. So retrieving their substance requires as much generosity as care. Practicing on them can help build good instincts. Consider the following:

Editor—

I wonder if the employees of the Department of Motor Vehicles could stop complaining about having to work on Saturdays long enough to realize who is footing the bill for their paychecks.

As a taxpayer, I'm getting more than a little tired of government—federal, state, county and city—employees who are too busy thinking of themselves to give a "tinker's dam" about the general public for whom they are supposed to work. If hospital services can be available 24 hours a day, 365 days of the year, I would hope the DMV could stay open 4 hours on Saturday. They certainly get more than enough holidays to compensate.

Were we to happen on this letter in our casual reading we might simply laugh at the hospital analogy and think no more of it: somebody else whining about life. But if, in the interest of discipline, we fight our dismissive instinct we will find some paraphrasable substance here. Instead of a simple complaint, we get a proposal and a bit of rationale.

The DMV should be open on Saturdays for the substantial convenience of many taxpayers who support it.

Here we try to look past the shaky analogy, and some awkward, intemperate expression, to the sober sentiment just beneath the surface. We may not agree with the sentiment, but we can see that it is not simply whining. Let us try the same routine on the following piece.

We are pleased to see the Legislature has approved and sent to the governor a bill that will require motorists to produce proof they have auto insurance when stopped for traffic violations. The bill further provides uninsured motorists will be fined and reported to the Department of Motor Vehicles, which could suspend the driver's license.

It is time for the state to get tough with scofflaws like this who are contemptuous of the rights of other motorists. They drive merrily along, causing loss and injury to others, expecting someone else to pick up the bill for the damages they cause. The "someone else" who gets stuck for the costs are all the law-abiding insured drivers whose rates are increased to cover the costs of accidents caused by the uninsured motorists. It is time to tell the deadbeats of the highway the free ride has ended.

Here again we must force ourselves to read charitably somebody who is not being very generous himself. Stripping away all the hyperbole about scofflaws and deadbeats we can find an unsensational and perfectly human view:

It is good that the legislature has passed this bill because the cost of accidents involving uninsured drivers has fallen unfairly on those who do buy insurance.

You do not have to share this perception to see that it is a respectable part of the debate on the topic.

Both of these letters, but especially the last one, illustrate a specific hurdle that contentious passages throw in the path of sympathetic paraphrase. For both are not just expressing a view but advocating it as well. And when we become advocates, our enthusiasm naturally intermingles with the substance of the views we defend and both are expressed in the same words. So the major burden of paraphrase then becomes charitably disentangling the two.

Our aim should be to read enthusiastic overstatement here just as we would "exaggeration for effect" in less abrasive contexts. If I tell you I can't have lunch with you because "I have a million things to do before five," you do not believe that I have a list of 1,000,000 distinct things on my afternoon calendar. You understand that a half-dozen will easily use up the time. The "million things" expresses something else, perhaps my panic or despair at the thought of my schedule. No competent speaker of English seriously takes "a million" as a literal description when used like this. In something like the same way, "deadbeat" and "scofflaw" may be viewed as mixing description with enthusiasm in the passage above. The terms clearly refer to (all) drivers who do not buy insurance, for whatever reason. Charging them all with a character flaw (deadbeat, scofflaw) may be read as simply the excited restatement of the evaluative part of the main point: it is good that these people will be newly inconvenienced. We need not uncharitably burden the central thesis with the implausibility that drivers not buying insurance always do so from malice of some sort. We may ignore that insinuation as merely intemperate expression, exaggeration for effect.

Exercise 1.16
....

"You'd better finish this job yesterday or there will be hell to pay." Generously paraphrase this sentence in more literal and temperate terms. (Suggestions on p. 32.)

THINGS TO KEEP IN MIND

The request for paraphrase (in our exercises, for example) provides its own special context, usually quite different from that of the passage you are trying to paraphrase. Simply trying to be clear in that special context will get you most of the required technique: You'll want to use words adapted to the context of paraphrase, and this will automatically avoid the intemperate exaggeration and rhetorical flourishes contained in a passage, and produce properly sober expression. And if you try genuinely to elucidate the author's perception, you will automatically be appropriately charitable.

Two rules that will capture much of this advice are these:

1. Try to use your own words, rather than quote directly from the passage.

2. Think of how the writer of the passage would view your paraphrase.

To these, let us add three more that extend points already made. Because they supplement the discussion of this chapter, each is briefly illustrated.

3. Pay attention to irony, sarcasm, and understatement.

If something said in any of these ways is part of the point of a passage, make sure it is expressed more soberly in the paraphrase. The artificial seriousness of academic contexts sometimes tempts students to read literally sentences they would immediately recognize as sarcastic or ironic in conversation with a friend. So this is just another reminder *not to leave your skills and good sense at home*. For instance, if somebody says, caustically,

Of course I drive home at rush-hour on purpose, because I like to visit.

This might mean something like,

I would gladly work different hours, if only to avoid the traffic, but I can't.

4. Rewrite rhetorical questions as declarative sentences.

For example, as used in the burger ad,

Where's the beef?

would be paraphrased,

There's not much beef here,

or

The patties are pretty small.

You might think "Where's the beef?" should be read as saying there is *no* beef at all. But this would be an uncharitable paraphrase: some hyperbole needs to be toned down here too. Rhetorical questions frequently contain sarcasm and hyperbole and might have been discussed under either of those headings. But questions that are not really questions form such a clearly identifiable group that a separate rule is reserved for them.

5. Reformulate the point of common clichés and exotic allusions in more straightforward terminology.

In some contexts,

Charlie got a little of his own medicine,

would best be paraphrased,

Charlie deserved to be humiliated,

or

I'm glad he was humiliated.

And read

He was, like Caesar, not of woman born,

as,

His birth was cesarean.

Exercise 1.17

(a) "Limiting the President to a single term would doubtless eliminate certain political distractions; but not having to stand for reelection would do nothing to increase a President's accountability for his actions." Rewrite this last clause to eliminate the sarcastic understatement and say what it's trying to say more straightforwardly. (b) Rewrite the following rhetorical question in simple, declarative form: "What right do YOU have to tell me what to do?" (c) "The fleeing suspect shot himself because he evidently felt he was in a no-win situation." Paraphrase this sentence to eliminate the cliché. (Suggestions on p. 32.)

SUPPLEMENTAL EXERCISES

A. Review Questions

1. Describe the difference between "background" and "dispensable detail" as padding categories.

2. What's wrong with saying that in a passage items of padding are those things that could as well have been omitted from the passage to begin with?

3. What is the point of reading charitably?

B. Passages for Analysis

1. KIEV, Ukraine—A school district in western Ukraine, facing a severe financial crisis, has reached an agreement with its teachers to pay their salaries in vodka and other products. Teachers in the Novoselitsky district, who hadn't been paid since November, agreed to accept back wages in vodka, grain and butter, the ITAR-Tass news agency reported Monday.

The unconventional solution was prompted by a district-wide payment crisis. Novoselitsky's education department is broke, in part because a local distillery is failing and cannot afford to pay taxes to the local administration, the report said. Teachers across Ukraine frequently protest chronic wage delays and shrinking salaries.

(The Associated Press)

a. Write a headline for this article.
b. Write out a bare-bones paraphrase.
c. Choose one item from the article you did not mention in the paraphrase and explain what kind of padding it is.

2. A sailor in a round-the-world yacht race sliced open his own arm to repair an inflamed tendon, operating mid-ocean with a flashlight strapped to his head for illumination. Peter Goss, 35, followed faxed instructions from a French doctor on how to perform the makeshift surgery aboard his yacht, the 50-foot Aqua Quorum, currently 1,300 miles off Chile's south coast.

Goss said the inflamed tendon started causing problems soon after he set sail three months ago in the Vendee Globe solo competition, a 22,000-mile race around the globe. This week, the skin split open, exposing the damaged tissue. If all goes well after his surgery, Goss is expected to pass South America's Cape Horn and enter the Atlantic Ocean early next week for the final stretch of the trip back to France.

(The Associated Press)

a. Write a headline for this article.
b. Write out a bare-bones paraphrase.
c. Describe two different kinds of padding you omitted from the paraphrase.

3. Researchers long have wondered why people usually gain a few pounds when they quit cigarettes. Studies have shown that people often eat more food, especially sugar, after quitting, but there also was evidence that they burn fewer calories. The new research, based on measurements of the effects of nicotine, suggests that the drug's effect on the body's metabolism—the rate at which it uses up calories—is larger than experts had suspected. Smokers burn significantly more calories than nonsmokers engaged in the same physical activity. Furthermore, the difference is substantially greater if people smoke while they are busy, instead of only when resting. The finding helps explain why some people put on more weight than others when they stop smoking.

a. Write a headline for this article.
b. Write out a bare-bones paraphrase, noting that there are two internal connections.
c. Describe the padding you omitted from the paraphrase.

ANSWERS

1.1 "Would you like your groceries in paper bags or plastic ones?"

1.2 "Take five":
a. Let's take a short break.
b. You will need five of these chips if you want to play the game.
"Put that on the board":
a. Write that on the chalkboard at the front of the room.
b. You may leave that package on the plank over there.
"He made the connection":
a. He suddenly saw what the conversation was about.
b. He soldered the two wires together.

1.4 a. Oh, that noise is our neighbor's burglar alarm, which has been acting up lately; try to ignore it.
b. Try not to worry about that, my neighbor herself warned me that the alarm would go off while the electricians worked on it this morning.
c. There it goes again; it must be a pretty serious problem.

1.5 a. i. Headline: New pulsars found
ii. Paraphrase: Astronomers have found a cluster of millisecond pulsars that may help us understand galaxy formation.
b. i. Headline: French business lunches decline
ii. Paraphrase: French business lunches have become less extravagant lately for a number of distinct reasons.
[Since the piece is complex, many variations on this are possible, e.g., you might briefly give the four reasons.]

1.6 a. The first paragraph is entirely background: the traditional French concern with eating, some details on the nature of their past business lunches, and the contrast with those in England and America. The case of the troubled telecom executive at the end is on the borderline between background and illustration.
b. Because the substance of this article concerns the levees that collapsed recently, the entire last paragraph describing what the levees are made of and how they saturate will be background padding.

1.7 The two quotations, from Barry Cupp and Donald Davis, are illustrations of the gun-sales boom, which is the main point of the article.

1.8 a. The bacterium is dispensable detail. Mentioning *Vibrio cholera* would simply clutter the paraphrase.
b. (label all padding in millisecond pulsar piece):
Setting: the astronomers were from Australia, Britain, and Italy.
Background (four items):
• Only about this number known before

- Only one discovered here before
- Thought to send out a rotating beam

Definition: Millisecond pulsars are dense stars that emit bursts of radio waves only thousandths of a second apart.
Dispensable detail: Found in the cluster 47 Tucanae
Illustration: An Earth-bound observer detects energy bursts every time a beam of radio waves crosses Earth.

1.9   Three possible paraphrases of "we've had a little accident."
   a. "a pipe has burst" (and you'll get your shoes wet).
   b. "someone has vomited" (and it's pretty disgusting).
   c. "an elderly lady has ripped her clothes" (and would be embarrassed to be seen).

1.10   a. The ladies of the church have accumulated cast-off clothing, which may be examined in the church basement on Friday afternoons.
   b. The plot is less than the sum of its parts. It concerns an unconventional family—a free-spirited mother and her three young-adult children—that visits an English seaside resort. There they meet a young dentist (who happens to fall in love with the older daughter), his grumpy landlord, the mother's nervous solicitor, the friendly waiter, and a stuffy barrister.

1.11   a. Three bits of background: the flap about speed limits, the indeterminate problem on Walnut, and the new mall.
   b. Dispensable detail: Richmond is a major route to Hamilton Elementary; one hundred twenty cars observed in a fifteen minute period.
   c. Restatement: "accident waiting to happen" restates the danger; "inexcusable to wait" restates the recommendation.

1.12   We should devote more attention to reducing reproduction by the nonpoor and less to the poor.

1.13   (c) Several levees failed in a recent flood. Of the others, (d) is not presupposed, it is actually stated; and the others are not part of the article at all.

1.14   (Possible paraphrases, depending on details of the context:)
   a. You should have gone for a cheaper repair.
   b. You're wasting your money fixing that worthless car.
   c. You should think about getting another car.

1.15   a. HONOR SOCIETY INDUCTS 26
   b. "Bond fires" should be "bonfires."

1.16   (Possible paraphrases)
   a. It's important to finish this job very soon.
   b. If this job isn't finished very soon, there will be terrible consequences.
   c. This job must be finished faster than seems possible without superhuman effort or your life will be miserable.

1.17   a. Not having to stand for reelection will decrease a President's accountability for his actions.
   b. You have no right to tell me what to do.
   c. The fleeing suspect shot himself because death was preferable to the open alternatives or because the thought of captivity was unbearable.

CHAPTER 2

READING FOR STRUCTURE
Dependency and Subordination

.... The bare-bones paraphrases of complex passages will have an internal structure to reflect that complexity. In this chapter we exam-
OVERVIEW ine that structure. A central aim will be to distinguish reasoning from
.... other kinds of structural elements.

COMPLEXITY

What we read varies in complexity, and this will be reflected in our paraphrases.[1] To a small degree we have already observed such variation. The paraphrase of the El Niño article was extremely simple, summarizable in a single thought: El Niño is unlikely this year. Other examples from Chapter 1 were more complex. In the paraphrase of the Cholera article (on p. 7), for instance, we may distinguish two distinct items:

a. Somebody caught cholera within the city limits of San Francisco

and

b. It was the first case in years.

Cathleen Barney's letter (p. 18), also contains two distinct points:

a. The recommendation that stop signs be placed at First and Richmond.

and

b. The danger that traffic presents to local school children.

---

1. When we speak of paraphrases in this chapter we will always mean "bare-bones paraphrases."

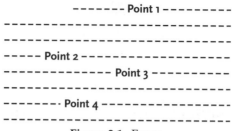

Figure 2.1. Essay.

When we find separate points in a paraphrase such as this, they are usually connected, related to each other in some obvious way. These connections are the links that structure our expository writing, and they are the topic of this chapter. The two points in the Barney letter, for instance, are connected in our paraphrase by the word "because." This signals a connection of a certain kind. There are many other kinds of connection, some signaled by other words and some simply understood from the context. The task of this chapter will be to develop a way to recognize and talk about these different kinds of expository links or relations. Our picture of a paragraph or an essay will be of **lumps of substance linked together in different ways** (Figures 2.1 and 2.2).

But first, one other observation about items of substance: they will usually have different *priorities*. That is, when a paraphrase contains two points, one will be more important, more central to the passage than the other. When there are more than two points, we can usually find one that's most important, to which the others will be secondary, or subordinate. The primary thing in the cholera article, for example, was simply reporting the case (that somebody came down with it). The fact that cholera is rare in the United States is interesting, but wouldn't be mentioned on its own. The article was written because there was a case to report. You will soon see that our normal way of talking about the connections among the various points in a paraphrase always presumes a priority. The connections are always taken to be ways in which one point *depends on* another. A dependent point is always *subordinate*, that is, of lower priority, than the one on which it is dependent. So when the priorities are not obvious, we will have to assume an order we think the author would find congenial. In Cathleen Barney's letter, for instance, the proposed stop sign seems

PICTURE OF STRUCTURE

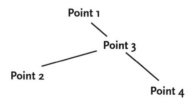

Connecting lines = links

Figure 2.2. Picture of structure.

primary, and the dangerous traffic is there in its support. That is, the danger is mentioned *in the service of* the proposal, and is dependent on it for its role in the piece. Ultimately, nothing hangs on this, because we will eventually be able to easily convert from one priority to another. It is just that we must begin with some order or other.

Because everything in this chapter concerns these connections between points of different priority, we will adopt some vocabulary to make them easy to talk about. We will call the more important point in a paraphrase the **Main Point** (MP for short) and the others **Secondary Points** (SPs). In the cholera article, the case itself is the main point (MP) and the rarity the secondary point (SP). In the Barney letter, the need for traffic control seems clearly to be the main point (MP) and the danger is subordinate (SP). Note that in writing complex paraphrases in single-sentence form, **we always state the MP first, then give the various secondary points later in the sentence.**

So, to summarize, secondary points connect to main points in a way that makes them dependent on the main point for their role in the passage. SPs are always there *in the service of* MPs. This service will take a number of different particular forms, but they will all have one thing in common: they will all be *comments on* the MP. In other words, the service that a SP provides its MP is to *say something about it*. The rarity of cholera says something about the cholera case; the danger to kids says something about the need for traffic control. We will discuss the variety of possible connections shortly. But all of the different SPs provide structure by commenting on their MPs. This is what makes them *dependent on* main points for their role in a piece.

One more preliminary point and we will be ready to articulate structure. We mentioned earlier that in the single-sentence paraphrase of the Barney letter, we naturally connected the MP and SP with the word "because."

> We should make First and Richmond a four-way stop *because* the heavy traffic is a danger to children crossing there on the way to school.

Words such as this will help us recognize the connections we will be looking for. In this use grammarians call "because" a *subordinating conjunction*; by that they mean to indicate exactly the priority difference with which we are concerned here. What follows the "because," in a sentence like this, depends for its role in the piece on what went before the "because." When we say "A because B," the second part (B) is there in the service of the first part (A). So subordinating conjunctions signal the very links we are looking for in this chapter. Other useful subordinating conjunctions are "although," "if," "since," "unless," and "in order to." Thinking about what these words typically do in a sentence will help you see what we are looking for here. The grammarians' interests are much narrower than ours, however. So our category of subordinating connections will cover much more ground, and they will be signaled by many other kinds of words. Coordinating conjunctions ("and," "but," "for," "yet," "so"), for instance, will indicate expository connections as reliably as subordinating conjunctions. And we will find other useful indicator expressions as well.

Some Conventions

Because the "points of substance" in an essay will be complete thoughts (clauses), displaying the lumps and links as we did in Figure 2.2 will be messy and cumbersome. Instead, to display structure in our bare-bones paraphrases, we will adopt the ordinary outlining practice of separating the points, writing one below the other, and *indenting* to show subordination. So, for example, to create a structured paraphrase from a basic two-part passage, simply label the main point "MP," the secondary one "SP," and write the latter below the former and indented to the right.

> MP: First and Richmond needs a four-way stop.
>> SP: The heavy traffic is a danger to children crossing there on the way to school.

We will call this a "structured bare-bones paraphrase," or (for simplicity) just a "structured paraphrase."[2] We will soon show how to make more complicated ones.

Exercise 2.1
....

For practice, write out in indented form the structured paraphrases of the following passages of Chapter 1: (a) Cal Scepti's letter on p. 20; (b) Mrs. Holtz's letter on p. 23; (c) the uninsured motorist passage on p. 27. (Answers on p. 87.)

The various words that can link an SP with an MP begin to suggest the different kinds of connections they may have. Because secondary points say something about main points, the various connecting words will be our first clue to *just what sort of thing is being said* by the SP. If the paraphrase reads, "First and Richmond needs a four-way stop, BUT the city refuses to provide one," we know immediately that *this* SP says something very different about the need for a stop sign than Cathleen Barney's SP did. Points connected with a "but" relate to each other very differently from ones connected with a "because." So the question we need to ask is, What is a good way to think about the different kinds of things an SP may say about an MP? For our purposes, we may begin with just four basic kinds. First (as in Cathleen Barney's letter), an SP may give a *reason or argument* for the MP. Second, it might *explain why it happened* (if it is something that happened). Third, it might *give a result or consequence* of it. Fourth, it might simply *qualify it* in one way or another.

Let us indicate each of these kinds of subordination with a letter: [s] for support or argument, [e] for cause or explanation, [r] for result or ramification, and

---

2. The notion of "bones" in bare-bones paraphrasing will actually take on more significance as the complexity of a passage increases. For we may think of our structured paraphrases as the "skeleton" of a passage, with main and secondary points as the bones and their connections as the "joints."

[q] for qualification. We will use these letters to mark the kind of subordination that holds between the points in our indented paraphrases. In the Barney paraphrase, the SP (danger) is a reason or argument for the MP (stop sign), so it would get an [s] to the left of the SP:

> MP: First and Richmond needs a 4-way stop.
> [s]   SP: The heavy traffic is a danger to children crossing there on the way to school.

Other single-sentence paraphrases may be used to illustrate other connections.

> Much of downtown Davenport lost power last night because a van skidded in the rain and knocked down a power pole.

Here the "because" does not signal "reason to think," but rather "cause." The skidding van caused the blackout; it *explains why* downtown Davenport was dark.

> MP: Much of downtown Davenport was without power last night.
> [e]   SP: A van skidded into a power pole.

An example of "result" or "ramification" would be this:

> Nighttime gunfire became more and more common during the late eighties, so my parents finally abandoned the old place and moved us out of the city.

Its structured paraphrase would be something like this:

> MP: Nighttime gunfire in our neighborhood increased during the late eighties.
> [r]   SP: We moved out of the city.

"Qualification" is not as neat a category as the other three. It covers a variety of things that might be said about a main point. It will nevertheless turn out to be a very useful heading that will become clearer as we go along. The subordination in the cholera article was in category [q]. A qualification such as this is often indicated by the word "but" as in this simple paraphrase of an article on postage rates:

> The cost of mailing a letter will go up four or five cents early next year, but after that, automation and other economies will keep future rate increases below inflation.

This would be structured as follows:

> MP: First class postage will rise about a nickel early next year.
> [q]   SP: Planned economies should hold down subsequent increases.

For now you may think of qualification as a catch-all category covering everything not covered by support, explanation, and ramification.

The subordination code (s, e, r, q) takes the place of the connecting word or phrase in the passage. The connection will not always be so simply indicated, of course, and we will soon examine more subtle cases. But when you have a "but" or "so" or "because" doing the job, as in these cases, you will normally omit them from a paraphrase and indicate the kind of connection with a code in the left-hand margin. The code is both more reliable and more systematic than the indicator words themselves. For the same word (e.g., "because") can indicate different kinds of subordination, and different words can indicate the same kind (e.g., both "so" and "hence" may indicate [r]).

> **Exercise 2.2**
> ....
>
> (a) Put the subordination codes in the paraphrases you wrote in Exercise 2.1.
> (b) Structure and label: "The door was locked so they broke a window to get in." [Remember that in single-sentence paraphrases, the MP is always given first.] (Answers on p. 87.)

As passages increase in complexity you will of course find more than one secondary point. Consider an article with this paraphrase:

The roof of the gym collapsed due to the heavy snowfall, so the tournament had to be canceled.

Because it occurs first in the sentence, the collapse is the MP and it has both a consequence and an explanation. This would be structured as follows:

	MP: The roof of the gym collapsed.
[e]	SP: The weight of snow was too great.
[r]	SP: The tournament was canceled.

> **Exercise 2.3**
> ....
>
> Structure and label the following: (a) I have a very slow modem, so I can't download graphics, but it's okay for e-mail. (b) The microwave failed because we ran it empty and now we can't easily reheat the coffee. (Answer on p. 87.)

Independent Subordination

Sometimes, though rarely, a secondary point will be subordinate *only* because it is of lower priority: it will be less important than the MP in the context, but *will not say anything directly about the MP*. So it will not fall into any of our categories.

> BRIDGEPORT—No criminal charges will be filed against the operator of a probation camp in the drowning deaths of three juvenile residents and four would-be rescuers, prosecutors said. "I feel there is insufficient evidence to establish criminal liability beyond a reasonable doubt as it related to the actions of individuals or Camp O'Neal Inc.," Mono county district Attorney Stan Eller wrote in a memo to the sheriff on Tuesday.
>
> Three juvenile offenders housed at Camp O'Neal fell through thin ice and drowned during an outing to the frigid Convict Lake Feb. 19. Four adults, including two counselors, drowned while trying to save the youths.

While the district attorney's investigation clears the camp operator of criminal wrongdoing, a civil complaint filed by the state Department of Social Services is still pending.

(The Associated Press)

Here the main point is that criminal charges have been dropped. This is the substance of the first paragraph, and the second provides it with some helpful background. The third paragraph provides further substance, however: the still-pending civil suit. The order in which the material is presented makes clear that the article's main business is reporting on the criminal case, whereas the civil suit is secondary. But the fact that the civil suit is still pending does not connect to the MP in any of our four ways. It isn't an argument for it, and it doesn't explain it, result from it, or qualify it. The fact that the civil suit continues is merely added as a related matter, "something else you would doubtless find interesting while we're on the topic." Therefore we would still get an indented structure, but with no dependency code.

> MP: The Mono Co. D.A. will not file criminal charges against Camp O'Neal in the recent drowning deaths of 7 people.
> [i]   SP: A civil suit on the matter is still pending.

Secondary points such as this, on a related topic but not otherwise connected to the main point, will be called "independent" secondary points (thus the [i]). They are far less interesting structurally than the dependent secondary points we have been examining up to now. The value of this example lies in pointing out that subordination is not the same thing as dependence. Dependence involves some connection between points (s, e, r, q), not just a different level of importance. *Dependent* subordinating connections are the ones that will serve to structure our paraphrases.

Higher Order Subordination

Expository writing will commonly make use of subordination under secondary points too. That is, some information in a piece will say the same sorts of things about secondary points that we have seen them say about main points. This can happen again at any level, creating a cascade of subordination that you will recognize as having the same form as the outlines you yourself use in writing reports and essays.

MEXICO CITY—Smoking will be banned in classrooms, auditoriums, health facilities and some other public areas under a federal decree that takes effect in May, according to officials in Mexico City. The decree, signed by Health Secretary Jesus Kumate Rodriguez and published on Tuesday, said the restrictions fall under the constitutional right to health and promotion of individual and community health in the 1989–1994 National Development Plan. The officials said the measure was likely to draw opposition because heavy smoking is common in Mexico.

(The Associated Press)

The main point is obviously the ban itself; so the information about exactly where the ban would apply, and under what constitutional auspices, may be left out of our paraphrase as "dispensable detail" (padding).[3] But the last sentence gives a ramification of the ban. We begin with a structure like our first simple cases:

> MP: The federal government will ban smoking in many of Mexico's
> public places beginning in May.
> [r]   SP: The ban will likely draw opposition.

But in the passage this SP is connected to something else (heavy smoking) with a "because." How do we represent this? Well, obviously, secondary points can be explained, supported, qualified and have results too, just as the MP can; so we may include the heavy smoking by indenting it under the SP. This shows that it is commenting on the SP, not on the MP. Heavy smoking provides reason to think the ban will draw opposition, it is *support for the prediction.* So the paraphrase would then look like this:

> MP: The federal government will ban smoking in many of Mexico's
> public places beginning in May.
> [r]   SP: The ban seems likely to draw opposition.
> [s]   SP: Heavy smoking is common in Mexico.

Note that when we indent in this more complicated way, an SP always comments on the point under which it is indented. So we may have several SPs indented under an SP before returning to others commenting on the MP.

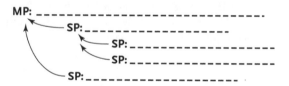

And others might be indented under each of these in a complex passage. Look ahead to the article beginning with "Manhattan firefighters" (p. 43) for an illustration.

Exercise 2.4
....

Indent and label the following. (a) The staff met at noon today, but one member was absent, so we had a meal left over. (b) I have a very slow modem, so I can't download graphics, except very simple ones. (Answers on p. 87.)

---

3. Were it important in the context, this detail could be included in the paraphrase as a qualification of the MP. This is just how the category of "dispensable detail" works, and why it was given an asterisk (*) in the list of padding categories. Our interest here lies in material at the end of the passage, however, so we will ignore the detail for now.

Recall that the examples we have been using in these illustrations might well be single-sentence summaries of longer passages, with the padding already stripped from them. This suggests a useful technique on which to fall back when paraphrasing a longer passage is difficult. We often identify subordination more easily when structure is presented briefly, because brevity requires the connections to be captured in a simple word or phrase. So for tricky cases, try to generate a headline (which will require thought in a longer piece), then flesh it out into a more complicated sentence. Often the connecting terms you naturally use will be useful clues to the proper subordination type.

Exercise 2.5
....

Write a single-sentence paraphrase for each of the following two articles and then indent and label the subordination connections within each. (Answers on p. 88.)

a. MONGOLIA—An airliner crashed in northern Mongolia on Thursday, killing 34 passengers, news reports said. The Antonov-24 plane, belonging to Mongolia's MIAT Airlines, crashed on a flight from the capital of Ulan Bator to the town of Moron, about 300 miles to the northwest. One of the 35 aboard did survive, but with serious injuries, according to Chinese and Mongolian news reports. The crash occurred about noon in the town of Duurengiinam, China's official Xinhua news agency reported.

(The Associated Press)

b. An elderly man died early Tuesday when fire engulfed his home on 20th Street. Shortly after 3:30 a.m. firefighters received a call that the house was ablaze, according to Los Angeles Fire Department spokesman Brian Humphrey. "It took 20 firefighters 14 minutes to extinguish the blaze," Humphrey said. Firefighters found the 75-year-old man, whose identity has not been released, inside the house after extinguishing the blaze. Cause of the fire was careless smoking, officials said. Damage was estimated at $40,000.

TECHNIQUE AND VOCABULARY

The examples of dependent subordination we have examined are typical of the structural relationships you will find in your expository reading: Some passages describe events with their causes and effects; some spell out policies and their consequences; others will offer proposals with arguments for them; and each may involve various qualifications. The central aim of this chapter is to learn how to identify these different connections between MP and SP (s, e, r, q), and to develop a systematic way to talk about them. So we will stop looking at new examples for a moment and introduce some vocabulary and apparatus for that purpose.

Technical Vocabulary

The first thing to notice is that words we are using to name kinds of subordination, "support," "explain," "result," "qualify," are functioning in somewhat special ways. So [s], [e], [r], and [q] represent the beginning of a *technical vocabulary* designed to help us talk more clearly about what we read. We begin with the four English words because the basic technical concepts we need are reasonably close to a normal everyday use of those terms. The technical concepts will develop their own identity in application.

For a first level of refinement, let us look more closely at each of these categories. [e] is supposed to cover things such as causes. But we use [e] (instead of [c]) because we want it to cover the whole range of "explanations of why the MP took place," including motivations and purposes. Of course, we may explain all sorts of things about an MP in addition to why it came about, such as who was involved or how funny it was. These would not be [e]s. So perhaps we should think of [e] as standing for "etiology." Etiology does mean specifically "explanation of what brought something about," which is just what we want here. ("Etiology" is a good word to add to your vocabulary.)

The other things to explain about an MP would be what kind of thing it is, or how it works, or who was involved, and so on. All these other kinds of explanation will fall under [q], since they are something like *elaborations of the MP*. They help us better understand what the MP is, but not how it came about. This is why [q] is a catch-all category for things that do not fit in the others. The name was chosen because most of these elaborations do qualify the MP in a reasonably straightforward way. Others will become clearer as we examine more examples.

Support [s] and result [r] are less problematic headings. We use [s] to cover *arguments for* the MP, that is, *reason to think it is true*. This will often show up as an SP saying *how we can tell* the MP is true, or why the author thinks so. The category [r] on the other hand covers anything that follows on, or follows from, the MP. Therefore very often an [r] SP is better described as a "ramification" of the MP than as a result or consequence of it. (Look up the word "ramification" if it is not familiar; it too will be very useful.)

Exercise 2.6

Look again at all the structured paraphrase illustrations in this chapter (and on the answer pages) and try to read them substituting one of the phrases from this section for [s], [e], and [r] in the left-hand margin. If A and B are connected by [s] read, "A and reason to think so is B"; if connected by [e] read, "A and this happened because B"; if by [r] read, "A and as a consequence, B."

Interrogating Structure

We are now ready for our first bit of technique. What we have learned so far may be used to actually construct paraphrases of complicated passages, if we can first determine the MP. This is often easy because, even in a complicated piece, the main point will stand out in a "headline" summary. And when it does we will usually be able to find the rest of the structure by following a simple procedure. The procedure is this: just run through the piece asking of *each clause* whether it fits into one of the subordination categories:

Does this provide support for the MP?

Does this explain why the MP happened?

Is this a result or consequence of the MP?

Does this qualify or elaborate on the MP?

We may then repeat this procedure under the SPs until we run out of them. Answers to these questions are often obvious, and they will naturally structure your paraphrase. Consider this passage:

> Manhattan firefighters responded to a smoky electrical fire on the ground floor of the World Trade Center yesterday afternoon. A spokesman for the Center said the fire resulted from a malfunctioning circuit breaker, which had been giving trouble for the past few weeks, but was thought to be fixed. No one was injured in the fire but the dense smoke required evacuation of many offices and concessions on the first three floors.

The main point is obviously the fire, so let us ask our questions of it first. Any support offered? No, it is simply reported. An explanation of it? Yes, a malfunctioning circuit breaker (so that is one SP). Any results or consequences? Yes again: the evacuations (another SP). Any qualifications? No.[4] So our initial, rough structure would look like this:

	MP: There was a fire in the World Trade Center yesterday.
[e]	SP: A circuit breaker malfunctioned.
[r]	SP: Nearby offices and concessions were evacuated.

Now let us ask the questions of the secondary points (the circuit breaker and the evacuation). No support offered for either. No explanations either. No further consequences. No qualifications of the evacuation, but something is added about the circuit breaker: that it has been giving trouble. This sort of comment falls under [q] in its "catch-all" function. And this qualification is *further* qualified (signaled by "but") as having been thought fixed. So if we insert these SPs under the malfunctioning circuit breaker we get the following:

	MP: There was a fire in the World Trade Center yesterday.
[e]	SP: A circuit breaker malfunctioned.
[q]	SP: It had been giving trouble lately.
[q]	SP: They thought they had fixed it.
[r]	SP: Nearby offices and concessions were evacuated.

You would of course produce a paraphrase this elaborate only if asked to display all the structure you can find. The second- and third-order qualifications of [e] would normally be relegated to padding as "dispensable detail."

---

4. "Smoky," "electrical," and "ground floor" obviously qualify "fire" in a standard, grammatical way. But when expressed like this, they are either simply part of the MP, or omitted as unneeded detail. We will discuss simple adjectives and adverbs later in the chapter (see p. 66).

Let us try out this technique on a tougher example:

INDIANAPOLIS—An explosion at a motel blew a guest out of bed and brought down the walls and ceilings of 13 rooms yesterday morning injuring five people, two of them critically.

Fire investigators speculated that the blast was set off when a worker, responding to complaints of lack of hot water, lit a match and ignited propane at the 150-room Comfort Inn on the south side. "It blew the window frames and a lot of the false ceilings," Fire Capt. Gary Campbell said. The blast knocked out the exterior walls of some rooms, exposing them to the street.

Campbell said the blast occurred at 9:30 a.m., and some guests may have left by then. "It could have been a potential disaster," Campbell said. "They had 100 percent occupancy last night. How many (rooms) were occupied this morning, we don't know."

Maintenance worker Emery Bradley, 61, of Beech Grove, who may have lighted a match and caused the explosion, and maid Rae Voorhies, 51, of Greenwood, were listed in critical condition yesterday in the burn unit of Wishard Hospital.

(The Associated Press)

The main point is pretty clear:

> MP: A motel in Indianapolis blew up yesterday.

So, let us ask our four questions of this MP:

1. Is any support offered for this statement? No, the event is just given to us by the author.
2. Does anything explain why it happened? Yes, a cause is mentioned: a maintenance worker touched it off.
3. Are there any results or ramifications? Yes, five people were injured by the blast, two seriously.
4. Are there any qualifications of the MP? This is arguable: you might count the observation that the consequences would have been worse had the blast occurred earlier as something like a qualification. But we will omit it here as "dispensable detail."

Now ask the same questions of each of these secondary points: are there any support, explanation, results, or qualification offered for any SP? Yes, some support is offered for the explanation (some reason to think it is true). A maintenance worker had been called to investigate the lack of hot water, and he was one of the most seriously injured in the explosion. Each of these facts supports the diagnosis made by the investigators.

This leaves us with two secondary points, a result and an explanation, and two further secondaries under the explanation, each offered in support of it. Thus, the paraphrase would look like this:

> MP: A motel in Indianapolis blew up yesterday.
>
> [r]   SP: Five people were injured.
>
> [e]   SP: It was probably caused by a maintenance worker checking a gas leak.

[s]   SP: A maintenance worker had been called to investigate a
            lack of hot water.

[s]   SP: The maintenance worker was one of the most seriously
            injured.

The first secondary point is limited to the injuries (the most notable of the consequences) simply to emphasize economy. Were more detail called for by the context, we could, of course, list more of the damage.

Exercise 2.7

a. Structure a paraphrase of the following article by interrogating it using the following MP: "A school district in western Ukraine has had to pay its teachers in produce."

> KIEV, Ukraine—A school district in western Ukraine, facing a severe financial crisis, has reached an agreement with its teachers to pay their salaries in vodka and other products. Teachers in the Novoselitsky district, who hadn't been paid since November, agreed to accept back wages in vodka, grain and butter, the ITAR-Tass news agency reported Monday.
>
> The unconventional solution was prompted by a district-wide payment crisis. Novoselitsky's education department is broke, in part because a local distillery is failing and cannot afford to pay taxes to the local administration, the report said. Teachers across Ukraine frequently protest chronic wage delays and shrinking salaries.
>
> (*The Associated Press*)

b. Structure a paraphrase of the following article by interrogating it using the following MP: A nearby star exploded about 35,000 years ago. Take all the physics of supernovas and cosmic rays to be background.

> SAN FRANCISCO—Traces of a rare element found deep in Antarctic and Greenland ice suggest a nearby star blew up 35,000 years ago, zapping Earth with radiation that could have speeded evolution, a researcher said yesterday. The supernova was located in our own galaxy only 150 light years, or 880 trillion miles, from Earth. That is closer than any other known exploding star, said astrophysicist Grant E. Kocharov, vice chairman of the Soviet Academy of Sciences' Cosmic Ray Council. By comparison, a 1987 supernova that was the closest exploding star seen by scientists in 400 years was 1,000 times more distant and located in another galaxy.
>
> When stars explode as supernovas, the incredible blasts produce a wide variety of radiation, including powerful cosmic rays, which continually strike the entire Earth. When cosmic rays enter Earth's atmosphere over the poles, they can smash into nitrogen and oxygen molecules and produce beryllium-10, a metallic element that then falls from the atmosphere and is incorporated in the polar ice sheets. Kocharov drilled ice cores at the Dye 3 and Camp Century research stations in Greenland and the Vostok, Byrd and Dome C stations in Antarctica. He found the amount of beryllium-10 was doubled in ice that formed 35,000 years ago, at what is now about 2,000 feet below the surface.

That indicates a powerful supernova exploded nearby about 35,000 years ago, doubling the cosmic radiation bombarding Earth, Kocharov said during the American Geophysical Union's fall meeting. Supernova remnants of about the same age are still detectible in space, suggesting they and the increased cosmic rays came from an exploding star 150 light years away, he added. Cosmic rays are so energetic they can break chemical bonds in living cells, causing cancer.

(The Associated Press)

(Answers on p. 88.)

Refining the Taxonomy

One further distinction is crucial. The category [r] (results or ramifications of the MP) combines two very different kinds of consequences: **Effects** and **Implications**. That is, a secondary point may tell you what the MP causes (its effect), or it may tell you what you can infer from it (its implications). For instance, suppose a newspaper story about a burglary contains the sentence

Grabbing his revolver from the nightstand, the startled homeowner fired six shots in rapid succession, fatally wounding the intruder.

If we take the order of the points mentioned to determine priority (MP first, SP second), then the subordination here is [r]: the killing is a result or consequence of the shooting. And the type of consequence is *effect*: the six shots *caused* the intruder's death. But suppose instead the sentence had read,

Grabbing his revolver from the nightstand, the startled homeowner fired six shots in rapid succession, so [we can tell that] the revolver must have been fully loaded.

Here the MP/SP relation is also [r], but the SP is not an *effect* of the six shots, but an *implication*: something we may *infer* from them. The shooting did not cause the gun to be loaded, it just implies that it was. We can *tell* it was loaded from the MP. We will usually want to keep effects distinct from implications in our thinking, so we will adopt a notation to mark this difference. $[r_e]$ will stand for effects (explanatory or causal results) and $[r_i]$ will represent implications (inferential results). The two illustrations would then be labeled as follows:

1.   MP: He fired six shots in rapid succession.
   $[r_e]$ SP: They fatally wounded the intruder.
2.   MP: He fired six shots in rapid succession.
   $[r_i]$ SP: The gun had been fully loaded.

Exercise 2.8
....

(a) Structure and label: "Joe forgot to reset his watch, which caused him to miss his bus." (b) Structure and label: "Joe missed his bus, so he probably forgot to set his watch." (c) Add proper subscripts to the "r" subordinations you found in Exercise 2.7 (both a and b). (Answers on p. 89.)

This distinction exactly parallels the support/explanation distinction we made earlier. There we distinguished SPs that explain the MP from those that provide support for it. Here we are distinguishing SPs that the MP explains (its effects) from those it supports (its implications). To organize our thinking, then, we may say that these four SPs fall into two kinds: explanatory (etiological) and inferential.[5] When the relation is explanatory, sometimes the MP is explained *by* an SP and sometimes it explains an SP [r_e]. When the relation is inferential, sometimes the SP supports the MP [s] and sometimes it is supported *by* the MP [r_i]. These pairs of relations are displayed below.

1. Explanatory (etiological) SPs
   a. SP explains MP [e]
   b. MP explains SP [r_e]
2. Inferential SPs
   a. SP supports MP [s]
   b. MP supports (implies) SP [r_i]

These four subordination types[6] plus qualification [q] provide the basic categories of dependent subordination. They contain most of the concepts we will need to create good structured paraphrases.

Exercise 2.9
....

Label as explanatory (e) or inferential (i) the subordination in the following single-sentence paraphrases. In each case ask the following: Is the relation (between MP and SP) cause or explanation (e) or is the relation evidence or indicator (i)?

a. The airplane clipped the transmission lines, causing a local power failure.

b. The pilot hit the transmission lines, so he must have been flying well below the flight path.

c. The pilot must have been incompetent, because he hit wires well below the flight path.

d. The pilot kept the plane very low because he wanted to hit the transmission lines.

e. The pilot hit wires well below the flight path, so he was either incompetent or badly wanted to interrupt local power.

(Answers on p. 89.)

---

5. The word "inferential" suggests itself here because in these cases ([s] and [r_i]) we will typically be either inferring the MP from something or inferring something from it.

6. You may wish to note a systematic difference between etiological and inferential MPs. Etiological MPs are events or actions (things to be explained), whereas inferential MPs are *statements* (things to be supported or argued for). Because events get into passages only by being described (in statements) you can see that the same MP could be treated as an event or as a statement (its description) in the same passage and hence be subject to both kinds of subordination. We will not emphasize this further here (though it is obviously relevant to the discussion in the next section), but it will become important in Chapters 3 and 5.

Nevertheless, one more layer of complexity will sometimes come in handy. This involves distinguishing three different kinds of [e], two of them directly related to human action. First, all events (including human action) may have causes. But sometimes we explain a human action by appeal to the agent's *motivation* for doing something, in contrast to a mere cause. This contrast may be illustrated in explaining any action, let us say: Sarah's arriving late for dinner (question: "why was she late?"). The explanation might be something beyond her control, say, she was held up in traffic: this would be a *cause*. On the other hand, she may have been late *intentionally*, say, because she was angry with the host for not inviting a friend of hers. The reason a person has for doing something intentionally is recognizable as at least a very special kind of cause, and we will find it useful to have a way to record this distinction. So, whenever it is either obvious or important, we will note this distinction by adding the subscript m (for motivation) to our [e] category: [e$_m$].

But explaining something as intentional may take two importantly distinct forms: backward-looking and forward-looking. That is, a reason for doing something intentionally may concern what has already happened, as in the case we just looked at (the host did not invite Sarah's friend). But we may also explain an action by appeal to something in the future, something we hope to *accomplish* by the action. Sarah may explain that she was late *in order to* make a grand entrance. Hence, we need these two forms:

BACKWARD-LOOKING:

Sarah was late because the host did not invite her friend.

FORWARD-LOOKING:

Sarah was late so that she could make a grand entrance.

This last sort of explanation is typically called "purpose." So we will reserve [e$_m$] for backward-looking explanations, and use [e$_p$] for forward-looking ones, whenever that distinction is useful. The context will sometimes allow us to easily convert a motive (she came late because of the host's offense) into a purpose (she came late in order to show her displeasure at the offense), so which way we phrase the explanation will depend on the context. But you will find it generally useful to have all three kinds of explanation available as you paraphrase. We now have a total of eight types of subordination. They are listed and illustrated on p. 49.

Exercise 2.10

Label the subordination in the following sentences [e$_c$], [e$_m$], or [e$_p$].

a. She left California because she lost her job.

b. She left California to find work.

c. She left California because she found the climate boring.

d. The Croatians ignored the cease-fire because the Serbs had ignored the previous one.

e. The Croatians violated the cease-fire for the sake of a tactical advantage.

f. The cease-fire broke down because fireworks were misinterpreted as artillery fire.

(Answers on p. 89.)

SUBORDINATION CATEGORIES

The following list contains the eight basic categories we will use in structuring bare-bones paraphrases. Each is illustrated and a typical single-sentence description is provided. The first seven are the dependent subordination headings we have just examined. The last is the contrasting category of "independent" secondary points discussed earlier.

A secondary point may be:

[e$_c$] 1. A **cause** of its main point.
(The dynamite went off [MP] because the fire reached the storage shed [SP].)

[e$_m$] 2. A **motive** (reason) for its MP (action/policy).
(They set off the dynamite [MP] because it had become unsafe with age [SP].)

[e$_p$] 3. A **purpose** of its main point (action/policy).
(They set off the dynamite [MP] in order to bring down the building [SP].)

[r$_e$] 4. An **effect** (explanatory result) of its main point.
(The dynamite went off [MP], killing the guard and a passerby [SP].)

[s] 5. **Support** for its main point.
(The dynamite must have gone off spontaneously [MP], because nobody was near it when it blew [SP].)

[r$_i$] 6. An **implication** (inferential result) of its main point.
(The dynamite went off without provocation [MP], so it must have been unstable [SP].)

[q] 7. A **qualification** of its main point.
(The dynamite went off [MP], but the sound was muffled [SP].)

[i] 8. **Independent** of the main point.
(The dynamite went off (MP), and authorities said the owner had no permit to store explosives (SP).)

These are the relationships to look for in paraphrasing. Sometimes the kind of [e] or the kind of [r] will be unclear or unimportant, and *you may omit the subscript.* Less frequently, an MP/SP connection will be ambiguous, and you may display two codes in the left-hand margin (though you should resist doing this without strong reason). As passages become more complicated, you will find many different ways to use these categories to express your understanding of them.

Illustration

Let us practice our paraphrasing technique, including the latest refinements, on the following complicated piece, extracted from a longer article about the former Soviet Union.

> A spokesman for the Soviet Navy said yesterday it plans to retrieve a nuclear submarine that sank off Norway to learn what caused the accident that killed 42 sailors. "We consider that we must raise it," Vice Adm Sergei P. Vargin said on the nightly television news program Vremya. Vargin, who is with the Soviet Baltic Fleet, said details of how to bring the submarine up from nearly 5,000 feet below the surface had not been worked out. "The experts will deal with it," he said, adding that the hull was believed to be cracked but intact. The sub caught fire and sank Friday in the Norwegian Sea.
>
> Vargin repeated the Soviet position that there is no danger of radiation leakage. He said the reactors were shut down before the crew evacuated and neither of the two nuclear-tipped torpedoes was armed for combat.

The quick "headline" summary would be something like "The Soviet Navy plans to recover a recently sunk submarine to find out what went wrong." This gives us the main point and its purpose, omits a bit of setting (who said it and where), and relegates the fire and fatalities to background.[7] The second paragraph exactly fits our notion of an independent SP (something you might want to know while on the topic, but not connected to it by an s, e, r, or q). So, the backbone of the paraphrase would be as follows:

	MP:	The Soviet Navy will try to raise a nuclear sub that recently sank (off Norway).
$[e_p]$	SP:	They want to discover why it sank.
$[i]$	SP:	The sub poses no radiation danger.

To complete the structure, let us ask our four questions about these points. First about the main point.

MP:	Any [e]?	Yes: $[e_p]$ above; no others.
	Any [s]?	No: MP just announced.
	Any [r]?	No: no consequences of the intent are given.
	Any [q]?	Yes: "The details . . . have not been worked out . . . the experts will deal with it."

So we have uncovered another first-order SP, one that qualifies the MP by saying (in our words), "raising the sub will be tough to do." So the complete first-order structure will look like this:

> MP: The Soviet Navy intends to retrieve a nuclear submarine that sank recently (near Norway).

---

7. Note that the fire and fatalities are cause and consequences of the sinking itself, not of the MP of this article. The MP of this article takes the sinking as background. Look again at the description of background in the padding taxonomy in Chapter 1.

[e_p]   SP: They want to find out why it sank.
[q]   SP: It will be difficult to raise.
[i]   SP: The sub presents no radiation danger.

This gives us three SPs to ask our questions about. Can we find

Anything under [e_p]? No: Nothing further about the purpose.
Anything under [q]?   Yes: Two reasons are given to think it will be tough
                       to raise: it's 5000 feet down and its hull is cracked.
                       So we have two [s]s under the [q].
Anything under [i]?   Yes: Again, two reasons to think there is no radia-
                       tion danger: the reactor was shut down and the tor-
                       pedoes were not armed.

Because this is an exercise in searching for structural connections, let us ask our
questions of each second-order SP as well (even though this will reveal structural
detail far beyond anything a bare-bones paraphrase would usually require). This
turns up just one further (third-order) SP: "cracked" is qualified by "but intact."
So the complete array would look like this:

           MP: The Soviet Navy intends to retrieve a nuclear submarine that sank
               recently (near Norway).
[e_p]   SP: They wish to discover the cause of its sinking.
[q]   SP: It will be difficult to raise.
[s]   SP: The sub is in 5,000 feet of water.
[s]   SP: The sub is probably cracked.
[q]   SP: (But) it seems intact.
[i]   SP: The sub presents no radiation danger.
[s]   SP: The reactors were shut down.
[s]   SP: The torpedoes were not armed.

Here the three first-order secondaries ([e_p], [q], and [i]) all relate directly to the
MP, whereas the others relate directly to the secondaries under which they are
indented.

Exercise 2.11

Structure a paraphrase for the following article by interrogation. Use as its MP
"Artificial flavorings may lower heart attack risk." (Answer on p. 89.)

SAN FRANCISCO—A new study suggests health-food enthusiasts got it all
wrong: Artificial flavorings in everything from barbecue potato chips to tooth-
paste may actually be good for you. The reason: All sorts of artificial flavors
contain salicylates, a chemical cousin of aspirin. And aspirin is known to reduce the risk of heart attacks by preventing blood clots.
    The new study found that people take in the equivalent of one baby aspirin
a day from the artificial flavorings put in processed foods. The researchers say
that Americans' taste for artificial flavorings may help explain why fewer peo-

ple are dying from heart attacks. "We are presenting what we consider to be a plausible hypothesis, but it needs a lot more exploration," said Lillian M. Ingster of the National Center for Health Statistics in Hyattsville, MD.

Deaths from heart attacks rose steadily through this century until about 30 years ago, when they began to fall. Experts have searched for reasons to explain this and have come up with several, including less smoking, lower consumption of saturated fats, better medicines and more exercise. The problem, though, is that heart disease began to drop before most of the healthier living habits came into vogue. "The decline in heart disease started rather abruptly in the mid-'60s. Within about three or four years it spread across the country. It's hard to imagine that something like cholesterol lowering or blood pressure treatment could explain it," said Ingster's colleague, Dr. Manning Feinleib. Salicylates in food "may be the missing link in explaining why this decline occurred when it did as widely as it did."

Feinleib and Ingster presented their case for this new explanation Thursday at a conference sponsored by the American Heart Association. The researchers said they are not telling people to change their eating habits. Certainly, eating more junk food would be an unhealthy way to take in more salicylates.

(The Associated Press)

USEFUL PATTERNS

The seven types of dependent subordination obviously relate to each other in many different ways. Some are the "opposite" of others, some are subtypes of the same general kind, some occur in pairs, and some overlap in function. We will explore these relations in the rest of this chapter. But let us begin by looking at some patterns in them that will be useful in organizing our thinking about structure. The first pattern is functional: Secondary Points have just three general functions: explanatory, inferential, and qualificatory. The pattern looks like this:

Function Taxonomy
1. Explanatory (etiological) SPs
   a. Explanations of MP
      i. Cause [e_c]
      ii. Motive [e_m]
      iii. Purpose [e_p]
   b. Explanations by MP
      i. Effect [r_e]
2. Inferential SPs
   a. Support for MP [s]
   b. Implications of MP [r_i]
3. Qualifications of MP [q]

Because the following chapters examine reasoning, they will be exclusively concerned with the inferential SPs of Function 2. So we will devote some time to distinguishing those from the others.

Antecedents and Consequents

We have occasionally noted that subordination is often carried by certain characteristic words: "because," "but," and "so," for example. We will refer to these indicator words as *flag terms* and speak of them as *flagging* different kinds of subordination. "But" flags a certain kind of qualification, for instance. Now if we confine our attention to explanatory and inferential subordination (see Function Taxonomy, above), an interesting pattern stands out. Of the six "types" that fall under these two headings, three are flagged by "because" ([e_c], [e_m], and [s]), and the other three by "so" ([e_p], [r_e], and [r_i]). This is displayed in Table 2.1, together with other characteristic flags of each type.

When we contrasted [e_m] with [e_p] we found it natural to think of the first as backward-looking and the second as forward-looking. This is the pattern that stands out in Table 2.1. "Because" looks backward (to what came earlier). "So" looks forward (to what comes later). We can assimilate arguments to this pattern by thinking of them as "going from" support to conclusion (to implication). So the labels "antecedent" (for what comes before) and "consequent" (for what comes after) display the similarities.

Figure 2.3 displays geometrically the various relations that secondary points may bear to a main point. In Figure 2.3 the main point is surrounded by the eight different kinds of secondary point, antecedents at the top and consequents at the bottom. The connecting lines represent dependency and display the structural possibilities in a passage: answers to all the different questions we can ask about the MP. Higher order subordination (more complex structure) may be displayed by constructing smaller versions of this same diagram around any SP: taking that secondary point to be the main point of a sub essay.

TABLE 2.1 Flag Types

Type	Type Flag	Other Characteristic Indicators
Antecedent		
[e_c] Cause	Because	Due to, owing to
[e_m] Motive	Because	
[s] Support	Because	For, since, after all
Consequent		
[e_p] Purpose	So (so that)	In order to, for the sake of
[r_e] Effect	So	Which caused, and as a result
[r_i] Implication	So	Therefore, it follows that

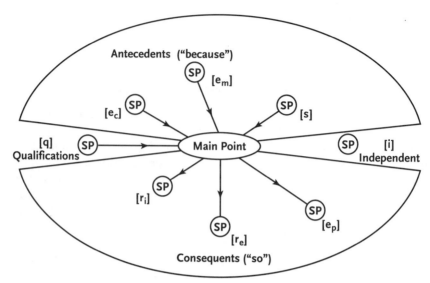

Figure 2.3. Dependency diagram.

Exercise 2.12

For each of the following single-sentence paraphrases (a) label the subordination, (b) locate it in Figure 2.3, and (c) reformulate the sentence with "because" or "so." (Answers on p. 90.)

a. The small trailer was flattened when the boulder hit it.

b. You'll never find him; he's been missing too long.

c. He set two alarms to make sure he'd get up on time.

d. The boulder rolled down the hill and flattened the small trailer.

e. He's been missing too long for there to be any chance of finding him now.

Explaining and Inferring

One striking feature of Figure 2.3 is that different *kinds* of subordination have the same characteristic flag term. Both [e] and [s] may be flagged by "because," but they are wholly different kinds of SPs: one explains why the MP happened and the other gives an argument for it. Similarly for [r_e] and [r_i]: the word "so" is characteristic of each, though again they are of very different kinds: [r_e] tells you what the MP caused whereas [r_i] tells you what you can infer from it, what it is an argument for. The following mnemonic will help you hold the distinction in mind:

Mnemonic
When the passage (or paraphrase) reads "MP because SP," then either

a. the "because" is an [e] if the SP *causes* the MP,

or

    b. the "because" is an [s] if the SP is *reason to think* the MP is true.

When the passage (or paraphrase) reads "MP so SP," then either

    a. the "so" is an [r_e] if the MP *causes* the SP,

or

    b. the "so" is an [r_i] if the MP is *reason to think* the SP is true.

You might think that using the same word to do such radically different jobs would risk great confusion. It turns out, however, that a systematic feature of the way we use these flag terms allows us to easily distinguish explanation from inference in the vast majority of cases. Let us take a look.

First, note that we seldom confuse the two in actual cases. The context usually provides enough information to make the proper identification easy. For instance, sometimes the MP and SP are *not things that can be caused* or brought about, such as events or actions. In such cases they can't be related by our explanatory categories ([e] or [r_e]). A "because" or "so" in that case will have to flag inference ([s] or [r_i]). For instance,

    The square root of 289 must be 17, because that's what Mike put down.

Here, the MP is "the square root of 289 is 17," and that isn't caused by anything, so we know the subordination cannot be [e], it must be [s]. And, of course, that was pretty obvious to begin with. Mike's putting down 17 is being used as *an argument* here, as reason to think the answer given in the MP is right.

Even if the MP and SP are things that have causes, however, the subordination is often clear because one or the other type simply will not make any sense in the context. For example, a passage may read,

    It seems to be raining, because water is dripping through the kitchen ceiling.

Here, though both the rain and the drip doubtless have causes, the drip can't be *causing* the rain in any normal context. So, here again we can easily determine that subordination is [s]: the drip is an argument for the claim that it is raining.

                 MP: It is raining.
[s]   SP: Water is dripping through the kitchen ceiling.

Exercise 2.13

Which of the following "becauses" and "sos" make sense as causal? (Answers on p. 90.)

a. The trailer looks like that because a boulder hit it.

b. The plane crashed so it must have been out of fuel.

c. The light is burned out because it doesn't go on with the switch.

> d. The light was burned out, so it didn't go on with the switch.
>
> e. The light didn't go on with the switch, so it must be burned out.

In some passages, however, none of these simple tests works, yet the subordination is clear. How do we tell? The key is **Indirectness.** When both MP and SP are events or actions, and make sense as related in either explanation or inference, the question to ask is whether we know about one of them only *through* the other. Let us consider the two pairs separately.

Antecedents ([e] versus [s])

If an MP is an event or action, and an SP is given *in support of* it, then the SP is our "reason to think the MP happened." That is, we do not know about the MP *directly*, but only *through the SP*. So if the passage reads:

"MP because SP"

and we are unsure whether the subordination is [e] or [s], ask the following:

Do we know about the MP *directly*, through observation or simple report of it, or only *indirectly* through knowing the SP?

If we know of it directly, then the subordination is [e]; if indirectly, then the subordination is [s]. So, in the usual sort of context, if a newspaper article reads,

The plane crashed because it was out of fuel

the subordination would be [e]. For we would normally know about the crash directly, through observing it or from reports of it. We would normally not know about it by first finding out that it was out of fuel. So the structured paraphrase would be as follows:

	MP: The plane crashed.
[e]	SP: It was out of fuel.

This is a valuable tool because the English language contains numerous *indirectness flags*. These are words whose job is to point out the indirectness that signals inference. Authors will often use them explicitly for this purpose, and we will naturally put them in our paraphrases, even when they are not in the passage. The most obvious example of an indirectness flag would be the "seems to be" in the sentence about rain. Saying "it seems to be raining" tells you we did not just look out the window and see rain, but only know about it *indirectly* through the drip in the kitchen. Perhaps the most common indirectness flag like this is "must." This occurred naturally in our first example. When the passage said, "the square root of 289 *must* be 17," you could tell the author was inferring it from something: they did not just *know* it. In this case we were inferring it from the fact that Mike had given that answer. Many other words and phrases play this same role: "probably," "I suspect," "doubtless," "I'm sure that," "I'll bet," and more.

If you run into a case in which the SP makes sense as either [e] or [s], look around for indications of indirectness *in the MP*. For instance, if a single-sentence paraphrase is "It's raining because they seeded the clouds this morning," the seeding might be a cause [e] or an indicator [s] of rain. So you need to look back at the passage to see how we know about the rain. If the passage reads

I'm sure it's raining by now, because they seeded the clouds this morning

this makes it clear that we know about the MP only through the seeding. "I'm sure . . . by now" is an indirectness flag. Therefore, the structured paraphrase would be

> MP: It is raining.
>
> [s]   SP: They seeded the clouds this morning.

What you are looking for, of course, is the indirectness itself, whether or not it is flagged. So if the passage makes it clear that we are supposed to know about the MP only through the SP, then the subordination is [s] even without a flag. You may put the proper flag in your single-sentence paraphrase, if you wish, because you understand the subordination. On the other hand, you leave indirectness indicators out of the indented paraphrase, just as you would any connection flag.

Now suppose we change the example a little so that it reads as follows:

It's been raining nonstop all day because they seeded the clouds this morning.

This makes it pretty clear that the author knows about the rain directly, has seen it or heard it and possibly even gotten wet in it, and is explaining the downpour by appeal to the cloud seeding. The structure of the passage would then look like this:

> MP: It is raining.
>
> [e$_c$]   SP: They seeded the clouds this morning.

Exercise 2.14

Indent and label the following. (a) Termites had evidently damaged the structure because it almost disintegrated in the earthquake. (b) That must have been some windstorm last night, every tree in the yard has major damage. (Answers on p. 90.)

CONSEQUENTS ([r$_e$] VERSUS [r$_i$])

Indirectness flags inference when the subordination is [r], too; but in this case it is the *Secondary Point* that we know only indirectly. We know it *through* the MP. So for [r$_i$], the indirectness flags will be in the SP, not the MP. And we have already seen one clear example of this:

He fired six shots in rapid succession, so the gun must have been fully loaded.

Here the "must" signals that we know the SP only *through* the MP; that is, we are inferring the SP, and the subordination is [r$_i$]. All the now familiar indirectness flags help distinguish [r$_i$] from [r$_e$]. But again, if the context makes clear that we know the SP only through the MP, then the subordination is [r$_i$] even if no indirectness flags appear in the passage.

The other tests work with [r] too. Sometimes an SP will make sense only as one or the other, eliminating one alternative. For instance,

The light doesn't work so the switch must be broken

Here the MP makes no sense as a *cause* of the SP, so the subordination cannot be [r$_e$]:

	MP: The light doesn't work.
[r$_i$]	SP: The switch is broken.

But again, we could also tell this from the indirectness flag.

Two rules summarize this section, and may help you make this distinction in practice:

1. Sometimes only inference ([s] or [r$_i$]) will make sense.
2. When both explanation and inference make sense, indirectness will usually tell us whether inference is going on and, if it is, what is inferred from what (whether it is [s] or [r$_i$]).

Exercise 2.15

Write in the kind of subordination most plausible in the following single-sentence paraphrases of passages. Routine: First look for indirectness flags; if there are none, see if the sentence makes sense as explanation; if it does not, see if an indirectness flag makes sense somewhere. (Answers on p. 90.)

a. We can see better because they cleaned the windows.
b. They must have cleaned the windows, because we can see better.
c. The ruler moved because I didn't hold it securely.
d. I didn't hold the ruler securely, because it moved.
e. The ruler moved and smudged the ink.
f. The sun is out so it must have stopped raining.
g. The sun is out so I am happy again.
h. He limps because he has arthritis.
i. He must have arthritis because of the way he limps.
j. He has arthritis, but not bad enough to complain about.
k. She lost her job and had to sell her house.
l. We made a lot of noise so everybody must be up by now.
m. We made so much noise that everybody must be awake.
n. We made a lot of noise and woke everybody up.

TABLE 2.2 Common Qualifications

Type	What It Says about MP	Flag Terms
1. Means	How they did it	By
2. Condition	Under what conditions	If, when, only
3. Mitigation	It's not as bad as it seems	But
4. Obstacle	Anticipated difficulties	But, although
5. Prevailing	Difficulties overcome	In spite of
6. Elaboration	Gives relevant detail	Which, including
7. Comparison	Relation to similar cases	More, less
8. Amplification	Worse/better than it seems	Moreover
9. Sense/respect	Character, nature	In that, because

Qualification Types and Flags

The explanatory and inferential SPs form a tight functional cluster: all six either explain or support the MP, or are explained or supported by the MP. And all are flagged by a closely related group of terms. By contrast, qualifications say an enormous number of very different things about the MP, and they are flagged by a wide variety of different words. Table 2.2 lists a number of common types. It will provide a useful reference.

Exercise 2.16

Identify the kind of [q] in the following:

a. They cleaned the windshield by rubbing it with newspapers.

b. The Earth's atmosphere did not warm much in the nineteenth century, even though the industrial revolution put a lot of carbon dioxide into the atmosphere.

c. The deficit is projected to increase by 37% in the next ten years, if some effort is not made to reduce middle-class entitlements.

d. Four people were killed in the incident, and two of them were residents of the board and care facility sponsoring the event.

e. The crew managed to keep the ship on course in gale-force winds.

f. He's a worthless friend: he has no sense of loyalty.

(Answers on p. 90.)

TRICKS FOR TOUGH CASES

After reading a passage carefully a couple times, your understanding of it will usually be adequate to guide a competent paraphrase. You will normally not need special rules or tricks to find the proper structure. Occasionally, however, a passage will not fall easily into the categories we have laid out here, and when that happens, the strategies examined in this section will be of some help. They deal with three problems: (1) sorting out all the different things that might be indicated by "because"; (2) distinguishing four different roles played by consequences; and (3) using your discretion wisely to combine various items into a single point.

Distinguishing [e] from [s] in Human Action

We have already learned how to distinguish [e] from [s] and [r_e] from [r_i] when the passage concerns simply whether something happens or not. Some passages explain *why* it happened (or happens), and others give us reason to *think* it happens (or happened). And we can tell which is which by noticing (a) what makes sense and (b) indirectness. But when the substance of a passage concerns human action, the possibility of *evaluation* arises. We talk not only of whether something was done, but also whether it *should* have been done. This requires a slightly different treatment of the distinction between explanation and inference. It will also reveal some contextual flexibility in our paraphrases.

The notion of a "reason" is famously ambiguous in human affairs. When we give a reason for something we did, it is sometimes simply an explanation [e_m] of the action and sometimes a justification [s]. There is nothing invidious in this distinction. It is just a function of what the passage is about. Sometimes it will be trying to justify and sometimes simply to explain. So when "MP because SP" concerns human action, the trick is to notice whether the MP is *descriptive* or *evaluative*. In other words, does the MP simply describe an action, or does it also say it is a good or bad idea. The subordination is [s] only if the MP is evaluative (what philosophers call "normative"): if it concerns what *should or should not* happen. If it simply describes the action, the subordination is [e_m]. For instance, in our illustrative example,

They set off the dynamite because it had become unsafe with age

the subordination is [e_m] because the MP is simply the action of setting off the dynamite, not whether they should have or should not have.

	MP: They set off the dynamite.
[e_m]	SP: It was old and unstable.

But if the sentence had read

We should set off the dynamite, because it has become unsafe with age

we would have an argument. The SP is offered in support of a proposal. We could even do this in the past tense and third person: "They were right to set off the dynamite, because it was old and unstable."

	MP: They were right to set off the dynamite.
[s]	SP: It was old and unstable.

All this works in the same way if the connection is "so" instead of "because." If the single-sentence paraphrase is "The dynamite was old and unstable, so they blew it up," the subordination would be explanatory. But if it read, "The dynamite was old and unstable, so they should have gotten rid of it long ago," the subordination would be inferential.

Exercise 2.17

Indent and label these last two single-sentence paraphrases. (Answers on p. 90.)

This rule will be most helpful when a passage describes a person or group offering a *proposal* or *recommendation*. Then the subordination in "MP because SP" would depend on whether the MP is the recommendation itself (which would then have a "should" or "right" in it), or the *action* of making the recommendation. An article discussing the restrictions on Iraq imposed after the Gulf War, for instance, might have the following paraphrase:

The United Nations proposed trade sanctions against Iraq because that country refuses to allow biological warfare inspections.

Here the subordination would be [e$_m$], because the MP is a description of the proposed action. On the other hand, it might be written from the point of view of the UN and be paraphrased like this:

Trade with Iraq should be restricted because it will not allow biological warfare inspections.

In this case the MP is the proposal itself, containing the normative "should," so the subordination would be [s].

> MP: Trade with Iraq should be restricted.
> [s]   SP: It won't allow inspections.

Sometimes the same article may be summarized either way depending on the context.

WASHINGTON—A children's advocacy group said yesterday it wants the government to investigate whether a long-range microphone marketed in a line of high-tech toys is an illegal eavesdropping device. "Part of it is just a pretend spy kit," said Peggy Charren, president of Action for Children's Television. "The problem is that the listening device works. It is not then a toy; it is an eavesdropping device."

Tyco Industries Inc. manufactures the "Spy-Tech" toy line, which includes the microphone, an undercover vest, binoculars, an intruder alert, periscope, fingerprint kit, walkie-talkies and a hidden camera. The toys, each sold separately, are designed for children 8 years and older.

(The Associated Press)

The way the first sentence introduces this case, we naturally take the topic to be the group's action in objecting to this toy, rather than the objection itself. So the overall structure would be something like this:

> MP: A pressure group (ACT) wants the government to ban a long-range toy microphone.
> [e]   SP: They feel it falls under statutes outlawing eavesdropping devices.

Were the article written from the group's point of view, however, or if your instructor had asked you to paraphrase the group's argument, then we would make the recommendation the MP, and the subordination would be [s]:

	MP:	The government should ban a long-range toy microphone.
[s]	SP:	Its use falls under statutes outlawing eavesdropping devices.

Beginning with Chapter 3 our interest will turn exclusively to reasoning. There we would look at the passage simply for the sake of the reasoning it contained, and so we would usually want the second of these paraphrases.

We may summarize this section in a simple rule: *if the passage is normative, look for an argument* ([s] or [r_i]). But very often we may be even more specific. When the "should" (or other normative term) is in the MP followed by "because," the subordination will be [s]. If it is in the SP preceded by "so," it will be [r_i].

Exercise 2.18
....

Give the subordination type for each of the following single-sentence paraphrases. (Answers on p. 90.)

a. The Fed lowered interest rates because the economy is sluggish.

b. The Fed should lower interest rates, because the economy is sluggish.

c. The economy is sluggish, so the Fed should lower interest rates.

d. They ought to clean the windows because they are so dirty.

e. They cleaned the windows to improve visibility.

f. The windows are filthy; they should get somebody to clean them.

Distinguishing Etiologies from Qualifications ([e] from [q])

Earlier in the chapter we noted that qualification [q] covers explaining things about the MP other than why it occurred. Explaining who was involved in the MP, or what kind of thing it was, or how it compares with other similar cases all fall under [q]. These explanatory [q]s will often be introduced by our multipurpose subordinator "because"; but whether it is a [q] or an [e] will usually be clear. For example, suppose a passage condenses into "The house is too small because the builder misread the plans." This explains how the house came to be too small and what brought it about, so the subordination is clearly [e].

	MP:	The house is too small.
[e_c]	SP:	The builder misread the plans.

Now consider a similarly structured passage having the same MP: "The house is too small, because there is no room for my grand piano." This subordination is not an [e] because it does not tell us how the house came to be too small; it just describes the *way* it is too small (what it is about it that makes it too small). So the subordination is [q].

[q]
                MP: The house is too small.
                     SP: There is no room for my piano.

Other examples of [q]s flagged by "because" would be "Ravens are annoying because of the racket they make" and "That tie doesn't go with the shirt because
it's too busy."

When "Because" Might Be Either [q] or [s]

In some cases very much like the [q]s in the last section, the author of a passage
will be treating the SP as support for the MP, not merely a qualification. And
because this is a reasoning text, we will want to keep our eyes open for arguments that may not be easy to identify. The cases in question will sound right
with either a "because" or an "in that." Nevertheless, the author will be using
the SP as *grounds for* the MP. We have already seen some examples. One part
of the nuclear sub illustration, for instance, attributes the following argument
to Admiral Vargin: "The sub will be difficult to raise because it is in 5000 feet
of water." Here we might have used "in that" instead of "because" without
changing the sense of the paraphrase. But since the difficult raising is in the future, we have no problem seeing the subordination as [s]. The only way Vargin
knows about the difficulty is *through* the depth, so the indirectness flags fit perfectly: the sub will "probably" (or "surely," or "no doubt") be difficult to raise
because it is so deep.

When the MP does not concern a future event, however, this distinction is
harder to make, so we must pay special attention to context to make the deter-
mination.

His presidency was a failure because he was unpopular when he left office.

Here the author might be saying that unpopular is *all that failure comes to* here, all
it means to be a failure. Unpopularity would simply be a *kind* of failure, and hence
the subordination would be [q]. By contrast, the context may make clear that failure refers to something more substantial than mere unpopularity, such as not having a coherent set of policies or not reacting competently to the problems arising
during his term. And in this case the author might be using unpopularity as a
symptom of these more substantial things, a recognition by his constituency that
he had done some things poorly. If so, indirectness flags would fit in the paraphrase before "failure" ("it must have been a failure," "probably was a failure"),
and the subordination would be [s].

Exercise 2.19
....

In which of the following is the subordination plausibly [q]? (a) The talk was
boring because it went on so long. (b) The leftovers are probably unsafe to eat
because they're covered with little green specks. (c) My printer is a pain because the roller's contaminated and messes up the copy. (Answer on p. 90.)

A more difficult but similar case would be one in which the author is listing characteristics of failure, not symptoms, but also not simply cutting off debate and saying this is all failure amounts to.

> I'd say he was a failure, because he did not get a single major piece of his program through Congress, and was unable to whip up public support for his diplomatic initiatives.

Here everything would rest on signs of indirectness or insecurity in the passage, and the "I'd say" here is one such sign. The author is not simply saying "this is a kind of failure" but offering these two particular items in support of the charge that the presidency failed in some larger way.

So to distinguish between [s] and [q] in cases such as this, we must pay special attention to indirectness: whether the author is using the SP *as an indicator of something further* or just giving us a particular way or sense in which the MP description fits. As a rule, *if there is no indirectness* a "because" that can be paraphrased "in that" will be [q].

Exercise 2.20
....

Explain why the "annoying ravens" example and the "busy tie" example at the end of the last section would be [q]s and not [s]s. (Answer on p. 90.)

The Various Roles of Consequences

Talking about the consequences of actions and events can play four different roles in structuring exposition: when an SP is (or concerns) a consequence of the MP, the subordination may be $[r_e]$, $[r_i]$, $[e_p]$, or [s]. And although your understanding of them will often be perfectly clear, it will be worth gathering all four of them in one place, to point out their contrasting features. This will provide some guidance when your confidence falters.

Let us illustrate these roles using a commonplace example. When the Federal Reserve Board changes interest rates, that will have more or less regular consequences for the American economy. Much economic journalism has recently discussed these, and the discussion has involved each of the four possible subordination types. So let us look at single-sentence paraphrases illustrating each. Consider first a simple causal consequence: "The Fed lowered interest rates last summer, which led to a healthier economy this spring." Here we have simply "A caused B," so the subordination is $[r_e]$.

$[r_e]$ MP: The Fed lowered interest rates.
               SP: The economy is growing.

A different passage might say, "The Fed lowered interest rates to stimulate the economy." Here the MP is an action and we can recognize that the connection "to" is short for "in order to," so the SP gives the *purpose* of the action.

$[e_p]$ MP: The Fed lowered interest rates.
               SP: To stimulate the economy.

TABLE 2.3 Clues to the Role of a Consequence

Type	Constraints	Characteristic Flags
[r$_e$]	SP an event or action	So, caused
[r$_i$]	SP treated as a statement	So, must, probably
[e$_p$]	MP a human action	So that, to, in order to
[s]	MP a recommendation	Should, right to

A third kind of subordination is found in "The Fed recently lowered interest rates, so they must have thought the economy was losing steam." Here the indirectness flag "must" tells you an inference is being made, and since it is in the SP, *that* is what we know indirectly. So the SP is an implication of the MP:

	MP: The Fed lowered interest rates.
[r$_i$]	SP: They were worried about the sluggish economy.

Finally, we might find a consequence at work in the following way: "The Fed should lower interest rates because that would stimulate the economy." Here the "because" tips us off that we're dealing with one of the *antecedent* forms of subordination ([e] or [s]) in the *top* of Figure 2.3 on p. 54. And the "should" tells us we're dealing with a recommendation, not an event, so that eliminates [e]:

	MP: The Fed should lower interest rates.
[s]	SP: That would stimulate the economy.

This is a very common argument form: supporting a recommendation (something normative) by appeal to some consequence it would have. This connection is most easily confused with purpose [e$_p$], which also may use "because it would" to flag a consequence ("they lowered rates because that would stimulate the economy"). But the two subordinations ([s] and [e$_p$]) *use* the consequence in different ways. One uses it to explain the action ([e$_p$]) and the other to give an argument for doing it ([s]). So in cases such as this, the crucial thing is to *look for normative terms* such as "should" and "right." These will be the clues that what you have is an argument.

When the MP is a recommendation (telling us what we *ought* to do), a link to a consequence such as this will virtually always be an argument [s]. This is an even more reliable test than looking for a "because," since the connecting flag in such cases will sometimes be typical of a consequent. For instance, had the passage read "The Fed should lower interest rates to stimulate the economy," it should be paraphrased exactly as would the previous example.

All these observations are gathered in Table 2.3.

Exercise 2.21

Label the subordination in the following:

a. The economic forecast was bad, causing the market to plunge.

b. There was no fire on impact, so the plane must have been out of fuel.

c. The plane was out of fuel, so there was no fire on impact.

d. They should clean the windows, to improve visibility.

e. The car was speeding and was unable to negotiate the turn.

f. They should slow down so that they can negotiate the turn.

g. They slowed down so they could make the turn.

h. The car was unable to negotiate the turn, so it must have been speeding.

i. Debris characteristic of termite activity was everywhere, so they decided against making an offer on the house.

j. Debris characteristic of termite activity was everywhere, so the house probably needs to be fumigated.

k. The Titanic sank with 1750 souls.

(Answers on p. 90.)

Comment and Explanation

Recall that the function of a dependent SP is to *say something about* the MP, to *comment on* it. If we are careful, we may think of **all** of these comments as explanations in a very broad sense. The etiologies we represent as [e] are only a very special kind of explanation: they explain why something happened. These are particularly important for our purposes, so we have singled them out for special use of the word. But all of the categories may be thought of as *explaining something or other*, so let us organize the points from the last few sections by thinking of the different SPs as (again: broadly) explaining different things about the MP.

[s]   Explains how we can tell the MP is true (how we can tell it happened, if it is an event).

[e]   Explains why the MP happened, what brought it about.

[r_e]   Explains what effect the MP had, what it caused.

[r_i]   Explains what we can tell from knowing the MP, what it implies.

[q]   Explains other things about the MP, such as the kind of thing it is, the sense in which it fits the description given, how it might be misunderstood, who was involved, and all the other things on the list on p. 59.

Combining [s]s and Combining [q]s

We have seen that some qualifications are so closely associated with an MP that they are essentially part of it (typically adjectives). Look again at the article on the World Trade Center fire (on p. 43). We might have begun its paraphrase like this:

MP: There was a fire in the World Trade Center yesterday.
[q]   SP: It was smoky.
[q]   SP: It was an electrical fire.
[q]   SP: On the ground floor.

But not only would this have distracted us from the structure of the article, which lay elsewhere, it would dwell on detail so fine that the paraphrase would rival the passage in length. So if we were to include these details at all, it would be better simply to make them part of the MP:

MP: There was a smoky electrical fire on the ground floor of the World Trade Center yesterday.

But even this is too much: the smoky and electrical aspects are covered by implication elsewhere in the paraphrase, and nothing much depends on the fire being on the first floor. So we settled on a simpler MP, without any of these qualifications. This is the sort of judgment call you will be constantly making as you paraphrase. And this judgment improves with practice.

Your discretion is tested in something like the same way when a passage offers several substantial qualifications at the same level. If the MP is qualified in three ways, A, B, and C (and unlike the previous case, they are important to the paraphrase), you still have the option of combining them into a single qualification. That is, you might structure it like this:

MP:

[q] SP: A
[q] SP: B
[q] SP: C

Or, you might choose this:

MP:

[q] SP: A, B, and C.

The same is true of support [s]. Several of the arguments we have examined have included more than one item offered in support of something; and in each case we might have combined them into a single item. For instance, in the motel explosion, instead of two separate supporting SPs, the evidence that the maintenance worker set it off could have been put in one SP:

SP: A maintenance worker had been called to investigate a lack of hot water, and he was one of the most seriously injured.

Similarly, the two separate items of support in Admiral Vargin's argument that the submarine will be tough to raise could have been put as follows:

SP: The sub is in 5000 feet of water and is probably cracked.

So the question is, why not always combine [q]s or [s]s when they are subordinate to the same point? There are actually two reasons, one obvious and the other more subtle. The obvious one is clarity of display. Sometimes it is simply clearer to list items of support or distinct qualifications separately. And if your aim is to display your understanding of a piece to your instructor, that is normally the safest course.

But there is another, more substantive reason to do so. For sometimes, one or another of the individual [q]s or [s]s will have something *subordinate to it*, that is

not connected to the others. And to display this in the structure will require separating it out for attention. For instance, the structure might be

	MP:
[s]	SP: A
[q]	SP: C
[s]	SP: B

Here, the two supporting SPs could not be combined, because C qualifies only
one of them. And this is exactly what happened in the Vargin example (look again
at p. 51): "intact" qualified "cracked," but not "5000 feet," so the two had to be
separated in the paraphrase. Of course, if we decided that "intact" was too fine
a detail to include in the paraphrase, then the two supporting items could be combined without this problem. They still might be worth keeping separate for simple clarity of display, however.

To illustrate this point, consider another short article:

> A meningitis epidemic sweeping through western Africa has killed more than
> 4,500 people and shows no signs of abating, the World Health Organization said
> Thursday. Most of the victims are children under 14, and millions of people are
> at risk, the U.N. agency said.
>
> The epidemic began in January, taking the highest toll in Nigeria. The num-
> ber of dead there rose to 3,386—an increase of more than 700 in a week—according
> to the latest U.N. figures. Almost 19,000 people have been infected.
>
> (The Associated Press)

Because of the compact presentation, you might be tempted to make the causal
claim in the first clause the MP.

	MP: A meningitis epidemic in Africa has killed 4500.
[q]	SP: It is not abating.
[q]	SP: Most victims are under 14.

And although it would not always be wrong to have a causal MP, it will not work
in this case. Because the two SPs are not subordinate to the causal claim (that the
epidemic killed so many), but rather one comments on the epidemic itself and the
other on its victims. It is the epidemic that is not abating, and the 4500 victims
who are mostly under 14. So we would have to break up the MP into the epidemic and its effect.

	MP: Africa is suffering a meningitis epidemic.
[r_e]	SP: It has already killed 4500.
[q]	SP: Most of them under 14.
[q]	SP: It is not abating.

Exercise 2.22

a. Paraphrase the following article two ways: first listing the [q]s separately
and then by combining them in an efficient way.

A coin-operated computer for public use will be available at the La Sierra branch Library beginning Monday. In addition to the PC, a printer and several software programs will be available. Paper is furnished for the printer, but patrons must supply their own disks, if needed.

The computer runs for 15 minutes for a quarter, and only quarters can be used. The Central Library on Seventh Street and other local branches already offer coin-operated computers. The La Sierra branch is at 4600 La Sierra Ave; hours are from 10 a.m. to 9 p.m. weekdays.

b. Paraphrase the following article two ways: first combining green tea's cancer fighting components into a single point and then distinguishing them to elaborate the subordination under them.

The evidence pointing to tea's cancer fighting ability is compelling. Epidemiological studies in Japan have shown that people who consume at least one cup of green tea a day exhibit lower rates of lung, stomach, esophageal and skin cancer. Researchers speculate it's because green tea is rich in catechin, which has been shown to slow cancer in laboratory animals, and high in certain flavinoids that attack free radicals, which may play a role in developing skin cancer.

(*The Vegetarian Times*, 9.96)

(Answers on p. 90.)

SYSTEMATIC FEATURES

Subordination Cascades and Padding

When you paraphrase longer passages (essays, chapters) you will naturally find yourself using more levels of subordination. Greater length allows more complicated structures, and our indenting procedure places no limit on the amount of structure you may represent. A very complicated structure might look like this:

MP_1: ....
  SP_1: ....
    SP_6: ....
      SP_{10}: ....
  SP_2: ....
    SP_7: ....
    SP_8: ....
      SP_{11}: ....
        SP_{12}: ....
  SP_3: ....
MP_2: ....
  SP_4: ....
    SP_9: ....
  SP_5: ....

Here, SP_1, SP_2, and SP_3 are all directly subordinate to MP_1, that is, each answers a question about MP_1. SP_4 and SP_5 are similarly subordinate to MP_2. None of the other secondary points lies directly under a main point, however: each of them is instead subordinate to one of the other secondary points. SP_6 is subordinate to SP_1, SP_{12} to SP_{11}, and so on. Complicated diagrams such as this will usually contain strings of subordination that we earlier described as "cascades." One such cascade is

$$MP_1 \rightarrow SP_1 \rightarrow SP_6 \rightarrow SP_{10}$$

another is

$$MP_1 \rightarrow SP_2 \rightarrow SP_8 \rightarrow SP_{11} \rightarrow SP_{12}.$$

A subordination cascade is recognizable in our bare-bones paraphrase form as a string of secondary points indented further and further to the right. Go back to the diagram and circle all of the subordination cascades just to train your eye to pick them out.

Sometimes the only thing that will end a cascade, and keep you from writing another line in the structure, is that not ending it would add too much detail to bother with in a paraphrase. You stop because the next line would count as padding; it would be too trivial to include.

The SPs linked together in a cascade may be of all different kinds, of course: the first may be a cause, the next support, the next a qualification, and so on. But cascades will sometimes be all of the same kind, a series of qualifications, for instance, or a sequence of causes, or consequences, or support for support for support. These are of special interest because they reveal an interesting pattern in our understanding of things.

Perhaps the most natural illustration would be a sequence of consequences in which the MP is the first item in the sequence. A famous homily thus records the sequence of events behind a great military defeat:

> For the want of a nail, a shoe was lost; for the want of a shoe, a horse was lost; for the want of a horse, a rider was lost; for the want of a rider, a battle was lost; for the want of a battle, a Kingdom was lost; all for the want of a nail.

Taking the nail to be the MP, this sequence would then be structured:

	MP:	Somebody left out a nail.
[r_e]	SP:	A horse lost a shoe.
[r_e]	SP:	The horse was disabled.
[r_e]	SP:	Its rider was missing.
[r_e]	SP:	His side lost a battle.
[r_e]	SP:	The kingdom was defeated.

Each item in the structure is offered as an effect (causal consequence) of the one before it.

Support might cascade in a similar way: He should be convicted of first-degree murder because the killing was clearly deliberate: he had plenty of time to think about it because he loaded six shots into the empty gun. I'm sure of this because the neighbors heard him fire six shots in rapid succession.

          MP: He should get first-degree murder.
[s]   SP: The killing was deliberate.
[s]   SP: He had plenty of time to think about it.
[s]   SP: He loaded the gun.
[s]   SP: The neighbors heard six rapid shots.

Here, each item is offered as an argument in support of the one before it.

You will find cascades like this, or hints of them, in much that you read. And very often some of the steps that you could dig out will amount to structure too fine for a bare-bones paraphrase. So, many of them will need to be combined with others or omitted as padding. In this last cascade, for instance, a reasonable paraphrase in some contexts might be simply, "He should get first degree murder because he had plenty of time to think about it as he loaded the gun." Nothing more.

All this is perhaps better seen in a real passage.

> Gun dealers yesterday reported heavy runs on semiautomatic assault rifles as collectors, shooters and investors reacted to widening national and local controls on the weapons.
>
> "Yeah, there's been a run," said Barry Cupp, manager of the Bulletstop, a gun shop and target range in Marietta, Ga. "I've sold every assault rifle and everything that looks like an assault rifle."
>
> Buyers of the weapons this week included gun enthusiasts worried that stocks soon would be depleted, and investors who have noted the rapid runup in prices and are hoping that they can profit. "It's hysteria running wild," said Donald G. Davis, owner of Don's Guns, a chain of three stores in Indianapolis. "My price has gone up from about $350 to $1,000 today, and when I sell half of what I have left the price will go to $1,500," Davis said.
>
> At the Gun Gallery in Dallas, an AK-47, a type of gun used in the Stockton school shooting that triggered the attack on assault weapons, cost $369 on Monday, $599 on Tuesday, and $799 yesterday.
>
> *(The Associated Press)*

This article hints at a fairly substantial explanatory cascade: prices are skyrocketing because buyers have panicked because legislation threatens to restrict sales because legislators are reacting to the Stockton incident. But that would attribute more structure than this small piece could stand. About the right amount of detail would be this (omitting from the structure a [q] giving the source of the demand):

          MP: The assault gun business is booming.
[e$_c$]   SP: Legislation threatening to restrict sales.
[e$_c$]   SP: Legislators reacting to the Stockton incident.

Even this would be too much, however, because the Stockton incident is simply thrown in as background at the end of the article, so it should be omitted as padding.[8]

---

8. This shows the practical, rough-and-ready nature of padding categories. For the Stockton incident might also be omitted as "dispensable detail": something that actually fits into the structure, but too far from the MP to justify mention. Again, the padding categories are there more to guide the eye in recognizing what needs to be omitted, than as a fixed classification.

Exercise 2.23
....

a. Indent and label the following:

  i. She saved the event by generating donations by recruiting volunteers by word of mouth and newspaper advertising.

  ii. The road was wet, so when I tried to stop, the brakes locked and I lost control, ending in a ditch with a rumpled fender. So I had to spend my $360 fixing the fender and couldn't afford tickets to the Super Bowl. That's why I'm watching it on television.

  iii. The plane must have been out of fuel because there was no fire. I can tell because there was no obvious charring of the stubble in the field.

b. Write out a structured paraphrase of the following article, using order of occurrence to determine priority (i.e., MP first).

  A torrential downpour fell on Las Vegas yesterday, stranding motorists and filling houses with mud. Among those stranded was a team of surgeons driving from their hotel to a conference at the convention center where they were to demonstrate some new applications of cryogenics, according to conference spokesperson, Mabel Hamilton. The surgeons were not injured, but their demonstration had to be postponed until Saturday, Hamilton said.

(Answers on p. 91.)

Reversing Connections: Same Case, Different Priority

We mentioned earlier in the chapter (p. 35) that the connection between two points A and B does not depend on which is subordinate, even though the way we describe the connection does. For instance, if A is caused by B, this will not be affected by whether we choose A or B as the MP. But our *description* of the relationship will change from $[e_c]$ in the first case to $[r_e]$ in the second. Diagrammatically, we could represent the connection either way:

	MP: A
$[e_c]$	SP: B

or

	MP: B
$[r_e]$	SP: A

The first would say "A is caused by B"; the second would say "B causes A." These are just two different ways to describe the same connection.

This is typical of subordinations flagged by "because" and "so": if you have "A because B," but describe it starting with B instead of A, you will get "B so A." Since inferential connections are described with the same words, the same point applies to them. "The plane must have been out of fuel because there was no fire when it crashed" would be structured thus:

[s]
> MP: The plane was out of fuel.
> SP: There was no fire on impact.

But if we changed priority, we would have, "There was no fire on impact, so the plane must have been out of fuel":

[r$_i$]
> MP: There was no fire on impact.
> SP: The plane was out of fuel.

Since [e$_m$] is also flagged by "because," this sort of reversal works for it too. If a passage reads "She sent a card because she didn't want to talk to him on the phone," that would look like this:

[e$_m$]
> MP: She sent a card.
> SP: She didn't want to talk to him.

But if we change priority, and make avoiding conversation the MP, we get "She didn't want to talk to him on the phone, so she sent a card."

[r$_e$]
> MP: She didn't want to talk to him.
> SP: She sent a card.

When you reverse priority, [e$_c$] and [e$_m$] switch to [r$_e$], and [s] switches to [r$_i$], and vice versa. These switches are reliable because they are simply talking about the same relationship in each case, but looked at from a different point of view. An [s] is an inferential relationship looked at from the point of view of what is *being supported*; [r$_i$] is the same relationship, looked at from the point of view of what is *doing the supporting*. It is similar for cause (or motive) and result.

Even though every connection will change in this way when priorities alter, few other reversals are as reliably systematic as the exchange of "because" with "so." Hence, the others we examine will be more closely tied to specific contexts. One that is reliably systematic involves the explanatory category of purpose ([e$_p$]), which was not covered in the last paragraph. Purposes already are consequences, of course, so they cannot reverse into any form of [r]. But they do reverse reliably into a certain kind of [q]. This might be called "the means/end switch." One sort of qualification is the *means* by which something is done, and it is flagged with the word "by." "They brought the fire under control by cutting off the oxygen supply."

[q]
> MP: The fire was controlled.
> SP: They cut off the oxygen supply.

When the priority is reversed in a case such as this, the secondary point naturally becomes the *end* (or purpose) for which the means was employed: "They cut off the oxygen supply in order to control the fire."

[e$_p$]
> MP: The oxygen supply was cut off.
> SP: To control the fire.

Exercise 2.24
....

Indent and label "They've switched off the power so they must have finished early." Then reverse priority and do it again. (Answers on p. 91.)

The reason to dwell on these switches is that sometimes the connections structuring a passage will be clearer than its priority. One way to deal with such a passage is to sketch out the connections in the simplest fashion possible, and then try a number of different priorities by selecting different items as the MP and seeing how the rest works out. This will involve switching back and forth between subordination types, depending on the particular arrangement. For instance, consider again the homily of the lost kingdom. We took the order of occurrence in the passage as determining priority, resulting in a neat cascade of causal consequences:

	MP: Somebody left out a nail.
$[r_e]$	SP: The horse lost a shoe.
$[r_e]$	SP: The horse was disabled.
$[r_e]$	SP: Its rider was missing.
$[r_e]$	SP: His side lost a battle.
$[r_e]$	SP: The Kingdom was defeated.

Suppose, however, that in the passage telling this melancholy story, the author's main concern was clearly the lost kingdom. That would mean that we have the structure upside down, but, given what we now understand about priority switches, it can be put right simply by reversing the order and changing the $[r_e]$s to $[e_c]$s.

	MP: The kingdom was defeated.
$[e_c]$	SP: It lost a battle.
$[e_c]$	SP: A rider disappeared.
$[e_c]$	SP: His horse was disabled.
$[e_c]$	SP: It lost a shoe.
$[e_c]$	SP: Somebody left out a nail.

And we might choose any item in this structure as the MP and then determine the resulting structure in this manner. Suppose we select something in the middle such as the missing rider. This would give us a double cascade: causes going off in one direction and effects in the other.

	MP: A rider disappeared.
$[e_c]$	SP: His horse was disabled.
$[e_c]$	SP: It lost a shoe.
$[e_c]$	SP: Somebody left out a nail.
$[r_e]$	SP: His side lost a battle.
$[r_e]$	SP: The kingdom was defeated.

(a) Do the same for the [s] cascade in the "First degree murder" paraphrase on p. 71. That is, make the third item the MP and rewrite the structure. (b) Do the same for the Superbowl cascade of Exercise 2.23 (a, ii). (Answers on p. 91.)

Illustration

NEWPORT NEWS, Va.—A tampered switch diverted an Amtrak train onto a siding Wednesday, causing it to derail and injuring 74 people, federal investigators said yesterday.

Four people were hospitalized, including the engineer at the controls when the train, Amtrak's Colonial, jumped the track shortly after 9 p.m. Investigators from the National Transportation Safety Board suspected tampering when they found a pair of bolt cutters, and some metal shavings that might be from a lock, on the siding switch. They said the lock itself is still missing.

Here is a case in which what is being described has a simple underlying structure. The story concerns some things that happened because somebody tampered with a railroad switch; and they fall neatly into a cascade of consequences and qualifications, with some support offered for the tampering itself.

	MP:	A switch was tampered with.
$[r_e]$	SP:	An Amtrak train derailed.
$[r_e]$	SP:	Injuring 74 people.
$[q]$	SP:	Four required hospitalization.
$[q]$	SP:	Including the engineer.
$[s]$	SP:	Some bolt cutters and shavings that might be from a lock were found nearby.
$[s]$	SP:	The siding switch lock itself is missing.

This structure does not accurately represent the priorities of the article, however. For as the lead paragraph emphasizes, the wreck itself is the plausible MP. But we can now easily correct for this by reversing one connection and letting the rest reshuffle to fit.

	MP:	An Amtrak train derailed at a switch.
$[r_e]$	SP:	Injuring 74 people.
$[q]$	SP:	Four required hospitalization.
$[q]$	SP:	Including the engineer.
$[e_c]$	SP:	The switch had been tampered with.
$[s]$	SP:	Some bolt cutters and shavings that might be from a lock were found nearby.
$[s]$	SP:	The siding switch lock itself is missing.

Exercise 2.26

a. Write out a structured paraphrase for the following short article, finding all the structure you can.

> The blood supply at the county blood bank is running low after four weeks of heavy demand, and the agency is searching for donors. The agency's director of donor resources said the shortage is due to a greater than usual number of open heart surgeries coupled with fewer blood donors because of the bad weather.

b. Write out a structured paraphrase for the following article, but do it in the following two steps: First write out the causal cascade unleashed by the earliest event mentioned (Galway's illness); then choose a better main point and rewrite the structure to accommodate the changed priority.

> Flutist James Galway missed his operatic debut because he was hospitalized, and his wife stepped in to fill the role. Galway was scheduled to play the lead role in a new production of Rossini's "The Thieving Magpie" with the Opera Company of Philadelphia. He was hospitalized for an inflammation of the intestinal tract, said Betsy Samuels, spokeswoman for Thomas Jefferson University Hospital in Philadelphia. He was in stable condition.
>
> Galway was scheduled to perform at the McCallum Theatre for the Performing Arts in Palm Desert tomorrow with the Tokyo String Quartet. The concert will be held with flutist Ransom Wilson replacing Galway.
>
> *(The Associated Press)*

(Answers on p. 91.)

Paired Roles: Inference and Explanation

In the interest of economy, we often make language serve several functions at once, and we will occasionally need to note that an SP bears more than one subordination relationship to an MP. In the most important and systematic of these, an SP will relate to an MP both *explanatorily* and *inferentially*. Two of these pairings are worth special attention.

[e$_c$] AND [s]

One standard kind of informative passage will suggest a causal connection between two things and then go on to give an underlying story explaining just *why* these things are connected the way they are. For instance, an article might inform us that excessive exposure to the sun causes skin cancer, and it does so *because* ultraviolet rays genetically alter skin cells. Here, the causal connection itself would be the MP, and the SP would explain the connection:

> MP: Excessive exposure to the sun causes skin cancer.
>
> [e$_c$]   SP: Ultraviolet radiation genetically alters skin cells.

But very often such an article will be written because there is some doubt about the *truth* of the MP. In this case we may assume some resistance to thinking that sun causes skin cancer. And when that is the context, finding an underlying explanation will *also count as support* for the MP: a reason to think the two things are causally connected. Before discovering the underlying mechanism we may simply dismiss a correlation between sun and cancer as an accident of statistics, or due to something else at work in the population. But after finding the underlying story, we must be less skeptical.

In cases such as this, the SP will deserve *both labels*: [e_c] and [s]. And if the article goes on to give results of a study supporting the underlying explanation, those results will *directly* support only the SP; but they will of course *indirectly* support the causal MP, through the explanation they endorse.

$$\begin{array}{ll} & \text{MP: Excessive exposure to the sun causes skin cancer.} \\ [e_c]/[s] & \text{SP: Ultraviolet radiation genetically alters skin cells.} \\ [s] & \text{SP: [Results of physiological study.]} \end{array}$$

As always, if the article telling this story has a different priority, making the underlying account the MP, the subordination categories reverse in the usual way:

$$\begin{array}{ll} & \text{MP: Ultraviolet radiation genetically alters skin cells.} \\ [r_e]/[r_i] & \text{SP: Excessive sun exposure causes skin cancer.} \\ [s] & \text{SP: [Results of physiological study.]} \end{array}$$

This is a fairly common pattern in our reasoning and will become of special importance in Chapters 3, 6, and 7. For whenever we have an impressive correlation between two things that do not seem obviously connected, finding an underlying story that would *explain* their connection will always provide *support* for it too.

Of course we do not need an underlying account in order to be certain of a causal connection. People who know nothing of physiology understand that drinking too much alcohol causes the complex unpleasantness known as a hangover. An underlying physiological story about hangovers would for most of us function only as an [e_c]: there would be no doubts to allay.

Exercise 2.27

Write structured paraphrases of the following articles. (Answers on p. 92.)

a. Eating fish at least once a week cuts in half the risk of sudden cardiac death in men, according to a pair of studies in the Journal of the American Medical Association. In the first, an analysis of 20,551 male physicians aged 40 to 84 found that the incidence of sudden heart failure among those eating fish at least once a week was 52% lower than among those who did not. In a second study, a team of scientists led by Dr. Christine Albert of Harvard University's Brigham and Women's Hospital in Boston uncovered a physiological explanation of this phenomenon. Substances specific to fish, known as n-3 or omega-3 fatty acids, help stabilize the heart's rhythm by preventing clotting and clumping, allowing the blood to flow freely.

    (Los Angeles Times)

b. COLUMBUS, Ohio—Lowering temperatures in water heaters to save energy
    may have touched off the sudden outbreaks of Legionnaires' disease [some
    time] ago a researcher says. An Ohio State University study concludes that
    lowering the temperature of water heaters in hotels, hospitals and other build-
    ings to conserve fuel probably created a near-perfect environment for the bac-
    teria, *Legionella pneumophilia*.

    Joseph Plouffe, associate professor of medical microbiology and immunol-
    ogy, said that in the 1960s most buildings, including hospitals, kept their hot
    water at a temperature of about 140 degrees. But in the 1970s, energy conser-
    vation measures coupled with rules by the Joint Commission on the Accredi-
    tation of Hospitals caused thermostats to be turned down to 110 degrees.
    "When they brought it down to 110 degrees Fahrenheit, they provided the
    ideal temperatures for the growth of the organism," Plouffe said.

    The organism is known to flourish in both large and small water systems
    and causes an often-fatal form of bacterial pneumonia. The study's conclusion
    is based in part on survey of six buildings in the Ohio State University Hos-
    pital's complex. Researchers compared water temperatures to the presence of
    the *Legionella* bacteria in the buildings. Because of special requirements, two
    of the six buildings maintained their water temperatures at 135–140 degrees.
    The other four lowered their water temperature to 110–120 degrees in the 1970s.
    The first two buildings showed no bacterial colonization, while tests on the
    water supplies in the other four did turn up the bacteria. In one building, re-
    searchers killed the *Legionella* by flushing the system with water heated to 160
    degrees, Plouffe said.

    (The Associated Press)

A very common source of $[r_e]/[r_i]$ pairs is prediction. For we often predict an
occurrence when we discover something that might *cause* it and the discovery of
the cause gives us *reason to think* it will occur. If a passage reads,

Consumer confidence is back, so the economy will recover

the "so" is obviously inferential: consumer confidence is *reason to think* the economy will recover. The subordination would be $[r_i]$. But consumer confidence is
reason to expect recovery mostly because it will *cause* it: spending by newly confident consumers will drive the recovery. Hence, the SP plays both roles:

	MP: Consumer confidence is back.
$[r_e]/[r_i]$	SP: The economy will recover.

Note that if the priorities were reversed, we would simply reverse the subordinations.

The economy will recover because consumer confidence has returned

would be structured:

	MP: The economy will recover.
$[e_c]/[s]$	SP: Consumer confidence is back.

This is the same connection, looked at from the other point of view.

> ### Exercise 2.28
> ....
>
> Structure and label the following. (a) The liner sank because the iceberg punctured the hull below the water line. (b) The liner will certainly sink, because the iceberg punctured the hull below the water line. (Answers on p. 92.)

[e] AND [r$_i$]

Explanations double not only as support, but also as implications. For in much of our thinking about the world we *infer explanations* from the things they explain. Driving along, the car starts to sputter and die; we may infer we are out of gas. Why? Because that would explain the sputtering and dying. Or: the house shakes violently for a few seconds, and we infer there's been an earthquake on a nearby fault. Why? Because that would explain the shaking. It is called "inference to the best explanation": we infer one thing (X) because it is the best explanation of something else (Y) *that we know about directly*. This is another common pattern in our experience, and one reflected in much of what we read. Many passages will contain SPs such as this that are *both* explanations and implications of the MP (both [e] and [r$_i$]).

$$[e_c]/[r_i] \qquad \begin{array}{ll} \text{MP:} & \text{The house briefly shook.} \\ \text{SP:} & \text{We've had an earthquake.} \end{array}$$

Not every explanation will also be an inference, of course, and the passage will normally make clear which ones are. As usual, what makes an explanatory connection *also* inferential is *indirectness*. If A is explained by B, and we don't know about B directly, but only *through* A, then B is also inferred from A. When we suspect that this is going on, we may test the suspicion by trying out the single-sentence paraphrase both with and without an indirectness flag. What makes the earthquake illustration a good one is that both do work in a normal sort of context.

> "The house shook, so we must have had an earthquake,"

sounds as reasonable as,

> "The house shook because we had an earthquake."

In any case, if an author seems to be both inferring and explaining, we should use both labels. This double labeling will be important to bear in mind when we begin to structure arguments in Chapter 3.

This particular double subordination is so important to our reasoning that we will devote two entire chapters to it later in the text. So let us explore it a bit further, using a different account of the discovery described in an earlier exercise.

> Scientists drilling into the Greenland icecap have found traces of a star that blew up nearby about 35,000 years ago. When stars explode as supernovas they emit cosmic rays of staggering intensity, some of which smash into the nitrogen and oxygen in the air to produce beryllium-10 atoms. If the star is close enough to re-

ally zap the Earth, this beryllium will fall to the ground in amounts large enough to detect.

The scientists drilling in Greenland have found twice normal levels of beryllium-10 in the ice 2000 feet below the surface. This ice formed about 35,000 years ago, which suggests that about that time a star exploded so close to the earth that it doubled the normal amount of cosmic radiation reaching our atmosphere. To do this, the scientists estimate that the star would have to have been within the Milky Way galaxy itself, probably within 200 light years of Earth.

If we take the MP of this article to be that a nearby star exploded about 35,000 years ago, then the beryllium buried in the Greenland icecap will, as an SP, play both a causal and inferential role in the paraphrase. The beryllium is both *evidence of the explosion* ([s]) and an *effect of the explosion* ([r_e]):

> MP: A nearby star blew up 35,000 years ago.
>
> [r_e]/[s]   SP: Unusual levels of beryllium-10 have been found at the 2000-foot level in the Greenland icecap.

Of course, if we changed the priorities around and made the evidence the MP, the subordination would look just like the earthquake example:

> MP: Unusual levels of beryllium-10 have been found at the 2000-foot level in the Greenland icecap.
>
> [e_c]\[r_i]   SP: A nearby star blew up 35,000 years ago.

Exercise 2.29

Indent and label the following: "The Apollo 13 explosion occurred just when the oxygen tank fans were turned on, so it must have been due to something in the fan circuitry." (Answer on p. 92.)

You will sometimes be able to make a case for two labels (explanation and inference) even when an author does not say anything directly relevant to one of them. We will consider this possibility in Chapter 3. For now we will want two labels only when the point of the article requires mentioning both. In particular, do not give two labels when the article does not say anything explicit about one of them.

Useful Discretion

As the author of a paraphrase you will always have some leeway in expressing the main point and various secondary points of a passage. This will sometimes allow you to combine items in different ways to experiment with different structures. Difficult passages will often require some trial and error to come up with an acceptable arrangement, and the combination that works will sometimes surprise you. Consider the following simple illustration.

A planned Organization of American States mission to Haiti to discuss the restoration to power of ousted President Jean-Bertrand Aristide hit a snag yesterday because the group planned to fly on an Argentine plane. An OAS announcement said the mission originally scheduled to depart today would leave later this week. "The authorization for the landing rights of an Argentine aircraft at Port-au-Prince have not yet been worked out," it said without elaboration.

However, OAS sources said the Haitian military was sensitive about Argentine involvement since Argentina has openly supported using military action to restore Aristide to power.

(*The Associated Press*)

Just ticking off this article's major points as they occur would yield something like this: "The OAS could not send a mission to Haiti yesterday because it planned to fly on an Argentine plane and Argentina has openly supported using force to restore Haiti's former government, so the Haitians wouldn't grant it landing rights." This in turn would yield the following structure:

MP: The OAS was unable to send its mission to Haiti yesterday as scheduled.

[e$_c$]   SP: It planned to use an Argentine plane.

[e$_c$]   SP: Argentina had advocated force to restore a former government to Haiti.

[r$_e$]   SP: The Haitians would not grant its plane landing rights.

Although this structure does capture the connections as they occur in our single-sentence synopsis, it is inadequate in a number of ways. For one thing, it misrepresents the role of the last SP as simply a consequence of earlier Argentine action. The refusal to grant landing rights is actually why the OAS could not send its mission. That is, it explains the MP. So it should be an [e$_c$] directly subordinate to the MP. The other two SPs would then be subordinate to this SP, and consequently changed to [e$_m$]s.

MP: The OAS was unable to send its mission to Haiti yesterday as scheduled.

[e$_c$]   SP: The Haitians would not grant its plane landing rights.

[e$_m$]   SP: The plane belonged to Argentina.

[e$_m$]   SP: Argentina had advocated force to restore a former government to Haiti.

A less important problem is that the two [e$_m$]s actually work together in explaining the Haitians' refusal, and so it should really be combined into a single SP. But this assimilation may be represented in a number of different ways without distorting the point. Besides simply combining them, we might combine the first of them with the [e$_c$] immediately above, which would allow the second to carry the explanatory burden:

MP: The OAS was unable to send its mission to Haiti yesterday as scheduled.

[e$_c$]   SP: The Haitians would not grant landing authorization for the Argentine plane the OAS chose to use.

[e$_m$]   SP: Argentina had advocated using force to restore a former government to Haiti.

Exercise 2.30
....

The first sentence of the following article offers three items that might constitute the MP, together or separately. They are (a) the British government's conviction that the tubes are a gun, (b) their confiscation of them, and (c) the disabling of the gun by the confiscation. Sketch paraphrases under a number of
these choices to find the best organization of this piece. Work out at least three.
(Answers on p. 92.)

> LONDON—The British government said yesterday it is convinced that Iraq
> was attempting to build a giant gun but that customs officers set back the proj-
> ect by seizing eight steel tubes last week. "Let me make it absolutely clear that
> the gun itself cannot be in operation without all its parts, and it is a great suc-
> cess on behalf of this country to have been able to prevent that happening,"
> Trade and Industry Secretary Nicholas Ridley told the House of Commons.
>
> Some weapons experts have said that a gun on the scale of the seized parts—
> 131-feet long with a bore of 39 inches—would have the potential to lob nu-
> clear or chemical warheads hundreds of miles. The Iraqi government and the
> manufacturer, Sheffield Forgemasters, have insisted the tubes were designed
> for a petrochemical plant.
>
> Ridley's statement was the first Cabinet-level statement that the tubing had
> military potential. Ridley said the government believed Iraq's gun project fol-
> lowed the designs of Gerald Bull, a Canadian-born American ballistics expert
> who was found shot to death in Brussels, Belgium, on March 22. He confirmed
> that his own department cleared the production of the tubes for Iraq two years
> ago. But he said his agency had no knowledge the goods were designed to
> form part of a gun "until a few days ago."
>
> (*The Associated Press*)

TRIAL AND ERROR EXERCISE

The following article contains enough structural complexity to allow us to try out
many different aspects of our paraphrasing technique and apparatus.

> PASADENA—NASA prepared yesterday to turn the spacecraft Galileo away from
> the sun's heat in an effort to free a trapped antenna and salvage the craft's $1.3
> billion mission to Jupiter. Engineers believe the drop in temperature might shrink
> the stuck ribs of the 16-foot-wide antenna and allow the umbrella-shaped device
> to open fully for its 1995 exploration of Jupiter.
>
> The craft was to be turned 165 degrees away from the sun for 50 hours starting
> last night, said Bob MacMillin, spokesman for the National Aeronautics and Space
> Administration. A similar effort in July, when the craft was nearer the sun, failed to
> fix the problem. But MacMillin said Galileo will be cooled further this time. Engi-
> neers at NASA's Jet Propulsion Laboratory in Pasadena also will shut down heat-
> generating instruments on Galileo in hopes of allowing the jammed metal to cool
> and contract. "In a week or so we'll know if they [the ribs] pulled loose," MacMillin
> said. If the main antenna can't be fully opened, the promised flood of data Galileo
> sends from Jupiter will be no more than a trickle transmitted by a smaller antenna.

Even if the effort is successful, the antenna won't be deployed for the asteroid fly-by on Oct. 29, MacMillin said. The instrument is not needed to provide data on the asteroid, and NASA would prefer to keep it closed until Galileo reaches Jupiter.

Galileo, now 146 million miles from Earth, was launched from a space shuttle in 1989. The antenna—gold-plated mesh stretched over graphite-epoxy ribs—failed to open fully when NASA first tried on April 11. Engineers believe three to five of the 18 ribs are stuck.

(The Associated Press)

The first paragraph links together a number of things, in complex ways, but underlying it all is a contemplated action directed at a goal. Let us begin with a purpose cascade, and see if we can build the structure from that.

		MP: NASA is going to turn the Galileo spacecraft (away from the sun).
$[e_p]$		SP: To cool it.
$[e_p]$		SP: To unstick its antenna.
$[e_p]$		SP: To save the mission.

The first problem with this arrangement is that "turning the spacecraft" is not a very plausible MP. Either of the first two SPs would be better. Let us choose "unsticking the antenna" as the MP. This will convert part of the purpose cascade to a qualification cascade: "NASA will try to unstick the antenna by cooling it by turning it, in order to save the mission."

	MP: NASA will try to free the stuck antenna.
$[q]$	SP: They will cool it.
$[q]$	SP: By turning it away from the sun.
$[e_p]$	SP: To save the mission.

Because something like this had been tried before, we can find a further qualification cascade under "cooling," beginning with the comparison. So we can display this, just for practice, even though it is pretty fine detail for a bare-bones paraphrase.

	MP: NASA will try to free Galileo's stuck antenna.
$[q]$	SP: They will cool it.
$[q]$	SP: By turning it away from the sun.
$[q]$	SP: (But) more than before.
$[q]$	SP: Also by shutting off equipment.
$[e_p]$	SP: To save the mission.

This structure accounts for 10 of the article's 12 sentences (look through to check this). The exceptions are sentences 9 and 10 (next-to-last paragraph). These concern the asteroid fly-by, which is more substance, clearly secondary, but also clearly independent of what we have so far. It is included in the article as interesting "while we're on the topic" information, not connected with the rescue by any of our dependency relations. So it counts as an [i].

As they stand, the sentences of the paraphrase are pretty austere. It would not defeat the spirit of bare bones to make some of them more informative. So let us flesh out a final, complete structure:

	MP: NASA will try to free the stuck antenna.
[q]	SP: They will cool it.
[q]	SP: By turning it away from the sun.
[q]	SP: It will be cooled further than it was in an earlier, unsuccessful attempt.
[q]	SP: By also shutting off equipment.
[e$_p$]	SP: So that it can send back the data the probe was sent to retrieve.
[i]	SP: The antenna will not be needed for an asteroid fly-by in October.

In most contexts you would want to omit the higher order secondaries as "dispensable detail," perhaps leaving just the MP and three first-order SPs. But a number of variations are possible. Because we were ambivalent between "freeing" and "cooling" as the MP, one strategy would be simply to combine the first [q] with the MP. And another option we have is to convert the [e$_p$] to an [e$_m$]. One more possibility would look like this:

	MP: NASA will try to free Galileo's stuck antenna thermally.
[q]	SP: By turning it away from the sun.
[q]	SP: It will be cooled further than it was in an earlier, unsuccessful attempt.
[q]	SP: Also by shutting off equipment.
[e$_m$]	SP: A stuck antenna will dramatically reduce the value of the mission.
[i]	SP: The antenna will not be needed for an asteroid fly-by in October.

Exercise 2.31

For practice, work through some of the Passages for Analysis at the end of this chapter. (Suggestions: numbers 3, 4, and 7.)

SUPPLEMENTAL EXERCISES

A. Review Questions

1. If the MP and SPs are the "bones" in a structured paraphrase, what is the "flesh?"

2. Mark the following true or false.

a. A dependent secondary point answers a question about the main point.

b. Support is an inferential secondary point.

c. Explanatory SPs treat the MP as a statement.

d. Independent SPs answer a question about the MP.

3. In the following examples choose the right functional description from the alternatives offered.

a. If an SP falls in category [e_m],
  i. It explains the MP.
  ii. It is explained by the MP. ✗
  iii. It supports the MP.   ✗
  iv. It is implied by the MP. ✗

b. If an SP falls in category [r_i],
  i. It explains the MP.
  ii. It is explained by the MP.
  iii. It supports the MP.
  iv. It is implied by the MP.

c. If an SP falls in category [s],
  i. It explains the MP.
  ii. It is explained by the MP.
  iii. It supports the MP.
  iv. It is implied by the MP.

d. If an SP falls in category [e_p],
  i. It explains the MP.
  ii. It is explained by the MP.
  iii. It supports the MP.
  iv. It is implied by the MP.

e. If an SP falls in category [r_e],
  i. It explains the MP.
  ii. It is explained by the MP.
  iii. It supports the MP.
  iv. It is implied by the MP.

f. If an SP falls in category [e_c],
  i. It explains the MP.
  ii. It is explained by the MP.
  iii. It supports the MP.
  iv. It is implied by the MP.

B. Passages for Analysis

1. A satellite that provides weather information for the Western United States and the Pacific failed last week. Investigators speculate that the failure was due to a solar flare because one occurred shortly before the failure and there were magnetic disturbances on earth shortly afterward typical of such flares. Solar flares produce streams of subatomic particles that can easily damage certain electronic devices not protected by the atmosphere.

a. In this article, something is known indirectly. What is it?
b. What tells you it is indirect?
c. What does the indirectness tell you about the "because"?
d. Write out a structured paraphrase of the article, making sure it reflects all this.

2. *Dear Editor,*
   Another week has gone by and more people have been killed in robberies. Robbers kill their victims because the penalty for robbery is almost as great as that for murder. The only rea-

sonable solution is to cut down the penalty for robbery to something significantly shorter than the murder penalty—perhaps eight months in jail. Then there would be no incentive for robbers to kill their victim.

Able Blan
San Dimas

Write out a structured paraphrase of this letter, labeling the subordination.

3. Estrogen replacement therapy is known to reduce the risk of death by heart attack in post-menopausal women by about 50 percent, ~~but scientists were puzzled about how estrogen produced this dramatic protective effect.~~ Reporting in the medical journal *Circulation*, a team of Johns Hopkins University researchers said they found the answer: Estrogen increases blood flow to the heart, including diseased hearts.

A study of post-menopausal women showed that almost all of them had an average 23 percent increase of blood to the heart after receiving an intravenous dose of estrogen, said Dr. Steven Reis. Estrogen also appeared to increase blood flow through arteries that were already partly narrowed from heart disease, he said.

(*The Associated Press*)

Write out a structured paraphrase of this article, labeling the subordination.

4. A group of researchers at America's National Institute of Mental Health (NIMH), in Bethesda, Maryland, has just given a new significance to the old Latin tag *mens sana in corpore sano*. They recently reported in the *New England Journal of Medicine* that it is true—or at least likely—that an unhealthy mind can lead directly to an unhealthy body. Specifically, they found that clinical depression may be linked to broken bones. This is not because depressed people are more accident-prone, but because their bones are weaker. David Michelson and his team measured the bone-mineral density in 24 women suffering from major depression, or with a history of it, and compared this with the density in 24 healthy women of similar age, size, weight, menopausal status and race. The team found that bone density in the depressed group was somewhat lower all over the body—and up to 14% lower at the neck of the femur (the thigh bone). This means that, according to standard measures, these women face a significantly greater risk of fractures than the population at large.

In searching for an explanation of their findings, Dr Michelson and his colleagues were able to rule out the effects of the anti-depressant drugs that patients often have to take for long periods. Instead, they believe that their results are due to an increased secretion of a hormone called cortisol. Excess cortisol production is a common feature of depression, and it has been known for some time that high cortisol levels can lead to decreased bone density. Dr Michelson's result is not the first to link mental state with physical well-being. Stress, for example, appears to affect the immune system adversely. Indeed, links between the mind and physical disease are now widely accepted, and disciplines with unwieldy names such as "psychoneuroendocroimmunology" (the study of the relationship between the mind, the brain, the hormones and the immune system) are emerging to look at them.

But Dr Michelson's findings are not simply a scientific curiosity. According to Philip Gold, the head of neuroendocrinology at NIMH, depression may affect as many as 9% of American women, so early treatment could improve physical as well as mental public health by reducing the risk of bone fractures. The affected women in Dr Michelson's study had an average age of 41. Their degree of bone loss, according to Dr Gold, was that of 70-year-olds.

(*The Economist*)

Write out a structured paraphrase of this article, labeling the subordination.

5. Seventeen people were injured last night as explosions rocked the coal-fired generating plant in Hammond that supplies power to Chicago. Four of the injuries were serious. The explosions set off fires that took six hours to extinguish and left thick black plumes of smoke towering over the Lake Michigan shoreline. For the most part power was interrupted only briefly across Chicago as backup systems kicked in, but some customers on the city's South Side were without power for as long as thirty minutes, according to Edison spokesperson J. Kennefick.

Write out a structured paraphrase of this article, labeling the subordination. Find as much structure as possible.

6. On several orbits astronauts aboard the shuttle *Endeavor* could see broad plumes of smoke obscuring much of the forested area of South America. The plumes formed an orderly pattern and were confined to jungles and otherwise sparsely inhabited areas. From these signs it was obvious that recent policies designed to encourage farmers to use alternative land-clearing methods had failed: people were intentionally burning off portions of the rain forest for agriculture.

Write out a structured paraphrase of this article, labeling the subordination. Use as the MP "attempts to get South American farmers to use alternative land-clearing methods have failed."

7. TURKEY—Southeastern Turkey, swept by some of the worst fighting between Turkish troops and Kurdish guerrillas since the rebels' insurgency began in 1984, seems to be on the edge of full-scale rebellion. Neither side appears willing to yield. After clashes in recent days that left scores of people dead and wounded, the Turkish government, despite censure from powerful benefactors like Germany, has imposed curfews in half a dozen towns, shipped in elite counterinsurgency battalions, arrested several hundred people and moved aggressively to track down Kurdish rebel positions. But many Kurds in the southeast, who in the last year have seen the Kurds in northern Iraq move to establish autonomy and neighboring Central Asian republics free themselves from the grip of the Soviet Union, have decided that it is their turn.

(The Associated Press)

Write out a structured paraphrase of this article, labeling the subordination.

ANSWERS

2.1   a. MP: We should not pass Proposition 14.
           SP: Its funds are not specifically targeted to the reduction of class size.
      b. MP: A Moreno Valley airport is a bad idea.
         SP: It would cause too much development.
      c. MP: The legislature was right to require proof of insurance.
           SP: Insured motorists have unfairly borne the expense of covering accidents
                by uninsured drivers.

2.2   a. Each SP in 2.1 should be labeled [s].
      b. MP: The door was locked.
         [r]   SP: They broke a window to get in.

2.3   a. MP: My modem is slow.
         [r]   SP: I can't download graphics.
         [q]   SP: It works for E-mail.
      b. MP: The microwave failed.
         [e]   SP: We ran it empty.
         [r]   SP: We can't easily reheat coffee.

2.4   a. MP: The staff met at noon today.
         [q]   SP: One member was absent.
         [r]   SP: We had a meal left over.

b. MP: I have a very slow modem.
   [r]   SP: I can't download most graphics.
   [q]   SP: Just very simple ones.

2.5 **a.** Sentence: An airliner crashed in northern Mongolia killing 34, one survived but was seriously injured.

Structure:
MP: An airliner crashed in northern Mongolia.
[r]   SP: 34 on board died.
[q]   SP: One survived.
[q]   SP: The survivor was seriously injured.

b. Sentence: An elderly man died Tuesday morning when his house burned down due to careless smoking. (Optional: "it took 14 minutes to extinguish the blaze.")

Structure:
MP: An elderly man died early Tuesday.
[e]   SP: His house burned down.
[e]   SP: Owing to careless smoking.
([q]   SP: It took 14 minutes to put it out.)

2.7 **a.** MP: A Ukrainian school district has had to pay its teachers with produce.
    Any support offered for this? No, it's just reported.
    Any explanation? Yes, district is broke (payment crisis).
    Any consequences? No, nothing direct.
    Any qualification? No, nothing notable.

SO THE FIRST-ORDER STRUCTURE LOOKS LIKE THIS:

MP: A Ukrainian school district has had to pay its teachers with produce.
[e]   SP: The district is broke.

NOW ASK, under the SP:
    Any support offered for this? No, it's just reported.
    Any explanation? Yes, a local distillery is failing and can't pay its taxes.
    Any consequences? Yes, teachers not paid since November.
    Any qualifications? No.

BECAUSE THERE'S NOTHING FURTHER UNDER THESE POINTS, THE FINAL STRUCTURE LOOKS LIKE THIS:

MP: A Ukrainian school district has had to pay its teachers with produce.
[e]   SP: The district is broke.
[e]   SP: Distillery is failing.
[r]   SP: Teachers haven't been paid since November.

NOTE THAT YOU COULD HAVE BROKEN THE DISTILLERY'S INVOLVE-MENT INTO TWO STEPS (the "and" is actually causal) AND MADE THE STRUC-TURE SLIGHTLY MORE COMPLEX AS FOLLOWS (though the simpler one is better as bare bones).

MP: A Ukrainian school district has had to pay its teachers with produce.
[e]   SP: The district is broke.
[e]   SP: Distillery can't pay its taxes
[e]   SP: It's failing
[r]   SP: Teachers haven't been paid since November.

b. MP: A nearby star exploded about 35,000 years ago.
  [s]? Yes, the beryllium and the nearby supernova debris.
  [e]? No.
  [r]? Yes, zapped Earth.
  [q]? (Optional: closest recorded supernova.)

SO FIRST STRUCTURE (omitting [q]):

MP: A nearby star exploded about 35,000 years ago.
[s]   SP: Cosmic ray products 2000 feet down in ice caps.
[s]   SP: 35,000-year-old supernova debris nearby.
[r]   SP: Showered Earth with intense cosmic rays.

BECAUSE WE'RE TAKING THE PHYSICS AS BACKGROUND, THERE'S NOTHING FURTHER UNDER EITHER OF THE FIRST TWO SPs AND NOTHING UNDER THE THIRD EXCEPT THE EVOLUTIONARY CONSEQUENCE. SO THE FINAL STRUCTURE WOULD BE THIS:

MP: A nearby star exploded about 35,000 years ago.
[s]   SP: Cosmic ray products 2000 feet down in ice caps.
[s]   SP: 35,000-year-old supernova debris nearby.
[r]   SP: Showered Earth with intense cosmic rays.
[r]   SP: This probably speeded organic evolution.

2.8 **a.** MP: Joe forgot to reset his watch.
         [r_e] SP: He missed his bus.
         b. MP: Joe missed his bus.
         [r_i] SP: He forgot to set his watch.
         c. The [r] in 2.7a is [r_e].
         The first [r] in 2.7b is [r_e], the second [r_i].

2.9 (a) explanatory [r_e]; (b) inferential [r_i]; (c) inferential [s], (d) explanatory [e]; (e) inferential [r_i].

2.10 (a) [e_c]; (b) [e_p]; (c) [e_m]; (d) [e_m]; (e) [e_p]; (f) [e_c].

2.11 MP: Artificial flavorings may lower heart attack risk.
  - [s]? Yes, two things:
    i. Heart attack death rate began to fall just after they were introduced. (SP_1)
    ii. Nothing else seems able to explain this correlation. (SP_2)
  - [e]? Yes, Artificial flavors contain salicylates. (SP_3)
  - [r]? No.
  - [q]? No.

NOTHING UNDER TWO SUPPORTING SPs EXCEPT DISPENSABLE DETAIL BUT CONSIDER THE SP_3:
  - [s]? No, just given.
  - [e]? No, why they contain salicylates not explained.
  - [r]? No, nothing further (we don't need MP again).
  - [q]? Yes, salicylates prevent blood clots.

SO THE STRUCTURE WOULD LOOK SOMETHING LIKE THIS:

MP: Artificial flavorings may lower heart attack risk.
[s]   SP: Heart attack death rate began to fall just after artificial flavorings were introduced.
[s]   SP: Nothing else seems to explain this correlation.

[e_c]   SP: They contain salicylates.

[q]   SP: Which prevent blood clots.

2.12 (a) [e_c], top, . . . because the boulder hit it; (b) [s], top, . . . because he's been missing for so long; (c) [e_p], bottom, . . . so that he'd be sure to get up on time; (d) [r_e], bottom, . . . so the small trailer has been flattened; (e) [r_i], bottom, He's been missing for a long time, so there's no chance of finding him now.

2.13 (a) yes; (b) no; (c) no; (d) yes; (e) no.

2.14 **a.** MP: Termites had damaged the structure.
  [s]   SP: It almost disintegrated in the earthquake.
  b. MP: The wind was very strong last night.
  [s]   SP: Every tree in the yard suffered major damage.

2.15 (a) [e_c]; (b) [s]; (c) [e_c]; (d) [s]; (e) [r_e]; (f) [r_i]; (g) [r_e]; (h) [e_c]; (i) [s]; (j) [q]; (k) [r_e]; (l) [r_i]; (m) [r_i]; (n) [r_e].

2.16 (a) means; (b) "in spite of"; (c) condition; (d) elaboration; (e) "in spite of"; (f) sense/ respect.

2.17 **a.** MP: The dynamite was old and unstable.
  [r_e]   SP: They blew it up.
  b. MP: The dynamite was old and unstable.
  [r_i]   SP: They should have gotten rid of it long ago.

2.18 (a) [e]; (b) [s]; (c) [r_i]; (d) [s]; (e) [e_p]; (f) [r_i].

2.19 (a) yes; (b) no; (c) yes.

2.20 **a.** The racket is offered as "what it is about" ravens that is annoying; it's not an indicator of further annoyances.
  b. That it is busy is offered as "what it is about" the tie that doesn't go with the shirt; again, it is not an indicator of something more that might be wrong with it.

2.21 (a) [r_e]; (b) [r_i]; (c) [r_e]; (d) [s]; (e) [r_e]; (f) [s]; (g) [e_p]; (h) [r_i]; (i) [r_e]; (j) [r_i]; (k) [r_e].

2.22 **a.** **i.** MP: A computer will be available for public use at the La Sierra branch public library starting Monday.
      [q]   SP: It will be coin-operated.
      [q]   SP: It will run 15 minutes for a quarter.
      [q]   SP: A printer will also be available.
      [q]   SP: As will some software.
      [q]   SP: Paper will be free.
      [q]   SP: Users will have to supply their own disks.
      [q]   SP: The branch address is 4600 La Sierra Ave.
      [i]   SP: Other branches already have computers.
    ii. MP: Beginning Monday, a coin-operated computer will be available for public use at the branch library at 4600 La Sierra Ave.
      [q]   SP: It will run 15 minutes for a quarter.
      [q]   SP: Some software and a printer with free paper will also be available.
      [q]   SP: Users will have to supply their own disks.
  b. **i.** MP: Drinking green tea fights cancer.
      [s]   SP: Its drinkers have low rates of four cancers.
      [e_c]   SP: It contains catechin and flavinoids.
      [q]   SP: Which have cancer-fighting credentials
    ii. MP: Drinking green tea fights cancer.
      [s]   SP: Its drinkers have low rates of four cancers.

[e_c] SP: It contains catechin.

[q]   SP: Which slows cancer in animals.

[e_c] SP: It contains flavinoids.

[q]   SP: Which attack free radicals.

[q]   SP: Which may play a role in skin cancer.

2.23 a. i. MP: She saved the event.

[q]   SP: By generating donations.

[q]   SP: By recruiting volunteers.

[q]   SP: By word of mouth and advertising.

ii. MP: The road was wet.

[r_e] SP: The brakes locked.

[r_e]   SP: I lost control.

[r_e]   SP: I crashed in a ditch.

[r_e]   SP: Rumpling a fender.

[r_e]   SP: Costing me $360.

[r_e]   SP: No Super Bowl tickets.

[r_e]   SP: I'm watching on TV.

iii. MP: The plane was out of fuel.

[s]   SP: There was no fire.

[s]   SP: The stubble was not charred.

b. MP: A downpour hit Las Vegas, yesterday.

[r_e] SP: Motorists were stranded.

[q]   SP: Including a team of surgeons.

[q]   SP: Who were not injured.

[q]   SP: They had to postpone a demonstration.

[r_e] SP: Homes were flooded.

2.24 a. MP: They've switched off the power.

[r_i] SP: They've finished early.

b. MP: They've finished early.

[s]   SP: They've switched off the power.

2.25 a. MP: He had plenty of time to think about it.

[s]   SP: He loaded the gun.

[s]   SP: The neighbors heard six rapid shots.

[r_i] SP: The killing was deliberate.

[r_i]   SP: He should get first-degree murder.

b. MP: I lost control.

[e_c] SP: The brakes locked.

[e_c]   SP: The road was wet.

[r_e] SP: I crashed in a ditch.

[r_e]   SP: Rumpling a fender.

[r_e]   SP: Costing me $360.

[r_e]   SP: No Super Bowl tickets.

[r_e]   SP: I'm watching on TV.

2.26 a. MP: The county blood supply is low.

[e_c] SP: Heavy demand.

[e_c]   SP: More open-heart surgery.

[e_c] SP: Fewer donors.

[e_c]   SP: Bad weather.

[r_e] SP: They're looking for donors.

b. i. MP: Flutist James Galway is ill.
  [r_e]   SP: He missed his operatic debut.
  [r_e]   SP: His wife took his place in the opera.
  [r_e]   SP: He will also miss an appearance tomorrow with the Tokyo String Quartet.
  [r_e]   SP: Another flutist will take his part.
  ii: MP: Flutist James Galway missed his operatic debut.
  *[r_e]   SP: His wife took his part.
  [e_c]   SP: He is ill.
  [r_e]   SP: He will also miss an appearance with the Tokyo String Quartet.
  *[r_e]   SP: Another flutist will take his place.

[*Note that the two asterisked subordinations might have been flagged as easily by "but" as by "so," and hence might appear here as a [q]. [r_e] was chosen to illustrate the cascade.]

2.27 **a.** MP: Eating fish reduces the risk of heart attack death in men.
  [s]   SP: Study of physicians reveals 52% lower incidence of cardiac death among men who eat fish regularly.
  [e_c]/[s]   SP: Eating fish adds fatty acids to the blood that reduce clotting and improve heart rhythm.

  b. MP: Lowering water heater temperatures caused outbreak of Legionnaires' disease.
  [e_c]   SP: The lower temperatures provided the perfect environment for *Legionella* bacteria.
  [s]   SP: In a test case, only lowered systems had *Legionella* colonies.
  [s]   SP: One of these was eliminated with a hot-water flush.

2.28 **a.** MP: The liner sank.
  [e_c] SP: The iceberg punctured the hull below the water line.
  b. MP: The liner will sink.
  [e_c]/[s] SP: The iceberg punctured the hull below the water line.

2.29 MP: The Apollo 13 explosion occurred just when the oxygen tank fans were turned on.
  [e_c]/[r_i] SP: Something was wrong in the fan circuitry.

2.30 **a.** MP: The British government thinks large tubing it confiscated on its way to Iraq is part of a long-range gun.
  [s]   SP: The tubing resembles a gun design by American ballistics expert Gerald Bull.
  [s]   SP: Bull was mysteriously shot to death recently.
  [i]   SP: Gun is inoperable without the confiscated parts.

PROBLEM: disabling looks more part of structure than [i].

  b. MP: The British government thinks some large tubing sold to Iraq by a British firm is part of a long-range gun.
  [s]   SP: It resembles a design by American ballistics expert Gerald Bull.
  [s]   SP: Bull was mysteriously shot to death recently.
  [r_e]   SP: The British government has confiscated some of the tubing.
  [e_m]   SP: Gun is inoperable without the confiscated parts.

SAME STRUCTURE WOULD WORK WITH A DIFFERENT MP:

MP: The British government thinks large tubing manufactured by a British firm is part of a long-range gun.

YET ANOTHER POSSIBILITY:

MP: British customs has confiscated some large tubing en route to Iraq.

[e_m] SP: British government thinks the tubing is part of a long-range gun.

[s]   SP: The tubing resembles a (gun) design by American ballistics expert
              Gerald Bull.

[s]   SP: Bull was recently shot to death.

[e_m] SP: The gun is inoperable without the confiscated parts.

CHAPTER 3

READING FOR REASONING
Paraphrasing Arguments

.... When we read for a specific purpose, we may place greater demands
OVERVIEW on a paraphrase and hence create a more ambitious and useful apparatus. In this chapter we begin to focus exclusively on the *rea-*
.... *soning* in what we read.

READING FOR A PARTICULAR PURPOSE

The aim of paraphrasing has so far been simply to understand a passage, to unearth an author's perception. So the techniques we have developed apply naturally to a very broad range of informative writing. Descriptions of events, warning labels, arguments, assembly instructions, explanations, and complaints are all
expository, and our understanding of each may be captured in a bare-bones paraphrase. Sometimes, however, our aim in reading is not to digest everything an
author has to say, but rather to get something specific out of a text. We may come
to a piece asking not simply "What did the author have to say?" but rather "What
was her advice about job hunting, or her view of Cromwell, or her argument for
economic sanctions?" In cases such as this we may streamline our paraphrasing
a bit by shaping it to our particular interests. We still must understand the author's project, but may concentrate on how it bears on the advice or perception
or reasoning that particularly interests us.

The last of these, reasoning, is important enough and complicated enough
to warrant separate treatment, and this chapter is devoted to that topic. Many
of the things we noted about our reading skill in Chapter 1 are equally true of
our reasoning skill. We constantly deliberate: on what's causing a draft, how
much salt to add, what to do about a spill, when to leave for the appointment,
what route to take, whether to take an umbrella. And our thinking about such

94

matters is normally so effortlessly successful that it hardly draws our attention. We just do it naturally, in the right circumstances, like breathing and walking and reading. But this very effortlessness creates occasional problems, of three different kinds, and of the same sort we had thinking about reading. First, the limits of our skill are hard to detect, and we can be over our heads without noticing it. Second, even when we do notice that reasoning has become difficult, we often do not know what to do about it or where to go for help. And finally, as with reading, our first attempts to deal with such difficulties can easily make things worse (see the centipede effect in Chapter 1, footnote 5).

To solve these problems we begin by examining the reasoning we find in our reading. To see just what the topic of reasoning is supposed to encompass, we will find it useful to isolate and articulate examples of reasoning that others have taken the trouble to write down. This will provide the subject matter for analysis in the rest of this text.

READING FOR REASONING

When we read for reasoning we focus on the part of a passage in which one point is offered as a reason to think another point is true or false. These will be the connections between points that we have been paraphrasing either as support [s] or implication [r$_i$], which fall under the functional head "inferential subordination." Sometimes reasoning will be the purpose of the entire passage; but often just one part will contain reasoning and we will then confine our attention to that one part. In any case, reading for reasoning will change our paraphrasing priorities in two distinct ways. First, it will allow us to omit from a paraphrase those aspects of the structure not involved in reasoning. Second, and just as important, it will provide a reason to unearth details related to reasoning that we would naturally omit from a general-purpose paraphrase. These two differences will take some getting used to.

Exercise 3.1

Look through all the structured paraphrases in the body of Chapter 2 and in the Chapter 2 answer pages and circle the parts that contain reasoning-subordination. (**This Is a Very Important Exercise**: it will make the following discussion much easier and prepare you for the next exercise.)

Vocabulary and Technique

Let us first introduce the slightly technical notion of "an argument," as it is used by philosophers in discussing reasoning. You have an argument, in this sense, whenever one thing is offered as a *reason to think* something else. And "the argument" then refers to the entire package, the reason, together with what it is a reason for thinking,[1] and it is represented schematically in this way:

$$\text{ARGUMENT} = \frac{\text{Reasons for thinking something}}{\text{The something}}$$

So if somebody offers a draft as a reason to think the door is open, they would have offered an argument looking like this:

$$\frac{\text{I feel a draft}}{\text{The door is open}}$$

The major activity of this chapter will be schematizing arguments such as this: the reasons go on the top, what they are reasons for goes on the bottom, and they are separated by a dashed line.[2] To standardize the jargon we will call the reasons "support." What they are reasons to think (the something), we will call "the conclusion" of the argument.

$$\text{ARGUMENT} = \frac{\text{SUPPORT}}{\text{CONCLUSION}}$$

This schematized "picture of an argument" is meant to paraphrase the reasoning in a passage—to display inferential connections. And, as mentioned earlier, these are *exactly the same connections* we represented by [s] and [r$_i$] in the paraphrases of Chapter 2. That is, the top of the schematic argument (support) is offered as "reason to think the conclusion is true" or "how we can tell the conclusion is true." So you might wonder why we want this new schematic arrangement to do the same thing we were doing before by indenting and labeling. We do this for a number of reasons. One is that schematic form is commonly used in the literature on reasoning, and you should be familiar with it. Another is that it handles complex arguments more easily than indented outline form (see p. 105 for an example). But the main reason (which is why it is in general use) is that this schematic form displays the connection between support and conclusion in the same way no matter which was subordinate to which in the passage itself. In other words, the schematic argument will look the same whether the connection shows up in the passage as an [s] or an [r$_i$]. So we get a picture of the *direction of the reasoning* quite independent of the author's particular priorities. This is just what we want.

Because we are dealing with the familiar inferential connections, one way to schematize the reasoning in a passage is to first write out a structured paraphrase and then simply locate the inferential parts and convert them into schematic form. Of course the two inferential subordinations ([s] and [r$_i$]) schematize differently,

---

1. In ordinary conversation we often use "argument" for the reasons alone. But context will make this ambiguity harmless.

2. We will eventually use different lines for different kinds of argument; but for now the line will always be dashed.

but that is easy to keep straight. Because the support goes on the top and the conclusion on the bottom, [r$_i$] schematizes "right way up" and [s] schematizes "upside down." For in [r$_i$], the MP supports the SP:

	INDENTED FORM	SCHEMATIZATION
	MP	MP
[r$_i$]	SP →	----------
		SP

While for [s], the SP supports the MP:

	MP	SP
[s]	SP →	----------
		MP

So if we had

       MP: The plane was out of fuel.
[s]   SP: There was no fire on impact.

it would schematize

S: There was no fire on impact.

C: The plane was out of fuel

But

       MP: He fired six shots in rapid succession.
[r$_i$]   SP: The gun had been fully loaded.

would schematize

S: He fired six shots in rapid succession.

C: The gun had been fully loaded.

And all this naturally applies also to two secondary points connected by either
[s] or [r$_i$].

    To pull all this together in a practical application, look again at the Motel Blast
example in Chapter 2 (p. 44). The paraphrase we derived from the article was as
follows:

MP: A motel in Indianapolis blew up yesterday.
[r$_e$]   SP: Five people were injured. [r$_e$]
[e$_c$]   SP: It was probably caused by a maintenance worker checking a gas
              leak. [e]
[s]   SP: A maintenance worker had been called to investigate a lack
              of hot water.   [s]
[s]   SP: The maintenance worker was one of the most seriously in-
              jured.   [s]

Here, only the last three points are connected by reasoning, therefore all we would schematize would be the relation between them: the last two supporting the one labeled [e]. Of course, because the pronoun "it" in this SP (the one labeled [e]) refers to the MP, some information from the main point will have to be imported into the schematic picture for simple understanding. So it would look like this:

S_1: A maintenance worker had been called to investigate the lack of hot water.

S_2: He was one of the most severely hurt in the explosion.

C: He set off the explosion.

Sometimes we will schematize reasoning directly from a passage. But when we extract it from an indented paraphrase like this, some of the sentences will often need rewriting to make sense in schematic form.

Of course both kinds of inferential subordination may occur in the same paraphrase, which can make extracting the reasoning complicated. But it will always follow the patterns sketched above. For instance, let us suppose a passage reads, "On my way home the car sputtered to a stop, so I figured I must have run out of gas. This was confirmed when I was towed to a gas station: it took more fuel than I have ever put in the tank." The author's reasoning would be paraphrased like this:

MP: The car sputtered to a stop.

[r_i]   SP: It was out of fuel.

[s]   SP: It took more gas than ever before.

Here the MP and the SP on the bottom both support the SP in the middle. So the reasoning would schematize:

S_1: The car sputtered to a stop.

S_2: Filling it required more gas than ever before.

C: The car had run out of fuel.

Exercise 3.2

a. Go through all the reasoning examples circled in the previous exercise (3.1) and indicate the conclusions.

b. Schematize the reasoning in the Soviet submarine article on p. 51 of Chapter 2. (Answer on p. 130.)

Adding Detail

An interest in reasoning will also justify looking through the padding, naturally omitted in deriving a paraphrase, to see if anything there might be relevant to an argument we have found. In particular, the two categories of padding we asterisked in the original list, "dispensable detail" and "background," often contain items of additional support for a conclusion. When we schematized the argument in the Motel Blast article, for instance, we found two items in the paraphrase were offered in support of a third: (a) the fact that the maintenance worker was called to investigate the lack of hot water and (b) his severe injuries both supported the conclusion that he caused the subsequent blast. If we look back through the article, however, something else plainly implied by the author is clearly relevant to the reasoning: that the water was heated by propane. So this additional item should be included in a schematization of the reasoning in the article, even though it was not included in a perfectly adequate paraphrase. In other words, the schematization would look like this:

S_1: A maintenance worker had been called to investigate the lack of hot water.
S_2: He was one of the most severely hurt in the explosion.
S_3: The water was heated with propane.

C: He set off the explosion.

For a more complicated illustration, consider the following letter.

Dear Editor,
It is a crying shame that so many performances at our elegant new Arts Center play before a half-empty house. Why not give some of those seats to senior citizens living on social security, who deserve a break? Simply calling a senior citizens' center would yield a lot of happiness, as well as an appreciative audience.

For the rest, why not try high school drama teachers? Many of their students cannot afford these expensive productions, but by attending could better learn their craft and thus benefit us all one day. And wouldn't the performers rather play to a full house?

The rhetorical questions here contain a proposal and some support, a modestly austere bare-bones paraphrase of which would look something like this:

MP: The many empty seats at the Arts Center's performances should be given to senior citizens and (drama) students.
[s] SP: This would do some civic good.
[s] SP: The performers would appreciate it.

Putting this in schematic form would yield the following:

S_1 Giving the extra seats at Arts Center performances to students and senior citizens would be good for the community.
S_2 The performers would also enjoy the crowd.

C We should give the unsold tickets to students and senior citizens.

But some detail we have omitted in the austerity of a general paraphrase is clearly important to the reasoning. Part of what makes the proposal reasonable is the fact that it would directly enhance the education of drama students. The detail that seniors on social security cannot afford the tickets and deserve a break is relevant in the same way. Similarly, that this particular audience would *appreciate* the show clearly increases the support provided by S$_2$. So these three things at least should be added to the schematization to register that we recognize their force.

S$_1$ Drama students would better learn their trade, and hence benefit us all, if given the opportunity to attend Arts Center performances.
S$_2$ Senior citizens on social security deserve a break and can't afford the tickets.
S$_3$ The performers would enjoy a large, appreciative audience.

C We should give the unused tickets to students and senior citizens.

The general rule is to include in a schematic representation anything in a passage that affects the strength of the argument. So, schematizing from a paraphrase will always have two stages: *First*, schematize the reasoning you have labeled ([s] or [r$_i$]) in the paraphrase. *Then* look for *omitted detail that makes a difference* to the argument.

Exercise 3.3

A structured paraphrase is given immediately below the following passage. (a) Schematize the reasoning in the paraphrase; (b) look through the passage for anything else relevant to the reasoning and add it to the schematization. (Answer on p. 130.)

Steve's car had almost certainly been burgled. When he returned from the late movie he noticed that the change holder on the center console, which he was compulsive about keeping full, was completely empty—not a coin remained. And something hadn't felt right when he unlocked the door: nothing of the familiar resistance to the twisting key, no satisfying "click" as it unlocked. Could he have forgotten to lock it? No, he remembered walking back half a block to recheck, mentally rebuking himself for not paying more attention in the first place. With growing alarm he checked the glovebox, where he remembered leaving the travelers checks remaining after his trip to Europe last month, and found it too was empty. Looking for signs of break-in, Steve found an inch-wide pattern of new scratches, right at the bottom of the driver's door window, just where a competent thief would insert a "slim jim" to open a locked car.

MP: Steve's car was burgled.
[s] SP: Valuables were missing.
[s] SP: Door did not seem locked.
[s] SP: Pattern of scratches on driver's door window.

One special kind of detail that we will want to watch for is the explanation that is also an implication. We saw these in the section on "paired subordinations" in Chapter 2: a secondary point that is both [e$_c$] and [r$_i$] at the same time. Rather often, one or the other of these connections will not be explicitly flagged, so you will have properly left it out of your paraphrase. Consider a simple example.

> There was an explosion onboard the Apollo 13 command module when the crew turned on the circulating fans in an oxygen tank. This was very likely caused by damaged insulation on the wires carrying current to the fans. Records indicate that the system was mistakenly subject to 65 volts, many more than it was designed to stand, during a procedure carried out weeks before launch. And this mistake was not noticed until after the explosion, despite many checks and reviews.

Here the MP is the explosion, and the first SP gives its cause. But the "very likely" suggests the cause is being inferred from something, and, sure enough, some support follows. So the paraphrase would look something like this:

MP: The Apollo 13 explosion occurred when power was fed to circulating fans in a tank of liquid oxygen.

[e_c]   SP: Insulation had burned off wires in the tank during a procedure weeks earlier.

[s]   SP: Records indicate far too high voltage was used.

[s]   SP: This was not noticed before launch.

The reasoning would schematize like this:

S_1: Far too much voltage was applied to the circuits of an Apollo 13 oxygen tank during a prelaunch procedure.

S_2: This was not noticed before launch.

C: Damaged insulation on the circulating fan wires caused the explosion that aborted the mission.

But this does not capture all of the reasoning in the passage. One important reason to think the insulation had burned off the wires was that the explosion occurred when the fans were activated. That is, the MP also provides some support for the first SP, making that SP not just an [e_c], but also an [r_i] of the MP. This was simply taken for granted in the article and so would not be mentioned in paraphrase. It is centrally important to the reasoning, however, so we must add it to our schematization. We might even go back and add the [r_i] to the paraphrase, remembering that it is there because of *our interest in the reasoning*, not the author's priority. In any case, it is relevant detail just like that we found in the earlier letter on the Arts Center audience. So the complete schematization would be as follows:

S_1: Far too much voltage was applied to the circuits of an Apollo 13 oxygen tank during a prelaunch procedure.

S_2: This was not noticed before launch.

S_3: The explosion occurred just after the crew turned on the circulating fans in the tank.

C: Damaged insulation on fan circuit wires caused the explosion that aborted the mission.

In looking for reasoning in a passage, you will always need to watch for causes that are also implications. This sort of detail will sometimes sneak up on you in surprising ways, and we will devote all of Chapter 5 to it. For now, we can use a simple test. Whenever you suspect an explanatory "because" hides an inferential "so," or vice versa, test your suspicion by trying the paraphrase both ways: with both explanatory and inferential flags. If you begin with

MP because SP [e]

try   MP so it must have been SP $[r_i]$

to see if it fits as well. Or, if you begin with

MP so SP $[r_e]$

try   It must have been MP, because SP [s].

Exercise 3.4

a. Describe circumstances in which the following causal connections would also be inferential (use the flag-term hint immediately above). Give the two subordination codes.

  i. The dynamite exploded because the shack got too hot in the sun.

  ii. Tony lost his job, so he had to sell his house.

  iii. The plane crashed because it was out of fuel.

b. Below is the paraphrase we offered for the train wreck article on p. 75 of Chapter 2. Find and label the double subordination (consult the article for guidance). Then schematize the reasoning it contains.

MP: An Amtrak train derailed at a switch.
$[r_e]$ SP: Injuring 74 people. $[r_e]$
[q]   SP: Four required hospitalization. $[q]$
[q]   SP: Including the engineer. $[q]$
$[e_c]$ SP: The switch had been tampered with. $[e]$
[s]   SP: Some bolt cutters and shavings that might be from a lock
           were found nearby. $[s]$
[s]   SP: The siding switch lock itself is missing. $[s]$

c. Write out a structured paraphrase of the following passage (take the whole first paragraph as background); then schematize the reasoning it contains.

One thing physicians thought they could count on was that there was good and bad cholesterol. Low-density lipoprotein (LDL) was bad, because it deposited cholesterol on artery walls where it could interfere with blood flow, high-density lipoprotein (HDL) was good because it helped rid the body of excess cholesterol.

The Pima Indians of the American Southwest appear to have a special form of LDL, however. Instead of depositing cholesterol on artery walls, it seems to transfer it to HDL, which then transports it out of the body. This is according to physiological research by Dr. John Bagdade and his colleagues at Rush Medical College in Chicago and at the National Institutes of Health Laboratory in Phoenix. Dr. Bagdade and his colleagues think this finding explains why the Pimas have relatively low rates of heart disease, despite their high-fat diet and high rates of extreme obesity and early-onset diabetes, all of which are strongly linked to heart disease.

(Answers on p. 130.)

Complex Arguments: Cascades and Tributaries

The reasoning we have examined so far in this chapter has all been of a very simple structure: a great deal of support is offered for a single conclusion.

$$S_1$$
$$S_2$$

$$C$$

Reasoning may be far more complex than this, of course, and we have already seen examples of such complexity in the support cascades of Chapter 2: For example:

MP: He should get first-degree murder.
[s] SP_1: The killing was deliberate.
[s] SP_2: He had plenty of time to think about it.
[s] SP_3: He loaded the gun.
[s] SP_4: The neighbors heard six rapid shots.

Here we have four distinct arguments laced together in a particular way. We think he should get first-degree murder because the killing was deliberate. And we think the killing was deliberate because he had time to think about it. And we think that because . . . , and so on. SP_4 is support in an argument that has SP_3 as its conclusion; and SP_3 is support in an argument that has SP_2 as its conclusion; and so on until we get to the MP, which is supported by SP_1. Schematically, such complex reasoning would look like this:

$$SP_4$$

$$SP_3 \rightarrow SP_3$$

$$SP_2 \rightarrow SP_2$$

$$SP_1 \rightarrow SP_1$$

$$MP$$

In a complex argument such as this, we will call the last argument, at the bottom of the chain, the *main argument,* and the others *tributary arguments.* An argument is a tributary if its conclusion is support in a further argument.

$$S_2$$
$$----$$
$$S_1 \longrightarrow S_1$$
$$----$$

Tributary   C
Argument

                    Main
                 Argument

Although schematic form makes reasoning easier to see even in simple cascades, its real advantage becomes apparent only in irregular cases that are more typical:

$$S_4$$
$$S_5 \qquad\qquad S_6$$
$$---- \qquad\qquad S_7$$
$$S_1 \longrightarrow S_1 \quad S_8$$
$$S_2 \qquad ----$$
$$S_3 \longleftarrow S_3$$
$$----$$

$$C$$

Here the main argument is (obviously) the one in the middle; and only two of its supporting statements have tributaries. Consider the following illustration.

MP: A badly latched cargo door caused the crash of a DC-10 outside Paris.

[s] SP$_1$: The door was found 10 miles from the crash site.

[s] SP$_2$: A baggage handler latched the door improperly just before take-off.

[s]   SP$_3$: He couldn't read the directions on the door.

[s]   SP$_4$: He remembers having to force the latch handle.

[s] SP$_5$: Sudden depressurization of the baggage compartment would collapse the cabin floor, disrupting the control of the rear engine and control surfaces.

[s]   SP$_6$: The floor was not designed to withstand the pressure difference an open baggage door would cause.

[s]   SP$_7$: In a similar incident two years earlier, depressurizing the baggage compartment at a lower altitude caused the floor to collapse partially, nearly severing connection to the rear.

This would schematize as follows:

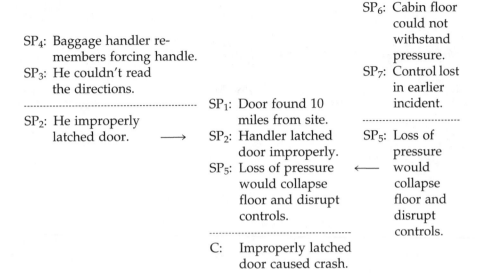

One common locus of tributaries are the SPs that are double labeled [e_c]/[s] (see the discussion of "paired roles" on p. 76 of Chapter 2). Very often we will support a hypothesis about something indirectly by supporting an underlying explanation of it. We may, for instance, support the claim that smoking causes cancer by discovering a connection between some component of cigarette smoke and the physiological preconditions of malignancy. Then we might give the experimental results underwriting the connection.

     MP: Smoking causes cancer.
[e_c]/[s] SP: Component X of cigarette smoke interacts with lung tissue to
           initiate malignancy.
    [s]   SP: [Certain laboratory results.]

The reasoning would schematize as follows:

        S_1: Lab results

        C': X initiates malignancy
            in lung tissue.   ⟶ S_2: X initiates malignancy
                                           in lung tissue.

                                   C: Smoking causes cancer.

Exercise 3.5

Accept the following as the paraphrase of the Legionnaires' disease article in Exercise 2.27b on p. 78. Locate and label the double subordination in this structure (consult the article for guidance) and then schematize the reasoning.

MP: Lowering water heater temperatures caused the outbreak of Legion-naires' disease.
[e_c] SP: The lower temperatures provided the perfect environment for *Legionella* bacteria.
[s]   SP: In a test case, only lowered systems had *Legionella* colonies.
[s]   SP: One of these was eliminated with a hot-water flush.

(Answer on p. 131.)

A Subtlety: Qualification of Support

We saw in Chapter 2 that it is sometimes difficult to decide whether a particular subordination is [q] or [s]. This is relevant here because it can affect how we schematize the reasoning in a passage. For we have already seen that support for support yields complex structure.

$$
\begin{array}{lll}
\text{MP} & & \text{SP}_2 \\
[\text{s}] \quad \text{SP}_1 & & \text{------} \\
[\text{s}] & \text{SP}_2 \quad \text{Converts to:} \quad \text{SP}_1 \;\; \rightarrow \;\; \text{SP}_1 \\
& & \text{-------} \\
& & \text{MP}
\end{array}
$$

Qualification of support, on the other hand, although almost always an important part of the argument, does not add complexity.

$$
\begin{array}{ll}
\text{MP} & \\
[\text{s}] \quad \text{SP}_1 & \text{SP}_1 \text{ qualified by SP}_2 \\
[\text{q}] \quad\quad \text{SP}_2 \quad \text{Converts to:} & \text{----------------------------------} \\
& \text{MP}
\end{array}
$$

In the Soviet submarine case (see p. 50), for instance, we find the following reasoning:

SP: The sub will be difficult to raise.
[s] SP: It is in 5,000 feet of water.
[s] SP: Its hull is probably cracked.
[q]   SP: (But) it seems intact.

Because whether the hull is intact affects how difficult the sub will be to raise, it is clearly relevant to the argument. But the fact that the hull is intact does not support the SP it comments on, it just qualifies it somewhat. So the argument would schematize like this:

S_1 The sub is in 5000 feet of water.
S_2 Its hull is cracked but intact.

C It will be difficult to raise.

Exercise 3.6
....

Why are "probably" and "seems" not indicators of reasoning (indirectness flags) in the submarine paraphrase? (Answer on p. 131.)

Consider a different kind of example.

As a private citizen I wholeheartedly support the current method of recycling used in California. In my living room there is a stack of Times newspapers which is given to a neighbor when it reaches three feet high; on the back porch are bags of aluminum cans and glass containers which are taken to a recycling center at a local high school.

However, as a retailer and franchisee of a 24-hour convenience store, I am against Proposition 11. It will require retailers to become recycling centers. It will require me to take back all empty soda and beer containers brought into my store; however, I cannot call the distributor for a pickup of these empty containers unless I have at least 25 cases of each brand sold in my store.

I currently have available to the consumer 20 different brands of soda and 10 of beer. I carry some because of a small contingent of customers who will buy them, but they are not fast sellers. If this proposition is passed, I can assure one and all that I will limit the number of brands available at my store to only those items that will sell quickly enough and be returned quickly enough to ensure me the required 25 cases for a pickup by the distributor.

I will also have to cut down on the selling space of other items that I carry in order to provide storage space. Additionally, I will be forced to have my store serviced more often by the fumigator to ensure that whatever "crawly" items are returned inside these empty containers do not infest other merchandise.

An additional problem with Proposition 11 concerns its enforcement provisions. Who is going to enforce the law and levy the fine?

Harriet Markman
Alhambra (LA Times)

This whole letter is a sustained argument against Proposition 11, giving reasons it should not become law. Three large components may be distinguished. Most of the letter details ways in which the proposed law will hurt small retailers. But it begins by urging that the current system is fine; and it ends by raising questions about enforcement. So it would paraphrase as follows:

MP: Proposition 11 is a bad idea.
[s]   SP: It would hurt small retailers.
[s]   SP: It contains no enforcement provisions.
[s]   SP: We already have an adequate recycling program.

Which would schematize as this:

S_1 Proposition 11 would hurt small retailers.
S_2 It contains no enforcement provisions.
S_3 We already have an adequate recycling procedure.

C Proposition 11 should not become law.

When we go back to the article for relevant detail, we find a number of items related to S_1. How do we include them? This involves resolving the [q]/[s] ambiguity we looked at in Chapter 2. And in this case, the detail is most naturally captured as qualification of S_1: ways in which it will hurt small retailers, connected to S_1 with "by."

> SP: Proposition 11 would hurt small retailers.
> [q] SP: It would limit stock.
> [q] SP: It would restrict shelf space.
> [q] SP: It would increase fumigation expense.

So the fleshed-out schematization would look like this:

S_1 Proposition 11 would hurt small retailers by limiting stock, restricting shelf space, and increasing fumigation expense.
S_2 It contains no enforcement provisions.
S_3 We already have an adequate recycling procedure.

C Proposition 11 should not become law.

Had we represented the subordination here as [s] rather than [q], and put the additional detail in a tributary on the original S_1, that would not have seriously misled us about the argument. The additional structural complexity would have given us no further insight into the reasoning, however, so this simpler structure is best. In the next chapter we will see another reason to resist thinking about qualifications such as this as arguments.

Exercise 3.7

Below is the simplest paraphrase we gave for the green tea article in Exercise 2.22b on p. 69. Locate and label the double subordination and schematize the reasoning. (Consult the article for guidance.)

> MP: Drinking green tea fights cancer.
> [s]   SP: Its drinkers have low rates of four cancers
> [e$_c$] SP: It contains catechin and flavinoids.
> [q]   SP: Which have cancer-fighting credentials.

(Answer on p. 131.)

A SHORTCUT: SCHEMATIZING DIRECTLY FROM A PASSAGE

Once we can reliably distinguish inferential connections from other kinds of subordination, we will often be able to schematize directly from a passage, without first writing out a complete indented paraphrase. We may refine the tricks we used to identify inferential connections in the last chapter to make the extra step unnecessary for most everyday passages. Of course if the passage is particularly complicated, you may always fall back on a complete paraphrase to help you see its structure. But in this section we will practice the short cut.

Reasoning Clues

To extract the reasoning from a passage requires us to do two different things. The first is simply *to recognize that some reasoning (inference, argument) is going on* in a passage. The second is to see just what supports what. Normally we do both of these things at the same time, as we did in Chapter 2. There, recall, we thought about whether something was reasoning (as opposed to explaining or qualifying) only as we were sorting out what supported what in a paraphrase. But if we want to extract reasoning without working through a paraphrase, we will need to keep the two activities separate, at least in our thinking.

The reason to do this is that all the words and phrases that help us discern argument structure also do many other jobs in the language. Before we can use them to find the structure, we need to make sure they are involved in reasoning. If you miss the big picture you can trick yourself into thinking you're piecing together an argument, when you're simply misunderstanding the passage. So we must learn to recognize the features of a passage that tip us off to reasoning.

Reasoning clues come in three basic kinds, and they *usually work in pairs*. The three basic kinds are (a) general common sense indicators, (b) indirectness flags, and (c) [s] and [r$_i$] indicators such as "because" and "so." If a passage contains indicators of one kind, you have some ground to look for reasoning. If it contains indicators from two different categories, then it almost certainly contains reasoning. If they pair in specific ways, we will see, it is certain. Let us look at the indicators.

A. General Indicators

The general common sense indicators are simply *Investigation* and *Controversy*. If a passage—or part of a passage—concerns an investigation into something, or takes a position in a controversy, that will be a good sign that some part of it will be offered in support of something. So you should not be surprised to find inferential connections in an article about new evidence in an unsolved aircrash, for instance, or one offering proposals to raise taxes or restrict abortion.

In practice, your ability to recognize investigation and controversy depends on how much you know about what's going on in the world. You must be acquainted with things such as the history of the abortion debate and the fate of TWA's Flight 800. But even here we can expand our ability to spot such things, beyond our current grasp of public affairs, by noting key words that sometimes accompany them. Very general indicators of investigation will be terms such as "evidence," "clue," "discover," and (of course) "investigators." So if a headline reads

CLUE FOUND IN MYSTERIOUS DISAPPEARANCE

or a paragraph contains the sentence

"Investigators have found evidence that the fire was started by transients."

you will not be wasting your time looking for inferential connections.

Exercise 3.8
....

Both the headline and the sentence extracted from the paragraph above give us part of the argument we're likely to find in the passages they concern. What is it? (Answer on p. 132.)

The most general indicators of controversy will not be particular words as much as the proposals and recommendations around which controversy swirls. But since proposals and recommendations often contain the normative terms we pointed out in Chapter 2, they will function as the same sort of clue to reasoning that the investigation words do. So watch for words such as "should," "ought," "right," and "wrong." If a passage reads:

> We should not dismantle outcome-based affirmative action programs.

or

> It would be a mistake to immediately expand NATO to include former Soviet Satellites.

you might reasonably expect some support to be offered for these sentiments.

B. INDIRECTNESS FLAGS

We noticed in Chapter 2 that indirectness was a sure way to distinguish inference from other subordinations. So, just as you would suspect, indirectness *flags* turn out to be another indicator that a passage contains reasoning. The major ones are "must," "may," "probably," "likely," "apparently," and "seems." When these words do flag indirectness, they indicate that something in the passage is not known directly, but through something else, from which it is inferred. So if you find a sentence such as

> The door may have been left unlocked.

or

> The children were apparently playing with matches.

you might well check around for a schematizable argument.

Exercise 3.9
....

If "may" and "apparently" turn out to be indirectness flags in these cases, what part would these sentences play in the argument we've found? (Answer on p. 132.)

C. [s] AND [r$_i$] FLAGS

The third class of reasoning indicators includes "because" and "so" and other words that flag the support and implication subordinations we codified in Chapter 2. Other terms that behave like "because" include "since," "for," and phrases such as "after all." Expressions that work like "so" include "thus," "hence," "therefore," and "it follows that." These are the weakest indicators of reasoning, which need the most help from context. But finding one of these terms in a piece of writing should at least alert you to the possibility that it contains reasoning.

Powerful Pairs

We saw in Chapter 2 that when b and c flags go together, it virtually guarantees inferential subordination.

The door may have been unlocked, because there was no sign of forced entry.

The kitchen ceiling has begun to drip, so it is doubtless raining quite hard now.

These sentences are perfect pictures of schematizable reasoning.

Exercise 3.10

Schematize the reasoning in each of these sentences. (Answer on p. 132.)

Another strong pair indicating reasoning is the occurrence of indirectness flags *in* an investigation. If a newspaper article on Flight 800, or a political corruption probe, contains a "must" or "may" or "apparently," you should suspect an inference is being made. These are from categories a and b. But an a–c combination is also powerful. If a proposal or recommendation comes attached to a "because" or a "so," that makes a good case for schematizable reasoning. For (as we saw in Chapter 2) these words do not do their explanatory jobs in normative statements. So an "ought" together with a "because" or "so" ("since" or "therefore") almost guarantees inference.

Exercise 3.11

List the general indicators that reasoning is going on in the following passage, that is, indicators not closely linked to the particular argument being offered. (Answer on p. 132.)

WASHINGTON—Secret Service officials suggested Monday that a dramatic suicide, rather than an assassination attempt, was the most likely motivation behind the crash on the White House South Lawn of a light plane piloted by

> Frank Corder, a 38-year-old truck driver with a history of alcohol and drug
> problems. The plane's dive onto the White House South Lawn at 1:49 a.m.
> Monday "does not appear directed toward the President," Secret Service
> spokesman Carl Meyer told reporters, warning that the conclusion was "very
> preliminary."
>
> The plane contained no explosives or other weapons, Meyer noted, and in-
> vestigators have found no evidence that Corder had any political grievance
> against President Clinton nor that he had ever threatened the Clintons. Inves-
> tigators did discover that Corder, who lived in Perryville, Md., northeast of
> Baltimore, had been treated last year for alcoholism at the Perry Point Med-
> ical Center, a Veterans Administration Hospital in Maryland, had separated
> three weeks ago from his wife and had been distraught over the death of his
> father last spring.
>
> (David Lauter, *Los Angeles Times* Staff Writer)

Structural Clues

Once we find evidence that a passage contains some reasoning, we may then exploit these very same indicators to determine just what supports what.[3] Let us assume for the moment that the argument is simple, not compounded of tributaries.
We will shortly see that this assumption is self-correcting: if it is wrong, that will
show up in our attempt to schematize it. So, assuming a simple one-step argument, let us explore ways to locate its components.

Link Flags ([r$_i$] Indicators)

Although they do not occur very frequently, words that indicate [r$_i$] subordination ("so," "therefore," "hence," "it follows that") actually contain the most information about argument structure. Once you know they are doing their reasoning job, you may be pretty sure that they come directly between the support
and the conclusion of an argument. That is because they are *consequence-drawing
words*: they give you both a consequence *and* what it is a consequence of. They
point back toward support and forward toward a conclusion. We will call these
words *link flags*. When you find one of them in what you recognize as reasoning,
look back at what precedes it to find the support and forward to what comes afterward to find the conclusion. An example from normal driving experience will
illustrate this:

> The oncoming cars are all using their windshield wipers, so we must be driv-
> ing into rain.

Here what comes before the "so" is the support in an argument, and what follows is the conclusion. Link flags work so well because they simply make no sense
in any other arrangement. If the points occurred in a different order, or if we omit-

---

3. We may still find out we were wrong to think the passage contained reasoning;
and this will come out in our inability to find a satisfactory structure.

ted one as too obvious to mention, or put much irrelevancy between point and link, the link flag simply wouldn't work. You might try the various possibilities to see for yourself.

For a more complex example, consider this:

> The government of Iraq has violated the sovereignty of its neighbors and the human rights of its citizens. It has engaged in chemical warfare, sponsored international terrorism and considered the genocide of its Kurdish minority. It has also attempted to build atomic weapons with the obvious intent to employ them in these vicious activities. Therefore all civilized countries should join in the boycott of Iraqi oil until convinced that the country has renounced its rogue barbarousness.

Here the link flag "therefore" divides this passage into support (above it) and conclusion (below). Schematization will then consist simply in deciding how to condense the material into supporting claims and conclusion.

Exercise 3.12
....

Schematize the last two arguments (wipers and Iraq). (Answer on p. 132.)

Conclusion Flags (Indirectness Indicators)

If reasoning contains no link flag to make things transparent in this way, the best strategy is to first look for the argument's conclusion. And (in the absence of a link flag) the best indicators of conclusions are our familiar *indirectness flags*: "must," "may," "probably," and the rest. When we use them to find structure we will call them "conclusion flags," and sometimes they will occur right before the conclusion, just like link flags. For example, assuming we have found some reasoning, if a sentence reads:

> Apparently the children were playing with matches.

this will be the (or a) conclusion. You should look around for some support. But unlike link flags, the support need not have come immediately before this sentence: it can occur anywhere else in the passage, before or after. It can even be unstated: so obvious as to be taken for granted.

Exercise 3.13
....

Schematize the following:

a. Evidently there had been inadequate preparation, because the earthquake drill caught everybody off guard.
b. The drill caught everybody off guard; apparently the preparation had been inadequate. (Answers on p. 132.)

Most conclusion flags will not be like this example, however. Usually indirectness flags are so intimately connected to a conclusion that they will be tangled up in the very statement of it, and require careful removal just to state C properly. In the windshield wiper illustration above, for instance, the conclusion is "We are driving into rain." But to derive that from what's given we need to get rid of the "must" and change the form of the verb "to be."

Sentence in Passage	Schematized Conclusion
We must be driving into rain.	We are driving into rain.

This is similar in the following example:

> The door may have blown open, since the breeze is coming from that direction.

Here the conclusion is "The door has blown open." But stating it requires dropping the "may" and, again, reworking the major verb. So the rule is that a conclusion flag occurs either just *before a conclusion or is part of it.*

Exercise 3.14

Schematize the following: "There seems to have been inadequate preparation, since the drill caught everybody off guard." (Answer on p. 132.)

SUPPORT FLAGS

In this last example (the breeze) the support is also flagged by the characteristic word "since." Occasionally an author will introduce the support in an argument with something explicit and obvious, such as "the reason to think so is . . ." or "we can tell this is true from. . . ." But usually this will be done more simply with "because" and the other words that function similarly. When they have this function we will call them *support flags,* and they say that what is coming up is support in the argument: it goes above the line in schematic form. Sometimes, when the conclusion is stated first, these flags will also occur directly between conclusion and support:

> We must be driving into rain, because the oncoming cars are all using their windshield wipers.

But, again unlike the link flags, support flags work with the points in any order, and the conclusion may even be unstated. So the general rule is that terms such as "since," "for," and "after all" indicate that *some support is coming up.*

Exercise 3.15

Schematize the following: "Because we haven't seen them in a while and yellowing newspapers are collecting in their driveway, the Wendlestadts must be away on vacation." (Answer on p. 132.)

Remove Structural Flags before Schematizing

In schematic form, a statement's location within the diagram tells you whether it is support or conclusion: support on top, conclusion below. So the geometry of the diagram takes the place of all argument-structure flags. Being on top takes the place of "because" (and all similar flags); being below the line takes the place of "must" and all the other conclusion flags. The line separating S from C replaces all the link flags (because it comes right between them). Just as subordination flags in general paraphrases are redundant, so are inference-structure flags in schematizations. But their redundancy is much more troublesome here, so omitting them will be even more important. Including flags in an indented paraphrase can be harmless, when necessary to make it read well. But you must make it a rule to *strip* **All Structural Flags** *from your schematized arguments*. Either of the one-sentence arguments about driving into rain would schematize like this:

S Oncoming cars are all using their wipers.

C We are driving into rain.

No "because." No "must." No "so."

Exercise 3.16
·····················

a. Schematize "Something awful must have happened to Angela over the summer, because she's been in a terrible mood ever since she got back." (Answer on p. 132.)

b. Check the schematizations you gave for Exercises 3.12, 3.13, 3.14, and 3.16 to make sure you omitted all structural flags.

Mental Flags and Attributed Arguments

The reasoning we find in print, and even in conversation, will often be credited to a particular individual or group. As we saw in Chapter 2, an article may give the President's argument for trade sanctions against China, or investigators' argument that the maintenance worker caused the motel to explode. When arguments are attributed to people in this way you will find another group of verbs appearing as indirectness flags, and hence as conclusion flags. Words such as "think," "believe," "suspect," and "presume" will then stand in for the verb "to conclude" or "to infer." These words indicate that the person doing the thinking or suspecting does not claim to know the thing in question *directly*, and hence must infer it. So if a passage reads "Investigators believe the driver fell asleep at the wheel, because no attempt to steer or brake was made before impact," the investigators are giving *reason to think* the driver fell asleep. They are offering an argument, which should be schematized:

S No attempt was made to steer or brake
  before impact.

C The driver fell asleep at the wheel.

Because the word "believe" simply flags the investigator's conclusion it does not appear in the schematization: it is a structural flag.

If you miss this point you may write the conclusion,

> C′ Investigators believe the driver fell asleep at the wheel.

And this makes it seem that the argument concerns the investigators' mental state (their beliefs), which it does not. The investigators' argument concerns what went on out on the road, not what went on in their heads. So it is important to recognize "believe" as a conclusion flag and keep it out of the schematization.

Exercise 3.17
....

What is the mental flag in the Motel Blast article on p. 44 of Chapter 2. (Answer on p. 132.)

We may accumulate the various structure flags conveniently in Table 3.1. These are the terms to omit from schematizations.

Exercise 3.18
....

a. In the following sentences, pick out and describe the flag terms, then schematize the reasoning. (Answers on p. 132.)

   i. Because there was no fire at the site of its impact, the plane must have been out of fuel when it crashed.

   ii. The plane was probably out of fuel, because there was no fire at the crash site.

   iii. Many days of newspapers have accumulated on their porch and no lights went on at dusk, so the neighbors may be away on vacation.

   iv. Earthquake retrofitting was apparently inadequate: many bridges suffered severe damage in last night's modest temblor.

   v. Members of the school board think the building needs replacing because the cost of renovation is so high.

   vi. Twenty minutes have elapsed since the last shot was fired from the second floor window, so I'm sure there is nobody left alive in the house.

b. In the article below, five different indicator words flag three different versions of a conclusion drawn by various authorities in a coroner's investigation. (i) List the five flags. (ii) State what kind of conclusion flag each is. (iii) List the three versions of the conclusion. (iv) These three versions have one claim in common. Schematize the argument given in the passage for that common claim. (Answer on p. 133.)

   Dogs May Have Eaten Dead Woman's Body
   HESPERIA—The skull and one foot of a woman whose body apparently was eaten by her pet dogs were discovered in her home by her nephew, author-

ities said. "We think the dogs completely chewed up the rest (of the body) . . .," said Dave Hammock, a San Bernardino county deputy coroner. "We dug everywhere (in the yard), but with the rain and everything, it's hard to locate anything." Hammock said he believes Mary Ethel Hessey, a 61-year-old cancer patient, died naturally and her body later was eaten by the dogs. "There is no visible trauma to the skull, and no indication what caused her death," Hammock said, adding that with the few remains it will be impossible to determine how the victim died or whether she was dead when the dogs attacked her.

San Bernardino County sheriff's deputies believe the woman died inside her home and was dragged outside through a broken sliding glass door by the dogs when they became hungry. The woman had been dead between three and four weeks before the remains were discovered Tuesday by her nephew, Raymond Nuccil, Hammock said. He said the dogs, described as medium-sized mongrels, "looked in pretty good shape to me—not like they were starving or anything." The dogs were to be destroyed by San Bernardino County Animal Control Services.

(The Associated Press)

c. In the White House suicide crash article on p. 111 (Exercise 3.11) the secret service draws a conclusion indicated by a typical indirectness flag, but in a slightly complicated manner. (i) What is the flag? (ii) Write out the conclusion. (iii) List the support offered in the article for this conclusion.

(Answers on p. 133.)

Proposals and Recommendations

Proposals and recommendations all have the basic form,

"We should do X" (or "We should not do X").

All the key terms may be reduced to this form. Saying we ought to do X, or that it would be right or good to do X all may be paraphrased "We should do X." Similarly saying that X would be wrong or bad or a mistake or a tragedy comes to saying "We should not do X."

When reasoning concerns "normative" statements such as this, we need not worry much that support and link flags ("because," "so," and similar terms) might be doing their explanatory jobs. So we can reasonably confidently determine the

TABLE 3.1 General Inference-Structure Flags

Link	Support	Conclusion (Indirectness)	(Mental)	
So	Because	May	Think	Implies
Hence	Since	Must	Believe	Entails
Thus	For	Probably	Suspect	Suggests
Therefore	After all	Possibly	Guess	Indicates
It follows	In as much as	Doubtless	Presume	
This means		Seems	Conclude	

form of the argument using these terms as structural flags. If a recommendation is connected to something else in a passage with a "because" or "so," you can be reasonably sure these terms structure an argument. That is, whatever comes after the "because" is support, and the tools we have just examined should get you the rest of the argument. Similarly for "so": it will connect support and conclusion in an argument. Consider:

> Since rain is forecast for later in the day, we should plough the field before taking off for lunch.

Here the normative term "should" tells us that the "since" is doing its reasoning job. That job is to flag support, so we know that the forecast is support for something; and, of course, that something is the recommendation that we plough before lunch. So the schematization would be as follows:

> S: Rain is forecast for later in the day.
> --
> C: We should plough before lunch.

Note that we do not leave normative terms out of the schematizations. Normative terms such as this are part of the *substance* of the conclusion, not mere structural terms telling us where to find it; so they stay in the schematic argument. "Since," on the other hand, is a support flag, so we leave it out.

Recommendations come in a nearly infinite variety of forms. But usually what is being recommended is transparent, and we may, if we wish, check our understanding by translating an unusual form into a more standard one.

> The United Nations General Assembly today called for an end to economic sanctions against Iraq, arguing that they cause too much suffering among the civilian population, especially children.

Here we recognize the "calling for" as a recommendation: the General Assembly thinks we should end the sanctions. "Arguing" looks like a definite indication of reasoning, but what sort of flag is it? "Because" could easily replace "arguing that" in the sentence, so it is a support flag: the suffering is support in an argument. The conclusion, of course, is the recommendation: they are arguing that we should end sanctions because of their harsh consequences.

Exercise 3.19
· · · · · · · · · · · · · · · · · · ·
Schematize the General Assembly's argument. (Answer on p. 134.)

Two more observations will complete this section. First, when they are conclusions, recommendations sometimes come disguised as *imperatives*. That is, instead of saying "We should do X," because of something or other, the author will simply say "Do X" for that reason. Suppose you lend me your car and say, "Avoid heavy traffic, because it overheats in stop-and-go driving." Alerted to the possibility, we have no difficulty paraphrasing it as saying that I *should* avoid heavy traffic for this reason. That is, we can see it as schematizable reasoning for a recommendation.

And finally, a group of normative statements in some sense weaker than recommendations functions similarly in reasoning contexts. These merely claim that doing something is *permissible*, not particularly recommended, or a fine thing to do. So if your driving instructor says, "you are free to pass the truck now if you wish, because the road ahead is clear," he is given support for a proposition, but has not actively recommended the pass. He has just argued that it's now okay if you want to. Although indirectness flags may flag any sort of normative conclusion, they are far more common in permissibility arguments.

I guess it's okay to leave: it's a half hour after they said they'd be here.

Here the "I guess" is an indirectness flag, telling us that the "okay" statement is the conclusion of an argument. This in turn allows us to recognize that a colon has been used in place of "because."

Exercise 3.20

Schematize this last argument. (Answer on p. 134.)

One More Trick: Flags in Partial Paraphrases

Sometimes an author will not flag—or even mention—a major piece of his or her argument because it is simply too obvious. This will be especially common when the argument concerns a proposal or recommendation. Harriet Markman does not explicitly say, "We should vote against Proposition 11," even though that is clearly her conclusion. The argument about the Arts Center's seats casts its recommendation not in any of our standard forms, but as a rhetorical question, "Why not give the unsold seats to . . . ?" One step that often helps in such cases will be to adapt the "headline" device of Chapter 1 to the task of finding reasoning. To do this, first assure yourself that the passage contains reasoning, using the tools described above. Then simply summarize the part of the passage you take to contain the reasoning, using a single sentence with natural flags.

Sentence summary: She thinks we should oppose Proposition 11 because it will be hard on small businesses.

Sentence summary: We should give the seats to senior citizens and drama students for all those reasons mentioned there at the end.

Sentence summary: The cabin temperature reached 400 degrees, so everybody must have been dead before impact.

You may then use your own flags to structure the argument, and go back to the passage itself for detail to make the argument robust.

Exercise 3.21

a. List all the inference structure flags in these summaries and describe the kind of flag they are in each case.

b. (i) Write a one-sentence summary of the following article, displaying the (new) reasoning. (ii) Schematize the argument, being sure to add relevant aspects of the omitted padding to the support made explicit in your sentence.

> According to historical accounts, Southern California suffered several earthquakes in 1812, including a severe one on December 8 that collapsed part of the mission at San Juan Capistrano. Scientists had always assumed that the Dec. 8 temblor occurred on a fault near the coast of Southern California because most reports of the quake came from areas near the coast. That opinion has recently changed, however, as the result of data from tree ring cores taken near the town of Wrightwood, which lies on the famous San Andreas Fault.
>
> Core samples taken from older trees near the fault in that area show wide bands of growth through the year 1812. The following year, and for many years thereafter, the growth rings are bunched close together, suggesting "a long and painful recovery from trauma," in the words of one scientist. Samples were taken from enough trees to conclude that they suffered from an event that devastated a large area along the fault. A similar drop in tree growth was found in tree rings along another part of the San Andreas Fault that suffered a major quake. The rings become bunched and narrow after 1857, the year the quake occurred.

(Answers on p. 134.)

Finding Complex Structure

If we pay proper attention to flag terms and other indicators of reasoning, we may be able to tease more complex reasoning out of a passage. Consider the following:

> It will probably rain here within twenty four hours. Because if you look at the map you can see that radar's showing rain across the entire valley, and temperatures are dropping sharply on a line to the south. And that means we've got a storm system just south of Elko. So unless something unusual happens the storm will be here sometime tomorrow.

Four inference flags provide a sure sign of complexity: two link flags, one conclusion flag, and a support flag. Because every link flag stands between some support and a conclusion, the fact that there are two of them *and* a conclusion flag means we must look for three conclusions. Fortunately, the conclusion that is flagged by "probably" at the beginning and the one flagged by "so" at the end are actually the same proposition: namely, the rain forecast, which is given twice in the passage. This suggests that there may be only two conclusions to worry about. But having the same point occur twice in a passage also makes paraphrasing it tricky, so this is a good place to try our shortcut.

How then should we tease out the structure? Well, the two link flags tell us that the storm system is both a conclusion and support: one link comes before it ("that means") and the other one after it ("so"). So it must be the conclusion of a tributary, which in turn shows up as support in the main argument. What is the main conclusion? Whatever the system is linked to by the second link flag. This turns out to be the rain forecast. So the main argument is this:

> S: There's a storm system south of Elko.
>
> ---
>
> C: It will rain here tomorrow.

If S is also the conclusion of an argument, what support does it have? Again, look at what comes before the link flag (that means) preceding the storm front in the passage. It is all the data on rain and temperatures: just what we should expect to support the claim that a storm front exists somewhere. This gives us the tributary:

> S_1: Characteristic rainfall patterns in the valley.
> S_2: Temperature is dropping along a line to the south.
>
> ---
>
> C': There's a storm system south of Elko.

All that's left is to make sense of the support flag "because" and the "no unusual circumstances" proviso. The support flag merely tells you that what's coming up is support for the forecast that precedes the "because." But we already have that in the schematization (because the forecast is mentioned twice), so we need add nothing. The proviso, on the other hand, adds a caution to the normal time line assumed in the main argument: that the prediction holds only in the absence of meteorological surprises. So the whole structure would look like this:

> Characteristic rainfall
> patterns in the valley.
> Temperature is dropping
> along a line to the south.
>
> --
>
> | There is a storm system south of Elko. | $\rightarrow$ | There is a storm system south of Elko. |
>
> Such systems normally get here the next day.
>
> --
>
> It will rain here tomorrow.

Exercise 3.22

The following article starts off in one direction, but then shifts gears after the first paragraph, giving a coherent argument for an unexpected conclusion. Two indirectness flags and a support flag should allow you to schematize this compound argument offered by Samuel Epstein. (Answer on p. 134.)

PASADENA—Analysis of a meteorite that fell on Australia in 1969 supports a hotly debated theory that the chemical building blocks of life on Earth came from deep interstellar space, a scientist said yesterday. Researchers long have known that meteorites, including one that fell near Murchison, Australia, [so many] years ago, contain amino acids, which are organic chemicals needed for the formation of life. But many scientists argue that the chemical building blocks of life already were available on Earth after its formation 4.6 billion years ago, and there was at most a negligible contribution from meteorites or asteroids that struck the planet.

Scientists at the California Institute of Technology and Arizona State University analyzed the hydrogen in amino acids and fragments of such acids taken from a sample of the Murchison meteorite. They found unusually high levels of a heavy form of hydrogen named deuterium. Because deuterium is rare on Earth but much more common in gas clouds in interstellar space, the analysis suggests the amino acids, or at least the simpler organic chemicals that formed them, came from space beyond our solar system, said Caltech geochemist Samuel Epstein, principal author of the study.

If these building blocks of life were present not only on Earth or in space within our infant solar system but in space between the stars, the chemicals might also have been "a possible source of life in other solar systems," Epstein said in his study, which was published in April in Nature, a British science journal.

(*The Associated Press*)

In subtler cases, the rule urging us to keep inference flags out of our schematizations can help us determine when a complex structure is necessary. The purpose of schematizing arguments is to display support relations clearly: to diagrammatically separate support from what it is supporting. So when we find it hard to avoid a reasoning flag in one of the schematized statements we may suspect that we do not yet have the schematization right. It suggests that some reasoning is going on *within* one of the statements that needs to be made part of the diagram. So if a schematization ends up looking like this:

$$S_1$$
$$S_2$$
$$S_3 \text{ because } S_4$$
$$\text{-----------------------}$$
$$S_5$$

you have simply discovered the need for a tributary argument:

$$
\begin{array}{ccc}
S_1 & & S_4 \\
S_2 & & \text{----} \\
S_3 & \longleftarrow & S_3 \\
\text{----} & & \\
S_5 & &
\end{array}
$$

If the flag turns up in the conclusion:

$$S_1$$
$$S_2$$

$$S_3 \text{ because } S_4{}^4$$

it may indicate that you have simply misplaced some support, and it should be schematized like this:

$$S_1$$
$$S_2$$
$$S_4$$

$$S_3$$

or it might indicate the need for a tributary like this:

$$S_1$$
$$S_2$$

$$S_4 \longrightarrow S_4$$

$$S_3$$

Which of these is required will, as always, depend on the context.

To see how this helps in practice, consider the following article.

> Aspirin, which has long been known by doctors and laymen alike to have many uses, may have yet another: It may be able to play an effective part in weight loss. When combined with the allergy relief medicine ephedrine, aspirin is believed to have, at least theoretically, the ability to help people lose weight.
>
> Researchers at Harvard Medical School and the University of London recently published the findings of their aspirin-ephedrine studies in the *American Journal of Clinical Nutrition*. In one study, laboratory mice were fed a combination of the two drugs, and their metabolic rates increased as a result. This is important news at a time when interest in using metabolic-rate increase to reduce weight is being rekindled.
>
> The researchers think it's possible that a mixture of the two drugs could be used to help humans control obesity. They think the active ingredients in aspirin and ephedrine should be safe for such use by humans, if only because doctors have been using them in standard, everyday medicine for centuries.

Two indicators that this article contains reasoning are (a) that it concerns an *investigation* into the way this drug combination works and (b) that it makes a *proposal* about how they might be used. These two general clues then make it very

---

4. A conclusion flag (such as "therefore") could have just as easily been used in either of these illustrations simply by reversing the two connected statements. When used as reasoning flags, "A because B" expresses the same relationship as "B therefore A"; so resolving the difficulty with a conclusion flag would be a very similar process.

likely that the typical reasoning terms ("may," "believed," "think," "because") really are argument flags. As is usual in such cases, the proposal, flagged by "may," is the conclusion of an argument: it is that a combination of aspirin and ephedrine can be useful in combatting obesity in humans. In support of this it offers three distinct considerations: that this combination raises the metabolic rate of mice, that elevating metabolic rate is a general means of reducing weight, and that the drugs are safe for human consumption. Or, schematically,

S_1 A mixture of aspirin and ephedrine raises metabolic rates in mice.
S_2 Raising metabolic rates is an established means of weight reduction.
S_3 Aspirin and ephedrine are safe for human consumption.

C A mixture of aspirin and ephedrine can be useful in treating human obesity.

The only flaw in this schematization is that it omits a small but clear part of the reasoning. Some support for the eventual conclusion is to be found in the article's reference to our long experience with these two drugs. This is obvious not just from reading the piece, but also from the fact that reference to this long experience follows the support flag "because" in the passage. It must be part of the support, but it does not occur in the above schematized representation of the reasoning. What should be done?

A quick solution would be to simply include it in S_3, since our experience with the drugs is directly related to our estimate of their safety.

S_1 A mixture of aspirin and ephedrine raises metabolic rates in mice.
S_2 Raising metabolic rates is an established means of weight reduction.
S_3' Aspirin and ephedrine are probably safe for human consumption, because they have been used unproblematically for years.

C A mixture of aspirin and ephedrine can be useful in treating human obesity.

But if we do it this way we have reasoning going on within S_3', which is displayed in the occurrence of the reasoning flag pair "probably" and "because." So as the diagrams above would suggest, we need a tributary to express this reasoning, to get rid of the flags. S_3' should be broken into a separate argument with S_3 as its conclusion.

S_1 S_4 Aspirin and ephedrine have been in use for centuries.
S_2 --
S_3 ⟵—— S_3 They are safe for humans.

C

Exercise 3.23
....

Using everything we have covered so far, schematize the reasoning in the following article. This presents a tricky case for analysis because its main conclusion is only implied and structural flags are sparse. But you should be able to schematize the reasoning **with the following hints.** (a) The main conclusion answers the question the investigation concerns, which is made explicit in the article. (b) Three relevant things are known directly and hence can be used as support in an argument. (c) One thing not known directly is inferred from (supported by) two of these three things and then is used in another argument for the main conclusion. Write out responses to each of these three hints and then assemble them into a schematization. (Answers on p. 134.)

> TEXAS—Crews searching farm fields near Eagle Lake, Texas, found an airplane part yesterday that came off a Continental Express commuter flight last week before a crash that killed all 14 people aboard. The part, a 9-foot deicing attachment, is considered a vital clue in the investigation into what caused Flight 2574 to crash Wednesday, en route from Laredo to Houston. Three crew members and all 11 passengers died.
>
> Investigators speculated Saturday the de-icing boot fell off because 43 screws were missing from the leading edge of the plane's stabilizer, where the de-icer would have been attached. The sudden loss of the de-icer would stall the tail and cause the plane to nose dive, Kolstad said at a press briefing on the crash. It was found about three-quarters of a mile northeast of the crash site.
>
> *(The Associated Press)*

CHARITABLE SCHEMATIZING

A narrow focus on reasoning makes charity easier to deal with too. One problem we encounter in applying the principle of charity to general paraphrase is that what counts as a generous reading depends so much on just what the author is up to, which is sometimes not obvious. Are they really upset at something that seems so trivial, or is something else bothering them? Or is this really just sarcasm? Even with the best will in the world some passages will remain ambiguous simply because we cannot be confident of what reading would be most congenial from the author's point of view.

Much of this indeterminacy is removed, however, when we consider just the reasoning in a passage. For then, no matter what the overall purpose of the passage, we may impose a clear and specific purpose on our paraphrase: to provide support for a certain conclusion. Doing *this* well then becomes our criterion of charity; and it is generally easier to tell whether you have done a sympathetic job of unearthing an argument than it is to say whether you've been faithful to some more general aim.

In practice, schematizing arguments charitably requires mainly that we avoid creating straw men. So the rule is simply: do not contrive to weaken an argument as you paraphrase it simply because you do not like it.[5] This is the greatest danger and it is also why the principle is called "charity." Human beings have a nat-

---

5. In case the term is unfamiliar, this is just what a "straw man" is: a weakened version of an argument that is easier to criticize than a more plausible version readily available.

ural tendency to make fun of views they despise, and this can lead to inaccurate and implausible paraphrases. Look again at the piece on the law requiring drivers to carry proof of insurance in Chapter 1 (p. 27). The intemperate language ("deadbeat," "scofflaw") might tempt us to caricature:

> S People who drive without auto insurance are deadbeats and sociopaths beyond the pale of civil society.
>
> --
>
> C It is a good thing that the legislature has passed a bill requiring drivers to carry proof of insurance.

Stated in this way, the support is so implausible that such an argument will have little appeal. But as we saw, a better, stronger argument lurks just below the effusive surface.

> S The cost of damage and injury caused by uninsured motorists is unfairly borne by those who do carry insurance, through the higher premiums they pay.
>
> --
>
> C It is a good thing that the legislature has passed a bill requiring drivers to carry proof of insurance.

No matter what you think of this argument, it is clearly more reasonable and more difficult to dismiss than the previous one. So you would automatically choose this one, rather than the former, as the charitable schematization.

Exercise 3.24

Schematize the reasoning in the following letter with care and generosity. The author should be able to comfortably endorse what you produce. (Answer on p. 135.)

Dear Editor,

Phil Kerby is up in arms against government restrictions requiring some public employees to submit their writings to an official review before publishing. He says this "directive's potential for censorship has no parallel in history." Many, like Kerby, who are concerned about censorship and civil liberty find it curiously hard to accept the realities of the atomic bomb and the new age it ushered in. In a world that contains nuclear weapons and the new missiles, is it seriously possible to believe that we can continue with the same 18th-century freedoms we used to dream were to be ours forever?

Back in the '30s some of us laughed at Father Caughlin, a vigorous advocate of U.S. isolation, as he spoke on nationwide radio in favor of what was called "Fortress America." His mix of message and media simply did not compute. Radio was one of the new inventions that knew no national boundaries and, with other revolutionary technologies, was working hard to shrink the world to its present more convenient but also more dangerous size. The nuclear breakthrough was only one tech-

nological change that spelled a reduction in liberty. With the dangers inherent in nuclear weapons it seems a sure bet that nothing is going to stop change to more powerful government and fewer personal freedoms. This will come about, I believe, no matter who is President or how much we may deplore it.

R. Carney
Los Angeles

Charity is not only more straightforward when we look for reasoning, it is generally more important too. Recall that simple understanding motivates the principle of charity: a generous disposition helps us share perceptions that may, for one reason or another, be difficult to share. This rationale, though weighty in general paraphrase, is even more so in our reading of reasoning. For the greatest threat to our reasoning lies in misunderstanding the strength of arguments for conclusions we find offensive.

The whole reason to read examples of reasoning here is to see how this complicated skill works in practice. So we waste our time unless we try as hard as we can to make sense of reasoning we do not like, and fight the temptation to make fun of it. This means that in schematizing arguments we use whatever discretion we have in the circumstances to make an argument *stronger*, never weaker. What we end up with should always be the best looking argument we can find in the context.

Exercise 3.25

Schematize the reasoning in the following article. (This will require fighting your way through some peculiar writing and malapropisms.) (Answer on p. 135.)

LOS GATOS—There is a "strong suspicion" that pesticide spraying over part of San Mateo county may have been extended unnecessarily due to a hoax, a Mediterranean fruit fly project official says. "There's a strong suspicion in my heart that spraying there is unnecessary. But we just can't be sure," deputy project manager Dick Jackson said yesterday. He said a hoax may have been responsible for the extension.

On at least three occasions, someone is believed to have planted Medflies in traps used to determine the spread of the infestation, Jackson said. The outbreak has been centered to the south and east of San Francisco Bay. The flies could have been planted by someone who doesn't like the project, Jackson speculated, or by a project employee trying to prolong his job. "Whoever it is, we're pretty sure that someone's been playing jokes on us," he said.

One of the incidents involved the discovery of flies in traps near Loma Mar, an isolated community on the mountains south of San Francisco. Six fertile flies were found in one trap in an area where only a single sterile fly—one of billions released by project officials—had been found before. "The chances of something like that happening are just too remote to believe," Jackson said.

Other suspicious finds occurred last week in south San Jose and Oct. 29 in Sunnyvale, where a fly with notched wings was trapped, indicating it might have been handled with forceps. "Those flies were so desecrated we know they had to (have been) put in there," Jackson said. More than 28,000 traps designed by Jackson are spread throughout the San Francisco Bay Area.

(The Associated Press)

SUPPLEMENTAL EXERCISES

A. Review Questions

1. Give one reason for reading reasoning charitably.

2. Why is indirectness such an important notion in reading for reasoning?

3. (a) Make up an example in which "after all" is a reasoning flag. What does it flag? (b) Give an example in which "must" is not a reasoning flag.

4. Write out a structured paraphrase containing $[e_c]\backslash[r_i]$ double-subordination and then schematize the reasoning.

B. Passages for Analysis

1. Fire department investigators suspect that the warehouse blaze was intentionally set, since nothing stored there was particularly flammable, but the fire spread unusually quickly, as though aided by something.
   a. What tells you that reasoning is going on in this passage?
   b. What locates the conclusion?
   c. What locates the support?
   d. Would the argument be clearer with the support broken into two separate statements or connected together in one?

2. Space Shuttle technicians believe tomorrow's launch should be delayed. Yesterday's hailstorm was so intense that it broke greenhouse windows and damaged cars in nearby parking lots, so it may easily have also damaged the insulation covering the Shuttle's external fuel tank. The kind of inspection possible at the launch site would not be able to ensure the integrity of the cover even if it detected nothing. Adequate inspection would require returning the Shuttle to its hangar, which would take more than a week. And launching with damaged fuel tank insulation would risk catastrophe.
   a. Write out a structured paraphrase of this article, taking the whole thing to be simply the technicians' argument. Pay special attention to the support cascade in the second sentence, which needs some rearranging to fit into a coherent paraphrase.
   b. Schematize the reasoning.

3. TEL AVIV, Israel—A five-year computer study of the Bible indicates one author, not three as widely held in modern criticism, wrote the book of Genesis. "The probability of Genesis having been written by one author is enormously high—82 percent statistically," a member of the research team said in an article published in today's Jerusalem Post. Professor Yehuda Radday, a bible scholar from the Technion, a Haifa university, said more than 20,000 words of Genesis were fed into a computer, which analyzed the text's linguistic makeup.
   Bible critics widely hold that Genesis had three authors—the Jawhist or "J" author, the Elohist or "E" author and a priestly writer, dubbed "P." "We found the J and E nar-

ratives to be linguistically indistinguishable," Radday told a news conference today. But the P sections differ widely from them. "This is only to be expected, since dramatic tales and legal documents must necessarily display different 'behavior,'" he said. "If you compared love letters and a telephone directory written by the same person, linguistic analysis would point to different authors."

The team combined statistical and linguistic methods with computer science and Bible scholarship to reach their conclusions. They used 54 analysis criteria, including word length, the use of the definite article and the conjunction "and," richness of vocabulary and transition frequencies between word categories. "These criteria are a reliable gauge of authorship because these traits are beyond an author's conscious control and furthermore are countable," Radday said. Radday would not comment on whether Genesis was written by Moses.

(United Press International)

Schematize the argument in this article with the following guidance. Three structure flags locate distinct parts of the argument. One locates the main conclusion, which is the MP of the passage. The other two locate tributaries on the support in the main argument.

4. The battle for market share between America's three main equity markets—the New York Stock Exchange (NYSE), the Nasdaq electronic stockmarket and the smaller American Stock Exchange (AMEX)—is getting hotter. . . . On March 20th, Nasdaq unveiled a new trading system that may go some way to appeasing its critics by improving its efficiency in handling orders for investors. That will not deter the two floor-based exchanges, which have been trying to tempt firms quoted on Nasdaq to leave it and seek a listing with them. The AMEX is even running advertisements trumpeting the number of firms that have switched to it from Nasdaq (although plenty have also gone the other way). The implicit assumption is that when a firm migrates to one of the two New York exchanges, this reflects well on them and badly on Nasdaq. Not so. According to a new study, such a move may reveal more about the firm than about the markets.

Bala Dharan and David Ikenberry, two economists at Rice University, Texas, analysed the performance of shares which left Nasdaq for either the NYSE or the AMEX between 1973 and 1990. They compared post-listing total returns (capital gains plus dividends) on these shares with total returns on similar shares already traded on the exchanges. Surprisingly, they found that in the three years following the switch from one exchange to another, the shares underperformed significantly. Total returns on shares that switched to NYSE underperformed by an average of 6% over three years compared with the benchmark; those joining AMEX by 15%.

This seems puzzling. One possibility suggested by Messrs Dharan and Ikenberry is that the tough pre-listing requirements (eg, a healthy earnings record plus good prospects) of both the NYSE and AMEX mean that if a firm is considering relisting, yet foresees a future decline in profits, it has a strong incentive to move before that deterioration becomes obvious to investors. That may explain why underperformance was greatest for shares of small firms with few institutional shareholders: at listing, such firms are likely to be unfamiliar to investors, who may therefore find it hard to spot problems ahead and rely too much on their impressive track records. Whether managers are so devious—or investors are so gullible—is debatable. But whatever the explanation, if a firm quits Nasdaq for one of the other exchanges, it may be time to sell.

(From The Economist)

a. The last half of this article contains two different arguments: two distinct conclusions drawn from some of the same data. Write each one out in a single-sentence paraphrase, modeled on those in the "flags in partial paraphrases" section. [*Hints*: They each use as support that shares switched to the New York exchanges do much worse than shares already on those exchanges for some years after the switch. One conclusion is normative.]

b. Write a structured paraphrase of each. [*Hint*: one involves a double-subordination.]

c. Schematize the two arguments [use the paraphrases in (b) as a guide].

d. You should now be able to see a stronger normative argument that isn't actually made in the article, but may be created by taking some support from the other argument and narrowing the normative conclusion. Schematize it.

ANSWERS

3.2 **a.** Every MP or SP that has an [s] directly subordinate to it (indented once under it) is a conclusion. Every SP labeled [r_i] is also a conclusion.

b. The submarine article contains two separate arguments:

i. S_1 The sub is in 5000 feet of water.
S_2 Its hull is cracked.

C It will be difficult to raise.

ii. S_1 The sub's reactors were shut down.
S_2 Its torpedoes were not armed.

C It presents no radiation danger.

3.3 **a.** S_1 Valuables were not where Steve remembered them.
S_2 The door did not seem locked.
S_3 The door window was newly scratched.

C Steve's car had been burgled.

b. S_1 Valuables were not where Steve remembered them.
S_2 The door did not seemed locked.
S_3 The door window was scratched.
S_4 The scratches were where a slim jim would be used.
S_5 It was late at night.

C Steve's car had been burgled.

3.4 **a.** **i.** "The dynamite exploded, so the shack must have gotten too hot in the sun." This would make sense if we knew it was hot and sunny and that nothing else was around to detonate the dynamite, but didn't know just how hot it was in the shack or how hot it had to get to be dangerous. [e_c]/[r_i]

ii. "Tony must have lost his job, because he had to sell his house." This would make sense if we perhaps suspected from other signs that Tony was unemployed, but the "For Sale" sign was final confirmation. [r_e]/[s]

iii. "The plane crashed, so it must have been out of fuel." This would make sense if we did not know about the fuel exhaustion in some other way, but inferred it from the crash, which would be fairly unusual. [e_c]/[r_i]

b. **i.** PARAPHRASE

MP: An Amtrak train derailed at a switch.
[r_e]   SP: Injuring 74 people.
[q]   SP: Four required hospitalization.
[q]   SP: Including the engineer.
[e_c]/[r_i] SP: The switch had been tampered with.
[s]   SP: Bolt cutters and shavings that might be from a lock were found nearby.
[s]   SP: The switch lock itself is missing.

ii. SCHEMATIZED REASONING

S_1 An Amtrak train derailed at a switch.
S_2 Bolt cutters and shavings were found nearby.
S_3 The switch lock is missing.

C The switch had been tampered with.

c. PARAPHRASE

MP: The Pima Indians have unusual LDL.
[s]   SP: Dr. Bagdade's research.
$[r_e]/[s]$ SP: They have little heart disease in spite of obesity, diabetes, and a
            high-fat diet.

SCHEMATIZATION

S_1 The Pima Indians have little heart disease in spite of obesity, diabetes and
      a high-fat diet.
S_2 Results of physiological research.

C The Pimas have unusual LDL

3.5   The first SP should be labeled $[e_c]/[s]$, so the reasoning would be schematized:

S_1 *Legionella* bacteria
      were found only in
      low temperature systems.
S_2 One of these was killed
      with a hot water flush.

C_1 Lower temperatures
      allowed *Legionella*
      bacteria to flourish. $\longrightarrow$ C_1/S_3 Lower temperatures
                                                       allowed *Legionella*
                                                       bacteria to flourish.

                                                       C   Lowering water heater
                                                            temperatures caused the
                                                            Legionnaires' epidemic.

3.6   Words such as "probably" and "seems" indicate reasoning (flag indirectness) only
          when they work with inference connectors such as "because" and "so," which they
          do not do here. If Vargin had said, "The sub is probably cracked, because . . . " and
          went on to give the evidence from which he inferred it, then "probably" would be
          an indirectness flag.

3.7   PARAPHRASE

MP: Drinking green tea fights cancer.
[s]   SP: Its drinkers have low rates of four cancers.
$[e_c]/[s]$ SP: It contains catechin and flavinoids.
[q]   SP: Which have cancer-fighting credentials.

SCHEMATIZATION

S_1 The drinkers of green tea have low rates of four cancers.
S_2 Green tea contains two known cancer-fighting chemicals.

C Drinking green tea fights cancer.

3.8   In both cases we know something about the argument's conclusion. In the first, we just know that C will concern a disappearance; in the second, we know the conclusion exactly: the fire was started by transients.

3.9   Indirectness flags indicate that we know these sentences indirectly, through inference from something else. So they will be the *conclusions* of arguments.

3.10 S There was no sign of forced entry.

C The door was unlocked.

S The kitchen ceiling has begun to drip.

C It is raining quite hard.

3.11 General indicators: "conclusion," "investigators," "evidence," "discover," as well, perhaps, as scattered indirectness flags.

3.12 **a.** S Oncoming cars are using their wipers.

C We're driving into rain.

b. S_1 The government of Iraq has violated the sovereignty of its neighbors and the human rights of its citizens.
   S_2 It has engaged in chemical warfare, sponsored international terrorism, and considered the genocide of its Kurdish minority.
   S_3 It has also attempted to build atomic weapons to employ in these vicious activities.

C Civilized countries should join in the boycott of Iraqi oil.

3.13 The schematization for (a) and (b) is the same:

S   The drill caught everybody off guard.

C Preparation had been inadequate.

3.14 Schematization is the same as for Exercise 3.13.

3.15 S_1 We haven't seen the Wendlestadts in a while.
       S_2 Yellowing newspapers are collecting in their driveway.

C They must be away on vacation.

3.16 S_1 Angela has been in a terrible mood ever since she got back.

C Something awful happened to her over the summer.

3.17 Mental flag: "speculated."

3.18 **a.** **i.** "Since" is a support flag.
             "Must" is an indirectness/conclusion flag

          S There was no fire at the site of its impact.

          C The plane was out of fuel when it crashed.

     ii. "Probably" is an indirectness/conclusion flag.
          "Because" is a support flag.
          S There was no fire at the crash site.

          C The plane was out of fuel when it crashed.

iii. "So" is a link flag.

"May" is an indirectness/conclusion flag.

S₁ Many days of newspapers have accumulated on their porch.

S₂ No lights went on at dusk.

C The neighbors are away on vacation.

iv. "Apparently" is an indirectness/conclusion flag.

S Many bridges suffered severe damage in last night's modest temblor.

C: Earthquake retrofitting was inadequate.

v. "Think" is a mental/conclusion flag.

"Because" is a support flag.

S The cost of renovation is high.

C The building needs replacing.

vi. "So" is a link flag.

"I'm sure" is an indirectness/conclusion flag.

S Twenty minutes have elapsed since the last shot was fired from the second floor window.

C Nobody in the house is still alive.

b. i and ii. • "may" (headline): indirectness
• "apparently": indirectness
• "think": mental
• "believes": mental
• "believe": mental

iii. Cₐ: Mrs. Hessey's dogs ate (most of) her body.

C_b: Mrs. Hessey died naturally and her dogs ate (most of) her body.

C_c: Mrs. Hessey died inside her home and the dogs dragged her outside and ate (most of) her body

iv. S₁ Mrs. Hessey had been dead for weeks when her body was found.

S₂ Of her body, only her head and one foot could be found.

S₃ Her pet dogs looked well fed.

C Mrs. Hessey's dogs ate most of her body.

c. i. "likely"

ii. S₁ Corder had no known grievance against the President.

S₂ The plane contained no explosives.

S₃ Corder had drug and alcohol problems.

S₄ He had just separated from his wife.

S₅ He was distraught over his father's recent death.

---

iii. C Corder's crash was a suicide, not an attack on the President.

OR   C Corder crashed his plane on the White House lawn to dramatize his suicide, not threaten the President.

3.19 S Economic sanctions against Iraq cause great
              suffering among the civilian population, especially children.

          C They should end.

3.20 S It's a half hour after they said they'd be here.

          C It's okay to leave.

3.21 **a.** Summary 1:   "thinks" (mental, conclusion)
                                 "should" (normative: so "because" isn't [e])
                                 "because" (support)
                  Summary 2:   "should" (normative: so "reasons" isn't [e])
                                 "reasons" (support)
                  Summary 3:   "so" (link)
                                 "must" (indirectness, conclusion)

          b. **i.** The December 8 1812 quake probably occurred on the San Andreas Fault be-
                  cause trees along a stretch of the fault all stopped growing vigorously that
                  year and did not recover for a while.

                  ii. S_1: A strong earthquake hit Southern California in
                           December of 1812.
                         S_2: Tree growth along a nearby stretch of the San
                           Andreas Fault slowed abruptly after 1812 and did
                           not recover for some time.
                         S_3: A similar abrupt decrease in tree growth occurred
                           along another stretch of the fault after a large
                           temblor struck that stretch in 1857.

                         C: The December 8 quake occurred on the San Andreas Fault.

3.22 The flags are "because," "suggests," and "might."

          S_1 An unusually large amount
                 of the hydrogen in the
                 amino acids found in the
                 Murchison meteorite is
                 deuterium.
          S_2 Deuterium is rare on Earth
                 but far more common in gas
                 clouds of interstellar space.

          C_1 These amino acids were formed
                 from material beyond our
                 solar system. $\longrightarrow$ C_1/S_2 The Murchison amino acids
                                                                                          came from outer space.
                                                                              S_3 Amino acids are the
                                                                                     building blocks of life.

                                                                              C Life could have developed
                                                                                 outside our solar system.

3.23 **a.** The investigation is into the cause of the crash, so the conclusion will answer
                  "What caused the crash?" The answer given is that it was caused by the de-icer
                  boot falling off.

b. We know three relevant things directly: (i) The boot was found some distance from the crash site; (ii) 43 screws were missing; and (iii) if the boot had fallen off, it would have stalled the tail and caused a nose dive.

c. The thing not known directly, but inferred from (i) and (ii) is that the de-icer fell off in flight. So the schematization will have a tributary argument in which (i) and (ii) are used to support this conclusion. Then this conclusion, together with (iii), forms the main argument supporting the main conclusion given in (a).

S_1 De-icer found 3/4 mile
    from crash site.

S_2 43 securing screws
    were missing.

C_1 De-icer fell off
    in flight. $\longrightarrow$ C_1/S_3 De-icer fell off in flight.
                                        S_4 Its loss would stall tail.

                                C The crash was caused by
                                    the de-icer falling off.

3.24 This is one of those cases in which cuteness of expression together with lack of context makes confident paraphrase difficult. One of the following two should work. If we place emphasis on the closing sentences, Carney seems to be simply grounding a forecast:

    S Advancing technology inevitably increases the power of governments.

    C Our civil liberties will substantially decrease with time.

If we emphasize the author's earlier chiding of Phil Kerby for not being able to "accept realities," the argument sounds more normative:

    S Advancing technology inevitably makes the world more dangerous.

    C Governments must curtail our liberty for our own safety.

3.25 The proposition needing support, known indirectly if at all, is that the medflies were being planted in the traps—i.e., they were a hoax. So the schematization would look like this:

S_1 For some time very few medflies had been caught in the 28,000 traps in the Bay Area.

S_2 Then a literally incredible number were found in a single trap in an area in which almost none had been found before.

S_3 At the same time, flies found in two other areas appeared to be long dead and handled by instruments.

    C Dead medflies were being placed in Bay Area traps as a hoax.

PART TWO

• • •

ANALYZING REASONING

ARGUMENT ANALYSIS

Answering Questions

INTRODUCTION

The schematic form of an argument is a fairly simple tool: it displays what we make explicit when we give reasons. By itself, however, schematic form does not say anything about the human significance of the reasons it displays. That is, nothing in Chapter 3 helps us talk about the *point* of assembling an argument, about why anybody would bring precisely these statements together in reasoning. The time has come to turn to this more complicated task. In this chapter we will develop some concepts that will help us see what's going on "inside" an argument that gives it value to us. This will allow us to see not only why arguments matter in our lives but also how easy it is to completely miss their point if we fail to pick up on the right detail in a context. The apparatus we develop here should help us avoid such failure.

Actually, we often do understand the significance of an argument perfectly well. We know why somebody would connect the Arts Center's wasted seats with a proposal about future tickets, or mention a storm front in connection with a weather forecast. But we have not yet developed a systematic way to talk about this connection. We have so far left it to whatever vocabulary strikes us as useful. That makes it difficult to keep our own interests and values from distorting the reasoning before we even know what it is about. To help us be more objective, in this chapter we will develop a systematic way to talk about what is at issue in an argument. To do this we must find very general concepts that underlie the whole human enterprise of asking for and giving reasons. And as the expression "asking for" here may suggest, the basic concepts will be Question and Answer.

Sometimes just getting clear about what's going on in an argument will enable us not just to grasp the reasoning it displays, but also to evaluate it. Simply seeing the broad structural outlines of the reasoning can sometimes make it clear whether an argument is good or bad, and even how to improve it. So as you master the vocabulary of this chapter, you will gradually find yourself able to use its terms to express judgments about the quality of arguments, in addition to articulating the issues they raise. Nevertheless, the main purpose of this chapter is simply to look at *the internal structure of argument*. This will require that we develop a systematic way to talk about those features of an argument that make it interesting, useful, or controversial. The major tools of evaluation will be introduced in Chapter 5. There we will show how the apparatus of this chapter can be used to bring our understanding to bear on reasoning. But first we must master the new vocabulary.

THE PURPOSE OF ANALYSIS

To survive even into early adulthood we all must develop a certain basic understanding of how the world works. This is the understanding required to make our way through the hassles and obstacles of everyday life. It is also the understanding that allows us to reason about the vast array of mundane concerns that constantly confront us as we live. Because the hassles and obstacles are pretty much the same for everybody at this level, we all develop very similar understandings of mundane reality. This is what allows us to reason together. On the routine matters of life, the same reasons support the same conclusions for virtually everybody. On a day when bad weather threatens, wet clothes and dripping umbrellas coming into the classroom are reason to think—very good reason to think—it has begun to rain. Everyone reaches the same conclusion. And rain, in turn, is a good reason to look for an umbrella to share, if I don't want to get wet walking back to the office after class. Nearly everybody finds such reasoning effortless to follow, which is the source of our sense that reasons are objective. Reasoning would be far less important to us if it did not fit into our lives in this way.

However, we do not always evaluate reasons the same way. Authors of newspaper columns, or letters to editors, commonly discover that the arguments they offer as persuasive and insightful are found silly and offensive by some readers. And this applies not just to broad public policy questions such as whether to legalize drugs or outlaw abortion, but even to relatively small, local issues of traffic control and leash laws. You have doubtless encountered public exchanges such as this yourself, and if you have paid close attention to them, you will have noticed what we call "cross-purposes" in many of them. That is, the participants in such exchanges often misunderstand each other as much as (or more than) they

disagree. The exchange may get heated—and even nasty—because the participants are not even clear about what the disagreement is, or even mistaken about whether there is one.

One reason for this is that we naturally talk about our reasoning in terms that depend heavily on the topic in question. When people have different "takes" on a topic, or are simply accustomed to different conversations about it, they will seldom use the topic's key words in exactly the same way. They will disagree as much about what counts as a drug, or a person, or murder, or fairness, as they will about any matter of fact. So it will be hard *not* to misunderstand each other. That is why we will devote this entire chapter to developing a particular way to talk about arguments. We want to find concepts that reveal the details of our reasoning but do not depend on the substance of an argument. Just as our paraphrasing concepts (padding, kinds of subordination) applied to our reading in general, we will aim for concepts that apply to argument in general and do not depend on the topic under discussion.

Our aim again will be to articulate our grasp of something, but this time it will be *reasoning* and not just reading. So far you have been able to recognize and even schematize arguments as you find them in your reading. Now we will try to say something about what you are recognizing when you do this. As always, you will have to hold on to your skills as we try to analyze them. For thinking and talking about reasoning are not things any of us do very easily. The centipede effect is a constant danger.

THE FUNDAMENTAL CONCEPTS: QUESTIONS AND ANSWERS

Let us begin by looking at the abstract form of an argument, as we schematized it in Chapter 3.

$$S_1$$
$$S_2$$

$$C$$

This picture offers S_1 and S_2 as reasons to think C is true. In other words, when we take something of this form out of a passage, we are saying that the author has offered the top part of this diagram in support of the bottom. We need some insight into this claim. What's a good way to talk about what the author is up to here? How should we "unpack" the claim that the top supports the bottom?

To find out, first notice that not just any stack of sentences will make an argument. For instance,

S_1: Napoleon was short.
S_2: Pennsylvania is the keystone state.

C: The economy will be okay in the short run.

does not look anything like an argument. We all can clearly see that S_1 and S_2 are just the wrong kind of things to provide support for this conclusion. By way of comparison, consider an argument from Chapter 3:

S_1: A maintenance worker was called to remedy the lack of hot water in a motel.

S_2: The motel blew up after he arrived.

S_3: He was seriously injured.

C: He somehow caused the explosion.

This looks like an argument. It may not be conclusive, or even very strong, but the supporting statements are the right sort of thing to offer in favor of a conclusion like this. They make sense as support.

So let us ask, what makes the difference? What tells us that one stack of sentences is an argument and another is not? The general answer is *context*. We must look to the circumstances in which the sentences arose. In the motel blast example, even if we had not already seen it in a newspaper article, we can easily imagine a context in which the statements on top would make sense as support for the one on the bottom. By contrast, it is hard to imagine a setting that would make sense of the earlier argument using Napoleon and Pennsylvania to support an economic forecast.

The Implicit Question

Because we want a special vocabulary for talking about arguments, the first notion in that vocabulary should be whatever it is that context supplies to make this basic distinction. What do we find in a context that turns a stack of sentences into an argument? We have already seen that the main thing a context supplies to help us understand each other is *motivation*. We understand somebody's words by having some sense of what they are *trying* to say in the context. And motivation is the key in arguments too.

What motivates an argument (giving reasons for something) can always be formulated as a *question its author is trying to answer*. Examples from earlier arguments would be "Why are oncoming cars using their wipers?" and "How will the smoking ban be received?" In the case just schematized it would be "What blew up the motel?" The authors of arguments usually take this question to be obvious and almost never formulate it anywhere in the passage. For that reason we will formally call this the argument's **Implicit Question.** It is the first part of our analytical vocabulary, and the most important concept we will introduce in this chapter. Let us use the abbreviation "IQ" for this central concept.

Sometimes the Implicit Question will be obvious to readers too. But very often it will not, and we will have to work to figure it out. Until we do we may not have a clear picture of the argument itself; so this will be an important step in our analytical work. How do we proceed? How do we determine what question is at work behind the scenes? The first clue in figuring out the implicit question is always the argument's conclusion. The conclusion is one of its *answers*, normally the author's *favorite* answer, and hence a good indicator of the question he

or she had in mind. So when you think you've found an argument's IQ, the first thing is to see whether the argument's conclusion makes sense as an answer.

Exercise 4.1
....

Look at the three arguments for which we gave IQs in the paragraph before last and note the way their conclusions answer those questions. Write out the questions and then write the conclusions in a way that makes clear that they answer them. (This will help train your ear: since we're developing a new vocabulary many seemingly trivial exercises like this will be useful in this chapter.) (Answers on p. 192.)

But the conclusion alone is never enough to give us the IQ. Because any conclusion—any declarative sentence—can be the answer to *many different questions*. To make this clear, consider a sentence such as "Rhonda stole your coffee." Think of it for a moment as the conclusion of an argument, but suppose you do not know anything more about the context. Now ask, What question does "Rhonda stole your coffee" answer? You immediately see that there are many possible questions. In the conversational sense we need for our analysis,[1] any of the following questions might have that answer (try saying it to yourself as you go down the list).

Who stole my coffee?

What did Rhonda do with my coffee?

What did Rhonda steal?

Whose coffee did Rhonda steal?

What happened while I was distracted?

What did Rhonda do while I was distracted?

What were you whispering about a minute ago?

To choose a question from this list we would need to know something of the circumstances of the reasoning. What else would help? Actually two more things.

One is the *support* itself. The part of the passage that ends up as support is often the most useful guide to the IQ. This is because the IQ is what links the support and the conclusion together in the author's thinking. We may think of the IQ as a puzzle, the conclusion as its solution, and the support as what solves it. So when it is not clear, you can get an idea of what puzzle the author was trying to solve (IQ) by looking at what the author thinks solved it (S). This will at least

---

1. Bear in mind that we are trying to make explicit what goes on in ordinary circumstances when we give an argument or try to understand one. So we must think of questions and their answers in an ordinary, everyday way. In particular, "Rhonda stole my coffee" is conversationally the same sentence as "She stole my coffee" when it is clear that "she" is Rhonda. The following lists can be thought of as displaying that ordinary question/answer relationship.

radically narrow the range of possible IQs, perhaps even to a single one. In the Rhonda example above, for instance, we feel cut off from the IQ by not having the rest of the argument. If we had the whole argument, instead of just the conclusion, we certainly would have a better idea of the IQ. The support is always a big help: pay special attention to it.

For a real example, consider the conclusion of an argument we have already seen: "The maintenance worker caused the explosion." This might, depending on the context, answer any of the following questions.

Why did the motel blow up?

How did an explosion occur in a locked room?

Why was the maintenance worker so badly hurt?

Why did they fire the maintenance worker?

What made the maintenance worker so depressed?

And so on.

But if we go back and look at the original passage (on p. 44 of Chapter 2), we can see immediately that the first of these is what the firefighters were "speculating" about. The puzzle in that context is why it blew up, and the sequence of events offered in support directly addresses that question. The locked room and the worker's job and mental state are not even mentioned; and his injuries are not central but are mentioned only in passing. With a little effort, however, we might imagine arguments in which each of the other questions would be preferred.

Exercise 4.2

(Note: these refer to examples from Chapter 3.)

a. Look at the Arts Center argument at the beginning of Chapter 3 (p. 99). Give an IQ for this argument that is sensitive to the context in which it arose. Note that the conclusion drawn naturally answers it.

b. Do the same for the argument about the burgled car in Exercise 3.3 (p. 100).

(Answers on p. 192.)

Sometimes the IQ will still not be obvious even after checking with S and C. We will not be out of luck, however, if the context supplies one other piece of data: the **other possibilities** with which C is supposed to contrast (C as opposed to what?). We will often have a good idea what these are, and they will allow us to sort through the list of possible IQs and eliminate questions that the contrasting conclusions do not answer. For example, if C is "Rhonda stole your coffee," we have already seen that it can be the answer to all the questions listed above. But if we can tell from the context that the issue is whether Rhonda did it *as opposed to somebody else*, then the conclusion's competition is a list of *other suspects*: me, Damion, the obnoxious practical joker from accounting, and so on. This tells us that the IQ must be some ver-

sion of "Who stole your coffee," because that is the question with the right sort of answers. Had we thought the IQ might be "What did Rhonda steal?" the contrasting answers would have to be *other things she might have stolen*, such as your lunch, the tape dispenser, or money from the cash register. She stole your coffee as opposed to one of these things. So if the natural competition is a list of suspects, we may eliminate "What did she steal?" as the IQ. It has the wrong kind of answers.

Exercise 4.3
....

Consider the following passage.

> The radio crackled madly and we lost radio contact with Flight 544 just as it entered an ominous-looking storm cell about six hours ago. It is now four hours overdue at its destination, and we've had no word from it. The terminal staff is doing its best to cheer the people in our waiting room, but I think the worst has happened.

a. Schematize the reasoning in this passage (in your own plain words).

b. Choose two different IQs that the conclusion answers and say why one is better. (Answers on p. 193.)

Again, an argument's IQ is not just any question answered by its conclusion, but the one that makes sense in the context. Although this judgment ultimately rests on your reading skill, you may check out any IQ candidate by explicitly asking three questions: (i) Does C answer it? (ii) Does the support make sense as recommending C as its answer? and (iii) Does C's natural competition answer it also?

The Basic Articulation

We may summarize what we have learned so far in a general paraphrase for practical arguments. This is the central piece of our analytical apparatus. When we schematize an argument like this:

$$S_1$$
$$S_2$$
$$S_3$$

$$C$$

what the schematic picture says is this:

(A)	S_1, S_2, and S_3 recommend C as the right answer to give the argument's implicit question.

There is much more to say about arguments, but this is a start. It articulates what you have been recognizing when you find a schematizable argument in a passage. (A) is *what you take the author to be saying*.[2]

Exercise 4.4
· · · · · · · · · · · · · · · ·

Look again at the Arts Center argument schematized at the beginning of Chapter 3 (p. 99) and the motel explosion argument schematized earlier in this chapter (p. 142). Plug them into (A) and write out the result. This may appear trivial, but it will be immensely valuable to have this in your head. (Answer on p. 193.)

Rival Conclusions

A conclusion's contrast, or competition, has even greater importance than we've given it so far. It does more than just help with the IQ, it actually helps us understand what the conclusion means. Recall from our discussion of "implied significance" in Chapter 1, that a large part of understanding what somebody says comes from seeing what gives their words human significance. And when they *assert* something, part of the significance is inevitably a *contrast*. For instance, suppose I were to say that Charles Barkley is short, even though he is six foot four. The significance of this characterization would be clear if you knew that Barkley is a forward in the National Basketball Association. For virtually all of the other forwards are substantially taller than six-four. Barkley *is* short, for a forward. He is tall, however, compared to most of the rest of us. So in a group of average people, I could point to Barkley and ask, "Who is that tall guy?" and be clearly understood. So whether "tall" is right or not depends on the intended contrast. *Understanding the implied contrast* is part of understanding language. This is what's at work in the First Mate's retaliatory entry in the ship's log. The significance of saying "The Captain was sober last night" seems to require the contrast, "unlike most nights."

When we select an answer for a question, as we do in argument, the contrast, or competition, may always be given in this way: it is **The Rest of the List of Answers** from which it was chosen. Part of the significance of selecting an answer is *to reject the rest of the list*. If you ask me who stole your coffee, and I answer "Rhonda," part of what I'm saying is that I, for one, did *not* steal it. If I stole it, and still answer "Rhonda did it," either I've lied or I didn't understand the question. Part of the significance of answering "Rhonda did it" is to reject "I did it" as well as the rest of the list of suspects.

This notion of a rejected contrast is the next important part of our apparatus. Our general argument paraphrase (A) tells us that an argument offers C as the IQ's right answer. But to know just what this means, we must have some idea of what are being rejected as **Wrong Answers** in selecting C as right. Rhonda took

---

2. It would not hurt to memorize the formula.

your coffee as opposed to what? Give the seats to seniors and students instead of what? We don't know what the support is being asked to support until we know just what C covers and what it excludes. We will call these competing answers of an argument's IQ, **C's Rival Conclusions.** They are the conclusions being rejected in recommending C as the right answer for the IQ.

One main reason to make rival conclusions explicit is to record the way a conclusion's contrast naturally varies with details of the context and subject matter. To illustrate again with our friend Rhonda, if the conclusion of an argument is "Rhonda did it" (IQ: "Who did it"), we need to know just what Rhonda is being accused of to know what contrasting possibilities are being ruled out. If the case is the one we've been following and Rhonda is charged with swiping a cup of coffee, then, in normal circumstances, simply saying "Rhonda did it" would rule out "Rhonda and Damion did it together." Because, normally, swiping a cup of coffee is a one-person job, so the simple answer would imply that nothing unusually complicated was going on.[3] In this case the rival conclusions would be not just other suspects, but all possible teams and conspiracies as well.

But what if Rhonda is accused of is selling me my new car (same C: "Rhonda did it")? We all know that car sales usually do involve teams of people, doing paperwork, servicing the car, and helping out with various details. Saying she sold me my car naturally gives Rhonda a more complex role than she would have in stealing a cup of coffee. It not only allows, but assumes she had all kinds of help in the transaction. In this case teams and cooperative efforts would *not* be ruled out by saying "Rhonda did it." The cooperation of others would be part of C. This feature of the context is often best articulated by giving rival conclusions. For stealing coffee we'd say Rhonda did it as opposed to me or Damion or anybody else in the office alone or together. For selling a car it would be Rhonda, together with the appropriate team, as opposed to another salesperson and her team, and so on. We might call these C's *natural rivals*: they are the conclusions taken to be rejected in the context, in a charitable reading.

The amount of our understanding captured in a list of natural rivals can be enormous in everyday reasoning. Consider, for instance, the truck-crash argument from the last chapter.

> S: No attempt was made to brake or steer before impact.
>
> --
>
> C_1: The driver fell asleep at the wheel.

Take this argument to be offered in the course of a normal crash probe, in which investigators, summoned to the scene of a fatal accident, try to piece together what happened. Part of their understanding would be represented by the schematization. Another part would be in the IQ, which could be simply "What happened?" or could be something more detailed, such as "What caused the crash?" or "Why did the truck crash?" But the rest of the understanding, which is substantial, would typically be captured in the rival conclusions the investigators had considered

---

3. If this point is difficult, reread the section on implied significance in Chapter 1.

and so far rejected on the evidence they have. In a normal sort of report the list would look something like this:

C_2: The driver died of something before the crash.
C_3: The driver crashed on purpose (suicide).
C_4: The brakes and steering failed simultaneously.
(And perhaps others like this, increasingly fantastic.)

It would be very difficult to incorporate the amount of information found in this list anywhere else in our analytical apparatus. That is why rival conclusions will play such a large role in articulating our reasoning.

Exercise 4.5
....

a. Look again at the Arts Center argument at the beginning of Chapter 3 (p. 99). Using the IQ from Exercise 4.2, list some rival conclusions that give the most important answers rejected in choosing the conclusion offered in that passage.

b. Do the same for the Flight 544 argument you schematized in Exercise 4.3 (p. 145), using the better of the two IQs in Exercise 4.3b.

(Answers on p. 193.)

Possibilities versus Rivals

Let us look again at the exploding motel argument. Its IQ is "What blew up the motel?" Now ask yourself how many different answers this question has. The natural list might begin with "maintenance worker," "gas leak unaided by anybody," "terrorists," "disgruntled employee," "suicide attempt by guest." But you could make the list more fine grained than this and vastly multiply the different answers. "Maintenance worker" covers many *different stories*, for instance. One story would have him coming from Ace Services and another would identify him as just a handyman employed by the owner. In one story he caused the explosion with a match, in another with a cigar lighter, and in yet another with a cigarette. Every different story you could tell about the explosion would, in some way, count as a different answer to the question. And there is no end to the fineness of detail. If we suppose he did it by striking a match, in one story he would do it by striking it on a match pack and in a different one he'd strike it on the seat of his pants. In one he'd strike it from left to right and in another from right to left. There is no limit to the number of different possibilities.

Obviously, however, most of these differences will not matter to the reasoning in question; only a few would be interesting or important in any given context. To investigators first on the scene—and to general newspaper readers—interest would lie in simply determining whether it was due to a gas leak and if the maintenance worker was involved. Just who he worked for and whether it was a match just don't matter at this stage; and which direction the match moved may never be relevant to anything.

In saying that C's rivals are the rejected competition, we mean them to mark out *Only Important and Interesting Differences*, not trivial ones. This is part of what we understand when an argument is clear: C as opposed to what? An adequate context will allow us to see which differences matter and which do not, and that will determine how much detail belongs in the rivals. In the case of our unfortunate motel, the favored conclusion is clearly something like "The maintenance worker somehow ignited the propane." From this we can tell that exactly *how* he did it is not important at the moment. He may have done it lighting a match, or turning a switch, or smoking a cigarette. They all fall under the same rival (C_1) in this case. Because the differences among them do not matter, they all *count as the same answer* here: "The maintenance worker did it." Other bunches of stories (answering "What blew up the motel?") will be collected under "terrorist attack" or "reprisal by a disgruntled worker."

Let us capture this graphically by representing all the possibilities in a case as points in a balloon. The dots in Figure 4.1 represent all the different possibilities covered by answers to a given IQ, no matter how trivially they differ. In the case we just looked at, each dot would be a story about what happened to the motel. Each would be a sequence of events different from its neighbors in the smallest possible way. One would have the maintenance worker setting off the explosion with a match lit in a certain way in a particular location. Another would be exactly the same story, except the match would have been struck slightly differently. And so on.

The context will then determine which differences are important and which are not, and this will decide how the dots are grouped together in rivals. The rivals will cover areas or slices of the balloon, like those marked C_1, C_2, etc. in the balloon in Figure 4.2. The rivals lump together possibilities that are not impor-

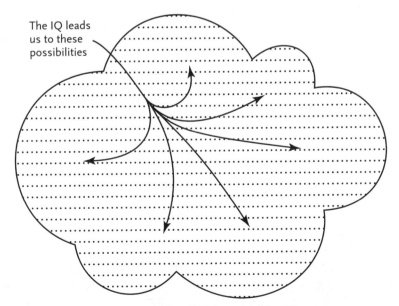

The IQ leads
us to these
possibilities

Figure 4.1. Possibilities raised by IQ.

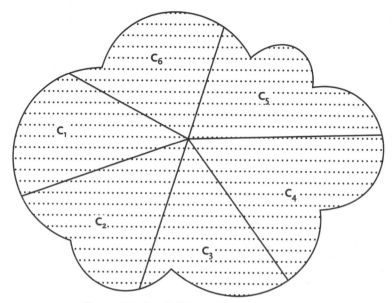

Figure 4.2. Possibilities grouped into rivals.

tantly different in the context of the argument. So which particular dot (story) falls in which rival will be determined in this way.

We may now see why our articulation requires *both* an implicit question *and* rival conclusions. The IQ leads us to a balloon of possibilities (that's what it asks about), whereas the rivals divide the balloon up into significantly different areas or groups of possibilities. Although each dot differs in some way from every other dot, the division of the balloon into rivals reflects the large-scale differences that are *significant* in the context. For instance, the difference between two stories about the motel blast that disagree only in the precise way the match was struck is insignificant for normal purposes. So they will not be different conclusions for us, even though they will be different dots in the balloon. They will both be in the C_1 wedge: "The maintenance worker did it."

Exercise 4.6

Consider the following case.

> I heard a crash in the kitchen. I immediately got up and rushed in to see what had happened. When I got there all I found was a glass, broken on the floor. No one was around and nothing else seemed out of place. I inferred that the crash was the glass breaking on the floor, though I was puzzled as to just how this came about.

[**Note on the Use of Sample Reasoning Like This:** always accept the data offered in an example like this as simply given, that is: take it to be true as stated. This determines the problem for analysis. Nothing in our analysis should conflict with the data that set the problem.]

a. Schematize my argument and take the IQ to be "What was that crash?"

b. Give some rivals I am obviously rejecting.

c. Give two possibilities that are not significantly different in the context.

(Answers and suggestions on p. 193.)

Finding Tough Implicit Questions

We noticed earlier that a conclusion's contrast can help us find an argument's IQ. We can now use what we have learned about rejected rivals to expand that insight into a powerful tool for finding the most difficult implicit questions. Consider, for instance, the case of Daisy Hiker, who has been following a trail through the high Nevada desert for most of the day, and is increasingly struck by the bleached and weather-beaten animal bones that litter the way. From a little anthropology and general experience she recognizes the bones as almost exclusively those of horses and cows. Suddenly the thought occurs to her: this must be an ancient pioneer route to California. That evening she articulates her reasoning in a note to a friend. It is schematizable thus:

S_1 The trail is littered with bones.
S_2 They are obviously very old.
S_3 They are mostly bones of horses and cows.

C The trail is an old pioneer route to California.

What is the IQ? Just looking at the conclusion and the support, we might try "What kind of trail is this?" or "What was the trail used for?" The conclusion surely answers these questions, and they are something Daisy would naturally wonder about. But they both miss the point of the reasoning, and this may be seen by noticing what Daisy is and is not rejecting in offering us C. First, in concluding that it is an ancient pioneer route, she is not saying it could not have been used for other things too. It could have been originally blazed by natives and simply followed by the pioneers; or it could have been—and could still be—a game trail; and it could still be used by ranchers' 4 × 4's as a shortcut. None of this would conflict with Daisy's reasoning. So different answers to "What kind of trail is this?" or "What was this used for?" are *not* being rejected by C. So neither of them can be the argument's IQ.

Second, if you think of the IQ as what connects support and conclusion for an author, we can ask, "Why would Daisy (or anyone) think the bones were connected to the pioneers?" The answer is obvious: she thinks that's how the bones *got there*. She is arguing that the pioneers were the *source* of the bones. So the competing rivals would be *other, different sources* of the bones. This is just the right set of rivals. She's saying the bones are from the pioneers, and *not*

C_2 Remains of livestock from local ranches.
C_3 A movie set that was abandoned.
C_4 A joke by some of Daisy's friends.
And so on.

These are the rival conclusions being rejected in offering C. The motivation of Daisy's inquiry is therefore better captured by an IQ such as "Why are so many domestic animal bones on this trail?" or "Where did all these old bones come from?" than either of the two earlier candidates.

Exercise 4.7

Consider the following passage.

> SALTON CITY—Authorities were searching yesterday for an Arkansas truck driver whose tractor-trailer rig was found idling and abandoned on the shoulder of Highway 86. Danny Paul Hamilton, 25 of Batesville, Ark., was last heard from about 5 p.m. Wednesday when he called his employer, Bob Alumbaugh of Mc-Crory, Ark., from Los Angeles. A California Highway Patrol officer found Hamilton's rig about 7 p.m. Thursday on the shoulder of the southbound lanes of Highway 86 near Salton City. Alumbaugh said Hamilton had just loaded some produce, cashed a check and was headed for Holtville, Calif. and eventually Arkansas.
>
> "If he was going to abandon a vehicle, he wouldn't just leave it out in the boonies," Alumbaugh said. "When they do that they leave it at a truck stop where they can get a ride. He also picked up part of his load, and he was en route to his next pickup." Alumbaugh said what disturbed him most was that the truck was left running with its windows open and radio on. The truck still contained Hamilton's clothing and billfold, Alumbaugh said.
>
> Imperial county Coroner Investigator Ralph Smith, who also investigates missing persons, said he was examining two sets of footprints leading from the truck to the highway's northbound lanes. Smith said the tire tracks near where the footprints stopped indicated that two people got into a vehicle heading north. Smith said he also was investigating a phone call Alumbaugh received Sunday from a man who claimed he had been in jail with Hamilton in Indio. Smith said there was no record of Hamilton being jailed in that area, and Alumbaugh said the caller provided little information.
>
> (*The Associated Press*)

Evidence from this passage might help us answer a number of different questions concerning Danny Hamilton's disappearance. For example:

a. What happened to Hamilton?

b. Why did Hamilton abandon his rig?

c. Why did he leave his rig there?

Instruction: Give some natural rivals for each of these possible IQs and note that they carve up slightly different (overlapping) balloons and group possibilities differently. (Answers on p. 193.)

An Important Formal Property of Rivals

Because we want rival conclusions to be, by definition, what's being rejected in accepting C, we need to build this into the concept itself. So when we call a conclusion "one of C's rivals," we will always mean that it is *incompatible* with C. That is, C and the rival cannot both be true. If one is true that simply means the other *must* be false. Usually this will be a natural part of our conversation. When I say "Rhonda swiped your coffee," the normal context makes it clear that this means I did *not*. In other words, "I did it" in the normal context is incompatible with "Rhonda did it." Only one of these can be true. We must take special pains to keep this incompatibility in mind, however, when we consider complicated stories that seem to make rivals overlap. If we want to consider the possibility, say, that the driver of the crashed truck committed suicide by taking a sleeping pill in the hopes of falling asleep and crashing fatally, where does this fall on the list of rivals: under sleep (C_1) or suicide (C_3)? It does not matter, so long as you assign it to one or the other and not both.[4] If it falls in both, they are no longer rivals. Ordinary answers may overlap in this way; rival conclusions may not.

To complete the picture, note that C and its rivals are all candidates to be the conclusion of the argument we are examining at any time. They comprise the list of answers from which the support is choosing. So each of the rivals ought to be suitable to play the role as *the* conclusion, as the *right* answer, in case things change. To do this the rivals must rival each other as well as C. This simply means that they must be incompatible not just with C, but with each other too. For if we choose any one of them, the others would be the ones rejected in doing so. We capture this by saying that rival conclusions are *mutually exclusive*: only one of them may be true. This feature was actually incorporated into the possibility balloon of Figure 4.2: the mutual exclusiveness of rivals is indicated by the sharp line separating them. Saying they are mutually exclusive simply means they do not overlap with each other, nor do they blend smoothly together. The difficult cases we have examined that tempt us to think the rivals overlap will occur at the boundaries of the slices. To consider them in our analysis, they will simply have to be placed in one rival or the other depending on what is most convenient for the analysis.

To practice thinking about overlap, consider again the motel explosion. This argument's IQ is "Why did the motel explode?" or, perhaps, "What caused the explosion?" The answer offered as right was something like "A maintenance worker touched it off accidentally while investigating a lack of hot water." What competition is being rejected in this case? Well, other ways of igniting leaking propane, for instance, as well as terrorist bombings, suicide attempts by overnight lodgers, reprisals by fired employees, and airplanes falling from the sky. Each of these carves out a different wedge in the balloon. What about a propane leak? One possible answer to give the IQ is "A propane leak caused the explosion." Is it a rival? No, it is not. Why not? Because it is compatible with the maintenance worker story; it may even be a big part of that story. One way the maintenance worker might have blown the place up was to have accidentally ignited leaking propane. So it is not being rejected in choosing the maintenance worker rival. This is why "propane leak" is not one of the rivals.

---

4. Another possibility would be to make it a separate rival altogether (call it C_5), and leave C_1 and C_3 pure.

Exercise 4.8
....

Continuing with the motel-blast example, explain how the following would fit with the list of rivals begun in the last paragraph: (a) carelessness; (b) poor ventilation of the water heater enclosure; (c) mortar fire; (d) a lodger cut the gas line in an attempt at suicide. (Answers on p. 194.)

Summary of Apparatus and Vocabulary

The picture of an analyzed argument, then, looks like this.

$$
\begin{array}{lll}
S_1 & & C_3\text{'S RIVALS} \\
S_2 & \text{IQ} & (\text{REJECTED ANSWERS}) \\
S_3 & & C_1 \\
\text{-----} & & C_2 \\
C_3 \quad \leftarrow & \text{rival answers} \rightarrow & C_4 \\
& & C_5 \\
& & \text{etc.} \\
& & . \\
& & .
\end{array}
$$

Internal structure of an argument.

We will add a bit more to this picture shortly, but for now note that it contains three essential items:

1. Schematized support and conclusion.
2. An implicit question.
3. The rival conclusions apparently rejected.

To display a clear grasp of an argument we will usually have to produce all three. Rival conclusions are the trickiest of these, however, because they do so much work. Let us collect their three most important properties in one place. Rival conclusions must

a. Answer the IQ (whatever it turns out to be).
b. Be mutually exclusive (contradict each other).
c. Express the contrast implicit in the context (what the author seems to reject).

REFINING THE APPARATUS AND EXERCISING OUR SKILLS

In this chapter, we are learning to think about our human resources. What do we bring to reasoning that allows us to do it? The general answer is an understanding of the context and subject matter. The support in a schematized argument

$$S_1$$
$$S_2$$
$$S_3$$

$$C$$

is offered as "reasons to think C is true." But to see the connection between support and conclusion, we must always understand quite a lot about the topic they concern *and* about the context in which the reasons are given. Some of this may be given in the discussion surrounding an argument, but most of it we must bring with us—must have inside us beforehand. This is why we reason best about topics we understand well, and we cannot begin to understand some arguments on exotic or technical subjects. When astronomers say a certain pattern in a computer readout is reason to think a planet circles a nearby star, we can only take their word for the connection. We would need to vastly increase our own understanding to make the connection ourselves. This text uses illustrations and exercises from everyday journalism because it operates at a level of understanding most of us have. Our understanding of things is always at work as we read and reason.

The project of this chapter is to say something helpful about how this works. We would like to discover *just what our understanding supplies* when reasoning is clear that might help us see what we lack when it is not. What we have found is this: When we have a schematized argument (S/C), the reasoning is clear when our understanding supplies a *question* and a *contrast*. This is what organizes the author's thinking,[5] and what we need to articulate in argument analysis.

To articulate question and contrast we invented the technical concepts of IQ and rivals, which have the properties elucidated in the last few pages. The understanding captured by these two concepts can be surprisingly complex and subtle, however. If they are to guide us in difficult cases, we need to work with them a bit to master their intricacies. That is the task of this section.

The Incompatibility of Rivals

The most artificial-sounding aspect of our apparatus is the strict incompatibility of rivals. In our normal talk, we allow different answers to a question to overlap without worrying too much about it. So we need to be clear about why we want our rivals to strictly exclude each other and how this happens very naturally in practice.

Rival conclusions are not just any sort of answer to an argument's Implicit Question, however. Rivals are the rejected contrast; and, as we have seen, to play that role they must be incompatible with each other. But there is yet another reason to keep rivals from overlapping. We will shortly want to talk about *evaluating* arguments. And the key item in evaluation is *how C stacks up against its competition*. Is it better? If so, how much better? A strong argument is one that makes its conclusion much better than the alternatives. To make this judgment, to compare alternatives with each other, those alternatives must be distinct from one another, not ones that cover some of the same ground (overlap). This is why we

---

5. Your own thinking, when you author an argument.

want rivals to be mutually exclusive: each possibility must fall in only one rival. Each dot in the balloon must fall in only one wedge.

Usually, the distinctness of rivals is simply understood in a context, and does not need explicit attention. In the coffee-snatching case we have been following, saying "Rhonda took it" naturally implies that the other suspects were not involved. So if we made a list of rival suspects (conclusions), it could look like this:

C_1 Rhonda
C_2 Tim
C_3 Me
C_4 Damion

and they would naturally be taken as mutually exclusive. That is, we would read C_1 as "Rhonda did it all by herself," and C_2 as "Tim did it acting alone," and C_3 as "I did it without help from anybody else," and so on. If we really wanted to consider the possibility that Rhonda and Damion were in this together, that would be a separate entry on the list:

C_{17} Rhonda and Damion

And similarly for other more bizarre possibilities.

Normal context and interests are enough to guarantee exclusive rivals. But when things are less clear, we will sometimes have to resort to trial and error to make the alternatives clear. Suppose you're examining an incident in which somebody's reading lamp flickers out during a violent windstorm. The victim argues that the winds make her think the cause is a failure of the entire neighborhood power grid. You realize that in doing this she's rejecting at least two house-bound rivals: a blown fuse and a worn out bulb. So your first analysis would look like this:

IMPLICIT QUESTION	RIVALS TO CONSIDER
Why did the lamp go out?	C_1 Local power grid failed.
	C_2 Fuse blew in the house.
	C_3 Bulb is shot.
	.
	.
	.

These would be graphically represented in the balloon in Figure 4.3.

Now suppose the victim goes on to speculate that what probably happened was that two power lines were blown together, shorting out the grid. That would obviously be a possibility to consider. Where does this go on the list? Well, as things stand, it would naturally be included in your first rival, because it is just one way for the grid to fail. So it is already on the list. It would not be an additional rival. But this need not be the end of the matter. If you think touching wires is a better version of the victim's conclusion, or just think the analysis would be clearer with that as a separate rival, you can always put it on the list *as long as you explicitly take it out of the more general rival.* You would have to **Split the C_1 Rival in Two,** one side containing the "lines touching," the other containing all the other local power failures. The list of rivals would then look like this:

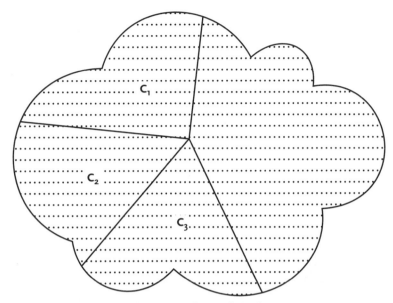

Figure 4.3. Original rivals.

C_1' The wind blew power lines together.
C_1'' Local power failed in *some other way*.
C_2 A fuse blew.
C_3 The bulb's shot.

Graphically this would look like the balloon in Figure 4.4. You may split up the possibilities in many different ways depending on what is important in the context. The requirement of incompatibility just limits your freedom in constructing the list: the different rivals may not overlap.

Exercise 4.9

a. Look at the rivals you gave for the Arts Center argument in Exercise 4.5a (or develop them now as suggested there). One rival you probably don't have on the list is "Reduce ticket prices slightly to fill some of the seats and give the remainder to senior citizens and drama students." Explain how we would have to understand the original conclusion to allow this one on the list. Would we have to modify any of yours?

b. Consider again the crash in the kitchen argument from Exercise 4.6. Suppose you wanted to include on the list of rivals, "It's just Charlie being clumsy again." (i) Explain how this overlaps with the original conclusion. (ii) Explain how you might deal with the overlap to get Charlie's clumsiness explicitly on the list.

(Answers on p. 194.)

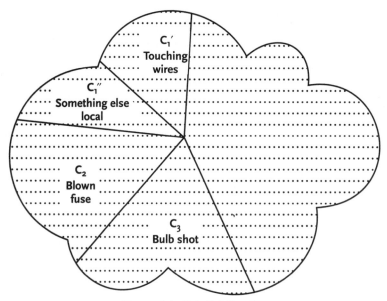

Figure 4.4. Subdividing C_1.

Using Rivals to Secure Understanding of IQ

The most useful IQs we encounter will begin with words such as "why," "who," "what," and "how." Questions such as "Why did the motel explode?" "Who stole the coffee?" and "What should we do with the empty seats?" will very often be the ones that best organize the reasoning we encounter in practice.[6] At the same time, our grasp of these questions, and what sort of answers they need, leans very heavily on our understanding of their contexts. A legendary illustration of this may be found in a "why" question posed by a journalist to Willie Sutton, a famous criminal of the early twentieth century. The journalist asked Sutton, "Why do you rob banks?" Sutton is alleged to have replied, "Because that's where the money is." He was of course just toying with the scribe, but we may characterize the joke as "getting the contrast wrong." The rival answers the journalist had in mind were other ways to make a living, not other things to rob. Sutton doubtless knew this, but exploited the context sensitivity of "why" questions to have a little fun.

The point is that all normal language users (including Sutton) will usually be clear about the contrast built into a question such as this, even though nothing in the question itself makes it explicit. We simply glean what it is from the context. But our task here is to *articulate* what we understand, so let us ask, "What can we say to make clear our grasp of an IQ in cases such as this?" As you should by now suspect, when we really understand a question, we already understand *the*

---

6. We will shortly see more clearly why this is so: their answers are ones with which human judgment has a particularly easy time.

right kinds of answers to give it. Our understanding lies in seeing what answers might be accepted and rejected in the context, as opposed to simply being irrelevant. In the Sutton case, we understand the question "Why do you rob banks?" and part of that understanding comes out in seeing immediately that "Because that's where the money is" is the wrong kind of answer (that's why it is a joke). So to express what we understand, we need to talk once again about what the right ones are: the list from which we wished him to choose.

Exercise 4.10
....

a. Give some rivals from the right list, the one the journalist had in mind in the Sutton case.

b. Give the rest of Sutton's list (the one's he'd be rejecting if we took him seriously). (Answers on p. 194.)

Of course we may sometimes insist on a more specific question. The journalist might respond to Sutton by saying something like, "No, what I meant was, Why did you choose to make a living by doing something dangerous and illegal?" But even here, if Sutton does not take the journalist seriously, he can still have fun playing with the question. The safer and easier thing to do usually is to keep the general question and give the contrast: the sort of answers relevant in a context. Why do you rob banks?—instead of any of a whole list of safe, legal things somebody clever and brave might do for a living. Similarly for "Why'd the lights go out?": the understood contrast is a fuse, the bulb, or something outside the house. Why'd the motel blow up? The understood contrast is the maintenance worker ignited leaking gas, or it ignited without his help, or it was unrelated violence of some sort.

Again, to articulate our understanding of an argument we need the whole package of concepts: support, conclusion, IQ, and rivals. Each helps in understanding the others. For the purpose of sketching our grasp of the IQ, our earlier picture of structure might be reconfigured like this:

SCHEMATIZATION	IQ	THE LIST OF RIVALS CHOSEN AMONG
S_1		C_1
S_2	The rival	C_2
S_3	answers →	C_3
----		C_4
C_3		C_5
		.
		.
		.

Internal structure: IQ articulation.

For some exercise, consider the following article.

> LOS ANGELES—A mistrial was declared yesterday in the trial of Catherine Stub-
> blefield Wilson when a single juror refused to convict the woman labeled by pros-
> ecutors as the nation's top child pornographer. U.S. District Judge Richard Gad-
> bois declared the mistrial after a jury deadlocked 11–1 to convict Wilson of
> distributing obscene material and exploiting children, said the prosecutor, U.S.
> Attorney Joyce Karlin. Gadbois set a Jan. 17 date for a new trial.
>
> "One of the jurors apparently made up his mind before he joined the deliber-
> ations," Karlin said outside the courtroom after she interviewed the jurors. "He
> was consistently late for court and he referred to witnesses who never testified.
> He said he didn't believe law-enforcement officers," Karlin said. "He made up
> his mind he wasn't going to vote guilty, no matter what."
>
> (*The Associated Press*)

Here attorney Karlin gives an argument, so let us articulate our understanding of
it with our apparatus. First, note that Karlin says five distinct things:

1. One juror made up his mind before deliberations.
2. He was consistently late.
3. He referred to witnesses that didn't testify.
4. He said he didn't believe officers.
5. He was not going to vote guilty no matter what.

The conclusion she is trying to support is pretty clearly statement 1, which is further confirmed by the indirectness flag "apparently" in the article. Statement 5
essentially restates this conclusion, whereas the other three make up the reasons
she has to think the juror was not listening to the case she was making. So we
may schematize her argument thus:

> S_1 One juror was consistently late for court.
> S_2 He referred to witnesses who did not testify.
> S_3 He did not believe law enforcement officers.
> ---
> C_1 He made up his mind before deliberations.

How do we find the IQ? Well, what question does Karlin take herself to be
answering by insisting on C? The context actually helps quite a lot here. Karlin's
argument is naturally defensive: journalists are writing articles about a case in
which she failed to get the conviction she was after. So she's telling us why it was
not her fault. She's arguing that the mistrial was not due to the case itself, or to
her presentation of it, but something else: namely, that one juror was not open to
persuasion on the matter. So the question is the one that attracted the attention
of the journalists: "Why was there a mistrial?" But to this question, Karlin wishes
to give *her* answer: there was a mistrial because one juror made up his mind before deliberations.

Our object in this section is to note how much of our understanding of an IQ
such as this lies unspoken in our grasp of the proper contrast. If we did not have
all the context provided by this article, and somebody asked "What caused the

mistrial?" the list of answers that might occur to us would be other things that might cause a mistrial:

C_A Hung jury.
C_B Error of law by judge.
C_C Improper evidence introduced.
C_D The jury died.

But because we have the context, we can see immediately that these give the wrong contrast. These are not the possibilities Karlin is anxious to reject in insisting on C_1. She's taking for granted that the jury was hung. All of her rivals will be *inside* C_A. They will be different accounts of a hung jury. So we might say that the IQ "What caused the mistrial?" is, in this context, just a stand-in for the more specific "What caused the hung jury?" In other words, Karlin is not interested in anything outside C_A: the whole balloon could be just what's inside C_A (Figure 4.5).

Even this is still too general to capture our understanding of the original IQ, however. Again, without our understanding of the context, we might divide up the hung-jury balloon in all sorts of ways (Figure 4.6). For example,

C_I The jury split evenly.
C_{II} All but three for conviction.
C_{III} All but two for acquittal.
C_{IV} All but one for conviction.
And so on.

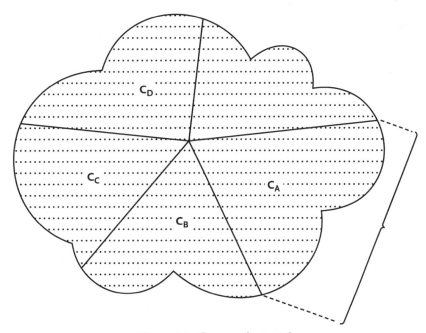

Figure 4.5. Causes of mistrial.

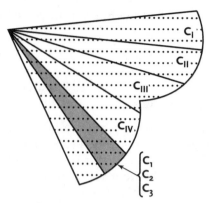

Figure 4.6. Subdividing C_A.

But, again, Karlin clearly takes the vote for granted too, so all of her rivals will be inside C_{IV}. And again we may restrict the scope of the original IQ by saying it was a stand-in for the more specific one: "Why did a single juror refuse to vote for conviction?" This does explicitly capture our understanding of Karlin's contrast, for what she is most concerned to reject are rivals in which the juror is a reasonable participant in the deliberations. For instance, the mistrial occurred because

C_2 The juror in question came in with an open mind, but did not find the evidence persuasive.

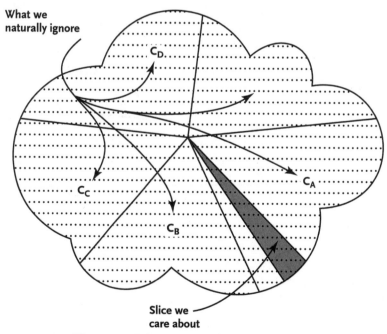

Figure 4.7. What context allows us to ignore.

or

C$_3$ The juror actually favored conviction at the outset but was convinced of Wilson's innocence by the evidence.

Both of these are to be found *within* C$_{IV}$.

So we may deal with a case such as this in either of two ways. We may work on finding a very specific IQ (such as "Why did this one juror vote against conviction?") *or* we may keep the more general IQ ("What caused the mistrial") and simply understand that we care only about a small slice of a single wedge in the possibility balloon naturally suggested by this question. You will find that the second way is usually easier and more useful in practice. For when you choose the very specific IQ, you must still keep in mind that the more general one still provides our motivation: we want to know why he voted against conviction *only because* that hung the jury. In any case, when you choose to keep a very general IQ, you may then point out the relevant (small) balloon slice by describing the specifically rejected rivals. This is pictured in Figure 4.7.

Exercise 4.11

a. Consider the following passage.

> An innocent outing to local snow-covered mountains turned into a grisly find for a couple of Air Force men and their families Sunday afternoon as they came upon a skeleton in a wrecked car. Steven Zarate of the coroner's office said the skeleton is that of a 54-year-old man from Rancho Mirage. The man's name has not been released pending notification of his family.
>
> Sgt. Jay Jones of the Banning Highway Patrol station said the man was reported missing on July 7 [six months ago]. The missing person's report indicated that the victim had left Escondido enroute to his home in Rancho Mirage prior to being reported missing. Jones said that the skeleton, hanging over the car's door, was mostly covered with snow. The wrecked car was situated about 250 feet down a steep cliff of the north side of Highway 243 north of Allendale Station and south of Lawlor Park, said Jones.
>
> Jones said the location where the car left the roadway is far enough from a populated area that no one may have heard the crash. The roadway opposite the crash area is popular for people playing in the snow but the other side "is so steep hardly anyone goes down there," said Jones.
>
> Jones said the highway patrol is assuming that the incident is a traffic accident and unless the coroner's autopsy finds something it will be investigated as an accident. (*The Hemet News*)

Take for granted that the IQ the highway patrol is trying to answer is "How did the unnamed Rancho Mirage man (URMM) die?" At the end of the article Sgt. Jones says the highway patrol "is assuming the incident is a traffic accident." This means they are, for the time being, going to ignore one part of the balloon that you get from the above IQ.

i. Just to test your understanding of this, give three rivals in that (neglected) part of the balloon—make them as different from one another as you can.

The conclusion probably favored by the highway patrol is "URMM died in a traffic accident," which of course comes from the part of the balloon they're taking seriously.

ii. Give a rival conclusion from this part of the balloon. (*Hint:* draw the balloon.)

b. Reread the article on medfly spraying in Exercise 3.25 (p. 127) and review the schematic argument you retrieved from it. A natural IQ suggested in the article would be, "What caused the spraying to be extended?" The controversy about the hoax, however, concerns only a small slice of the balloon determined by this IQ. (i) Give some rivals in the neglected (irrelevant) part of the balloon. (ii) Give rivals indicating the contrast in which Jackson is interested. (iii) What more specific IQ would specify the interesting part of the balloon?

(Answers on p. 194.)

The Significance of C

Note that in coming to understand the IQ in this way we are simply extending the use of rivals to articulate a conclusion's contrast. Rivals were originally introduced to flesh out our understanding of "C as opposed to what?" We may now say a bit more about the use of this contrast. To evaluate an argument, as we begin to do shortly, we need to know just which wedge of possibilities the support is asked to underwrite. And usually the sentence expressing an argument's conclusion ("A juror made up his mind before deliberation") may be taken in a number of different ways and hence taken to cover a number of different wedges. We nail down the wedge in the same way we narrow the IQ: by giving the rivals the argument's author is rejecting in the context.

Progress against Misunderstanding Each Other

We can now begin to see what is behind much of the misunderstanding that sometimes damages our reasoning with one another. The basic principle is this: **Arguments Work Well Only When Our Reasons Are Asked to Choose among a Small Number of Clear and Distinct Possibilities,** a few natural rivals. We are led to these rivals by understanding a question and a contrast. The (implicit) question gives us a balloon of possibilities and the contrast (rivals) divides it up in the right sort of way. In the easy, uncontroversial cases we have examined different people can do this independently with a considerable amount of agreement.

But in matters of controversy, such as the social and political issues we constantly argue about, people will often look at things so differently that the context will not guide them to anything like the same rivals. And they may well think of the rivals they do find as answering wholly different questions. When two people disagree strongly about a conclusion (concerning drugs or crime or welfare, for instance) they very often disagree about much else as well. Unless they realize how tricky getting the right questions and answers can be, they may talk past each other until they become angry and frustrated. Nothing in our apparatus guarantees the resolution of disagreement, of course. But it makes us alive to the fact that the same C can be reasonably taken to answer a number of different questions; and that even a single question will make sense with many different contrasts. Dealing with question and contrast in complex social and political issues is naturally far more messy and difficult than in the simpler cases we have looked at. That is part of the reason such issues are so hard to resolve. But noticing what needs to go right will at least allow us to see the source of much misunderstanding. And it may well go some way toward helping us reduce it.

We can take a large step in this direction by noticing that some IQs engage human skills more helpfully than others. Just which kinds and why will be explored in the next section.

EVALUATING ARGUMENTS: HOW GOOD ARE THE REASONS?

We have so far been simply learning to talk about arguments, to get clear about what is being claimed in giving reasons. The next step is to say something about how good that claim is. Because our judgment of the quality of reasons is just as subtle and dependent on context as anything else in reasoning, it will require the same care to articulate. So, as a preliminary, let us quickly review the basic points made thus far. In practice, an argument consists of some support being offered for a conclusion together with enough context to establish the question being addressed and the proper contrast among its answers. This gives us the picture we have seen before, repeated here for convenience.

$$
\begin{array}{ccccc}
 & & \text{SCHEMATIZATION} & & \\
 & & S_1 & & \\
 & & S_2 & \text{Implicit Question} & \\
\text{PRACTICAL} & & S_3 & \text{and} & C_1 \\
 & = & \text{----} & + \quad \text{Its Rival} & C_2 \\
\text{ARGUMENT} & & C_3 & \text{Answers} \rightarrow & C_3 \\
 & & & & C_4 \\
 & & & & \cdot \\
 & & & & \cdot \\
 & & & & \cdot
\end{array}
$$

The dots at the bottom of the list of rival conclusions indicate that, as we have seen in many cases, the list of rival conclusions can usually be extended more or less indefinitely.

Serious Rivals

We may begin thinking about evaluation with those dots. For when we know enough about something to reason about it, *we never have to extend the list of rivals very far*. If we list the natural rivals, brainstorm a bit, and perhaps get some suggestions from others, we can come up with a short list of *serious* rivals[7] and be reasonably sure we have the right answer covered. In the motel blast, we take the maintenance worker story seriously. We also seriously consider one having the propane find some other source of ignition, and perhaps one or two others. That's it, unless we learn something unexpected. Similarly when, on a calm summer evening, TWA Flight 800 fell into the ocean in flaming pieces, the investigators confined their attention to three rival causes: a bomb, a missile, and a mechanical failure.

Exercise 4.12
....

List four typical plane-crash rivals of this same level of generality that the investigators are *not* taking seriously in the Flight 800 case (that is, four substantial chunks of the "what caused the crash?" balloon they're neglecting because of what they already know). (Answers on p. 195.)

This means, of course, that part of the balloon of possibilities is *not* covered: the rival wedges leave some of the balloon without a name. But this is not just permissible, it is often the best sign that we know enough to reason about a topic. For we can always formulate fantastic rivals that, if we know what we are doing, *should* be ignored. One unserious rival in the motel blast would be that alien invaders blew it up to punish a turncoat spy. We don't take this seriously precisely because we understand a lot about how the world works here. We are right to ignore that part of the balloon.

Exercise 4.13
....

Draw the balloon for the motel-explosion case and generally describe what's in the serious part. (Answer on p. 195.)

The question of fantastic rivals comes up, of course, only because finding rivals at all requires exercising our imagination. Sometimes the only way to come up with serious rivals is to think up lots of possibilities and sort out the reasonably good ones. A good practical strategy is to be generous: make a list of all the obviously serious rivals and include as well one or two that are only borderline serious. Doing so virtually guarantees that we have the right one in there somewhere, and evaluation requires only that we begin with a short list.

The role of imagination poses yet another hazard to seriousness, however. As we think up answers to the IQ, we naturally entertain ourselves by embellishing the possibilities with detail. Sometimes the detail actually helps our brainstorming. To

---

7. Usually the serious rivals will simply be the natural ones: the ones we found trying to understand the author's contrast. But we may on reflection decide that some of the natural rivals should not be taken seriously. And we may think of serious possibilities the author neglected. The point is that seriousness is a crucial judgment to make, so we should make sure all reasonable possibilities are covered.

help us think about the exploding motel we might speculate: The maintenance man thought his sense of smell was good enough to tell there was no danger of propane, but maybe a marinated roast cooking nearby disguised the odor of the gas; so he lit a match and blew up the building. . . . But the degree of detail a serious rival may have *must be determined by the available support*; and the support we have is not specific enough to justify a separate (very thin) wedge for the marinating roast story. A million other similar stories are just as serious: they are all best lumped together in the C_1 wedge. That is why the rival reads simply, "The maintenance worker did it." The smaller the wedge, the more support is required for it to be serious.

Again, in the truck crash "the driver fell asleep at the wheel" is about the right level of detail for the support given. If someone offered instead "the driver nodded off four times since the last fuel stop, and was saved the first three times by the dead-straight road, but on the final time the road was cambered from years of weathering and bad drainage, and this directed the truck off onto the shoulder and into the bridge abutment," this would be too much detail to be taken seriously on the support we have. This story would be one of the dots within the wedge, but many others would be just as serious, which is to say none would be very serious by itself. You get a serious one only by lumping the bunch of them together under "the driver dozed off."

Consider the following illustration:

> SAN DIEGO—Authorities said Saturday they had found no trace of a 56-year-old man whose blood-spattered fishing boat was found drifting off Point Loma. A search for Travis J. Busby, of Colton, had been under way since he was reported missing Tuesday along with his 43-foot boat, Forever Amber.
>
> His boat was found Thursday, and a gun was discovered on board. The .22 caliber handgun apparently had been fired once. Coast Guard Lt. Norris Turner said Busby's wife and friends indicated that he had been depressed about financial problems. The Forever Amber had departed Kona Kai marina in San Diego on Jan. 4 after taking on 432 gallons of fuel. The Boat's fuel tanks were empty and its navigation lights were on when it was discovered.
>
> Five rounds remained in the gun. One had been expended, and the hammer was resting on the empty shell, Turner said. A billfold, a dinghy and an uninflated life raft also were on board. Busby was an experienced sailor who held a commercial fishing license and rented out the boat for fishing trips, Turner said.
>
> (*The Associated Press*)

If we consider an argument addressing the IQ, "What has happened to Travis Busby?" the support in this article suggests at most four general rivals as serious candidates.

> C_1 Busby committed suicide.
> C_2 Busby was murdered.
> C_3 Busby was killed in an accident.
> C_4 Busby faked his death to avoid his troubles.

Even the last of these may not be very serious, but we include it on the list as a borderline case. The point of this illustration is to think about the level of detail that allows a rival to be serious. As we brainstorm it might help to spell out possibilities such as "Busby was killed by a loan shark's hit man for missing a payment deadline." But this is just a small area around one of the dots in the C_2 slice of the balloon. If we made it a rival millions of others just like it would deserve the title as well. We can imagine many different murder stories, and the data give no reason to distinguish among most of them. Sketchy support means that the serious rivals can only be very general possibilities, relatively large wedges of the balloon.

Exercise 4.14

Look again at Exercise 4.5b on p. 148 (concerning Flight 544). (a) Explain why "Disappeared into the Bermuda Triangle" doesn't belong on the serious rival list. (b) What about "Hijacked to Cuba"? (Answers on p. 195.)

Right Answers and Sound Arguments

Recall that a schematized argument offers reasons in support of a conclusion:

$$S_1$$
$$S_2$$
$$S_3$$

$$C$$

And we have articulated the claim being made in offering this argument as our old friend (A):

(A) S_1, S_2, and S_3 recommend C as the right answer to give the argument's implicit question.

Once we have a short list of serious rivals, we may use (A) as a first step toward evaluating the reasons. For saying that C is the right answer says *at least* that C is a better answer than any of its rivals. And this is to begin to evaluate the reasons, to say that they are at least good enough to select C as the best of the list. Sometimes this is all we need, and sometimes it is the best we can do. But it is in any case the first crucial step in reaching something stronger. Let us introduce a bit more vocabulary. We will call an argument "sound" if it meets this criterion, that is, if the support *does* make its conclusion the best of the rivals.

Soundness is a purely comparative notion, which turns out to make it enormously useful. For even if we don't know all we would like to know about a case, we can often provide a **ranking** among the possibilities. That is, we can *rank the serious rivals* in a rough order corresponding to how good they are as answers to the IQ. Just given our general understanding of things, and the little bit we know about the motel explosion, we can say that the maintenance worker rival is the best answer so far, and others having to do with the hot water problem are the next best bet. Suicide attempts by lodgers and mayhem by disgruntled employees fall a bit lower in the ranking, followed by things falling from the sky, with aliens and other fantasies lower still. We can reasonably say all this even though we have more to learn that may eventually change our understanding of what happened. We can't be sure *just how good* the best rival is, but we do know it's the best of the bunch so far.

Rankings can be of many sorts. If we say rivals we can't distinguish between are "tied," we might end up with any of the following.

Ranking$_1$	Ranking$_2$	Ranking$_3$	Ranking$_4$	Ranking$_5$	Ranking$_6$
C_1	C_3	C_3	$C_1\ C_3$	C_1	$C_1\ C_2\ C_3\ C_4$
C_2	C_1	$C_1\ C_2$	C_2	C_3	
C_3	C_2	C_4	C_4	$C_2\ C_4$	
C_4	C_4				

For an argument with Ranking$_1$ or Ranking$_5$ C_1 would be the sound conclusion; for one with Ranking$_2$ or Ranking$_3$ it would be C_3. The other two would have no sound conclusion because there is no single best answer.

Exercise 4.15

Continuing with the Flight 544 case (Exercise 4.5b on p. 148), (a) rank the three most serious rivals. (b) Schematize the sound argument. (Answers on p. 195.)

Human Skill and Useful Questions

The ability to compare serious rivals and rank them in this way is the basic skill we apply to evaluate reasoning. It is the starting point from which we reach more sophisticated achievements, and to which we return when investigating tough cases.[8] But, as we should expect, this skill works well only in certain conditions. The first requirement is that our understanding is adequate to give us a short list of serious rivals to compare. We have already seen cases that meet this requirement for most of us, and we frequently know how to improve our understanding (learn more) to make it fit cases we find interesting. But another requirement is even more important: the rivals we compare must be serious attempts to answer the IQ—that is, real, substantive alternatives to one another.

In practice this means that C's competition should not simply be lumped together under some unhelpful heading such as "some other answer," or "something else besides C," or, simply, "not-C." Our understanding is not very good at coming to grips with such answers, and we often cannot even rank them. When TWA Flight 800 crashed in flames off Long Island, newspapers reported at first that investigator's suspected a bomb (C_1 = "A bomb did it"). How good an answer is this? (IQ = "What caused the crash?") Well, what's the competition? If we think of the competition as simply "It was not a bomb," that does not help at all. We might like this answer for its formal properties, because it nicely covers *all* the competition. It divides the possibilities balloon in two and covers all the dots (as in Figure 4.8). But to even begin to understand how good an answer C_1 is, we need to think about the

---

8. In this skill we find the roots of experimental design in science, as well as air-crash investigation procedures. We will say much more about this later in the chapter and in Chapter 5.

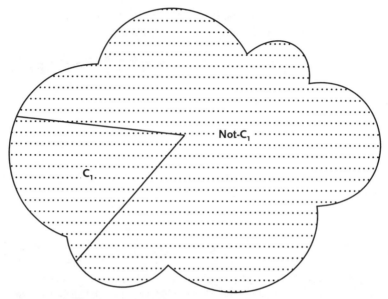

Figure 4.8. Unhelpful division of possibilities.

substantive possibilities covered by this very general rival. What's hidden inside "not-C_1" that we might have to take seriously? The serious, substantive competition would be C_2: "ground-to-air missile"; C_3: "internal fuel leak + spark"; and C_4: "collision with another aircraft." With these possibilities before us, we could begin using the available information to provide an initial ranking and begin working toward something better. Without them we are usually at a loss.

The importance of this observation about rivals is the restriction it places on the kinds of questions we can use as IQs. For some questions *have* only two answers, "yes" and "no" (C and not-C), and these will typically be wholly useless for human reasoning. In the TWA crash, if we make the IQ "Was it a bomb?" for instance, we guarantee that we will get the very picture (Figure 4.8) that we need to avoid. Every conclusion answers questions such as this, questions that essentially ask "Is C true?" and if we could use them that would make finding the IQ very easy. Unfortunately, we must almost always avoid these easy questions because they lump together all the interesting possibilities we must distinguish in order to think about an argument.[9] This is why most useful IQs will start with an interrogative word from the short list we gave earlier: who, what, when, where, why, how. These permit unlimited answers, and hence can be tailored to our needs and skills.

---

9. Sometimes we will find it very hard in practice to replace an easy, two-answer question with something more helpful. This usually means that the issue in question is just difficult to deal with. Strategies for turning questions we'd like to answer into questions we're competent to deal with will be addressed in Chapter 7.

Exercise 4.16
....

Look again at the URMM passage in Exercise 4.11a (p. 163) Which of the following would be unhelpful IQs for the highway patrol's argument?

a. How did the URMM die?

b. Was the URMM a victim of foul play?

c. What happened to the URMM?

d. Was this a traffic accident?

e. Did the URMM die here or elsewhere?

f. How did URMM get here and dead?

g. Did URMM die in a traffic accident?

(Answers on p. 195.)

Of course, when we are finished thinking about a case and wish simply to express what we think about it, we may say something like, "C_3 is better than all the other possibilities." There is nothing wrong with that as a summation. But our project here is to *articulate our reasoning*, that is, to say what we do to actually reach such a conclusion. For that we must see how our understanding actually works to discriminate better from worse answers. If we do think well of the proposal to give the empty Arts Center seats to senior citizens and students, it should be because we've thought through the alternatives. Is the proposal actually better than, say, lowering the price and improving access generally? How about doing a little of both (lower a bit and give away what's left)? Or can we find other groups just as worthy to be included on the free list? Might it be best to simply close the place down and save all the trouble? To articulate the work of our understanding in typical cases requires looking through real possibilities such as this. So we must always resist the temptation to fall back on easy, two-answer IQs such as

> Did X happen?
> Was it Y?
> Should we do Z?
> Is C true?

The best way to do this is, whenever possible, to begin your IQs with the standard interrogative words listed above.

Exercise 4.17
....

Describe the easy, fall-back IQ that we should avoid in the following arguments we've looked at in this chapter: (a) motel explosion on p. 142; (b) truck crash on p. 147; (c) pioneer trail on p. 151; and (d) hung jury on p. 160. (Answers on p. 195.)

Articulating Relevance

We are now in a position to use our apparatus to articulate another aspect of reasoning: the relevance of support. We have been relying on your ability to extract support from a passage simply by distinguishing it from other things that were not relevant to the argument. The way we phrased this in Chapter 3 was to look for things that "make a difference" to the argument. The concepts we have developed in this chapter will allow us to say a bit more about that difference: where it shows up and what it looks like.

The notion of "making a difference" suggests the following *thought experiment*. To articulate what we do when we decide whether to include a bit of information (call it "S?") as support, just compare the argument with and without S?. It is relevant if adding it makes the argument better or worse or changed in some important way. And where would this change show up? Mainly in the ranking of the serious rivals. If S? is relevant, the ranking would be one sort of arrangement when it is included in the support and another when it is not. But the difference could be of many kinds. For convenience we will divide the kinds into four groups, as follows.

1. The most important and obvious impact S? might have is to actually change the order of the serious rivals in the ranking. But even this can mean many things. The ranking would be changed if a different rival ended up on top, of course. But subtler changes count too. A swap further down on the list would be an important change in the ranking, as would making or breaking ties. Many of these changes would not affect the soundness of the argument but they will still be relevant to our evaluation of it (which we will talk about shortly). If adding S? changed the ranking from any one of the six patterns on p. 169 to another, that would make S? relevant, something to include in the support.

2. Information is also relevant if it *changes what the serious rivals are*. In the normal run of circumstances, for example, suicide might not be a serious rival in the truck-crash argument. But if we discovered (S?) that the driver had just lost custody of his kids in a bitter divorce, the cost of which had left him bankrupt, suicide could not be ignored as a possibility. So news of the divorce would be relevant support and should be included in the schematization. But we cannot articulate its relevance by talking of the rivals we already have. It is relevant because it *changes the list*: it makes suicide serious. Similarly, in the motel explosion, finding that the maintenance worker had just arrived at the motel, and was still talking with the manager at the time of the explosion, removes him from the list of serious rivals. So that information goes in the schematization, again, because it changes the list of serious rivals.

Exercise 4.18
....

Consider the following passage.

> The wind woke me from a sound sleep at about 4 a.m. I could hear it howling through the trees and pelting the bedroom window with bits of debris. In

the morning, when I tried to dispose of some kitchen scraps, our large, metal garbage can was not in its usual spot next to the garage. I finally found it wedged under a bush on the other side of my car, which had been parked in the driveway. The car itself had new scrapes and scratches, just about the height of a rolling garbage can, on the side facing the can's normal location.

a. Schematize the argument in this passage for the answer it suggests to the question "What scratched the car?"

b. Take the two most serious rivals to be C_2, some other windblown object, and C_3, vandals. Articulate the relevance of the wind.

(Answers on p. 195.)

3. Another kind of change is closely related to this, but it requires some new vocabulary to be described. This occurs when S? makes a rival that is already serious either more or less serious without changing its ranking, and without dropping it from the list altogether. To talk about these cases, let us introduce the notion of a "gap" in the ranking. If S? clearly helps a rival on the list, without changing its ranking, we can characterize this as decreasing the gap between it and the next best rival. It can also increase a gap by hurting the lower rival without dropping it from serious consideration.[10] In the disappearance of Travis Busby, for instance, if we found that he had just taken out a large life insurance policy on himself, that would be relevant even if we did not think it changed the ranking, because it would leave suicide (C_1), murder (C_2), and ruse (C_4) better looking answers than they were before. The thought experiment would look like this. Before discovering the life insurance, the ranking would be

C_1 Busby committed suicide.
C_2 Busby was murdered.
C_3 Busby was killed in an accident.
C_4 Busby faked his death to avoid his troubles.

perhaps with a bit larger gap between C_1 and C_2 than between C_2 and C_3, and an even larger one between the last two. When we find out about the insurance policy, that may not change this ranking, but it would at least increase the gap above C_3 and decrease the one below it. That would be enough to make it relevant.

4. Finally, information is relevant if it changes the proper level of detail in the serious rivals. This kind of impact always shows up in one or another of the previous three categories, but it is important enough to be worth separate treatment. For a common result of adding new information is that a very specific version of a general rival becomes a suspect. One point in one wedge of

---

10. Gaps are simply a measure of how hard it would be to raise the lower rival, or drop the higher one, so that they would be tied in the ranking. Because we could argue that any information changes a gap in some microscopic way, we must think of relevant information as having a serious or detectable impact on a gap, not an infinitesimal one.

the balloon takes on special importance. If we do find that Busby had taken out a loan from an underworld organization, for instance, and he had missed a payment deadline, and that this group had a reputation for hunting down people who miss payments, this would make the detail in "killed by a loan shark's hit man" perfectly reasonable. Before the new information, this possibility was just one dot in the C_2 wedge (murder). Now it can be a serious rival by itself. Exercise 4.19a below asks you to state how C_2 would have to be modified if we wish to include the "hit man" rival as C_5 on the list. Be sure to do that exercise.

Information is relevant support in an argument if

1. It changes the ranking of the serious rivals.
2. It changes the list of serious rivals.
3. It changes gaps in the ranking of serious rivals.
4. It justifies splitting a serious rival.

Four criteria of relevance.

Exercise 4.19

a. How would the C_2 rival in the Busby case have to be modified to allow the "hit man" rival on the list?

b. We noted that the fourth relevance criterion (changing appropriate level of detail) is actually included in the others. Explain how.

c. i. Articulate the relevance of the rest of the support in the windblown-garbage-can argument of Exercise 4.18.

   ii. Articulate the relevance to that argument of the following discoveries.

   S_6: Car-colored paint on a nearby lawn chair.
   S_7: A recent rash of neighborhood vandalism.
   S_8: No paint found on the garbage can.

(Answers on p. 196.)

INTERIM SUMMARY: WHAT WE HAVE LEARNED SO FAR

Articulation is a kind of explanation. When we articulate reasoning (either our own or that found in a passage), we are trying to explain three things: (a) how we came up with the argument we did; (b) what is being claimed by the argument; and (c) how good that claim is. This chapter has developed a picture of the "internal structure" of an argument to help us explain these three things.

At first, the picture contained just three basic concepts: schematization, IQ, and rivals. We have recently added two more concerning just the rivals: serious-ness and ranking. So the complete internal structure picture would be some-thing like this:

SOUND ARGUMENT

S_1		SERIOUS RIVALS		RANKING
S_2	IQ	(CHOSEN AMONG)		
S_3	+	C_1		C_3
----	Context →	C_2	Support →	C_2
C_3	determines	C_3	determines	C_5
		C_4		C_1
		C_5		C_4

Complete internal structure of argument.

These concepts fit together as a package, each helping to articulate the others and together explaining (a), (b), and (c).

We actually started with (b) "What does the argument assert?" To explain this we needed the IQ: the argument asserts that the support makes the conclu-sion the right answer to this question. The rivals were added here as a way to help flesh out C and the IQ. They give the conclusion's contrast (C as opposed to what?). All this was represented as a way of finding a balloon full of possibilities and dividing it up into wedges. We then moved to (c) and used the notions of seriousness and ranking to help us say whether the claim made by the argument was right in a minimal way (sound). These new concepts allowed us to return to (a) and explain why we chose the support we did to put in the schematization (relevance).

When reasoning is difficult, articulating it in these terms will usually help us see whether we have understood it. Using this apparatus, along with the Principle of Charity, we will often find a better expression of someone else's reasoning than they did themselves. In the next three sections we return to (c) (evaluation) and look at the most difficult issue: how to articulate the strength of reasons.

Exercise 4.20

Schematize the argument in the URMM passage of Exercise 4.11a (p. 163) and articulate the relevance of its support.
(Answer on p. 196.)

A Useful Distinction: Two Kinds of Support

Recall that the resource we exploit in reasoning is our general understanding of things. This is what we depend on to connect support and conclusion, and it is at work in our use of language to describe the things about which we reason. Both reasoning and articulation require substantial understanding just to get started, which is why we have confined our discussion to cases in which ordinary understanding is clear and uncontroversial.

In the simplest cases of reasoning we encounter, our general understanding overwhelms the case. What we know at the beginning is perfectly adequate to connect support with conclusion, to see what provides reason for what. I hear a crash in the kitchen. When I look in I see the cat on the counter and a broken jar of jam splattered on the floor just below. Nobody else is around. So I have good reason to think the cat knocked the jar off the counter. What I already understand about cats and glass and gravity and hard floors and other possible suspects is enough to figure out what happened. If I schematize my reasoning, the support will simply be details of the case in question:

S_1 There's a crash in the kitchen.
S_2 The cat's on the counter just above a broken jar of jam on the floor.
S_3 Nobody else is around.

C The cat knocked the jar off the counter.

But not all reasoning is like this. Sometimes our general understanding is inadequate to grasp the reasoning in a certain case. Some of my plants have wilted, for instance, in spite of having plenty of water. I started watering them more frequently at the first sign of wilting, but it did no good. I wonder why (IQ = "Why?"). A neighbor who knows something about gardening informs me that some plants are subject to a root fungus common in local soil, and must be allowed to dry out between waterings to keep the fungus at a tolerable level. This supplements my general botanic understanding enough that I can now figure out what's happening. That is, I now have reason to choose a particular answer to the IQ, and it can be formulated as an argument:

S_1 My plants are wilting.
S_2 I water them frequently.
*S_3 Overwatering can encourage a root fungus.

C They are suffering from root rot.

But here, unlike the cat argument, only the first two supporting statements concern this specific case. S_3 is more general "background" information.

Let us call these two kinds of support *Specific* and *General*. *Specific Support* provides details of the particular event or action or phenomenon inquired into by the implicit question. *General Support* supplements our understanding in a way required to appreciate the Specific Support. (The asterisk marks the item of General Support in the above schematic argument.) This distinction, like most useful distinctions, will allow borderline cases. Not every supporting statement will clearly fall into one category or the other. Nevertheless, we will sometimes be able to more clearly articulate our reasoning if we keep in mind these two different kinds of support.

Much of the reasoning we read about in popular journalism is like the plant case. To grasp the Apollo 13 crew's argument for abandoning the command module (for the return trip to earth after the power-supply explosion), most of us need some general information about the nature and properties of the two parts of the spacecraft, and maybe some help with problems of living in the vacuum of space. Crash investigations are similar. The general reader usually cannot infer much from patterns in the wreckage without some helpful supplement by the experts.

Exercise 4.21
....

The following article contains an argument with some general support. (a) What is the conclusion? (b) What is the general support? (Answers on p. 196.)

> The deftly skinned animal carcasses that have been turning up in Lakewood are the remains of coyotes—not dogs—that apparently were caught in steel traps and killed for their pelts, SPCA officers said Thursday. An autopsy performed on the last of the four carcasses that have been discovered since December showed that the animal had fed on small animals and possibly a bird, according to Cpl. Vicki Young of the Los Angeles SPCA. "This is typical coyote food," Young said.
>
> (Lee Harris, *Los Angeles Times* staff writer)

Because no argument can anticipate all the possible things somebody might misunderstand about a topic, every schematization must take a certain amount for granted. Reasoning always requires a certain level of understanding, and must be fashioned with a certain audience in mind. When the federal (NTSB) investigators formulate their reasoning *for each other*, they do not have to mention much of the General Support we would require. Their schematization might contain nothing but Specific Support (e.g., "this part of the front cargo door was found here and looked like this," and so on). But for us to reach the same conclusion, we would have to supplement their argument with general information about the effect of various kinds of impacts and disintegrations on airframes and people and baggage and food carts.[11]

We try to keep the arguments used in this text available to the normal level of understanding of an average current undergraduate in the United States. You will recognize that many of our illustrations would need additional General Support

---

11. In a pedagogic context such as this one, General Support has a peculiar instability. In ordinary circumstances, we read an argument, either appreciate it or don't, and let it go at that. But here, we pause, analyze, reparaphrase, schematize, and generally dwell on an argument far more than we would normally. As we do this, however, we tend to digest General Support and simply incorporate it into our own understanding of things. So it very quickly becomes unnecessary to mention such support to anyone who is part of the immediate conversation. To explain why we keep General Support in a schematic argument in such cases, therefore, we must usually appeal to the understanding we initially brought with us. The audience we *were* required it, even if we now do not. Specific Support does not have this problem.

were they aimed at audiences in other cultures or earlier historical epochs. Some-times, of course, what someone does not understand is so great that it cannot be remedied with a few lines of support. To understand an argument about the effect of India's balance of payments on its exchange rate, most of us would require some education in economics. Nothing in simple schematic form could help us enough. Similarly, if an audience knew nothing at all of air travel, or mechanical devices, it would need a whole range of experiences and education before it could make sense of an NTSB crash report. The notion of General Support is useful for filling small holes in our understanding, to allow us to grasp reasoning not too far from the com-fortably familiar. It cannot take the place of a curriculum, or years of experience.

Exercise 4.22
....

Look again at the article about the disappearance of Danny Hamilton in Exer-cise 4.7 (p. 152). Identify the item of general support and explain its relevance in an argument answering the IQ, "What happened to Danny Hamilton?" (An-swer on p. 196.)

Investigation: Making Reasons Better

We will sometimes be content to evaluate reasoning we find in a passage (or con-versation) and let it go at that. We judge the argument offered to be good or bad, sound or not, and move on to other things. When a matter is important to us, how-ever, we will often want to improve on what we're given. That is, when we find that the support offered does not favor any particular rival, or that it supports the one it does favor only weakly, we may care enough about the IQ to find this unsatisfac-tory. We would like a *good* answer, not just the best of an indifferent bunch.

We may do this by extending our *Relevance Judgment*. The skill that allows us to pull relevant data from a passage for a schematization may be adapted to lead us to *new* information. We already know how to recognize relevant support when we find it; we now have to figure out *Where to Look* for more. It turns out that the very same thing that guides our recognition also guides our search: the serious rivals.

Consider, for instance, our earlier example in which investigators concluded that a driver fell asleep at the wheel. They gave as their reason that the truck drove straight off the road, without any of the characteristic signs of braking or steering. This sounds reasonable, but let us suppose we are insurance under-writers and would like to be more certain of what happened. What do we do? Well, what's required is to look for more relevant information. And we know what makes information relevant: *impact on serious rivals*. If we already have an argument with serious rivals, we can look at the rivals and see what they sug-gest. And in this case, as often happens, they suggest quite a lot. Recall what those rivals were: suicide (C_2), died at the wheel (C_3), and comprehensive control fail-ure (C_4). So we can see immediately that autopsy results might affect C_3, and an examination of the truck's steering and brakes might have some impact on C_4, and looking into the driver's background and recent history would help us with the suicide rival, C_2. This history may also provide information relevant to C_1

(sleep), especially if it includes the driver's recent schedule. This is all reasonably straightforward, precisely *because* we began with a completely analyzed argument.

The point of this is to highlight some features of how investigations work. Implicit Questions, rival conclusions, and relevance judgments organize *inquiry* in the same way they organize arguments. So if we start with an argument, our tools for analyzing it give us everything we need for the investigation required to make it better. But when we start from the other end, we can now see that just having a question or a puzzle is not enough to launch an investigation. Before we can begin to look for information relevant to answering questions such as "Who killed the president?" "What blew up Flight 800?" "Is the earth warming?" we must first have a list of tentative answers, serious suspicions. Without some rivals, our relevance judgment has nothing to work on and nothing guides our data gathering: we know neither what to look for nor where to look. And as soon as we see that investigations must have rivals, we can see how intimately connected they are to arguments. Just as arguments simply become investigations when they look for more support, investigations become arguments when they pause to evaluate their progress. That is, the conclusion supported by an investigation at any given time simply is the answer to the IQ recommended by the data gathered so far: a classic, schematized argument. So just as investigations are dynamic arguments, arguments are slices, or cross-sections, of investigations.[12]

S_1		S_1 S_2		S_1 S_2 S_3		S_1 S_2 S_3 S_4		S_1 S_2 S_3 S_4 S_5		S_1 S_2 S_3 S_4 S_5 S_6
-----	→	-----	→	-----	→	-----	→	-----	→	-----
C_4		C_4		?		C_3		C_3		C_3
Ranking		Ranking		Ranking		Ranking		Ranking		Ranking
↓		↓		↓		↓		↓		↓
C_4		C_4		C_3 C_4		C_3		C_3		C_3
C_2		C_3		C_2		C_4				
C_3		C_2		C_1		C_2		C_2		
C_1		C_1				C_1		C_4		C_2

Progress of investigation: sequence of sound arguments answering a particular IQ.

---

12. One thing that may happen, of course, is that as you learn more you come to see that the original question (IQ) arose from a misunderstanding or was badly formulated as a result of limited information. So you may develop good reason to change the question motivating the inquiry (IQ). If you do this, you will get a different balloon of possibilities and different natural rivals, which is in a sense to start all over again. But the procedure will be the familiar one that got you this far; and your increased understanding from the initial investigation will often allow the new one to proceed more efficiently.

In many everyday contexts we are actually very good at extending our relevance judgment to increase the strength of an argument. As I get into my car after work I must decide which way to drive home in the rush-hour traffic. From long experience my understanding gives me only three serious possibilities: two distinct freeway routes and one that is mostly surface streets. Furthermore, I know that in normal traffic and barring accidents, one of the freeway routes is both shorter and faster than the other two alternatives. Let us suppose that on this day my sole interest is in getting home as quickly and easily as possible. The shorter freeway is thus the better choice, though not by much, because something often ties it up and makes the second freeway route the better choice. And occasionally both freeways will be so congested that the surface streets will actually be faster. So the information I have yields a sound argument for my number one choice, but not a very strong one.

I do, however, know of two specific ways to learn more that may be relevant to the rivals. A local radio station helpfully broadcasts reports on local traffic conditions every few minutes at this time of the afternoon. I also can see the street connecting my parking lot to the first freeway. I notice traffic flowing smoothly on that street and I tune to the traffic station as I start the car. The radio reports that traffic also flows smoothly on both of my freeway routes, but is especially sparse on the one I usually take. This additional information favors my number one choice, and so opens a gap between it and the next best. The argument now is stronger, the reasons better.

Exercise 4.23

Give some new information that would be relevant to the Flight 544 argument of Exercise 4.15 (p. 169). Articulate its relevance. (Answer on p. 197.)
[**Important Caution:** when thinking of new information in investigation exercises, you must **keep it in the spirit of an investigation.** This means that not only must you hold onto everything "given" in the description of the case (new information cannot simply reject what's given), you must find what would ordinarily be called "evidence." Most important, new information cannot simply be a rival: you can't simply discover C_5, for instance. That's not the skill we're trying to exercise here.]

Our illustrations of new information have been of Specific Support in each case. The new information in this case is Specific Support: that is, it all directly concerns my route home this evening. But what we learn in an investigation can be General, too. It can supplement our general understanding. Finding General Support can allow us to see the relevance of Specific Support we could not have otherwise appreciated. In the TWA investigation, for instance, one bit of information turned up by investigators was that the absolute altitude limit of the most commonly available ground-to-air missile is 12,500 feet. This is General Support because it is not specifically about this particular crash; and it is relevant, because it hurts the "missile" rival (drops it in the ranking). But it hurts this rival only because of some Specific Support, whose relevance is now clear: the plane was flying at almost 14,000 feet when it started to come apart.

Exercise 4.24
....

Suppose we launched an investigation into the Flight 544 case, beginning with the argument in Exercise 4.15 (p. 169). What general information might we seek that would be relevant? (Answer on p. 197.)

Keep in mind that we cannot compensate this easily for every lack of understanding we might have. Sometimes nothing we can simply add to an argument will allow me to appreciate an item of Specific Support. Grasping it might require years of study or training (understanding the reason physicists think quantum gravity requires so many dimensions, for example), and it could be beyond me altogether. But the genius of human practicality has invented a kind of argument explicitly crafted to get around just this difficulty. Sometimes we can exploit other people's understanding to supplement our own, and hence evaluate data that are directly beyond our comprehension. We appeal to "experts," which just means those who understand things we do not. To use the testimony of experts as support for a conclusion we still must understand a lot about human beings and their perceptions and motivation. But sometimes we can do this when we cannot understand an esoteric or technical matter that experts can. In this way, we can extend the reach of our reasoning indirectly.

For instance, a chemical analysis was required to identify explosive residue on a seat fragment in the TWA crash. For most of us, and even most of the investigators, to make this identification would require a course in chemistry—and perhaps some preparatory courses as well. But chemists were available who already understood everything necessary, and in the circumstances we had every reason to trust their analysis. Instead of including the analysis and making the argument inaccessible to almost everybody, the support simply read, "explosive residue was found on a seat fragment from row 23." This of course requires a tributary appealing to the testimony of chemists, and we will examine that kind of argument more closely in Chapter 6. For now we must merely note that our understanding can work in this indirect way.

Strength and Understanding

An argument is strong when nothing we might discover is likely to demote its conclusion from the top of the ranking. This is a judgment we can often make when we know a lot about a topic, as we do in the strong arguments at which we have looked. When we securely infer from dripping people that it is raining, or that the noise in the kitchen was a breaking glass, we imply that nothing further we might learn will likely overthrow these conclusions, no matter how thoroughly we search or what luck we might have. Our understanding of such everyday matters is what makes this implication secure. If we have doubts about strength, this is the question to ask: How likely is it that ideal evidence would de-mote the number one rival? When we know enough about a topic to estimate strength, which we do in everyday, easy cases, this is the judgment we make.

Successful investigations end when they satisfy this same criterion. We begin an investigation precisely because we think the top rival is vulnerable to new in-formation. We set out to either knock it off or confirm its status. In the process we try to educate ourselves about the case so that we can judge when the ranking is secure. That is, we try to learn as much about the case as we know about argu-ments that start out strong. If we worked on the truck-crash case long enough, we might find something that raised difficulties for the sleep rival, or we could elimi-nate all the others and find sleep the overwhelming choice. We would then know as much about that case as we did about the rain and broken glass arguments.

On the other hand, not all investigations are successful. Sometimes, as in the TWA Flight 800 case, we work very hard, look at everything available, and still do not find a single rival compelling. What do we lack when this happens? There are two general possibilities, corresponding to our two categories of Specific and General Support.

We may, as in the Flight 800 investigation, understand perfectly the sort of issues and phenomena with which we are dealing, but simply lack adequate in-formation about the case itself to reach a secure conclusion. The problem is avail-ability. We know what we lack, but our search has given us reason to think we will never find it. Something not recorded or irretrievable *would* make a differ-ence. In the TWA case videotape from a chase plane, or from inside the cabin, recording the sequence of events, would make a big difference, as would very precise radar scans of the area around the plane for the few minutes before the explosion. This is just what it means to know enough to estimate the strength of an argument even when it is not very strong: the top rival in the argument sum-marizing this investigation is vulnerable to evidence an ideal search might find.

Investigations that fail in this way do not cast doubt on our competence to deal with the matter. We understand the case well enough to know that Specific evidence we do not have may be significant and may scramble the ranking of serious rivals, just as we understand the successful cases well enough to know that anything we could turn up is *not* likely to be significant. We will call such investigations "tractable," just to contrast them with investigations that fail in a more frustrating way.

What we will call "intractable" investigations are those in which we are sim-ply baffled by the case. What we need can be provided only by General Support. Common problems with everyday appliances—the ones we finally attribute to gremlins—perhaps illustrate this best. My car mysteriously quits at random in-tervals on perfectly fine days and a series of mechanics has not found anything wrong. Or channel five has a distracting shadow that no amount of tinkering with antennae or swapping sets will diminish. We do not have a short list of serious rivals to guide us and may not even know what sort of rival to formulate. The problem is intractable: our general understanding needs supplementing just to make sense of the case. This means we do not know what we lack and have no way to estimate what an ideal investigation would turn up. Worse, without a list of rivals we have nothing to apply our relevance judgment to, no way to orga-nize an efficient investigation. All we can do is try to learn more about the case, guided by our imagination and whatever hints we have, and hope for the best. Only in special circumstances do we pursue such cases very far; and we will discuss some of them in Chapter 5.

Exercise 4.25
....

Suppose we learn nothing more in the Flight 544 case we've been following (see passage in Exercise 4.3 on p. 145) and are left speculating about what happened to it. Explain whether this is a tractable or intractable failure and why. (Answer on p. 197.)

Practical Strategies

When an argument is not yet strong for any one of the natural rivals, it may already be strong for a rival we can artificially construct by lumping two (or more) of the natural ones together. Rivals can usefully be lumped only when what they have in common is significant for us, but that happens occasionally. In the disappearance of Travis Busby, for instance, the top three rivals may be these:

C_1: He committed suicide.
C_2: He was murdered.
C_3: He died in a boating accident.

Given what we know, we may think none of them is very much better than either of the others. We would, nevertheless, be willing to say that *one of them* is certainly true: the IQ's answer almost certainly falls in the part of the balloon covered by these three rivals. So we can construct a superrival (C_x) covering that whole area, lumping together all three wedges (Figure 4.9). C_x says that Busby *either* killed himself, or was murdered, or died in a boating accident. And the evidence we have makes this superrival virtually certain. The argument is very strong when this rival is used as its conclusion.

This superrival would be interesting for most people connected with Busby, because what the three lumped rivals have in common is that he is dead. This would matter for Busby's family, his employer, his creditors, and his insurance company, because they all would be affected in one way or another by his death. That is to say, C_x is a significant rival in this context. And the evidence for that may be overwhelming, even when it is not for any of the smaller wedges.

Exercise 4.26
....

Suppose you turn on your computer and it seems to come to life (diodes flash, you hear characteristic beeps), but nothing shows up on the monitor screen. The problem could be anything from forgetting to plug something in to bad hardware. For the investigation, however, you might reasonably lump all the rivals into two big categories and concentrate your attention on one of these. What lumping would be reasonable? (Answer on p. 197.)

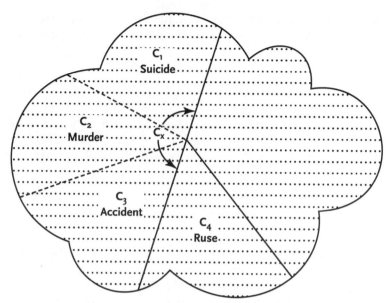

Figure 4.9. Joining rivals into superrivals.

Putting rivals together into superrivals is of course simply the opposite of the "splitting" of them we discussed earlier in the chapter. Our thinking about arguments—and investigations—will often be made easier if we remember both of these possibilities. When our interest is in distinctions "within" a particular rival, we may split it into many: $C_1 = C_a + C_b + C_c$, and argue for one of these as opposed to the others. This is what we did in thinking about the hung jury on p. 161 (see Figure 4.7). When we want to think about what distinct rivals have in common, we reverse the process and join rivals together: $C_x = C_1 + C_2 + C_3$, for instance. The "+" in each case corresponds to the word "or" in our locating of possibilities. Saying the right answer falls in C_x is saying it falls in *either* C_1 or C_2 or C_3. Joining them together in C_x means that, for the moment at least, we do not care about the differences. We split them, as we saw earlier, when the differences become important.

You will find many contexts in which joining rivals together will allow you to generate strong, useful arguments. A very different way to do this arises in arguments for recommendations, that is, for conclusions we have called "normative" (conclusions about what's the right thing to do, what we ought to do). What sometimes happens in cases such as our "route home" argument (IQ: which route should I take?) is that we may do a thorough investigation, learn all we can about the matter, and still find two rivals tied or close together at the top of the ranking. C_2 and C_3 are about equally good, so something quite trivial might reverse whatever order we now have. Here we cannot combine them in any useful sense: we cannot *do* both (take both routes), and what they have in common is simply "going home," which is not helpful.

But we may lump them together in another way. For what we have discovered is that there is little difference between them, so it doesn't much matter which we choose. I may do one *or* the other pretty much indifferently. Simply choosing one becomes more important than *which* one you choose. Flip a coin. Life is filled with decisions in which the alternatives are clear but of nearly indistinguishable merit. We choose among them more or less randomly. I may prefer a window seat to one on the aisle and the forward cabin to the rear. If I must choose between a forward aisle seat and one by a window at the rear, I may as well flip a coin. The important thing is simply to make a choice. Among closely ranked rivals, it is of little consequence which you choose. This is another sense in which the right answer is a superrival: $C_2 + C_3$.

DEALING WITH DISAGREEMENT

We began this chapter by talking of disagreement, but it has not figured much in the subsequent analysis. We started off with it to provide the project with some urgency: when two generally competent people draw different conclusions from the same data we feel most acutely the problems that can arise in our reasoning. But disagreement turns out to be inessential to understanding the problems. To see why, look again at the picture of reasoning and argument we have developed.

To give reasons for a conclusion, according to our analytical apparatus, is to make the complex claim that we have called (A). It may be paraphrased like this:

THE PROPOSITIONS OFFERED AS REASONS HAVE PLAYED THE CRUCIAL ROLE IN SORTING THROUGH POSSIBLE ANSWERS OF A PARTICULAR QUESTION TO FIND THE RIGHT ONE.

To further articulate this sorting process we needed, in addition to questions and answers, notions such as rivalry, relevance, contrast, seriousness, ranking, and gaps. Problems arise when something in a case makes any of these matters unclear. Reasoning becomes a struggle when we cannot settle confidently on an implicit question, for example, or we fail to grasp the conclusion's contrast, or have trouble deciding how to divide up the possibilities, or judging relevance, or the seriousness or ranking of the rivals. People can disagree about each of these things, of course. But we can just as well struggle with them when reasoning alone, or with others of the same mind. Disagreement is not required to raise these possibilities, nor is it part of articulating them. That is why it has not explicitly entered our analysis.

Our experience with disagreement does nevertheless provide part of our interest in reasoning. In this section we will look at the different ways disagreement can matter to our reasoning. But first we must deal with two preliminaries. Talking of disagreement necessarily makes our discussion personal in a way it has not been before. Instead of focusing on the contextual detail surrounding support and conclusion, we want to talk about different people reasoning differently about the same case. So to keep the individual reasoners straight, I will frequently use the first-person pronoun, and talk about *my* reasoning, and the contrast will then be with somebody else who does not agree with it.

The second preliminary concerns how I should think about disagreement when I find it. Since our central interest is in the reasoning, not particular reasoners, the answer is we should think of disagreement *as information*. When somebody disagrees with my reasoning, the intelligent thing to do is treat that fact as simply more data to be assessed as relevant or irrelevant, depending on detail and context. We are already familiar with the extreme cases. Sometimes someone's drawing a different conclusion is very important, and I may even substitute their reasoning for my own (the expert). Sometimes it is simply irrelevant, something to be ignored (the ignoramus).[13] We may use what we have learned in this chapter to say something about what makes the difference in such cases, and to articulate several other possibilities too.

Understanding the Disagreement

To use disagreement as information—to judge its impact on our reasoning—we must of course understand it. We should now be prepared to appreciate how much harder that is than it looks. For disagreement often catches us by surprise and our natural first reaction is too simple: "Here's the support, there's the conclusion. How could anybody not see that those are good reasons for that?" But our analysis of argument has revealed a great deal of complex detail under the surface that must be clearly in place before we can evaluate any S/C relationship. Disagreement can lurk anywhere in that detail. Two people may not have the same IQ in mind; and we have seen that the same conclusion may be a good answer for one question but a bad one for another. The two may even have the same question (sentence) in mind, but still be thinking of a completely different balloon of possibilities. So the support will not be choosing from the same list of rivals for the two interlocutors. Or they might get to the same balloon of possibilities but not divide it into rivals in the same way because they have different views on what is a trivial difference and what is significant. And so on.

Even though Willie Sutton was making a joke, he showed us that "Why rob banks?" might easily be taken to be asking about two wholly different sets of possibilities. But consider a case closer to ordinary reasoning. My friend Goran and I look at the same analysis of the national drug problem, for instance, and come away saying very different-sounding things. I say I think drugs should be legalized. He replies that such a suggestion is absurd and dangerous, and even making it shows I'm a lunatic. But as we discuss the issue it gradually becomes clear that what he means by "legalize" is not at all what I had in mind. He thought I simply meant to get rid of all laws governing drugs, allowing unrestricted buying and selling of any substance whatever. But that seems lunatic to me too. I explain that sensible legalization would require some fairly intricate regulatory apparatus, certainly more complex than that governing the sale of alcohol. After a bit of elaboration he may then concede that if that's all I meant, then we do not

---

13. Disagreement may of course affect my life without affecting my reasoning. If my passenger doesn't buy my judgment about the best route home, that may give me reason to take a different one (for the sake of peace), but may be irrelevant to my reasoning about which would be fastest. We are concerned here only with disagreement that affects my reasoning.

disagree very much at all. Here we had in mind the same balloon of possibilities, but had divided it up differently, generating merely an apparent disagreement.

Coming to understand such a difference does not automatically eliminate the disagreement, of course. We may each think the other has the *wrong* grouping of possibilities, or the *wrong* IQ, or the *wrong* contrast. Which is to say we really do disagree. But if I have pursued it this far, I at least understand where the disagreement lies, and this makes it more useful to me. I might come to see subtleties in the argument I had overlooked in my enthusiasm. On the other hand, I might find that Goran's interest in the matter is so far from my own that conversation between us cannot be productive. He has no reason to think about mine, nor I his.

Disagreement of any of these kinds is too varied and too personal to allow general treatment. The only general advice we have uncovered in our exploration is to avoid two-answer IQs. These are a real hazard in discussing large-scale social issues such as drug legalization. Seeing what's hidden in "not-C" will often be enormously revealing. Otherwise, no formula or mechanism will help much. But the apparatus we have designed to analyze arguments gives us both a way to discover whether disagreement is genuine, and some assistance in locating it when it is. This should help. Because I must be clear about *where* the disagreement lies before I can intelligently deal with it—or see that I do not have to deal with it—in my reasoning.

Using the Disagreement

Two people may agree on all of the structural preliminaries, of course, and still not draw the same conclusion. Goran and I may have in mind exactly the same question, exactly the same possibilities, exactly the same division of them into rivals, and even exactly the same support, and still disagree on the reasoning. We may not find the same rivals serious or agree on their ranking or find the same gaps even if we do have the same ranking. How can I use information such as this to benefit my reasoning?

Often quite easily. Differences of this sort indicate that Goran and I do not come to this issue with the same resources. We have understandings that differ on the matter in question. And this is the key to treating such cases. For sometimes Goran's understanding will be obviously better than mine and sometimes not. The section on investigations began exploring the way we can use superior understanding in our reasoning. So we can begin to deal with disagreement simply by expanding on the discussion started there. Then, it will turn out, the other cases can be handled by a further adaptation of the same considerations.

EXPLOITING SUPERIOR UNDERSTANDING

Finding a superior understanding can affect our reasoning in one of three constructive ways. In the simplest, a superior understanding may be able to supplement the inferior one with some General Support, which then allows it the same judgment as the superior one. When someone better informed tells me about the altitude limit of Stinger missiles, I may then be able to rank the "missile" rival in the TWA crash as well as those who knew all about such things from the beginning. The second way we may use a superior understanding in our reasoning is to exploit it in testimony form. Investigators may discover some suspicious-looking residue on a piece of wreckage and know that their own understanding cannot easily be supplemented to grasp its significance, so they turn it over to forensic chemists for analysis. To use what the chemist says as evidence the investigators must understand something of people and institutions (see Chapters 5 and 6 for more on this), but need not understand the *chemistry*. Finally, in this last sort of case, I may decide to bring my own understanding up to the level of the expert, by taking courses, getting degrees, or availing myself of training or experience of some other kind. If successful, what I thus gain cannot appear in an argument; but it allows me to judge Specific Support I could not judge before. My advanced understanding may then be exploited by others in testimony form.

Keep in mind that both whether Goran's understanding is better than mine *and* exactly how to exploit that fact are my judgments to make. My understanding of things must be up to that at least. But it often is. In clear and uncontroversial cases we are reasonably good at estimating the security of our own understanding, and, hence, the opportunity for expertise. I am very confident of my reasoning about rain, from the drips and the umbrellas; but I am far less secure in my thinking about the wilting plant, even before I run into my botanical friend. And I know I haven't a clue about the PETN residue on the piece of wreckage. So I have a good idea where to expect superior understanding. We also have resources that allow us to estimate the limits of expertise (again, see Chapter 6 for more on this). A chemistry Ph.D. may understand vastly more than I do about what's happening on the stove as I cook. But that may not make her a better cook and may not make her reasoning about *what to do* with the stuff on the stove any better (or even as good) as my own. I may know from experience that I can turn out a pretty good soufflé. I reasonably doubt that anything my chemist friend knows about oxidation, reduction, or the nature of the molecular bond will improve on my technique. The point is that there is nothing automatic about what to do with a superior understanding, once we've found it. It is simply more data to be taken into account in our reasoning.

Exercise 4.27
....

Look at the following cases and note where we exploit superior understanding in our reasoning. (a) Medfly hoax argument in Chapter 3 (p. 127). (b) Danny Hamilton's disappearance (Exercise 4.7, p. 152). (c) The coyote carcasses in Exercise 4.21 (p. 177). (Answers on p. 197.)

To raise one final possibility under the heading of "superior understanding," let us return to my friend and me, reasoning differently about some matter of common concern. It could be that Goran's understanding is superior to mine, and relevant to our reasoning, but that I have no way to know this. What should I then do? Well, if I really cannot see the superiority, then I cannot exploit it. And the best I can do is treat our disagreement as the simple discovery of a different understanding. That is the subject of the next section.

DIFFERENT BUT EQUIVALENT UNDERSTANDINGS

If Goran and I reach different conclusions because we have different understandings of a matter, but neither understanding is clearly superior, how can I use that in my reasoning? Well, at a minimum it should caution modesty. For it shows that this case is not like the best of our everyday reasoning, in which everybody with roughly normal understanding reasons the same way. Part of our confidence in our reasoning about traffic lights, hot stoves, and cloudbursts comes from the widespread *intersubjectivity* of it. When somebody, whose competence I cannot simply dismiss, does not reason the same way as I do about something, that should raise a flag: I cannot have the same confidence here, say, as I would driving through a green light (inferring that the cross street is red).

If the question is not terribly important to me, I can leave the matter there. I can simply note this sign of imperfect understanding and go on to other things. But, as always, I may do more if I wish: I may improve my reasoning on the matter by making an effort to *learn more*, by *investigating*. But here we need to improve our grasp not just of the substance of the issue (the route home, the drug problem) but also of the quality of understanding that Goran and I bring to bear on it. I know that my understanding of the matter is not good enough to simply dismiss his disagreement as irrelevant; so one thing an investigation can do is help see how much weight I should attach to his judgment. Although it can do this in many different ways, they fall into three interesting categories. I may discover that Goran's understanding is actually superior to mine, and hence to be exploited in the usual way. Or I may discover that my understanding is better, so I can ignore his. Or I may find that we are actually operating at about the same level.

Much of what we would do in such an investigation would be just like any other investigation. In particular, we might look for General Support that would improve either or both of our understandings and perhaps bring our judgments closer together. But discovering the credentials of someone's understanding does allow one further application of our analytic apparatus. This is discussed in the following section.

Exercise 4.28

....

Describe a case from personal experience in which you disagreed with someone about some issue that you both probably did not understand very well.

The Credentials of Understanding

Investigating understanding is as complicated as investigating anything else, so no simple guidelines constrain it. But the possibility of such investigations allows the vocabulary developed in this chapter one more useful application. We usually have a reasonably good feel for the adequacy of our understanding to reason about every-day, uncontroversial issues. (Remember things such as the rain, the plant, and the explosive residue.) If asked to say why I think better of my judgment in one area than another, I could doubtless say something useful about my particular experi-ence and training. But when the credentials of my understanding are controversial, as in the disagreements discussed in the last section, it would be useful to articu-late them in a general and topic-neutral way. As you might expect, we may achieve such an articulation using our new analytical concepts.

Ordinary investigations work by improving our understanding of a particu-lar issue, such as a crash, the roots of a plant, or current traffic conditions. The procedure is *systematic exposure to relevant data*. We purposely look in places where information relevant to various different understandings would show up and be hard to miss. We examine pieces of the crashed plane and interview witnesses. We talk to botanists about the plant problem and experiment with the watering schedule. We listen to the traffic report and check the local streets by eye. We know an understanding that arises and survives in *this* environment will be bet-ter than one not exposed to it. In the right conditions, what we learn can elimi-nate all rival understandings and establish one as uncontested. We find good signs of one and nothing of the others *in spite of looking hard for them*. We searched for signs of collision and nothing was found. We are confident because were we far wrong that would have shown up somewhere in one or another of the places we checked. We could not have missed it.

The credentials of our basic understanding may be articulated in a similar fashion. The part of our understanding in which we can have the most confidence is the part that is most "exposed," exposed to the world and exposed to the con-sequences of being wrong. We constantly depend on some parts of our under-standing for simply getting around—recognizing people, finding exits, telling time, avoiding various pains and obstructions. Consequently, that understanding is always being tested and refined. We would notice immediately if it were very far wrong. We would suffer incessant disappointment, bang into walls, fall off things, hurt ourselves, and terrify everybody. So it is self-correcting. Other parts of our understanding, by contrast, could be pretty awful and never have a bad consequence, never draw our attention at all. I could be confused about the eco-nomics of floating exchange rates or the topography of Peru and never notice it in the course of my life.

From a general point of view then, my basic, solid, understanding of things has accumulated just as though it had been the result of an investigation. It has survived in an environment that would have killed it off had it been far wrong. If called on to give the credentials of any bit of my general understanding of things, all I could do—and all I should have to do—would be to point out how well tested it is in the course of my life. This is not trivial: we can find that we're mistaken about such things. I can discover the particular experiences of my life have not tested my understanding of something as well as I thought, that I've gotten away with a misunderstanding because it does not cause much trouble. This is why perfectly intelligent people could think the earth is flat, or not know which pair of wheels drives their car. But for really basic things, such as what people look like and how doors work, fundamental misunderstanding could simply not go unnoticed in most twentieth (or twenty-first) century lives.

Exercise 4.29
....

Which of the following is more secure and why? Inflation is not much of a threat in the United States. Air will remain in the classroom during the lecture. You'd recognize a good friend if you saw her unexpectedly. (Answer on p. 197.)

SUPPLEMENTAL EXERCISES

A. Review Questions

1. Explain to someone unfamiliar with the notion what an argument's IQ is.

2. Describe the relation between the conclusion of an argument and its rivals.

3. How do a conclusion's "natural" rivals help you understand the conclusion?

4. Complete: An item of information is relevant in an argument if . . .

5. When people disagree in their reasoning, that may be traceable to several different aspects of an argument. Give three.

6. Why does an investigation require some suspicions?

7. How might a tractable investigation become intractable?

8. Identify the General Support offered in the argument of Supplemental Exercise 3 of Chapter 3. Explain why it is General and not Specific.

B. Passages for Analysis

1. On his way home from work, Ivan Potter's car crashed through a freeway guardrail and rolled down an embankment into a shallow stream. Examination of his corpse at the crash site by a qualified physician revealed no broken bones or external injuries. So it is reasonable to think that Ivan's death caused the accident rather than the other way around.
   a. Schematize the reasoning in this passage.
   b. What rival conclusion is being explicitly rejected in the passage?
   c. The natural IQ is "How did Ivan die?" but the conclusion and its rival do not provide very detailed answers to this question, but simply divide the possibilities balloon into three large superwedges. Describe the wedges and give more specific rivals in each of the two mentioned wedges.
   d. Think up some new support that might turn up in the investigation and explain its relevance.

2. The philosophy department secretary duplicated 100 copies of a Philosophy 7 homework assignment this week and entrusted them to the teaching assistants. Yet the last few students to leave class on Wednesday found that all the homework sheets had already been taken. Because only 81 students have registered for the class this term, it must be the case that the teaching assistants cannot be trusted to carry a handful of papers across campus without losing some of them.

    a. What conclusion is drawn in this passage?

    b. What IQ is it answering?

    c. Give two rival conclusions, one better (higher ranking on the data given) and the other worse (lower) than the one in a.

    d. What does your answer in (c) tell you about the soundness of the argument in the passage?

    e. Provide some relevant new information and articulate its relevance.

3. S_1 For as long as his parents can remember, eleven-year-old Johnny has had difficulty breathing, tired easily, and was thought to be asthmatic.

    S_2 Recently, physicians discovered a toy brick lodged in one of Johnny's lungs and when it was removed, Johnny's breathing difficulty immediately vanished.

    C Johnny's breathing problem was due to the toy brick.

    a. What is this argument's implicit question.

    b. No rival conclusions can be very serious given the support in this argument. Recognizing this, state two rivals that might become serious on easily describable discoveries (just give the rivals, not the discoveries).

    c. Think of some new information that would be relevant and articulate its relevance.

    d. Is the new information you added in (c) Specific or General support? Explain.

    4. On my way home from work the motor in my old car sputters to a stop. Before switching off the key I notice that the fuel gauge reads empty. On reflection, I don't remember filling up lately, so I figure I must be out of gas. I grab the can from the trunk and start walking.

    a. In this passage I do a little reasoning and reach a well-flagged conclusion. Schematize my argument.

    b. Give two rival conclusions I'm obviously rejecting (make them as serious as possible).

    c. Why would "something's wrong with the car" be a poor way to express a rival?

    d. What is the implicit question I'm trying to answer?

    e. Give an example of a rival that is not serious.

    f. Articulate the relevance of the fuel gauge reading.

    g. Think of some relevant new information and articulate its relevance.

ANSWERS

4.1   **a.** Q: Why are the oncoming cars using their wipers?
          A: We are driving into rain.

       b. Q: How will the smoking ban be received?
          A: It will meet with opposition.

       c. Q: What blew up the motel?
          A: A maintenance worker investigating the lack of hot water.

4.2   **a.** IQ: What should we do about the wasted seats?
          A: Give them to senior citizens and drama students.

       b. IQ: What happened to Steve's valuables?
          A: The car was burgled.

[*Note:* Though it would be clumsy, there would be nothing wrong with an IQ asking about all of the first three support claims. It would also be answered naturally by the same conclusion.]

4.3   **a.** S_1 Nothing has been heard from Flight 544 since contact was lost with it as it flew into a storm hours ago.

S_2 It is four hours overdue at its destination.

C It has crashed.

b. **i.** What happened to Flight 544?

ii. Why did we lose contact with Flight 544?

The first IQ would be better because main interest in the context is in different possible dispositions of the aircraft (and hence whether there's any hope for those on board), not different ways contact might be lost. A single answer to question (ii) (radio failure due to lightning strike) might correspond to radically different answers to question (i) (crash versus safe emergency landing at a remote airstrip), which, again, is the central concern.

4.4   **a.** The community would benefit from filling the Arts Center's empty seats with senior citizens and drama students, and performers would enjoy the larger crowd. This recommends "Give the surplus tickets to senior citizens and drama students" as the right answer to "What should we do about the Arts Center's wasted seats?"

b. The maintenance worker who had been called to investigate the lack of hot water was the one most seriously injured in the subsequent explosion. This recommends "The maintenance worker caused it" as the answer to "What blew up the motel?"

4.5   **a.** Rejected answers to "What to do about wasted seats?"

C_2: Lower ticket prices.

C_3: Give them to other groups of needy people.

C_4: Nothing.

C_5: Abandon unpopular plays and use the place for something else.

b. Rejected answers to "What happened to Flight 544?"

C_2: Made an emergency landing at an abandoned airstrip.

C_3: It is still flying somehow.

4.6   **a.** S_1 There was a crash in the kitchen.

S_2 A broken glass was found on the floor immediately afterward.

S_3 Nothing else was obviously out of place.

C The crash was the glass breaking.

b. Rejected answers to "What was that crash in the kitchen?"

C_2: The crash was a window breaking.

C_3: The crash was broadcast by a radio on the counter.

c. C_{3a}: The crash was an AM radio broadcast.

C_{3b}: The crash was a FM radio broadcast.

4.7.   **a.** Answers for "What happened to Hamilton?"

He died.

He's been hospitalized.

He decided to do something else for a living.

He's been abducted.

b. Answers for "Why did Hamilton abandon his rig?"

To help somebody in trouble.

He was tired of his job.

He was offered a lucrative scam.
He was abducted.
He was hurt and needed help.

c. Answers for "Why did he leave his rig there?"
That's where he'd arranged a rendezvous.
That's where he was forced to stop.
Somebody needed help there.
He had to go to the bathroom.

4.8 a. A carelessness rival would overlap with the maintenance worker (m/w) conclusion: one whole range of the m/w wedge would have him not being careful in investigating the leak.

b. Poor ventilation would overlap with the m/w conclusion in something like the same way: many different m/w possibilities would have the propane buildup he ignited be due to poor ventilation of water heater room.

c. Mortar fire would overlap with the terrorist rival.

d. A gas line cut in a suicide attempt would overlap with the m/w conclusion: that could be the source of the leak that made the water cold and that the m/w ignited when he came to investigate.

4.9 a. The original (C_1) rival would have to be read, "Keep the price the same and give whatever surplus tickets there are to seniors and drama students."

b. i. All the ways the glass could have gotten broken are included in C_1 (the broken-glass rival). So Charlie's clumsily knocking it off the counter is already on the list of rivals.

   ii. One way to include Charlie's clumsiness on the list would be to remove it from C_1, by making it read, C_{1a}: "The noise was the glass breaking, but Charlie didn't have anything to do with it." Then we could add to the list, C_{1b}: The noise was Charlie clumsily knocking the glass off the counter," as a distinct rival.

4.10 a. Journalist's:
Question: "Why do you rob banks?"
Contrast: Instead of doing something else for a living.
List of rival answers:
- for the excitement.
- because of the challenge.
- so much more money than I could make any other way.
- it's all I know how to do.
- revenge on capitalism for all its evil.

b. Sutton's:
Question: "Why do I rob banks?"
Contrast: Instead of robbing other things.
List of rival answers:
- because of the elegant architecture.
- they're quiet and the people are polite.
- you're indoors and out of the weather.
- they're clean and don't smell bad, like some places.

4.11 a. i. Rivals in the "it wasn't a car crash" part of the balloon:
- URMM was walking on the shoulder of the road, slipped and fell to his death, ending up tangled in the old wreck.
- He was killed elsewhere and his body dumped there.
- He suffered a heart attack while hiking and died leaning on the car.

    ii. Rivals to the CHP conclusion, in the car crash part of the balloon
- URMM died at the wheel and the car went off the road there.
- He survived the crash but was injured and couldn't escape hungry predators.

  b. **i.** C_1: The infestation continues apace, filling all the traps daily. C_2: Although spraying seems to be making progress, many areas are still producing large numbers of fertile fruit flies.

    ii. C_3: Local infestations of battered and unhealthy-looking fruitflies existed in a few areas. C_4: Somebody realized the infestation persisted but the traps were incompetent and so put some flies in the traps to keep the spraying going.

4.12 C_4 Bad weather. C_5 Pilot error. C_6 Collision with another aircraft. C_7 Hijacking.

4.13 Because all we know about the case is that there was a hot water problem, the other serious rivals would be related to that. So the serious part of the balloon would contain, in addition to the maintenance worker rival, other stories about how the heater's propane might have built up in the wrong place and been ignited.

4.14 **a.** The only kind of Bermuda Triangle rival that we'd take seriously is already part of the conclusion ("crashed"), and nothing in the support could justify separating this fraction of C_1 out and making it a rival on its own. Several million just like it would be as reasonable.

  b. Given what we know, hijacking in general would not be serious—so any particular hijacking would be even less so. Additionally, some version of "hijacked to Cuba" would already be on the list: the one in which it lands at a remote airfield to refuel.

4.15 **a.** Ranking

    Flight 544 has crashed.
    It has made an emergency landing.
    It is still flying somehow.

  b. S_1 Nothing has been heard from Flight 544 since contact was lost as it flew into a storm hours ago.
    S_2 It is four hours overdue at its destination.

    C: It has crashed. ($\leftarrow$ Whatever tops the ranking goes here)

4.16 Unhelpful (two-answer questions): b, d, e, and g.

4.17 **a.** Did the maintenance worker blow up the motel?
  b. Did the driver fall asleep at the wheel?
  c. Is this an ancient pioneer trail?
  d. Did one juror make up his mind before deliberations?

4.18 **a.** S_1 The wind blew hard last night.
    S_2 The garbage can moved from its normal location to some place on the other side of the car.
    S_3 The car is scratched on the side facing the can's original location.
    S_4 The scratches are about rolling-can height.
    S_5 The scratches are new.
    S_6 The can is metal.

    C The windblown can scratched the car.

  b. The serious rivals would be ranked:

    C The windblown can scratched the car.
    C_2 Something else blown by the wind did it.
    C_3 Vandals scratched it.

The relevance of the wind would then be articulated thus: If the wind had not blown hard last night, the first two rivals would not be on the serious list.

4.19 **a.** We could allow the hit-man rival on the list if we modified the murder rival (C_2) to read:

C_2': Busby was killed by someone other than a loan shark's hit man.

   b. The level of detail criterion could always be covered by criterion 1: "Changes the list of serious rivals." For lumping or splitting rivals always does this too.

   c. **i.** The movement of the can (S_2) elevates C in the ranking (makes it better relative to the other two than it would be without S_2).
   If the scratches were not where they are (S_3 and S_4), C would be lower than it is in the ranking (at least the gap to the others would be reduced, perhaps even its ranking would change).
   The newness of the scratches (S_5) is what makes any of these serious rivals: it determines the list.
   If we did not know the can was metal, that would make it a far worse rival: nonmetal cans would not easily scratch a car.

   ii. S_6 (paint on the chair) would help C_2: at least reduce the gap from it to C.
   C_7 (rash of vandalism) would help C_3 in the same way.
   C_8 (no paint on can) would drop C in the ranking (at least reduce the gap to the others).

4.20 **a.** S_1 URMM's skeleton was found in a wrecked car.
   S_2 He had been missing for six months.
   S_3 The wreck was at the bottom of a cliff, far from populated areas.

   C URMM died in a traffic accident.

   b. Both ends of this case are puzzles. So this argument has three characteristics typical of many puzzle solutions and that affect the way relevance is articulated. First, there are no serious rivals: the case is so bizarre that even C was not serious before discovering the skeleton. Second, and also typical, the support is tailored to its conclusion, not just the implicit question. And finally, each support claim contains a large piece of the puzzle, without which even C would not be very serious. So articulating relevance will consist in showing why C would not be serious without each piece.
   S_1: Being found tangled up in a wrecked car is what makes C a reasonable speculation. Without S_1 C would not be any more serious than many other manners of disappearance.
   S_2: Finding a skeleton in a wrecked car would not be evidence for death in a crash unless the crash took place a long time ago. So, again, C is serious, even *given* S_1, only because of S_2.
   S_3: Again, the accident must have happened months ago. So the fact that the wreck was found where a crash might have gone undetected is crucial to the seriousness of C. If the wreck were found in a public place, the possibility that the car crashed there and was not noticed is no longer serious: something else must be going on.

4.21 **a.** C: The carcasses are coyotes (not dogs).
   b. General Support: Small animals and birds are typical coyote food.

4.22 **a.** The item of General Support is the observation by Alumbaugh that when drivers abandon a truck "they leave it at a truck stop where they can get a ride."

    b. This is relevant to answering, "What happened to Hamilton?" because one of the options we must seriously consider on the sketchy information available is that he voluntarily abandoned the truck; and Alumbaugh's observation hurts that answer a bit in the ranking.

4.23   **a.** The sort of thing that would count as relevant new information would be (i) explosion and smoke spotted rising from a hillside along 544's flight path four hours ago; (ii) report of an airliner at an abandoned air strip nearby; (iii) an oil slick and pieces of a plane like 544 washing up on the shore of a lake in the area; (iv) observation of 544 (or a plane that could have been 544) refueling from an Air Force tanker two hours ago.

    b. Relevance would be articulated in the usual way, by explaining which rivals would be helped, hurt, or made serious by the information in question.

4.24 General information relevant to the Flight 544 case would be how well planes of that type do in violent weather, the airline's practice on carrying extra fuel, and perhaps the competence and resourcefulness of the flight crew.

4.25 This would be a standard case of a tractable failure. We know all sorts of specific support that would resolve the puzzle if we only had it: not just cockpit videotape, but radar traces, satellite tracking, observations by other aircraft, and an inventory of objects at the bottom of nearby bodies of water.

4.26 It would be reasonable to lump rivals into C_i: Things you can fix yourself and C_{ii}: Things you'd have to have an expert work on. You would then reasonably concentrate on C_i first.

4.27   **a.** Our reasoning about the medfly case depends on our accepting Dick Jackson's educated perception of what normal medflies look like when freshly caught and, to a lesser extent, what sort of changes in the daily catch would be surprising.

    b. Bob Alumbaugh's understanding of trucking clearly helps us see what kind of puzzle is raised by finding Hamilton's rig "out in the boonies."

    c. To the extent that we can reason about the mysterious animal carcasses at all, it depends on Vicki Young's understanding of what coyote's eat.

4.29 The obvious order of security (from most to least) would be as follows:

    1. Air will remain in the classroom during the lecture.
    2. You'd recognize a good friend if you ran into her unexpectedly.
    3. Inflation is not much of a threat in the United States.

And the reason is that this order reflects the competence your judgment has developed in simply leading your life. The part of your understanding relevant to air in the room is tested constantly under all sorts of different conditions. That related to recognizing people is tested somewhat less constantly and rigorously, but still quite a lot. And no matter how much you read about economics, your understanding will not underwrite an inflation forecast nearly as well as the other two.

CHAPTER 5

DIAGNOSTIC ARGUMENTS
Reasoning by Explaining

> **OVERVIEW** Arguments in which we reason by explaining data exploit our understanding so directly that they deserve to be singled out as basic. We call them "diagnostic" arguments, and they help us articulate our evaluation of reasoning.

INTRODUCTION

The apparatus introduced in Chapter 4 allows us to articulate the "internal structure" of argument. It gives us a neutral way to describe the key substantive elements of the reasoning: the question addressed, the answer given, the other answers possible, and the way they relate to each other. This by itself is enough to help us evaluate some arguments. Improving our articulateness about these issues will sometimes improve our judgment about which rival is best or what the serious competition is. But as yet we have no systematic way to talk about evaluation, even when it is clear. Our apparatus does not say much about what's going on when support makes a rival serious, or changes its ranking. For this we are again left with whatever vocabulary seems useful, which does not help much when reasoning is difficult.

In this chapter we expand our apparatus to include the *relation between support and rivals* in very basic arguments. Recall that our ability to judge the impact of support on rivals rests on our general understanding of everything relevant. We must add to our analytical vocabulary something about the way both support and rivals relate to that understanding. This should help us say something general about *how* support affects the seriousness and ranking of rivals. It should allow us to talk about what makes rivals better or worse. We will find that support may relate to rivals in these basic arguments in two very different ways. Taking note of this distinction will not just increase our articulateness, it will reveal some new and interesting patterns that we may exploit in our thinking about argument and evidence. It will also give us particular things to look for in the investigations to which these arguments naturally lead.

DIAGNOSTIC QUESTIONS

The very basic arguments we will deal with in this chapter are called "diagnostic." This is because their implicit questions request something like a *diagnosis*. They ask "What's going on here?" or "What happened there?" So their rival conclusions will be stories about what's going on or what happened somewhere. Many of the arguments we have already examined are diagnostic in this sense. Good examples of diagnostic IQs may be drawn from those examples:

Why did the truck crash?

What was that noise in the kitchen?

How did the motel blow up?

Where did all these bones come from?

Who killed the president?

Each of these would be answered by stories—sometimes very abbreviated stories—about what happened somewhere: stories about the crash, or the noise, or how all those bones got out there in the desert. Arguments with IQs and rivals such as these will help us peer more deeply into reasoning.

Of course not all questions beginning with our characteristic interrogative words request a simple diagnosis. "What should we do with the wasted seats at the Arts Center?" asks for a *recommendation*, a proposal for action, something very different from a simple story about what's going on. And "How high will the stock market go this year?" requests a *forecast*. Predictions and recommendations may be *based on* a diagnosis of what's going on in the case in question. But in offering a recommendation or prediction they go beyond merely telling a story about what's happening somewhere. Predictions and recommendations are treated in Chapter 7. We will first need to examine the reasoning behind simple diagnosis.

Diagnostic arguments are especially important because they are tied so closely to our understanding of how the world works, which is the main resource we use in reasoning. The rival conclusions in a diagnostic argument all answer an IQ requesting some understanding: questions of the form, "What's going on?" So diagnostic rivals are simply *rival understandings* of something, of what happened to Flight 800, for instance, or how the bones came to be on the trail in Nevada. Put another way, diagnostic rivals are different views on how one little chunk of the world works, or how it once worked (in the case of a past event). For a few minutes one evening over the Atlantic Ocean off Long Island, a Boeing 747 belonging to TWA disintegrated spectacularly. One understanding of what went on there involves a bomb on board the plane, another involves a missile launched from below, another alleges a malfunction of one of the plane's components, and yet another alleges collision with a second aircraft.[1] Diagnostic rivals are simply different (incompatible) ways in which a certain event or case may be understood. Because all reasoning—and everything else we do—rests on how we understand things in this way, diagnosis is the most basic reasoning we do.

Our general understanding of how the world works is simply the sum total of what we have learned from many diagnostic encounters with it over the years. Every time we have a new experience, we gain something else to add to our picture of the world. Our ability to do this has enormous survival value. We can make our way in the world only because we are so good at diagnosis. So, if we can articulate what goes on in diagnostic reasoning, we will be able to talk about the basic skill we all use when we reason. We will be able to say, in a neutral and systematic way, not just *what* rival is right, but also a bit about *why*.

DIAGNOSTIC CONCEPTS

Explanation

Fortunately, diagnostic arguments do permit a higher level of articulateness than is possible for reasoning in general. A systematic expansion of our analytical vocabulary applies just to these basic arguments. The object is to exploit the unique, explanatory relation between diagnostic rivals and support. Diagnostic rivals actually **Explain Some of the Support** in a diagnostic argument, and that will be immensely helpful in our project. To see why diagnostic rivals end up explaining their own support, notice where they come from. Diagnostic rivals arise in answer to questions such as "What's going on here?" or "What made that noise?" To know what the argument is about, you must know what "here" and "that noise" refer to. And we know this normally because *something happened to raise the question* in the first place: a plane exploded, a crash in the kitchen interrupted our conversation, a truck ran off the road into a barrier. Something like this will tell us where things are going on about which we're supposed to think.

In other words, in telling you what the argument is about, the initial data will actually give you *part of "what's going on"*:

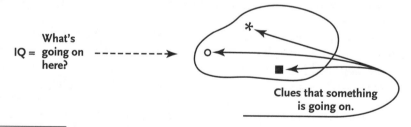

1. We referred to these as different "stories"; but, as we saw in Chapter 4, they might as well be described as "clusters of stories" about what went on at that place and time. The "bomb" rival (C_1) represents all the different stories about it that involve a bomb, and there are many of these. Many different kinds of bomb are possible, as are different locations, modes of detonation, and exact patterns in the flying pieces. Each is a different story (a different dot in the balloon), but we lump them together in a wedge of the balloon called "bomb" until we have reason to think of them separately.

These initial bits and pieces of what's going on naturally go in the argument's support: they are important clues. This tight connection between clues and IQ will allow us to advance our articulateness about diagnostic arguments in a very useful way. For the rival conclusions are stories explaining what's going on in the case in question—they all answer the question "What's going on here?" And because the initial bits are simply *part of what's going on*, the rivals will explain them too. They will explain the noise in the kitchen, the flaming debris, and the marks made by the crumpled truck. Furthermore, because these things are clues—support in the argument—we can now see how it happens that *diagnostic rivals explain some of the support* in diagnostic arguments. This is what we will exploit in this chapter.

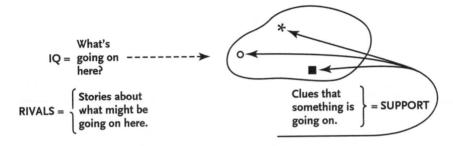

Trace Data

After we get interested in a case and look around a bit we will usually find more bits and pieces of what happened, and they will play the same role as the initial clues: they will be support explained by the rivals. We will notice patterns in the debris, glass on the kitchen floor, or the path of the truck's tires. Because it plays the crucial role in this chapter, we will need a suggestive name for this special kind of support. So let us call it **Trace Data**: these clues are *traces* of what's going on. Explaining such traces is what diagnostic argument is all about.

We will soon see that the concept of trace data (abbreviated TD) contains some complexities we will have to work on, but for now we may think of it under a rough-and-ready description: **trace data are parts or aspects or consequences of the thing the rivals are trying to explain.** They would be parts (or aspects or consequences) of the truck crash, or of the explosion of Flight 800, or of the noisy event in the kitchen. In each case we think some event has occurred, but we have only bits and pieces of it—traces of it. The rivals fill in the details of the event in different ways, and so they explain the traces as part of one kind of event or of another. With Flight 800, for instance, we begin (literally) with pieces of an event: a fireball, flaming ocean, and distribution of the wreckage. The rivals try piecing all this together as an event involving a bomb or a missile or a mechanical failure. Each tries to explain the traces in a particular way, to make sense of them as one kind of event or another.

Of course some rivals will usually explain the traces more easily than others, and this is how the concept of trace data helps us talk about *evaluating* arguments. For the more easily a rival explains the trace data, the more support those traces provide for that rival. That is, the easier time a rival has in explaining the TD, the higher it ranks. For instance, much of the TD in the Flight 800 explosion came from noting the way the pieces of the 747, recovered from the ocean floor, were bent or pierced or charred or not. These are traces left by what happened to the aircraft. And some of these things were more easily explained by one rival than by others. The particular way the central fuel tank was bent and buckled, for instance, was easily explained by a certain malfunction (fuel explosion), but harder for the rest. Lack of explosion damage on the engines is hard for a heat-seeking missile to explain but easier for the others. These and many other aspects of the debris field are traces for the rivals to explain, or perhaps to struggle with and fail to explain satisfactorily. In doing this, the rivals rise or fall in the competition for seriousness. So we may think of the relation between traces and rivals like this:

$$\text{explain} \left\uparrow \frac{\text{TRACE DATA}}{\text{RIVAL CONCLUSIONS}} = d \right\downarrow \text{support}^2$$

Diagnostic reasoning is *reasoning by explaining*, and trace data are what we explain in diagnostic arguments. These are the arguments we first noticed in the "Paired Roles" section of Chapter 2. Recall that in some of those cases an SP would have the two labels $[e_c]$ and $[r_i]$:

$$[e_c]/[r_i]$$

MP: The house just shook violently.
SP: We've had an earthquake.

The $[e_c]$ indicates that the SP is an explanation, and the $[r_i]$ indicates that it is the conclusion of an argument. Because the MP is the support in the argument, and it is explained by the conclusion of that argument, you can see that the MP must be trace data and the argument is diagnostic. All $[e_c]/[r_i]$ pairs will be diagnostic arguments like this.

Exercise 5.1
....

(a) Schematize the argument in the structured paraphrase above. (b) Identify the TD. (c) Say what makes it TD. (d) Provide one rival account of it. (Answers on p. 238.)

Recall that we chose diagnostic arguments as basic because our diagnostic skill is so deeply connected to our making our way in the world. We practice it every day of our lives,[3] so it is a very good skill and we naturally develop a rea-

---

2. We will adopt the convention of using a double line ending in a "d" to indicate that an argument is diagnostic.

3. Every perception is a diagnosis too. We tell what's going on simply by looking or listening. Many perceptions actually begin as diagnostic inference (indirect) and become perceptions simply by gaining familiarity (and losing their indirectness). When I first moved into a new apartment, I heard a peculiar, rhythmic noise coming from one part of the ceiling. I treated it as trace data, entertained rival explanations of it, and finally concluded that it was my upstairs neighbor exercising by running in place. After a few weeks I became able simply to *hear* my neighbor running in place: it had become a perception, it was no longer an inference. Innumerable perceptions have histories like this.

sonably clear sense of its limits. From our investigations so far in this chapter, we can now say something about just how it works. Our diagnostic skill is an ability to tell *what explains what*. In diagnostic arguments the second "what" will always be trace data. This is why the notion of a trace is central to seeing how our basic reasoning skill works.

Non-Trace Data (NTD)

Not all support in a diagnostic argument will be part of what's being explained, of course. Features of the surrounding circumstances can be relevant to understanding an event, for instance, without being part of that event. It is relevant to note, in the argument concerning the fate of TWA Flight 800, that the U.S. military was not firing missiles near the tip of Long Island on the evening of the crash. This hurts the ranking of the missile rival (eliminates a likely source) and hence it belongs among the supporting statements in that argument. Yet military exercises (or their lack) are not part of the event the rivals in that argument are trying to explain. The rivals answer the IQ, "What caused the plane to explode?" So they will just be stories explaining the plane's disintegration. They need not even attempt to explain all the other things going on in the neighborhood, even though those other things may be relevant to the disintegration.

Similarly in the truck crash, if we find that the driver had been driving all night, that belongs in the support: it makes the sleep rival look better. But, again, it is not a part of what the rivals are trying to explain. Sleep, suicide, and heart attack are offered as answers to the question, "What caused the crash?" In explaining this event they will explain various features and consequences of the crash as well; but they're *not even trying to explain* the many relevant things that came before it. In particular, they will not be asked to explain what made the driver think he had to stay up driving all night; things outside the argument will explain this. Nevertheless, the fact that the driver drove all night is relevant support. We will call support such as this "non-trace data" simply to give it a name, and we will abbreviate it NTD.

To exercise this distinction, consider a different example: the wilting-plant argument from Chapter 4.

> S_1 My plants are wilting.
> S_2 I water them frequently.
> S_3 Overwatering can encourage a root fungus.
> === d
> C They are suffering from root rot.

This argument is obviously diagnostic (IQ = "Why are my plants wilting?"), and all three supporting statements are relevant. But only S_1 is trace data. The conclusion explains why my plants are wilting (because the roots are rotting), and rivals would have to explain this too. The wilting is therefore trace data. The other two items of support, on the other hand, are obviously *not* trace data. The conclusion, and its rivals, are answering "Why are my plants wilting?" and in doing this they will not have to tell us *why* overwatering encourages root rot (S_3). They are just the wrong kind of thing to explain a general fact like that. Similarly for S_2, the rival accounts of my wilting plant will not even be trying to explain why I water the plants frequently.

Any diagnostic argument may contain non-trace data, of course. But arguments arising from investigations will almost always contain a great deal of it. This is because investigations typically turn up what we called "General Support" in Chapter 4. And *all* General Support (such as S_3 above) is NTD. The reverse is not true, however. Although most Specific Support will be trace data, some will be NTD, such as S_2 in the wilting-plant argument.

SUMMARY

Support in diagnostic arguments comes in two kinds, trace data and non-trace data. As a first approximation: TD are what the rivals explain; NTD are everything else that is relevant. We will refine these definitions as we go.

The basic picture of diagnostic argument looks something like this:

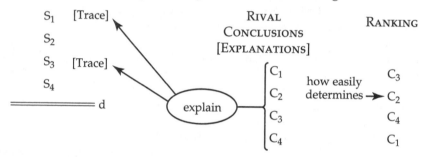

The rival conclusions are rival explanations of the trace data (S_1 and S_3). Their plausibility ranking is determined by how easily they explain the traces, given what we know generally and the additional information provided by the NTD (S_2 and S_4).

Exercise 5.2

a. The unswerving tire tracks are trace data because (T or F):
    i. They explain why the truck crashed.
    ii. This is a trick question; they are not TD.
    iii. Falling asleep at the wheel would explain them.
    iv. The tracks explain what the truck crashed into.
    v. This is something the rivals need to explain.

b. The pioneer trail argument in Chapter 4 (p. 151) is diagnostic. Answer the following T or F. The fact that the bones are from domestic animals is trace data because:
    i. That explains why Daisy thinks it's a pioneer trail.

    ii. This is something the rivals would have to explain.

    iii. This is a trick question: the domestic part isn't TD

    iv. If it's a pioneer trail, that would explain why the bones on the trail are from domestic animals.

c. The absence of nearby military exercises is NTD for the Flight 800 argument because (T or F):

    i. It can't explain a malfunction on board the plane.

    ii. It is irrelevant to the argument.

    iii. The rivals don't explain it or have to explain it.

d. Suppose we discovered and added to the wilting-plant argument the fact that fertilizer I always add to the water I give my plants contains a fungicide (a killer of fungus) (T or F):

    i. This is trace data because I'd need to explain it.

    ii. This is NTD because it is not relevant.

    iii. This is NTD because it is not something the rivals would explain.

e. Identify the NTD in the following argument, and explain why they are not trace data.

    S_1 A motel exploded while a maintenance worker was trying to discover why there was no hot water in the bathrooms.

    S_2 The water was heated by propane.

    S_3 Propane is highly explosive when properly mixed with air.

    $=\!=\!=\!=$ d

    C The maintenance worker set off the blast.

f. The following article contains a diagnostic argument. (i) Schematize it. (ii) Classify the support and explain the classifications.

> On the evening of January 24, 1978, several residents of a barren area of the Northwest Territories reported a spectacular fireball over Baker Lake, a body of water just west of Hudson Bay. For several weeks U.S. tracking stations had been warning that a Soviet satellite, possibly containing a nuclear reactor, had dropped very low in its orbit and was likely soon to fall into the atmosphere. Its orbit would have taken it over northern Canada about the time the fireball was reported to have occurred. Later that same week the Russians admitted losing a nuclear-powered satellite, but added that the danger of nuclear contamination was remote. Shortly following this announcement, two geologists hiking down a river just east of Baker Lake discovered radioactive debris, clearly of human fabrication, poking out of a crater in the ice.
>
> From all this, Canadian government officials concluded that the Soviet satellite had in fact returned to earth, burning up in the atmosphere in the vicinity of Baker Lake and showering that part of the Northwest Territories with radioactive debris.

(Answers on p. 238.)

DIAGNOSTIC ARTICULATION

Simple Evaluation

We began looking at diagnostic reasoning to develop a way to articulate our *evaluation* of arguments; we wanted to be able to say what it is about support that makes one rival better than another. We are now in a position to take the first step in that direction. *Explanation* is the link between S and C that determines how good a diagnostic argument is. The ranking of a rival depends on how plausibly it explains the trace data, given what else we know about the case (NTD and our general understanding). An argument is sound if its conclusion explains the traces more plausibly than its rivals; and it is strong if it is a *much* better explanation: if its rivals are clearly far worse.

Exercise 5.3
....

Using this basic vocabulary, say why sleep is the sound conclusion in the truck-crash argument. (Answer on p. 239.)

This is the rudimentary picture; and though it represents a considerable advance in articulateness, it is still fairly crude. It just provides an overall assessment of an argument, with no sense of how it was reached. But our judgment of argument strength depends on the way the individual bits of support relate to the serious rivals and to each other. How does S_4 help, exactly, and what does S_2 do for the argument? These, of course, are the *Relevance Relations* we explored in Chapter 4, where we looked at the impact bits of support had on the serious rivals. So to provide detail in our picture of evaluation, we must turn to *diagnostic relevance* relations. That is, we must articulate the impact of diagnostic support, of trace data and non-trace data, on the rival explanations. This will give us the fine structure we need to see evidence at work.

Diagnostic Relevance

Because relevance links connect the support bit by bit directly with the rivals—S_4 has this impact, S_6 has that impact—our relevance judgment is fundamental to all the others. When we decide on seriousness, ranking, soundness, and strength, those decisions actually derive from our judgment of relevance. In diagnostic argument, this is reflected in the fact that the basic concepts of trace data and non-trace data are themselves relevance concepts: they are distinguished by the different ways they affect the plausibility of the rivals. Hence, looking at diagnostic relevance will advance our understanding of every other diagnostic notion, including TD and NTD.

Recall that to show relevance we do a little thought experiment: estimate what the serious rivals would look like first with and then without the bit of information in question, for example, first with S_3 in the support and then without it. If the list of serious rivals changes in either of two basic ways the information is relevant. Either what's on the list changes (a rival joins or falls off) or something changes in the ranking (order or gaps). So what we'd like is the *diagnostic articulation* of what goes on when this happens in diagnostic arguments. Consider first the relevance of trace data.

Central Trace Data

If we try the experiment with some TD, it quickly becomes obvious that trace data can be relevant in two distinct ways: very generally or quite particularly. Recall that what raises a diagnostic IQ is usually some TD. Something happens and we ask, "What was that?" or "What's going on there?" Or we may ask more specifically, "What caused the crash?" or "Why is the trail littered with bones?" Because the IQ asks specifically about these traces, all of the serious rivals—any serious answer—will have to explain them. We call these "central" TD and their impact on the rivals is very general: *they determine which rivals are serious*; they shape the list. Whether a rival is serious or not is simply determined by how well it explains the crash, the bones, or my wilting plants.

Moreover, the central items explicitly mentioned in the IQ will have other features and properties that are just as central. The IQ asks about bones, but the bones are domestic animal bones. So the serious rivals will all have to explain this too. The IQ asks about a truck crash, but a key feature of *this* truck crash is that the tire marks went straight off the road; so the serious rivals will all have to explain this too. The point is that given our understanding of a case, the IQ may not have mentioned these other features, but *it might just as well have*. Instead of "Why is the trail littered with bones?" Daisy Hiker could as well have asked, "Why is the trail littered with domestic animal bones?" This would not be a different understanding of the case, just a more explicit representation of the understanding we had. So these features too have the same, very general impact: all of the rivals are trying to explain them and the serious list is simply the list of rivals that explains them plausibly.

Exercise 5.4

What are the central trace data in the following cases? In each case state what makes them central.

a. The Baker Lake argument of Exercise 5.2f (p. 205).

b. The Travis Busby mystery in Chapter 4 (p. 167).

c. CAMARILLO, Calif.—An explosion in the tomato-ripening section of a packing house leveled much of the building and critically injured one man Thursday night. There was no fire. "We know ethylene was involved, but we don't know how," said Ventura county fire dispatcher Shonna Matthews. The explosion rocked the Milton Poulos Corp. plant in the 300 block of East 5th Street at 5:25 p.m. The explosion occurred in the tomato-ripening area where a gas process is used to prepare the vegetables.

Basically what we've got is a building that came down. We're about five miles away and it hit us like a sonic boom," Matthews said. A 45-year-old man, assumed to be an employee, was hospitalized in critical condition with multiple injuries, Matthews said. Investigators did not know the cause of the blast.

(*The Associated Press*)

d. The Arts Center argument at the beginning of Chapter 3 (p. 99).

e. The URMM case, Exercise 4.11 (p. 163). (Answers on p. 239.)

PERIPHERAL TRACE DATA

Of course not all TD will be central and relevant in this way to every rival. Some will be explained, better or worse, by one or two rivals, but will not be directly relevant to any others. We will call such TD "peripheral," and it can have a large or small impact, depending on the case. In the crash-in-the-kitchen case (Exercise 4.6, p. 150), the pieces of a broken glass on the floor have a big impact: by themselves they put the "this glass broke" rival on the serious list. Without the shards, that rival is far too specific to be on the serious list. But with them, it explains both the shards and the noise (the central TD) so well that it clearly tops the ranking on what we know. On the other hand, the fragments would not be something *all* the rivals are trying to explain. The radio rival (noise came over the radio) is just trying to explain the noise, not the glass fragments. So the fragments would not be directly relevant to it.[4]

Peripheral TD can have a subtler impact too. In the Flight 800 case, for instance, the exploding central fuel tank rival is already on the serious list. But suppose investigators figure out that it (the exploding tank rival) can explain why the explosion occurred exactly 13 minutes into the flight. Thirteen minutes after takeoff is exactly how long it would take for a defective fuel probe to set off the fumes in the overheated tank. Getting explained in this way would make the 13 minutes trace data. But the other rivals might have nothing to say about the exact time of the explosion. They would not explain it or be hurt by not explaining it. It would still be trace data, because it is explained by one of the rivals; but it would not be central in the way the explosion itself is. Furthermore, it would not have a big impact, as the glass shards would, because the explaining rival is already serious, already on the list. Its impact is simply to boost that rival a bit in the ranking. It is a small but significant relevance.

Exercise 5.5
....

What TD in the Baker Lake argument are *not* central? Explain why. (Answer on p. 239.)

---

4. Of course they would be *in*directly relevant: they boost another rival so much that the radio is way down in the ranking. But this is indirect: it is not due to the radio rival's trying and failing to explain the broken glass.

Finally, it will turn out to be very useful to note that peripheral TD may be *negatively relevant* in this modest way. Sometimes one bit of TD will be especially tough for one rival to explain. As we noted earlier, the lack of blast damage on the engines of Flight 800 is a case in point. At least three rivals (bomb, missile, malfunction) explain the gross details of the crash equally well. All account easily for the fact that the plane exploded, how it came apart, and the general shape and contents of the debris field. But the missile rival cannot easily account for the absence of blast damage on any of the engines, the hot things on which a heat-seeking missile would home in. This hurts its plausibility, lowering it in the ranking. So the lack of engine damage belongs in the support and "hard to explain" articulates why. The hard-to-explain item is such a useful notion in diagnostic reasoning that we will coin a term just for it: **Explanatory Hurdle.** A bit of trace data is an explanatory hurdle for a certain rival if it is particularly difficult for that rival to explain. The absence of blast damage on the engines is an explanatory hurdle for the missile rival.

SUMMARY

We have found essentially four different kinds of impact TD may have on an argument and hence four different articulations of relevance:

    i. TD may determine the serious list (central TD)
       Relevance: All rivals must explain it.

    ii. TD may add one rival to the list.
       Relevance: C_n (some particular rival) easily explains it and that puts C_n on the list.

    iii. TD may move a rival up (change ranking or gaps).
       Relevance: C_n easily explains it and thus ranks higher

    iv. TD may move a rival down or off the list (hurdle).
       Relevance: C_n has difficulty explaining it and thus ranks lower.

Exercise 5.6
....

a. In the windblown garbage can example from Exercises 4.18 and 4.19c, one new bit of information in 4.19c (p. 174) is an explanatory hurdle for the garbage can rival. What is it and what makes it a hurdle? (Answers on p. 239.)

b. How is the fact that the bones are old relevant in the pioneer trail argument? What makes your articulation diagnostic? (Answers on p. 239.)

TWO USEFUL OBSERVATIONS

1. TD: The Basic Articulation We may use this latest advance in articulation to provide a systematic definition of trace data that will be useful in explaining why an item of support is TD. The general point is that "trace data" cover any item of support that gains its relevance in an argument as the *object of explanation* by the rivals. But this has three different manifestations, which will be useful to list. *Anything That Gains Relevance in an Argument in One of the Following Ways Is Trace Data*:

    i. All the rivals are trying to explain it (central TD).

    ii. One rival explains it easily.

    iii. One rival has difficulty explaining it (hurdle).

If an item of support is in an argument for one of these three reasons, that makes it TD.

2. The Importance of IQ in Articulation Keep in mind that the whole structure of an argument depends on our understanding of the case in question, and this understanding is reflected in the natural IQ. This is why we spent so much time and energy on it in Chapter 4. Accordingly, whether a bit of information is central TD or peripheral TD or TD *at all* will depend on the IQ. But this just means that if our understanding of a case changes much, so will the relevance articulations. Which is just what we should expect. If the rumpled truck turns out not to be an accident scene but rather an expensive sculpture, for example, and the tire tracks are from a road crew cleaning up the area last week, then we won't ask the same question and nothing will be relevant in quite the same way.

Exercise 5.7

The discovery that the maintenance worker was very badly injured in the motel explosion is obviously relevant to the (diagnostic) argument in that article (p. 98). Explain its relevance in diagnostic vocabulary. Would this make it TD or NTD? Why? (Answers on p. 239.)

Non-Trace Data

Since NTD are by definition *not* the object of explanation, not something the rivals even try to explain, their relevance cannot be articulated in anything like the way TD are. Nevertheless, the notion of explanation is crucial to describing the relevance of NTD too, just differently. For although trace data provide the items to be explained in a diagnostic argument, NTD provide *everything else needed for the explanatory task*. This comes primarily in two forms: (a) problem-setting NTD and (b) explanatory resources. The first, problem-setting NTD, help us see what needs explaining. The second, resources, tell us what is available to help in the explaining.

    In familiar cases, we usually know pretty well what needs explaining and have little use for type-a NTD. But sometimes a particular audience needs help to see just what the traces are, and type-a NTD will provide what's required. In the disappearance of Danny Hamilton (Exercise 4.7, p. 152), for instance, those of us unfamiliar with trucking may not realize that Hamilton's abandoning his rig "out in the boonies" is worth noting in the argument. (IQ: What happened to Hamilton?) But his supervisor provides some type-a NTD: that when truckers abandon their rigs, they usually "leave it at a truck stop where they can get a ride." We can now see that finding Hamilton's truck "out in the boonies" is a trace, something to explain, a clue in the mystery. So even though Alumbaugh's observation is NTD, it becomes relevant by *giving* us a trace: something hard to explain if we think Hamilton simply decided to abandon his job. Sometimes type-a NTD have a much greater impact on a case than this, determining by itself which rivals are serious (see Exercise 5.16, p. 217).

Exercise 5.8
....

Explain why Alumbaugh's observation is NTD. (Answer on p. 239.)

Type-b NTD are far more common. Even when we know what needs explaining, we may still require help in discovering plausible explanations. Consider again the argument about my wilting plants. If you did not know I watered my plants a lot, root rot would not be any more plausible than a number of other explanations of their wilting, perhaps much less. The soil might be too dry, for instance, or aphids might be lowering fluid pressure, or it might be too much sun. But when we add to the support the NTD that I water the plants frequently, that makes it easier for the root rot rival to explain the wilting. At the same time it makes it harder for dry soil (another rival) to explain wilting. This is the diagnostic articulation of its relevance. None of the rivals is even trying to explain *why* I water my plants frequently. So frequent watering cannot gain relevance through getting explained or being a hurdle. Its relevance lies in its *helping* one rival explain the TD and *hurting* another in its attempt. This is how it affects the serious rivals. This is also why we talk of "explanatory resources": type-b NTD help us see what's available in the context to do the explaining, just as type-a NTD help us see what needs explaining.

Sometimes the effect of type-b NTD is large, as in this case. Before we found out that I water frequently, the dry-soil rival was serious; but afterward it is not. Thus both kinds of NTD can affect what's on the serious list. Subtler effects on the serious rivals are just as interesting, however. Certain patterns in the Flight 800 debris made one version of the malfunction rival serious all by itself: a spark in the central fuel tank. The patterns are obviously TD and the ease with which the spark rival explains them places it among the serious rivals. But just where the spark rival falls in the ranking depends on how plausibly we can find a source of the spark. Because airliners are designed quite specifically to avoid sparks in their fuel tanks, this rival cannot rank very high without something to help it out. Help came in the form of "pickled" fuel probes recovered from the debris field. The "pickled" look was evidence of excess current flow and hence made the probes a possible source of a spark. This obviously makes it easier for the spark rival to explain the explosion. So the pickled probes are relevant—and relevant as type-b NTD.

SUMMARY

Non-trace data gain relevance in an argument by either showing what needs explaining or by showing what's available to do the explaining. Particular applications yield five distinct articulations:

    i. Type-a NTD show that some other item (S_n) is something to explain. This may have one of three articulations:

        Determines the serious list by giving central TD.

        Helps C_n by providing a trace it easily explains.

        Hurts C_n by providing a hurdle.

    ii. Type-b NTD provide explanatory resources

        Makes it easier for C_n to explain something.

        Makes it harder for C_n to explain something.

Exercise 5.9

In each of the two paragraphs before the Summary the relevance of a bit of NTD is given. Go back and underline the diagnostic articulations of their relevance. Then state what the two bits of NTD are. (Answer on p. 239.)

MORE USEFUL OBSERVATIONS

NTD: The Basic Articulation As with TD, we may use our new relevance articulation to provide a systematic definition of NTD that will help explain why a bit of support has that status. The general point is that "non-trace data" cover any item of support that gains its relevance in an argument *without being the object of explanation* by the rivals. But this has three different manifestations, which will be useful to list. *Anything That Gains Relevance in an Argument in One of the Following Ways Is Non-trace Data:*

    i. It shows that something needs explaining.

    ii. It helps a rival explain a trace.

    iii. It degrades a rival's ability to explain a trace.

The Importance of IQ in Articulation Again, whether a bit of information is type-a or type-b NTD, or even TD or relevant at all, depends on how we understand a case; and this will be reflected in the IQ. Hence if the IQ changes, you always have to reevaluate the status and even the relevance of the support you had before it changed.

Exercise 5.10

a. Flight 800 sat on the runway with its cabin air-conditioner running for an hour before being cleared for takeoff. This would have substantially raised the temperature of the central fuel tank. The ease with which kerosene fumes are ignited increases substantially with temperature. Explain the relevance to the argument about the crash of the Specific Support in this information. Does this make it TD or NTD?

b. Articulate the relevance of the following items to the Travis Busby argument in Chapter 4 (p. 167). In each case state in diagnostic terms why the particular item is relevant, and what kind of support that makes it.

   i. The once-fired handgun.

   ii. That Busby had been depressed.

   iii. The blood in the boat.

   iv. That an uninflated life raft was onboard.

(Answers on p. 240.)

Articulating Evaluation

As suggested at the beginning of the last section, once we see how to articulate relevance, we may refine our articulation of the other four evaluative notions. Seriousness, ranking, soundness, and strength all involve exactly the same explanatory connections, but looked at from other perspectives and grouped in different ways.

SERIOUSNESS

To explain in diagnostic terms why a particular rival is serious involves pointing out the traces it easily explains and perhaps also the NTD that help it explain them. Sleep, in the truck crash, is a serious rival because it very plausibly explains the tire marks going straight off the road. Sleep, suicide, and heart attack are the *only* serious rivals because they are the only plausible accounts of the traces on the original evidence. Similarly for Flight 800. Bomb, missile, collision, and malfunction are the only plausible accounts of an airliner's disintegrating in midair on a calm, clear evening. That is why they are the serious rivals. Before the investigation started, spark in the central fuel tank was by itself *not* a serious rival. It was no more plausible than a million other malfunctions all lumped together as "mechanical failure." *Some kind* of mechanical failure was all that was plausible at the outset. The spark rival *became* serious only when particular items were recovered from the seafloor. Some of them (pickled probes) helped it explain others (patterns showing how the plane came apart) so easily that it could be separated from the rest of the mechanical failure explanations and allowed in the ranking on its own. (Note that this is one criterion of relevance from Chapter 4.)

Exercise 5.11

(a) Without looking back at the paragraph, say why the sleep rival is serious in the truck-crash case. (b) Do the same for suicide and heart attack. (Reread the paragraph to check your answer.)

PLAUSIBILITY RANKING

To articulate ranking we must say how much better or worse the various rivals work as explanations of the traces. This is a complex judgment, requiring us to keep in mind the struggle the rivals have in explaining each trace and how much the NTD help or hurt each one. But in practice, the task is not overwhelming. Consider again the Flight 800 case, for instance. We can say that although the spark rival had a slight edge on the others, because it would easily explain patterns in the debris, it was not very far ahead given what else we knew. In particular, we have some NTD telling us how hard kerosene is to ignite and how tough it is to find a source of spark in the tank. These NTD make the spark rival less plausible as an explanation than it would have been otherwise. It is nevertheless still ahead of the others because they have explanatory troubles too. The collision and missile rivals both have trouble explaining the complete absence of signs of external penetration on the aircraft, for instance. This is an explanatory hurdle for each of them. They also have trouble with NTD. The collision rival was made less plausible by the failure to find any other missing aircraft in the entire northeast of the United States that afternoon and evening. And the missile rival's plausibility as the explanation was damaged by the absence of military exercises in the area.

Exercise 5.12

....

(a) Is the lack of external penetration TD or NTD? Explain why. Explain why (b) the lack of missing aircraft and (c) military exercises are NTD. (Answers on p. 240.)

SOUNDNESS AND STRENGTH

To show that an argument is sound we must say why its conclusion is the best of the rivals. This requires superlatives rather than simple comparatives, but otherwise looks like the ranking of explanations. Sleep, for instance, is the most plausible explanation of the tire marks (and hence of the crash) to begin with in the truck crash because the other two (suicide and heart attack) are relatively rare among truck drivers. If we had to mention this in the argument it would be (General) NTD, but we typically do not: it is just part of the vast general understanding we must take for granted in reasoning. The additional NTD that the driver had been up all night would make sleep an even better account of the crash. So we could say then that the argument (with sleep as its conclusion) was not just sound but *strong*. That is, the gap between the best and the next best rival is large.[5]

---

5. The ranking still might be reversed, perhaps by an autopsy showing heart damage. But saying the argument is strong is not saying it is conclusive—that *nothing* could demote the currently best rival. It is just saying that it would take something very impressive to do it (like an autopsy showing heart damage).

Exercise 5.13

Diagnostically articulate the soundness and strength of the Baker Lake argument in Exercise 5.2 (p. 205). (Answer on p. 240.)

As always, the point and value of articulating any particular reasoning will depend on our familiarity with the subject matter, on how well we understand the issues in question. When we know a lot about a topic (as we do for most passages we have examined in this text), our judgments can be confident and detailed. When the topic is difficult or exotic, on the other hand, we may still make evaluative judgments while realizing they are tentative and revisable. Their point will be more exploratory and less final.

So the diagnostic articulation we are working on will have different value depending on case and context. But every application will extend and refine the five major aspects of Chapter 4's project. Whether we're simply explaining our reasoning to someone, checking for simple oversights, locating disagreement, organizing an investigation, or seeing how to exploit the judgment of others, the diagnostic apparatus will add another dimension to our understanding of reasoning. Just what it will do will depend on how much you know and the problem you are trying to solve.

Articulation Recap

The following synopses should provide a quick reminder of the various diagnostic articulations we have just explored. **Note that each refers to the central diagnostic activity of explaining trace data.**

RELEVANCE: An item is relevant support in a diagnostic argument if it is either something for the rivals to explain (TD) or information that determines what's available to be explained (type-a NTD), or information that helps or hurts a rival in its attempt to explain the trace data (type-b NTD).

SERIOUSNESS: A rival is serious if it is a plausible explanation of the trace data.

RANKING: The ranking of a rival is determined by how hard or easy it is for it to explain the relevant traces, relative to the other serious rivals.

SOUNDNESS: The sound conclusion is the one that best (most easily or plausibly) explains the traces.

STRENGTH: An argument is strong if the sound rival easily explains all the traces and nothing else does. If two or more rivals are close in the ranking, then the argument cannot be strong for any.

REFINEMENTS

Diagnostic concepts relate to each other in many interesting ways. This section will explore some of the major ones to help you become more comfortable with the new vocabulary.

Interconnected Relevance

An item of information is relevant support in an argument (that is, it belongs in the argument) if it affects the list of serious rivals in one way or another. But sometimes a bit of information will have such an effect only because another item is also part of the support. That is, items of support may become relevant in pairs or groups, and may need each other for relevance. This interdependency of relevance gives us another tool to use in talking about arguments. It refines our ability to articulate our evaluation of them.

In discussing type-a NTD we have already examined a case in which one bit of support makes another relevant. For another example, consider the lack of blast damage on the engines of Flight 800. This, as we saw, is a hurdle for the missile rival: it is hard for the missile rival to explain and hence it drops that rival in the plausibility ranking. But, for the average person, it would have this effect only if we knew something else: that antiaircraft missiles work by seeking the hottest parts of their target and those are the engine exhausts. This is obviously background NTD, and without it, the undamaged engines would be of no particular interest. So here some trace data become relevant through learning about some NTD.

Exercise 5.14
....

Describe the relevance of this NTD in diagnostic terms. Explain why it is not trace data. (Answer on p. 240.)

But NTD can become relevant in the same way. We know, for instance, that Flight 800 was flying at 13,000 feet altitude when it exploded. Is that relevant? For an average audience we would again have to say not by itself. Against the understanding most of us have, the altitude would not hurt or benefit any of the rivals. But if we were to do some investigating and find that the altitude limit of the most common ground to air missile was less than 13,000 feet, then the plane's altitude would suddenly become relevant to the argument. It too would lower the missile rival's ranking, here by practically ruling out its most likely version. The 13,000 feet would have a distinct impact on the serious rivals and deserve to be included in the support.

Exercise 5.15
....

Describe diagnostically the relevance of the plane's altitude, given the altitude limit discovery; explain why altitude would be NTD. (Answer on p. 240.)

Of course for a superior understanding of the kind discussed in Chapter 4 (somebody who knows a lot to begin with), the altitude might have been immediately relevant. For someone who came to the argument already knowing about the Stinger's altitude limit, or much else about shooting down aircraft, would have realized the importance of 13,000 feet without anything further. This is just another way in which an argument must be sensitive to its audience. But it also reveals something about how those of us who needed this information would proceed. For our investigation, which revealed the missile's limit, almost certainly did not consist in actually testing missiles. What we would naturally do is read about them, or ask someone who knows. That is, we would find and exploit superior understanding: simply adding to the support something somebody else already knows.

Finally, some NTD and all peripheral TD are relevant *only* because certain rivals are on the list of serious ones. If those rivals fall off the list for other reasons, the data related only to them will become irrelevant. The 13,000 feet and the undamaged engines are relevant to the Flight 800 argument only because the missile rival is serious. If it were not there would be no reason to put either item in the support. They would only make an already unserious rival even less so.

Recall that we articulate relevance using the thought experiment introduced in Chapter 4: what difference does the information make to the serious rivals? We have devoted much of this chapter to showing all the ways diagnostic arguments allow a detailed and systematic articulation of this difference. Using our explanatory vocabulary and the concept of trace data we can often do more than simply describe the impact of a certain bit of information. We can say quite a lot about *why* it has that impact. The interconnections of this section add to that articulateness.

Exercise 5.16

The passage below contains an argument. (a) What IQ are you answering? (b) Schematize your argument (list the five relevant items separately). (c) Give two reasonable rivals. (d) Diagnostically articulate the relevance of each item of support. (e) Looking at (d), label the TD and NTD. (Answers on p. 240.)

> The campus is nearly deserted as you hurry in from the parking lot on your way to class. This is unusual. Normally there's a crowd of students going and coming. You look at your watch. It says 10:05, five minutes before class time, but it's been running slow lately and you don't remember setting it. You infer that you're late for class.

Assumptions: Articulating an Understanding

The whole institution of giving reasons (offering arguments) is possible only because we sharply limit the support to what has to be mentioned in a given context, for a particular audience. For, as we saw in Chapter 4, we are always rejecting countless possibilities in narrowing the list of rivals to the small number of serious ones we consider in argument. If we had to actually articulate—include in the support—all the aspects of our understanding that rule out these other possibilities, we would never be able to actually *give* reasons for anything. For there would be no end to them. We must simply take for granted, and not explicitly mention, *most* of the understanding we bring to reasoning. The NTD relevant to unserious diagnostic rivals are part of that unmentioned background.

Nevertheless, when done with care and in small doses, articulating some of this background understanding can be useful. We do this, for example, when we exploit a superior understanding. If somebody else ranks the rivals differently, we may sometimes find that they do so because they know something we do not. If we can get them to articulate the part of their understanding that we do not share, we may be able to add it to the support and end up agreeing about the argument. This is exactly what happened in the last section when we considered the possibility that somebody might come to the Flight 800 investigation already aware that the Stinger missile cannot reach 13,000 feet. They would judge the missile rival to be worse than I would, because I do not know this at the outset. But I might get them to reveal that part of their understanding; and adding it to the argument as NTD may then eliminate the disagreement. We will discuss the reasoning behind this move under "testimony" in Chapter 6. Exploiting superior understanding, it turns out, involves a very particular diagnostic argument.

A more common and interesting case is one in which somebody's understanding is not obviously better than mine, but it is different and leads to a different judgment. To deal with the disagreement, we may then try to discover what it is about our different understandings that leads to the different judgments. Sometimes we will find nothing. We just have different assessments. But we will sometimes find that we differ on a *particular proposition*, something definite and describable, that is relevant to the argument. We might call this "an assumption," some particular thing one of us assumes and the other does not.

Even this may be tough to figure out, but we are all familiar with cases in which it is obvious. Suppose I say, "These windows are so clean they must have been recently washed." A friend disagrees: "No, I'm sure there's nothing in the budget for something as frivolous as window washing." This is a diagnostic argument. I am offering "washed" as the best explanation of the windows being so clean; my friend offers some NTD lowering "washed" below some other undisclosed rival as an account of the transparency. He might then add: "You're just assuming that these are ordinary windows, and the air here is as filled with dust and smoke as any public place." And he would be right. He would have articulated a bit of my understanding, and something that might account for the difference in our judgments. But doing so would not settle the matter. Just articulating my presumption does not in this case give reason to think it is right or wrong.

Nevertheless, getting this assumption out in the open may be valuable. For it both locates the disagreement in a particular aspect of the reasoning and tells us what to investigate if the question is important to us. So far, all we have is a puzzle: how come the windows are so clean if my friend is right about the budget. So, if it matters, we can limit our investigation to whether these are ordinary windows, what the local air conditions are like, whether the budget is as strained as my friend thinks, and what the priorities are if it is. It is perhaps hard to imagine that the question of window washing would matter enough to either of us to justify such an investigation. But this simple case contains everything essential to showing that an assumption is what separates two people who disagree, and how to think about it when it does. So it makes a good model for understanding some genuinely important disagreements.

Note that if the question of what I am assuming becomes a matter of controversy, that controversy would also have diagnostic form. Someone might offer "You are assuming X" as the best explanation of our disagreement. But I might disagree with that as well. To settle the matter would involve the normal diagnostic procedure of looking at rival accounts of the disagreement, considering other traces and NTD, and making a plausibility judgment based on the whole package. The rival accounts would include *other* things I might be assuming, as well as the possibility that the disagreement does not stem from a single articulable source. And the list could also include all those things mentioned in Chapter 4 that two people could fail to share in an argument. (See the section on disagreement beginning on p. 185.) Locating a disagreement in this way will sometimes resolve the disagreement and sometimes not. But it will invariably give you deeper insight into your own understanding of the matter.

Often, however, even when resolving the disagreement is important, the matter will be so complicated that trying to actually locate it will be a waste of time. The best strategy might then be education: try to learn more about the issue and hope that works. The point of this section is simply to show how to treat unshared assumptions diagnostically. Nothing guarantees that a disagreement can be resolved within normal limits of time and patience.

Subtle Traces

One reason to think hard about diagnostic argument is to make us more alert to the trace data around us that we can exploit in reasoning. Just realizing that our basic reasoning involves explaining things should increase our awareness of the aspects of our environment that we can explain. Some of these will take some imagination to see. Consider the following example, a simple version of which we looked at in Chapter 4.

> The wind howled around the house as Rita sat in her living room absorbed in a book. Suddenly her reading lamp went out. She waited a moment to see if it would come back on, then got up and crossed the room to her study. The light in the study would not come on with the switch. She was on her way outside to check the fuse box when a small light in the kitchen caught her eye. Then she noticed that the clock on the electric stove was functioning perfectly. Momentarily puzzled, she returned to her study where she found the reading lamp was burning once again. It must have been a general power failure, she mused, perhaps due to the winds.

Here Rita infers an explanation of a collection of trace data she has encountered. She thinks it is all best accounted for by a general power outage in the neighborhood, as opposed to something more local in the house itself. How would we articulate her argument?

Well, the wind is important NTD; and if we were to list the traces, we would certainly include all the mentioned items: reading light out, study light unresponsive, kitchen light and clock okay, light in study back on. But the most important trace is only *implicit* in this list, and would be worth mentioning explicitly if we are to say why her inference is a good one. What is it? It is that all these things happened *in the order given in the story*. A general, wind-induced power outage typically interrupts power for a period, and then it comes back on on its own (this would be NTD if explicitly mentioned). So it would be a fine explanation of the *sequence* of events Rita observed. This surely was at work in her inference and is thus important to make clear in articulating her reasoning. Keep an eye out for this kind of thing when you find yourself involved in such detective work.

Exercise 5.17

(a) Schematize Rita's argument in a way that reflects this last subtlety. (b) Using the IQ "Why did the lamp go out?" describe a hurdle for the blown-bulb rival. (Answers on p. 241.)

Problems in Classifying Support

Explanation is obviously the fundamental diagnostic idea. Diagnostic reasoning is simply reasoning by explaining. The motivation for distinguishing trace data from non-trace data is primarily to make clear the *two fundamentally different explanatory roles* that support may play in diagnostic arguments. Support may become relevant either as the object of explanation (TD) or as information that shapes the rivals' explanatory task, but does not get explained (NTD). And for most everyday diagnostic reasoning, support will fall comfortably into one or the other of these types. But as you look through more and more arguments, and through more complicated arguments, you will occasionally find it hard to say which role a certain item of support plays in an argument. And sometimes, you will find one playing *both* roles at once: one for one rival and the other for another. Since our interest lies in being clear about how a given S relates to the rivals, not a particular pigeon hole, neither of these cases raises deep problems. We just have to articulate an ambiguous or complex relevance relation. But because this is new territory, it will be worth brief treatment.

AMBIGUOUS CASES

Because we have a lot of discretion in describing support and rivals, normal variations in those descriptions will occasionally change the natural way to describe the relevance of support. The troublesome cases will be Specific Support that is not central TD. General Support, you may recall, will always be NTD. But some NTD, along with *all* trace data, will be Specific Support: information particular to the case in question. Furthermore, there will seldom be any question of the status of central TD: what the case is about. But among the less central Specific Support you will sometimes find yourself torn: is this item explained or just helping? Take for instance the final resting place of the garbage can in the scratched car example of Chapter 4 (Exercise 4.18, p. 172). This (Specific) information is directly relevant only to the main rival, the plausibility of which it clearly helps. Is the fact that the can was on the other side of the car in the morning TD or NTD?

Well, if we stick to the simple conclusion, "The can scratched the car," it will be NTD: that conclusion does not explain the can's location. But we might naturally take that sentence to be shorthand for a longer story about what happened: "The wind blew the can over and it hit the car as it rolled along." This story, you might reasonably think, explains why the can was found where it was, which makes it TD. The point to recognize is that it doesn't matter which way you do it. Both formulations of C are fine; and either way you express the relevance of that item of support. In choosing you simply choose one formulation of C over another, and hence a particular articulation of relevance. There may be reasons to prefer one over the other in a given context, and you should be sensitive to that. But so long as you realize that your classification of support (as TD or NTD) simply expresses your picture of its relevance, your analysis will be clear.

Exercise 5.18

In Exercise 5.7 (p. 210) concerning the motel explosion case, we took the maintenance worker's injuries to be trace data because the conclusion (he set off the blast) would easily explain them. In doing this we were taking C to be a story with certain detail. Give the crucial detail. Explain why it is crucial to the status of the injuries as TD. (Answer on p. 241.)

Double Roles

Even with a stable formulation of C, however, Specific Support will sometimes also play *both roles at once*. In an earlier exercise on the TWA investigation, we had you explain how a long wait for takeoff could be important NTD in that argument. The answer was that the heat exhausted by the air conditioner during the delay would make it easier for the malfunction rival to explain the explosion with an ignition source likely to be on board. This is the classic relevance of NTD.

But this same delay might be trace data for one version of the bomb rival, for instance. That rival might explain the long wait as due to a cockpit warning light triggered by the way the bomb was installed in the galley (it interrupted a circuit showing that a hatch is secured). The light was declared defective after investigators could find nothing wrong and the flight was allowed to take off. So here the story explaining the explosion (bomb in galley) would also explain the delay (circuit interruption), making it trace data. The same item would be relevant in more than one way, as NTD for one rival and TD for another. This is nothing to be alarmed about, just one of the complexities you will encounter in the course of thinking through complicated reasoning. Your articulation of relevance should mention both roles.

Finally, remember that if our conception of a case changes very much, that may affect the status of the support in every possible way. For if we change our minds in a large way about what went on, we will also naturally change the question we ask about it. A change in IQ will usually revise everything dramatically. Certain rivals won't even answer it any more; and what was central trace data will no longer be central. All the relevance relations will change. Some things that counted as traces before may become irrelevant, or change to NTD; and some NTD may become irrelevant or change to TD. All this happens most naturally, of course, in the progress of an investigation.

DIAGNOSTIC INVESTIGATION

Investigation by Explanation

Recall from Chapter 4 that an investigation is what you get when you look for new information relevant to answering a question. The question may already be the IQ of an argument that you wish to make better by adding support. Or you may launch an investigation to answer a question you have. In this latter case, the question *becomes* the IQ of an argument after the investigation has accumulated some information and pauses to evaluate its progress. For the data you have gathered are then support in an argument; and the question's serious answers are the rival conclusions. This is just to point out once again the intimate connection between arguments and investigations spelled out in Chapter 4. Crucially, you must have some sense of what the serious rivals (answers) are to begin with, for this is all that tells you where to look for relevant data. Initially serious rivals are your reasonable *suspicions*; and without them you have no investigation, just a puzzle. [*Suggestion:* before going on, quickly reread the section of Chapter 4 entitled "Investigation: Making Reasons Better," starting on p. 178.]

Diagnostic investigations are special, however. We may say far more specific and useful things about diagnostic investigations than we can about investigations in general, because we can say so much more about relevance. Information is relevant to a diagnostic investigation in exactly the same ways it is in diagnostic arguments, as trace data and non-trace data. Diagnostic investigations therefore hunt for things to explain (TD) and for explanatory resources (NTD).

Exercise 5.19

Describe in diagnostic terms the relevance to the Travis Busby argument (Chapter 4, p. 167) of the following discoveries. In each case explain how it gains relevance and what kind of support that makes it.

a. Busby's body is found with a bullet hole in it.

b. Busby's fingerprints are not on the handgun.

c. Busby had just won the lottery.

(Answers on p. 241.)

General and Specific NTD[6] actually function in importantly different ways, however, so there are three different kinds of support to look for (and recognize) in a diagnostic inquiry. Let us briefly review these before applying them to an example.

TRACE DATA

What usually starts a diagnostic investigation is simply *noticing that something needs to be explained*: a plane falls from the sky, you do uncharacteristically badly on a quiz, or an epidemic strikes intravenous drug users. These we recognize as things that may be usefully explained, which is to recognize them as trace data. This gives us everything we need to begin. For the initial trace can provide both an IQ and a tentative list of rivals. The IQ may always be simply, "What explains this (TD)?" "What caused the crash?" for example, or "What brought about the bad grade?" "Whence the epidemic?" Although we can sometimes make the question more detailed than this, we usually need not. The serious rivals, then, are simply the plausible answers to this question. And *reflecting on those answers is what directs our search* for more things to explain: more TD.

Exercise 5.20
....

Why do investigators expect to find trace data by pulling pieces of Flight 800 from the sea floor? (Answer on p. 241.)

SPECIFIC NTD

The initial rivals also can guide us to information that, although not being something to explain, would help one of the rivals explain the traces we have. Fierce weather can crash an airplane, so checking weather records can obviously help or hurt weather-related rivals in a plane crash investigation. If we find calm, clear skies [Specific NTD], that will demote them all in the ranking. If the plane was flying through a squall line [Specific NTD], that makes the weather explanation more serious. Because the rivals would not be trying to explain the clear sky or the squall line, support such as this would function as NTD.

GENERAL NTD

We can sometimes tell that what we lack is *general* understanding of a certain matter and we may even know where to go to beef it up. Of course what we very often need is an education, not just more NTD. Nevertheless, in the right circumstances, a bit of General NTD will provide just the right supplement and allow us to proceed in an investigation that would have otherwise stymied us. I know I don't know much about how plants work, so I ask somebody in botany, agriculture, or

---

6. Just to avoid confusion, note that the General/Specific distinction is unrelated to the type-a/type-b distinction introduced earlier. Both types of NTD may be General and both types may be Specific.

some other related field. I find out about rotting roots [General NTD] and that suggests a plausible explanation of the wilting. Similarly for Flight 800. I don't know
enough about kerosene to evaluate the spark-in-the-tank rival, so I know what to
look up and ask about. When I find out how hard it is to ignite kerosene fumes
[General NTD], that makes it harder for the spark rival to explain the explosion.

General NTD almost always give us new places to look for TD and Specific NTD.
Learning of kerosene's poor ignitability [General NTD], we may look to see whether
this particular kerosene may have been special in this regard: perhaps hotter than
normal. We would then see the relevance of Flight 800's long wait for takeoff [Spe-
cific NTD] and the location of the air conditioning units under the central fuel tank
[more Specific NTD], which may have been easily ignored before. This compensates
for the earlier discovery, making the spark rival a more plausible explanation.

SUMMARY

In a diagnostic investigation we may say a good deal about how rivals guide our
search for new information, which we found to be the key feature of investigations in Chapter 4. Diagnostic rivals are explanations, so we can look for (a) things
they would explain, (b) information that would help them in this explanation,
and (c) General information that would increase our understanding of such explanations. Part of our diagnostic skill lies in knowing where to look for these
three things on topics we know something about. This is a picture of how we
learn. We will say more about how this works in Chapter 7.

Illustration

Consider the Baker Lake incident described in Exercise 5.2f on p. 205. It began as
the investigation of the fireball. We all recognize the fireball as something to explain, so it provides both the original trace and a pretty good IQ: "What was that?"
Our understanding of what's available to do the explaining gives us a list of rivals and a rough initial ranking:

C_1: Meteorite
C_2: Orbiting debris
C_3: Failed rocket launch
C_4: Flaming aircraft (perhaps)

This list of suspicions (initial rivals) would guide most of us along a path very
like that followed by the professional inquiry, though perhaps a bit more slowly.
Because the meteorite explanation is hard to check directly, the reasonable thing
to do is look at the others first and opt for the rock from space only if we can
eliminate the others.

An investigation by you or me would go more slowly than the professional
one precisely because we would realize our need for some General NTD. We
would need to learn where to look for explanatory resources: ideas about what
might explain the fireball. And, of course, our initial rivals would lead us to ask,
who, for example, keeps track of things such as airplanes in the area, worldwide

missile launches, or objects in orbit? This would take some time, effort, and luck, but we'd all realize when we were learning what we needed to. Let us suppose we are successful at this preliminary level and pursue more specific information.

Planes big enough to explain substantial fireballs usually do not go long unreported, but we could check to see if airline flights were scheduled over the area at the time and if any are missing. Similarly for military aircraft. And we could look into whether civilian or military radar installations had noticed anything at the time of the fireball. Much the same routine would work for missile tests. But by far the most interesting possibility would be to contact agencies that keep track of orbiting objects to see if anything in their catalogue looked like a plausible culprit. There we would have immediately encountered the interesting history of the Soviet satellite that soon became the most likely suspect. Let us diagnostically articulate the relevance of this history and how it tied together the rest of the investigation.

Exercise 5.21
....

Give the diagnostic translation of "plausible culprit" and "likely suspect" in the previous paragraph. (Answer on p. 241.)

To determine whether this particular satellite would be a serious rival by itself (split from the larger "orbiting debris" wedge), we would want three or four items of Specific NTD to help it explain the fireball. First, we would want to know whether the satellite's orbit had deteriorated badly enough that it should have been expected to soon fall into the atmosphere. Second, we'd have to see whether its orbit would take it over northern Canada at the time of the fireball. Third, we'd need to know the direction it would have been traveling had it been in the right place at the right time. This last item would lead us to look for a second piece of trace data: the direction of the fireball. For this satellite to be its explanation, the fireball's direction must accord with the orbit. If the fireball went east while the satellite was going west over Canada, that would be a tremendous hurdle for the satellite rival. Finally, it would be useful to know if any other bits of orbiting debris large enough to make a fireball were in similar straits.

We know from the article that everything discovered in such an investigation would have supported the satellite explanation of the fireball. So let us set out the first diagnostic argument, to which the initial rivals would have led us:

S_1 A fireball streaked eastward over Baker Lake on the evening of January 24, 1978.

S_2 The orbit of a particular Soviet satellite had recently begun to dip into the atmosphere.

S_3 It was due over northern Canada that evening.

S_4 Its orbit was from west to east.

S_5 No other candidates among planes, rockets, or orbiting debris were found.

$===d$

C_2 The flash was orbiting debris falling into the atmosphere.

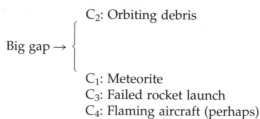

RANKING AT THIS STAGE:

C_2: Orbiting debris

Big gap →

C_1: Meteorite
C_3: Failed rocket launch
C_4: Flaming aircraft (perhaps)

We would of course not write the argument quite this way. Given what we discovered, we would naturally split the large C_2 wedge in two, separating the particular satellite as a separate rival, C_2'. So the schematization would look like this:

S_1 A fireball streaked eastward over Baker Lake on the evening of January 24, 1978.
S_2 The orbit of a particular Soviet satellite had recently begun to dip into the atmosphere.
S_3 It was due over northern Canada that evening.
S_4 Its orbit was from west to east.
S_5 No other candidates among planes, rockets, or orbiting debris were found.
_____ d
C_2' The flash was a particular Soviet satellite falling into the atmosphere.

RANKING AT THIS STAGE:

C_2': The Soviet satellite

Big gap →

C_2'': Other orbiting debris
C_1: Meteorite
C_3: Failed rocket launch
C_4: Flaming aircraft (perhaps)

But in discovering all this we would have also found other things relevant to the investigation. One thing was that the satellite carried a nuclear reactor; and another was that ground stations had been in constant radio contact with it as its orbit deteriorated. These would be relevant NTD because they would give us two further traces to seek. First, the radio contact should have been lost at the time of the fireball. If not, that would provide an enormous explanatory hurdle for this rival. Second, we might look for recently deposited radioactive debris on the snowy tundra.

Again, everything went in favor of our favorite rival: it could easily explain everything it needed to explain, leaving it virtually the only serious rival:

S_1 A fireball streaked eastward over Baker Lake on the evening of January 24, 1978.
S_2 The orbit of a particular Soviet satellite had recently begun to dip into the atmosphere.

S_3 It was due over northern Canada that evening.

S_4 Its orbit was from west to east.

S_5 No other candidates among planes, rockets, or orbiting debris were found.

S_6 Radio contact with the satellite was lost the night of the fireball.

S_7 A nuclear reactor was onboard the satellite.

S_8 Geologists hiking down a frozen river found obviously fabricated, radioactive debris sticking out of a crater in the ice.

$$=== d$$

C_2' The flash was a particular Soviet satellite falling into the atmosphere.

Exercise 5.22

....

(a) Label the eight support claims in this argument TD or NTD. (b) Three distinct aspects or components of S_8 are separately relevant. State what they are and how they are relevant. (c) Suppose you found out that the river in S_8 is east of Baker lake. Would that be relevant? State why and whether it would be TD or NTD. (Answers on p. 241.)

Ordinary diagnostic investigations into things such as the crashing noise in the kitchen (what was that?) or why the car won't start usually converge on a satisfactory conclusion in this same way. Diagnostic reasoning normally works so well that it does not draw our attention. This is why it is so useful and so basic. What does draw our attention, however, are the relatively rare tough cases. If an important investigation goes badly and we do not find a good answer, or even a best one, that tends to be unsettling. We have never discovered what happened to Amelia Earhart. She and her navigator simply disappeared one day over the Pacific Ocean, and we have no more than speculation about how and where. NASA lost contact with a survey probe just as it was going into orbit around Mars. Again, we have no more than a cluster of guesses about what went wrong, whether it still exists, and, if so, where it is.

Such cases are fascinating precisely because their mystery is a little frightening. They point out some limits in our ability to understand the world. But their celebrity can mislead us about our skills. We should take cheer from the fact that mysteries such as this are very rare and that most diagnostic investigations do not end inconclusively. And not just because they are about simple matters such as what broke a minute ago in the kitchen. Many genuinely challenging cases also resolve conclusively. In the Pan Am explosion over Lockerbie Scotland, investigators were able to determine such fine details as the suitcase that held the bomb, the kind of explosive involved, the model of radio it was planted in, and even where it was purchased. In another case, though it happened in the middle of the night, leaving few clues to go on, we have been able to piece together the events leading up to the sinking of the *Titanic* and even what happened after it disappeared from the surface on its way to the ocean floor. The investigative literature is filled with triumphs even more striking than these. It should not surprise us if occasionally, in the course of things, a case will deny us just those traces required for definitive settlement. More amazing is how much we can accomplish in chasing down leads when we're guided by a short list of initial suspicions about a case.

Strength and Success

A diagnostic investigation is successful only when its conclusion *has no serious rivals* left. This makes diagnostic investigations easier to deal with than normative ones, for example. For when the question is normative (What should we do?), we may find out everything we could want and still have two answers that were about equally good. We may know everything possible about the routes home and still have to flip a coin to decide. But when the question is diagnostic (What's going on here?) this is never so. Diagnostic rivals are incompatible stories about what happened or what's going on in a certain case, so only one can be right. A strong reason to prefer one will be a strong reason to discount the others. This means that "gaps" in the ranking play a major role in talking about diagnostic investigations.

The new information turned up in a diagnostic investigation may gain relevance in any of the standard ways, of course. It may affect the ranking of the serious rivals in all sorts of ways, or gaps in it; or it may change which rivals are serious. But an investigation makes genuine progress only when it actually eliminates some of the serious rivals, and one of them begins to stand out as much better than the rest. This is usually done in stages in which the gaps between rivals get larger and larger. If C_3 is already below C_1, and then we find more data that hurt it, or help C_1, the gap in the ranking between C_1 and C_3 has widened. When the NTSB first looked into the TWA crash, for example, "collision with another aircraft" ranked lower than "bomb" as a possibility. When it exploded, the 747 was still in contact with Kennedy Airport, and neither the crew nor air traffic controllers had detected another aircraft in the vicinity. Even though the disaster was observed by thousands on the ground, nobody reported another plane. So "collision" could not rank high. "Bomb" (and some other rivals) was a better bet. In the ensuing days an active search failed to turn up any other aircraft, civilian or military, unaccounted for in the vicinity. This NTD clearly makes "collision" an even less plausible explanation than it was at the outset, increasing the gap between it and "bomb." The gap got even wider as pieces of wreckage were brought up from the seafloor and assembled, because nothing could be found that looked the least like external collision damage (an explanatory hurdle). The collision rival thus becomes less and less serious as an explanation of the crash. This is typical of diagnostic investigations.

Recall that the concept of strength in an argument is linked to investigations. A strong argument is one in which an *ideal* investigation (unconstrained by luck or resources) is unlikely to find anything that will change the rival at the top of the ranking. So a diagnostic argument becomes strong, as opposed to merely sound, when the gap between the top rival and *all of the rest* is made large in the manner of this last example.

Conclusive Arguments

Sometimes diagnostic investigations will increase the gap between the top rival and all of the rest until none of the rest is any longer serious. When this happens, the information found during the investigation has then produced a *conclusive* argument for that remaining rival. The conclusion has no serious competition. Many investigations do yield results this impressive. We found out conclusively what disabled Apollo 13, what blew up Pan Am Flight 103 over Lockerbie, and what causes smallpox. It happens as well in countless mundane matters we investigate everyday, such as what broke the jar of jam and why the oncoming cars are using their wipers. At the end, the best of the competition is sometimes no better than rivals we dismissed as not serious at the outset. We know what explains what.

Of course some diagnostic arguments start off conclusively, that is, they have only one serious rival to begin with, such as our rain example. On a threatening day the latest people to come into the classroom have had increasingly wet clothes and dripping umbrellas. I conclude it has begun to rain. Our apparatus is designed to articulate such arguments transparently. The IQ is (something like) "Why all the wet?"; and the contrast would be other sources of wet. We might articulate its conclusiveness by formulating the best of the rival explanations and noting their unseriousness. One wedge of the balloon would be burst water pipes, another fire sprinklers run amok, and another conspiracies to deceive me about the weather. None is serious. Further investigation in the normal run of things is unlikely to change the ranking, or even reduce the gap much. This judgment stems from the understanding we all share simply as a result of growing up in the same world. We share an understanding because it is required to survive long enough to take a course on reasoning.

Exercises 5.23

Recall simple investigations you've made that have ended conclusively; describe what rivals you entertained and what discoveries reduced their plausibility.

Science as a Diagnostic Activity

This completes our development of the diagnostic model of basic reasoning. We will end the chapter by applying the model to the natural sciences, which will be helpful in a number of ways. It will first show how to apply diagnostic concepts beyond the matters of everyday experience we have relied on in our development. This should deepen your understanding of those concepts. It will also deepen your understanding of science by displaying some parallels between science and our everyday practical reasoning about the world. This will provide some insight into how science works at various levels. Along the way it will also reveal, and allow us to avoid, a common misperception of scientific progress.

The investigations of natural science are diagnostic.[7] Consequently, some of the key features of science—and of the individual sciences—may be expressed in our basic diagnostic vocabulary.

IMPLICIT QUESTION

A diagnostic question lies at the bottom of particular inquiries in every discipline from paleontology to physics. Questions such as "What killed off the dinosaurs?" for instance, or "What is the source of gamma-ray bursts?" or "How do bacteria relate to thermophilic worms?" all have this form; they all seek an understanding of something. One useful way to classify the different sciences is by the *form* of the diagnostic IQ they address. Basic sciences, such as physics, chemistry, and biology, address the present-tense version of the question, "What's going on?" How does the cell work, for instance, or the bond between atoms in a compound, or the nucleus itself? On the other hand, historical sciences (archaeology, paleontology) are devoted to finding out "What happened?" so the IQ is in the past tense. Other sciences (cosmology, geology) contain aspects of each of these and so will ask questions of each form.

TRACE DATA

Of course the various sciences are also distinguished by their characteristic trace data. They differ in the sorts of phenomena to which they apply these questions. Physics inquires into the basic nature of all matter, at the most general and abstract level; biology investigates organisms; chemistry inquires into the composition and behavior of compounds; geology into the development of the earth's crust; cosmology into the nature and evolution of stars and galaxies; archaeology into past civilizations; and meteorology into the weather. Explaining different subjects always requires somewhat distinct procedures and models, rewards different approximations and idealizations, and employs different tools and apparatus. This is why there are distinct disciplines, and different departments in universities. But the distinctions, though sometimes profound, are simply due to the practical problems encountered in explaining different kinds of trace data. They arise naturally out of the attempt to understand a certain aspect of the world. As disciplines advance, the practical problems they face constantly change, of course; so the relations between the disciplines are constantly evolving.

NON-TRACE DATA

Disciplines also overlap a great deal at their edges. Much of this occurs because the understanding developed in one field becomes non-trace data for another. Certain aspects of some disciplines are possible only because of the understand-

---

7. This is true of the social and behavioral sciences too, but they raise other special issues that will not be addressed in this section.

ing worked out in others. Physics provides General NTD of enormous value to cosmology; evolutionary biology does much the same for paleontology. Whole subdisciplines have been created out of such interdependency, for example, biochemistry as well as geophysics and physical chemistry.

The General Project of Science

Although the particular investigations carried out within a science look much like the practical ones we engage in every day, the overall project of science—or of the individual disciplines—is not like this at all. What distinguishes science—all the sciences—from more practical, everyday diagnostic enterprises is the **Generality** of the understanding to which it aspires. When I try to explain why my car won't start, I do so simply to solve a practical problem I have. When cosmologists look for the source of gamma ray bursts, they do so in an effort to piece together a general understanding of the universe. Explaining traces is not an end in itself for a science. It is always part of the broader endeavor of understanding the whole slice of nature falling under its purview. No matter how specific the investigation (Where did the diamonds come from in northern Indiana?), it is undertaken *as part of science* only if it promises to shed light on some General aspect of how the world works. As a consequence, the general project of a science resembles the most difficult and baffling kind of investigation we looked at in Chapter 4. This is probably why we find science so fascinating, but it is also why science is so easily misunderstood.

Recall that in practical matters, we found two very different kinds of investigation possible, which we called "tractable" (roughly: clear) and "intractable" (baffling).[8] An investigation is tractable if we understand it well enough to give the question we're trying to answer a short list of serious answers from which to choose. These answers guide exploration, as we have seen in every case examined so far; and comparing them in a ranking is what settles the matter. Like the particular scientific investigations we've looked at, most practical inquiries start out this way. TWA Flight 800, for instance, or choosing a route home, or the truck crash. In each case, an investigation can fail and still remain tractable, if what we find does not undermine our understanding of the case. It fails only because we cannot find what we know we need.

We normally do not waste our time investigating questions that are not at least tractable in this way, of course. But we do occasionally encounter an intractable investigation when one that starts off well enough turns up data that simply knock off all the initially promising rivals without suggesting anything to take their place. For instance, the computer crashes and nothing we or the technical assistants can think of checks out. Or cases in which someone is chronically fatigued, but nothing seems to help and all tests come up negative. We end up simply baffled. The data have undermined our understanding so that we do not

---

8. You may want to reread the section "Strength and Understanding" in Chapter 4 beginning on p. 181.

know what to think, and, hence, do not know how to proceed. The investigation must pause for some general education. We must read up on the topic or try some experiments to increase our understanding and restore direction to the inquiry.

Unless the problem is very special, we usually have neither time nor motivation to pursue the matter past this point. Standard strategy for baffling mysteries is to ignore them if we can (tool missing from the garage, funny noises the car makes), or remedy them without solving the mystery (buy a new tool, get rid of the car). We usually want to understand a problem only to rid ourselves of it; and when understanding is difficult we settle for ridding.

Science, on the other hand, specializes in just this sort of intractable case. The general project of each scientific discipline is to inquire into something we do not understand well, precisely to increase our understanding of it. One will look into the composition of the atomic nucleus, for instance, and another into how the living cell works, or the forces that shape the earth's crust, the dynamics of the atmosphere, the development of life, or of the universe. The aim in such an inquiry is not to solve practical problems (even though they must sometimes do that too), but to *find a way to think about some aspect of the world* that will increase our understanding of it. And at this general level, we almost never have a number of well-understood rival understandings to guide inquiry. We have at most one, and the entire discipline is struggling to work the kinks out of it. In this way basic scientific progress has all the characteristics of intractable practical investigations, except that there is very strong motivation to pursue them.

The neat-looking particular investigations (into dinosaur extinction, gamma-ray bursts, etc.) we examined in the previous section gain their neat, tractable form only from operating within the evolving general framework provided by their discipline's project. The extinction inquiry is tractable only if we take for granted very general aspects of genetics, stratigraphy, plate tectonics, climatology, and much else. Gamma-ray bursts exist only if we're right to assume all the complex physics and electronics involved in interpreting some very subtle instrument readings. So the contribution these particular tractable explorations make to our understanding of things depends deeply on the general disciplinary project within which they operate. When the nature of that project changes—which happens regularly in the history of any discipline—the internal investigations often lose their point and tractability. They may not even make sense any longer. More important, when we look at the sweep of its history, the very concept of "scientific progress"—the scientific increase in our understanding of the world—has always come through *wholesale changes in these big pictures*, the very changes that undermine the neat tractability of the internal investigations. This is the sense in which science is basically an intractable inquiry.

One such notable leap in our understanding of things occurred when we swapped an earth-centered picture of the universe for a sun-centered solar system. Another happened more recently when the old static picture of the earth's crust was replaced by the dynamics of plate tectonics. These are just the most easily visible examples in which a science replaces its basic theoretical framework—the picture that makes sense of its research. Even more radical transformations of our understanding took place when seventeenth-century geniuses replaced the classical (and quite sensible) way of thinking about bodies in motion with the one we learn today in high school; and when, a century later, chemists gave us our picture of the atmosphere as made up of different gasses; and when Einstein once again changed our picture of motion relativistically; and many many others like this. None of these advances has occurred in the way you would expect if you thought of science as a normal sort of tractable investigation. Evidence gathering is not guided by a list of serious rival understandings; nor does resolution at this general level come through comparing the explanatory facility of a number of well-understood alternatives. How then, you might ask, can it work at all?

The basic questions addressed by scientific disciplines are so hard for human beings to think about that the best we can do in normal times is to have a single, usually sketchy (rival) answer for each. We feel lucky to have one workable picture; competition among many is a luxury beyond hope. Everyday scientific progress consists in gradually fleshing out a single sketchy answer, working out the details of the current general theory. This is the function of the subordinate tractable investigations: to find out just how the elements of the current theoretical structure may be used to explain the details it must if it is the right way to look at things. The huge advances that come from swapping basic pictures occur only when the current one runs out of steam, when it seems no longer capable of helpfully adding detail, and when the subordinate investigations stop paying off. Historically this unhappy time in a science may go on for a long time, or a very short one. But it ends only when some genius, deeply familiar with both the success and failure of the current theoretical structure, thinks of a new kind of sketchy answer that will preserve much of the understanding accumulated under the old one, but point research in a new and more promising direction. Then the process starts all over again: more subordinate tractable inquiry fleshing out a new framework.

The Invisible Success of Science

When we first come to this topic we may have difficulty appreciating the huge advances in human understanding that science has accomplished over the ages. For most of them have simply been incorporated into the picture of the world we all share, and it is hard to think of how things could have ever been otherwise. We naturally dismiss ancient views of the world as unaccountably primitive, easily corrected by simply looking around. How could anybody think the earth is flat or is at the center of the universe? Only an ignoramus could fail to know that the heart pumps blood. But this radically misrepresents both how smart and thoughtful ancient thinkers were, and how hard it is to change our basic understanding of things.

To see this, however, requires the serious study of history. This is the only way to learn, for instance, how easily the human race got along for centuries without the quantitative notion of speed, the notion we find so familiar from car speedometers and police radar guns. This may allow you to appreciate how much genius and plain arduous work went into changing our picture of motion to incorporate that concept, which we could now hardly live without. You may also come to see that the earth-centered picture of the universe, which we now make fun of, was a great advance over the more primitive views it supplanted. Our current understanding could never have been reached without that intermediate step. The advance in our understanding it made possible was indispensable to Copernicus in proposing his sun-centered system. And so on.

The real and impressive ability of science to improve our grasp of the world can be seen only in this long perspective. Just as we (individually) can forget how hard it once was to get around in a now-familiar city, civilized cultures forget how much of their current understanding simply did not exist in earlier epochs. But the objective impact of science on our general understanding becomes clear when we compare ancient and modern pictures of the earth and planets, or the atmosphere, or chemical reactions, or even simple motion. The fact that the improvement is difficult to see just shows how much a part of our basic understanding it has become. It must be judged, like all of our understanding, by the contribution it makes to our competence in dealing with the world.

SUPPLEMENTAL EXERCISES

A. Review Questions

1. What makes information non-trace data?
2. What is an explanatory hurdle?
3. What's the diagnostic verb?
4. What makes an argument essentially *not* diagnostic? Give an example.
5. Describe the different roles of type-a and type-b NTD.

B. Passages for Analysis

1. During a series of operations on the surface of Mars, the scoop arm on the *Viking I* stopped responding to commands. When the *Viking* simulator on earth (a near twin to the mechanism on Mars) was subjected to the same series of operations, a pin malfunctioned and jammed the arm. Subsequently, a simple maneuver by the simulator caused the pin in question to fall out, freeing the arm. Delighted with this turn of events, the scientists in charge of *Viking I* on Mars commanded it to perform the same maneuver. When it did, the *Viking I* arm once again functioned normally. A television camera on board *Viking I* was then trained on the ground directly beneath the scoop arm; a pin just like the one that had jammed the simulator arm was observed lying in the Martian dust. The scientists concluded that the pin had been what jammed the arm on Mars.

a. Schematize the scientists' argument.
b. Give two rival conclusions (as serious as possible).
c. Label the trace data and NTD.

2. BOSTON—Divers found an uncharted rock near where the Queen Elizabeth 2 hit bottom that was scraped clean of vegetation and marked with red paint like that on the luxury liner's hull, officials said yesterday. Damage to the 937-foot cruise ship was much worse than expected, Cunard Lines officials said after dry dock inspections forced the company to cancel all trips through late September. They had hoped to resume next week. The ship suffered a series of gashes, cracks and dents extending along 400 feet of

the hull, said Leon Katcharian, a National Transportation Safety Board investigator.

The National Oceanic and Atmospheric Administration, which has been surveying the accident area off the southern coast of Massachusetts, has found "a number of uncharted rocks out there," said Lt. Cmdr. John Wilder. One rock, $34\frac{1}{2}$ feet deep, attracted the most attention. "Vegetation is not on the rock the way it is on surrounding rocks, and it has this substance that appears to be red paint," Wilder said. The QE2's hull, which is painted red, goes 32 feet below the water line. "We hope to get an analysis this weekend to get a (paint) match," Wilder said by telephone from NOAA headquarters in Rockville, Md.

In Boston, the local pilot helping guide the liner at the time told investigators he wasn't worried when the captain overruled him and altered their course slightly. Charts showed sufficient water depth. John Hadley, a Newport, R.E.-based pilot with almost 20 years experience, also said it was possible for the hull to dip below 32 feet because of certain ocean effects. The QE2 was using British admiralty charts. But Andrew Willis, spokesman for the British Ministry of Defense, said these charts use information from NOAA, which last surveyed the site of the accident in 1939. Wilder said the uncharted rocks were between the 1939 markings, which are spaced far apart.

(Robert W. Trott, *The Associated Press*)

Evidence offered in this article may be schematized in an argument with the IQ: What damaged the hull of the QE2? Two rival conclusions of such an argument would be as follows:

C_1: The QE2 hit the "uncharted rock" mentioned in the first sentence.

C_2: The QE2 hit some other rock, which has not yet been detected.

a. Give another rival (C_3).

b. What is the central trace data?

c. What other trace data are given in the article?

d. Articulate the relevance of the traces in (c) in diagnostic terms.

e. What item of NTD given in the article hurts C_1?

f. In diagnostic terms, explain how this hurts C_1.

g. What information given helps C_1 get around this objection?

3. WASHINGTON—Epidemiologists have concluded from blood tests and interviews with AIDS victims in the small South Florida town of Belle Glade that the disease is not linked to mosquitoes. Instead, the disease has spread in the migrant farming town through the same modes that it follows in some large urban areas: needle sharing among intravenous drug abusers, increased sexual activity with multiple sex partners, and prostitution. Belle Glade, a town of around 20,000, is said to have the highest AIDS rate in the United States with the equivalent of 560 cases for every 100,000 people. The rate in San Francisco has been reported at only slightly over 110 per 100,000. The unusually high rate and the fact that victims denied having homosexual contacts most often associated with the disease's spread had led a number of private researchers to blame the spread on mosquitoes.

A survey reported Friday in the scientific journal *Science* appears to rule out mosquito transmission of the virus in Belle Glade. Among other reasons cited by investigators was the fact that among Belle Glade residents surveyed, no one over 60 or between the ages of 2 and 10 had the human immunodeficiency virus, known as HIV. Investigators also said they were also unable to establish a relationship between persons who had been infected with other mosquito-borne viruses and those with the AIDS virus.

The survey was conducted by investigators from the Centers of Disease Control, the Florida Department of Health and Rehabilitation Services and the Palm Beach County Health Unit. "The evidence does not suggest transmission of HIV through insects," the investigators reported. The survey was based on interviews from 407 randomly selected households and on blood tests, the investigators reported. Of 93 persons reported to have AIDS . . . 34 could be directly linked to at least one other person with AIDS or

AIDS-related complex, the investigators said. No correlation could be established between the disease and exposure to mosquitoes or other insects.

(Jeff Nesmith, *Cox News Service*)

a. What two rivals do the epidemiologist consider?

b. Which rival do they consider to be more plausible?

c. One important item in the argument is the age distribution of those testing positive for HIV. What kind of data is this, trace or non-trace? Explain why it falls in this category.

d. To use the age distribution in this way, the investigators are obviously relying on two unstated items of nontrace data, one about mosquitos and one about human behavior. What are they?

e. Explain why the two items in (d) are non-trace data.

4. . . . A team including a Swedish dentist, Sten Forshufvud, and a Scottish professor of forensic medicine at the University of Glasgow were re-examining the death of Napoleon Bonaparte. "The Murder of Napoleon" by Ben Weider and David Hapgood presents Forshufvud's case.

Rejecting the accepted version that the emperor succumbed to cancer in 1821 on St. Helena, they argue convincingly that he was poisoned. Forshufvud, an amateur toxicologist and second-generation Napoleon buff, was unconvinced by the accepted version of Napoleon's demise. In pursuit of the truth he scanned the intimate records of the valet who accompanied Napoleon into exile. Reading the day-by-day descriptions of Napoleon's decline convinced Forshufvud that Napoleon displayed 22 of the 30 accepted signs of arsenic poisoning.

For instance, the edema that swelled Napoleon grotesquely toward the end, and that is recorded in numerous drawings, is a symptom of arsenic in the system and quite the opposite of the effects of cancer. To prove his suspicions, Forshufvud obtained six samples of Napoleon's hair that were documented as cut during the last months of his life. This was not as difficult as it might seem, since saving locks of hair was an early 19th Century obsession.

The strands went to Glasgow, where a new method of analysis verified the presence of arsenic. Neutron bombardment of a single hair indicated that Napoleon had had many hundred times the amount of arsenic in his body than was normal for the time. The analysis also revealed that the arsenic content of the strand appeared in waves, as if administered in weekly doses. That matched the valet's description of the attacks Napoleon experienced, as well as the recorded ingestion of wine from a particular source. According to these sleuths, Napoleon was slowly poisoned to death.

Capping the argument, Forshufvud recalls that in 1840, when the emperor's body was exhumed for reburial at Les Invalides in Paris, the grave diggers discovered the body as fresh as when it was interred 19 years earlier. They attributed this to a miracle. However, arsenic is a preserver of flesh and is, indeed, the principal ingredient used by taxidermists to preserve animal pelts. . . .

(From the *Los Angeles Times*)

a. What conclusion does Forshufvud favor?

b. What rival is mentioned in the article?

c. For each of the selections below, indicate whether it provides trace data (TD), or non-trace data (NTD), or is not part of the support at all (I).

_____ A Swedish dentist and a Scottish professor of forensic medicine were re-examining the death of Napoleon Bonaparte.

_____ Numerous drawings of Napoleon in his latter days depicted him as being swelled by edema.

_____ Edema is a symptom of arsenic in the system, and quite the opposite of the effects of cancer.

_____ The valet who accompanied Napoleon into exile kept intimate records.

_____ Neutron bombardment tests on a strand of Napoleon's hair indicated that Napoleon had had many hundred times the amount of arsenic in his body than was normal for the time.

_____ Saving locks of hair was an early nineteenth-century obsession.

_____ Napoleon was given wine once a week from a particular source, according to his valet's records.

_____ When it was exhumed 19 years after burial, Napoleon's body was reported to be as fresh as when it was first buried.

_____ Napoleon experienced weekly attacks.

_____ Arsenic is a preserver of flesh, used by many taxidermists to preserve animal pelts.

_____ Napoleon displayed 22 of the 30 accepted signs of arsenic poisoning.

_____ The arsenic content of Napoleon's hair appeared in waves, as if administered in weekly doses.

d. Which of these items provides an explanatory hurdle for he conclusion Forshufvud opposes? Explain what about it makes it a hurdle (that is: articulate in diagnostic terms).

e. Select one statement that you identified as NTD and explain why it is NTD.

f. What item is General Support? What about it makes it General Support?

5. GAINSVILLE, Fla.—A rat's jawbone, a pig's tooth and other artifacts found on the northern coast of Haiti could help pin down the location of Christopher Columbus's first settlement in the New World, a University of Florida researcher said. "We discovered deep in what looks like a well the jaw of a European rat and the tooth of a European pig," Kathleen Deagan, an archeologist at the Florida State Museum on the UF campus, says in the November issue of National Geographic. "Before Columbus, both of these animals were unknown in the New World."

A team of archaeologists and other specialists have been analyzing some seven tons of remains found on the northern coast of Haiti at the site believed to be La Navidad, the fort Columbus built after his flagship, the Santa Maria, ran aground on a coral reef in 1492. Columbus left 39 men at La Navidad. Upon his return a year later, he found the fortress burned and his men dead. The site was abandoned and its exact location lost to history.

The team, which visited Haiti in June, is trying to uncover conclusive evidence that the small Arawak Indian village is the site of La Navidad. Charcoal from a European-style well was carbon dated to the late 1400s. Zoo archaeologists Karla Bosworth and Erica Simons, working under museum curator Elizabeth Wing, identified the rat jaw and the pig bones, which were sent to the University of California at Irvine for further analysis.

"Jonathon Ericson analyzed the tooth for the stable isotopes of carbon, nitrogen and strontium," Deagan said. "Strontium reflects the composition of the soil and the plants that grew in it. Since the pig ate these plants while its bones and teeth formed, Ericson was able to show that the pig grew up in Spain and not Haiti. By comparing the amount of these elements in various Spanish soils with the pig tooth, he concluded that the pig grew up in the vicinity of Seville, not far from Palos, the port from which Columbus set sail," Deagan said.

Deagan and colleague Maurice Williams have been digging on and off for seven years with funding from UF, the National Endowment for the Humanities, the Organization of American States and the National Science Foundation.

(The Associated Press)

This article offers some evidence for the conclusion that the site of a well on Haiti's northern coast is the location of Columbus's fort La Navidad.

a. Describe the most plausible rival you can think of.

b. What question are these rivals answering?

c. For each of the selections below, indicate whether it provides trace data (TD), or non-trace data (NTD), or is not part of the support at all (I).

_____ The jaw of a European rat and the tooth of a European pig were found at the site.

_____ Before Columbus, the rat and the pig were unknown in the New World.

_____ The jaw and tooth were found in a European-style well.

_____ Charcoal from the well was dated to the late 1400s.

_____ Columbus built La Navidad in 1492.

_____ A year later he found the fort destroyed.

_____ The tooth was from a pig that grew up near the port from which Columbus sailed.

_____ The bones were sent to UC Irvine for analysis.

d. One of the items of support is the conclusion of a diagnostic tributary argument. Schematize that argument and label the trace data and NTD.

e. Diagnostically articulate the relevance of the first two items of evidence in (c).

6. Through the rain of embers and fly ash from a nearby brush fire, Herman scrambles up a ladder onto his roof carrying a hose. He must be trying to keep his house from catching fire.

a. What is the IQ of this brief argument?

b. Give the two most serious rivals you can think of.

c. Diagnostically describe the relevance of each item of support and say whether this makes it TD or NTD.

d. Describe some new information that would be an explanatory hurdle for the original conclusion.

e. What NTD would help that rival over this hurdle?

f. Describe some NTD that would boost the plausibility of one of your rivals.

ANSWERS

5.1   a. S The house just shook violently

$$\overline{\underline{\qquad\qquad\qquad\qquad\qquad\qquad\qquad\qquad\qquad}}d$$

C We've had an earthquake.

b. The violent shaking (i.e., S) is TD.

c. S is TD because C explains (or would explain) it.

d. The natural IQ would be typically diagnostic: "What's going on?" or "What was that?" or even "How come the house just shook?" So a natural rival would be C_2 They just blew up a building nearby; or C_3 A dump truck just missed a turn and took out the east wall.

5.2   a. (i) F; (ii) F; (iii) T; (iv) F; (v) T.

b. (i) F; (ii) T; (iii) F; (iv) T.

c. (i) F; (ii) F; (iii) T.

d. (i) F; (ii) F; (iii) T.

e. S_2 and S_3 are NTD. In answering "What set off the blast?" you would not explain why the motel chose propane to heat its water or why propane is explosive.

f.   i. S_1 A brilliant fireball streaked across northern Canada.

       S_2 A Soviet satellite disappeared that same evening.

       S_3 It was due over northern Canada at the time.

S_4 A nuclear reactor was on board the satellite.

S_5 Geologists found obviously fabricated, radioactive debris on a frozen river in the same area.

$$=== d$$

C The fireball was that Soviet satellite falling into the atmosphere.

ii. C explains S_1 (the fireball), S_2 (the disappearance), and S_5 (why there was radioactive debris on the river), so they are TD. In answering the IQ, "What was that flash?," C and its rivals would not be trying to explain the other two items of support. Saying the flash was this satellite, or a meteorite, or something else flaming in the atmosphere would not explain why the satellite was due over Canada, or why it carried a reactor. So these would be NTD.

5.3 Sleep is, at least so far, the best explanation we have of the trace data (crash, tire marks). So it tops the ranking.

5.4 a. The fireball is central, because all the rivals must explain it. This means that features of the fireball, such as its time and direction, are also central TD, for in explaining the fireball, rivals must account for these as well.

b. Busby's disappearance is central: it is what the IQ asks about and so what all rivals must explain. As things stand, the blood and the once-fired handgun are part of this, so they would be central too, as part of what counts as "the disappearance." As always, this could change if new information changed our sense of what happened.

c. The central TD would be the explosion: that the building came down with a bang. This is what the natural IQ would ask about and hence all the rivals would have to explain.

d. This is a trick question: the Arts Center argument has a normative conclusion (We should give the surplus seats . . .), so it is not diagnostic. It won't have TD.

e. Central TD would be URMM's skeleton in the car. This is what raised the question in this case, and hence what all the rivals must account for.

5.5 The radioactive debris is not central. The fireball is what raised the question and hence what the IQ will inquire into. So this is what all the rivals must account for. The debris is directly relevant only to the satellite rival.

5.6 a. The lack of paint on the can is a hurdle: it's hard for the "can scratched the car" rival to explain.

b. The age of the bones is, like "domestic," another key feature of the central TD. So its relevance is that any rival would have to explain it to be serious: it has a big impact on the serious rivals. This articulation is diagnostic because it appeals to explaining support.

5.7 The conclusion (that the maintenance worker set off the blast) would easily explain the severity of his injuries, and that increases its plausibility. So the injuries belong among the support. And because they are explained by C, they would be TD.

5.8 The conclusions of this argument (answering, What happened to Hamilton?) will not be trying to explain why truckers usually abandon their rigs at truck stops. So this is NTD.

5.9 The words you should have underlined are in the first paragraph: "that makes it easier for the root-rot rival to explain the wilting." . . . and . . . "it makes it harder for dry soil (another rival) to explain wilting." And in the second: "This made it easier for the spark rival to explain the explosion." These articulate the relevance of (first) my frequent watering, and (second) the pickled fuel probes.

5.10 **a.** The specific support is the long wait (and consequent heating). It is relevant because it helps the spark in the fuel tank rival explain the explosion (the main trace). Because it gets its relevance in this way it is NTD: it is not itself *being* explained.

  b. **i.** The once-fired handgun is relevant because it is easy for the suicide rival to explain (and not so hard for murder either). This makes it TD.

  ii. Busby's depression is relevant because it would make it easier for the suicide rival to account for the traces. This is the relevance of NTD.

  iii. The blood is relevant because it is something the rivals would have to explain (or at least benefit from explaining). This makes it TD.

  iv. Given what we know, the uninflated life raft does not (at least yet) have any impact on the serious rivals. So it is neither TD nor NTD.

5.12 **a.** Because "no sign of penetration" becomes relevant by being hard to explain (a hurdle for two rivals), that makes it TD.

  b and c. They are NTD because neither the lack of missing aircraft nor the absence of military exercises gains relevance by being explained or by being hard to explain. Their relevance lies in their damaging two rival's ability to explain the traces.

5.13 The Baker Lake argument is sound with the satellite conclusion because that conclusion explains the traces we have better than any other rival. It is strong because, given the NTD, no rival comes close to the satellite's plausibility as an explanation of the fireball.

5.14 The fact that antiaircraft missiles work by seeking engine exhaust makes it hard for the missile rival to explain the undamaged engines. This is not TD because it does not become relevant through being explained, but through affecting a rival's ability to explain.

5.15 Given the missile's altitude limit, the plane's altitude makes it difficult for the missile rival to explain the explosion and crash. Becoming relevant through affecting a rival's ability to explain is characteristic of type-b NTD.

5.16 **a.** The IQ is, "Why is the campus deserted?" (Answer: You're late.)

  b. S_1 The campus is deserted.
  S_2 It's normally crowded.
  S_3 Your watch reads 10:05.
  S_4 It's been running slow.
  S_5 You don't remember setting it lately.
  === d
  C You're late for class.

  c. C_2: It's a holiday (you forgot).
  C_3: It's not a holiday, but it is the wrong day (Tuesday has a different class schedule).

  d. S_1 is relevant because all the rivals must explain it.
     (It's what you're trying to explain.)
  S_2 is relevant because it makes S_1 trace data.
     (It shows that "deserted" is something to explain.)
  S_3 is relevant because it is hard for C to explain.
  S_4 is relevant because it helps C explain S_3.
  S_5 is relevant because it helps S_4 help C explain S_3.

  e. S_1 and S_3 are TD; the others are NTD.

5.17 **a.** S_1 The wind was blowing strongly outside.

   S_2 The reading lamp went out.

   S_3 Immediately afterward*, the study light failed to respond to the switch.

   S_4 Shortly thereafter* a small light was found to be on in the kitchen, and the electric stove clock was also functioning.

   S_5 Immediately* rechecking the reading lamp found it back on.

—————————————————————————————————— d

   C The neighborhood power grid had momentarily failed.

   [*The asterisked words reflect the sequence, hence are part of the trace data.]

   b. S_5 is an explanatory hurdle for the blown-bulb rival.

5.18 We're reasonably assuming (and making part of the explanation) that the maintenance worker was near the explosion when he set it off. The austere reading of "he set it off" does not include this and hence would not explain the injuries.

5.19 **a.** The bullet hole would be easy for the suicide and murder rivals to explain; so it would be TD.

   b. The absence of fingerprints would be hard for the most plausible suicide rival to explain; so it would be TD.

   c. Winning the lottery would make it harder for the suicide rival to explain the disappearance; so it is NTD.

5.20 Investigators know that each of the likely rivals would have characteristic effects on pieces of an aircraft they were responsible for bringing down. These characteristic effects would be trace data, and they would be found on the pieces of the aircraft, which were in the debris field.

5.21 Both would be translated "serious (rival) explanation."

5.22 **a.** S_1, S_6, and S_8 are TD; the rest are NTD.

   b. **i.** That they are radioactive is relevant because C would easily explain this.

   ii. That they are (or even appear to be) fabricated is relevant also because C would easily explain this.

   iii. That they were in a crater in the ice would be relevant because C would explain this too: they got there only recently.

   c. That the river is east of Baker Lake would help C explain the debris: that's where you would have expected them, given the satellite's orbit and the path of the fireball. It would of course be NTD (nothing here should explain why the river is east of Baker Lake).

CHAPTER 6

DIAGNOSTIC PATTERNS

OVERVIEW

In this chapter we will come to recognize many common patterns in our experience as trace data, and hence come to see that many familiar arguments are diagnostic. Each new *kind* of argument will introduce us to a distinct *kind* of trace data. Each also benefits from lumping rival conclusions together into large superwedges of the possibilities balloon.

INTRODUCTION

Diagnostic concepts articulate our basic, rock-bottom judgments about evidence. When something is offered as evidence of something else, the thing to do is throw it into diagnostic form and see how it checks out. In particular you want to see if anything fits as trace data, as something to be explained by rival conclusions. If it does, you may then use all the resources of Chapter 5 to schematize and evaluate the argument in question.

When this can be done with an entire category of evidence we can then see arguments exploiting that kind of evidence as all diagnostic in the same way. This invariably improves our ability to deal with them. In this chapter we will find that many familiar arguments belong to particular diagnostic *kinds*. That is, they have a particular *kind* of trace data, which in turn gives them other distinguishing features. After a few examples you will probably be able to find new kinds of diagnostic argument on your own.

CAUSE AND CORRELATION

Our first characteristic kind of trace data is the *correlation*. We are constantly bombarded by news of correlations between things such as sunburn and skin cancer, national savings rates and economic growth. And these correlations are almost always offered as evidence that the two correlates are *connected* in some way or other. Sunburn is connected to skin cancer; savings and growth are related. A problem arises, however, because sometimes this is done so quickly and naturally that we hardly see any reasoning going on: we read the correlation and simply *see* the connection. But all such cases actually involve an argument (even if an easy one), with the correlation as support and the connection as conclusion.

$$\frac{\text{CORRELATION}}{\text{CONNECTION}}$$

To see this—and to see that the argument is always diagnostic—we must first understand that the correlation is *not the same as* the connection: it is at most *evidence* for a connection. Giving a correlation between two things by itself does not say whether or how the two are connected. So we must find a way of talking about correlations that does not prejudge that question. Correlations must be neutral on the question of a connection.

The most natural way to describe correlations in general is to say that they are two things that "go together." A and B are correlated with one another when they "go together" in some way. This covers many different relationships, but the simplest is one in which A and B are events, and whenever A occurs, B does too. The light in my study comes on whenever I flip the light switch, so we have in this sense a correlation between flipping the switch and the light coming on. If we call the flipping "A," and the light coming on "B," we will represent a correlation between them as A/B. If I say to my mechanic that there's a terrible grinding noise every time I step on the brake, I have described a correlation between pressing the brake and the grinding noise. Other examples would be the correlation between bad weather and a pain in uncle Charlie's elbow and the correlation between eclipses and high tides. In each case we have a sequence of Bs regularly accompanying As:

$$A_1/B_1, A_2/B_2, A_3/B_3, A_4/B_4, \ldots \text{ and so on.}$$

Exercise 6.1

Just for practice, say what *counts* as a correlation in these last two cases (Charlie and eclipses). That is, state what's going on without using the *word* "correlation." (Answers on p. 306.)

We can now see why, when we use a correlation as evidence of a connection, the argument will be diagnostic: A correlation is *something to explain*. When two things "go together" we can always ask "Why?" and the answer will be some kind of explanation. So when a correlation is given to *support* a connection, the connection explains the correlation, making it **Trace Data** in a diagnostic argument.

$$\text{explains} \left\uparrow \frac{\text{CORRELATION}}{\text{CONNECTION}} = d \right\downarrow \text{supports}$$

Sometimes, of course, the explanation will be obvious, as it is for my study light: the flip goes together with illumination because the switch completes an electrical circuit allowing current to flow through the bulb. We all know that, so even though we have trace data and can make a diagnostic argument, it is not very interesting. We just see the connection. But most cases are not so boring. The correlation between my braking and the grinding noise, for instance, is something to investigate. An investigation with the IQ, "Why does the braking correlate with a grinding noise?" will almost certainly teach us something. We may learn that there is nothing to worry about, and I'll just have to get used to the noise; but we may find a problem to fix that will prevent future hazard and expense.

Exercise 6.2

....

A common correlation in our experience is between answering a ringing phone and somebody responding when you pick it up and say "hello." For practice, even though this is an easy case, answer the following: (a) What are the correlates? (b) Describe the correlation without using any form of the word "correlate." (c) What connection explains the correlation? (Answers on p. 306.)

Correlations need not be recurring sequences, however. We may also explain why two things occurred together on a single occasion, which would make them trace data in exactly the same way. Obvious examples would involve the correlation between an earthquake and an overpass collapsing onto the roadway below. What counts as a correlation in this case is simply the bridge falling down *during* the quake—or, at least, being down the first time anybody looked after the shaking stopped. It needs to happen only once for us to use it as trace data: evidence for the explanation that the shaking ground dislodged the bridge from its supports, hurling it to the ground below. It is similar for the correlation between the hornet landing on my arm and a sharp pain I then feel, or between the exploding noise and food all over the inside of the microwave. These, like the light in my study, are not terribly interesting because their explanations are so obvious. But such simple examples serve to point out a very common diagnostic argument. We have two things correlating and a story about why: trace data and explanation. Moreover, many one-time-only correlations *are* interesting, providing clues from which we can learn something valuable. The correlation that geologists have discovered between the extinction of the dinosaurs and a giant meteorite impact may help us understand much about our ancient history. At a more mundane level a correlation between a broken latch on the front door and the missing stereo equipment would certainly be worth investigating.

Exercise 6.3

....

(a) Describe the correlation in these last two cases without using any form of the word "correlate." (b) Describe the connection that probably explains the correlation in the second case. (Answers on p. 306.)

One reason to point out that correlations can be trace data is simply to address a controversy about correlational arguments. Sometimes thoughtful people raise public doubts about whether we should "infer causes from correlations." The present discussion serves merely to point out that such inferences are *diagnostic*, like so many others. So the answer to the question (Should we infer causes from correlations?) is "It depends." Sometimes a correlation (A/B) is evidence for a causal connection between A and B, and sometimes it is not, depending on what else is available for support and what the serious rivals are. The examples we have mentioned are all good candidates for a "yes" answer, just given normal understanding and NTD. The earthquake very likely caused the overpass to fall. The hornet almost certainly caused the pain. Flipping the switch unquestionably causes the light to come on. The likely connections among the other cases are somewhat more complicated, and we will look at them in detail shortly. But in each case the correlation is evidence for *some* causal connection. A connection would explain why A and B occurred together. The reasoning is diagnostic.

Finally, the concept of correlation has one more manifestation: differential frequencies. We have seen that when A and B invariably occur together there is always something to explain, even if the explanation is obvious. So we can always construct a diagnostic argument around them. But we can also have a correlation to explain when A and B go together only sometimes, when there is a *regular pattern* in their occurrence. For then the pattern is something to explain: why this pattern? Some of the most interesting and important correlations are like this: A does not go with B *all the time*, but it does go with B *more than its absence* does. Not everybody who sunbathes gets skin cancer, but more sunbathers do than those who do not sunbathe. So we say there's a correlation between sun exposure and skin cancer. There's a pattern to explain. Similarly, cancer does not correlate with smoking 100%. Far less than half of the people who smoke contract lung cancer. Yet there is a correlation, because one thing *is* regular. More people who smoke contract lung cancer than those who do not smoke. This is all it takes for a correlation to exist between smoking and lung cancer: a pattern to be explained. This kind of correlation is called a "differential frequency": As go with Bs *more often* than not As do. Lung cancer occurs more frequently in smokers than nonsmokers. Whenever you have As going with Bs more often *or* less often than not As do, you have a correlation: trace data to explain.

Exercise 6.4

The article below contains a correlation between two things. (a) What are the two things? (b) State the correlation as trace data, that is, as something to explain. (c) What explanation (connection) is offered in the article? (Answers on p. 306.)

> WASHINGTON—Caution: Dropping out of school may be hazardous to your health. That message was delivered yesterday in the government's annual report charting the nation's health. The National Center for Health Statistics said the death rate among adults ages 25 to 64 who failed to finish high school was 30 percent higher than those who got their diplomas.

That has held true for years, but the gap has widened recently, the center said in the 307-page book, "Health, United States, 1994." "We see better health outcomes for the more educated right from the start," said Dr. Philip R. Lee, the assistant secretary for health and head of the Public Health Service. There were 561 deaths per 100,000 adults among the dropouts, compared with 433 among those with 12 years of education.

(Christopher Connell, *The Associated Press*, abridged)

Let us then set out the general diagnostic picture of correlational arguments. The main or central trace data defining them will always be a correlation, A/B. Their implicit question will always be "Why have A and B occurred together?" and this will cover both observed sequences of As and Bs and also single occurrences of A and B that look as if they could use explaining. We will sometimes abbreviate this IQ simply as "Why A/B?"

FORM	IMPLICIT QUESTION	RIVALS
A/B (Trace) -other stuff- $$\frac{\quad\quad}{?} = d$$	Why have A and B occurred together? or Why A/B?	Stories relating how A and B came about.

General picture of correlational argument.

The General Superrival: Chance

All sorts of different connections might explain why A and B occurred together. But before we look at those, we must look at a more general contrast. For in the diagnostic reasoning about a correlation there is always one general kind of rival that says A and B occurred together *even though they were not connected at all*. It was simply a coincidence, mere chance. Sometimes this is a serious rival. Other times it is implausible. But it is always possible.[1] It may be, for instance, that a huge road-grader careened into a major support knocking down the overpass shortly before the earthquake. So the fact that the collapse correlated with the earthquake would be mere coincidence. The two were not connected. At the beginning of this century share prices on the New York Stock Exchange followed a cycle exactly parallel to that of contemporaneous sunspots. When sunspot frequency increased, so did share prices and vice versa. The correlation was so impressive that serious people began to suspect

---

1. In designing experiments in science the chance rival is known as the "null hypothesis." It says that the parameters being investigated are not related at all, and the results appearing to connect them have been unavoidable bad luck. A well-designed experiment sets things up so that this rival is as implausible as possible.

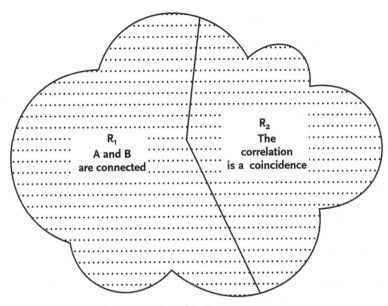

IQ: Why have A and B occurred together?

Figure 6.1. Superwedges grouping stories relating A and B.

some connection between the two phenomena. But, as you might guess, it turned out to be simply a long-running coincidence. No connection could be found.

Chance is a superrival because it covers many different stories about how A and B came about. Just as there are many ways A and B might be connected, there are many different ways in which A and B might occur together unconnected. If we use the IQ "How come A and B have occurred together?" to define a possibility balloon, as in Figure 6.1, we may divide it into two very general superrivals: R_1, which says that A and B are causally connected, and R_2, which says they occurred together by mere chance. R_1 covers all the stories about how A and B might be connected. R_2 covers all those in which they are not connected at all. Even though we will further divide this balloon shortly, this is one of the rare cases in which a single division into two large wedges is actually helpful.

It is helpful partly because our general understanding (together perhaps with some NTD) will often be enough to eliminate chance as a serious possibility. We know enough not to waste time thinking about whether it was merely coincidence that the pain happened right under the hornet, or that the light keeps coming on just as I flip the switch. That means we can dismiss all stories in the R_2 superwedge at once. We do not have to think seriously about any of the coincidence stories. By the same token, if so much as one coincidence story is plausible, we cannot rule out the possibility that A and B were not connected at all. A similar rationale for dividing possibility balloons will occur many times in this chapter.

Directions of Causal Influence

Again, the general picture is pure diagnosis. If we begin with a correlation (A/B), and an IQ asking "Why A/B?," we get a balloon full of stories explaining how the correlation came about (dots). We may add some other relevant TD and NTD, and lump the stories together in various ways before ranking them, and the procedure will be just the one discussed in Chapter 5.

In the last section we saw that one way to lump together the stories is in their answers to the general question "Are A and B causally connected?" The big division in Figure 6.1 corresponds to yes and no answers to this question. And if we get the answer no, that will sometimes be all we care about. But if the answer is yes (they are connected) we will often want to know more than that, because there are different *ways* in which two correlates may be connected, which have importantly different ramifications.

The (rival) stories that might connect A and B fall into three basic patterns. Some explain the connection by saying that A caused B; some say that B caused A; and some appeal to an outside factor we will call "X," which caused both A and B, but independently of each other. These three patterns are called "direct cause," "reverse cause," and "common cause," respectively; we will use the following arrow diagrams as abbreviations for them.

Direct cause: A → B
Reverse cause: B → A

Common cause: X $\begin{array}{c} \nearrow A \\ \searrow B \end{array}$

The three directions of causal influence.

To illustrate these in a single case, consider a racing car crash. The driver is killed. Nobody else saw it take place. All we have to go on is the crumpled car and the damaged scenery. The guardrail is severely scraped and bent near the car's final resting place, with recent-looking tracks leading up to the deformity and away from it again, toward the wreck. Investigators first on the scene note that, among other things, a part of the suspension important to the driver's control of the car is broken. Without looking any further, let us treat this as an interesting correlation: A is the broken part, B is the crash.[2] They may be connected in many different ways, or not at all. So they will illustrate the patterns we are concerned with here.

---

2. It does not matter which you call A and which B, of course. You may call the crash A and the broken part B if you wish. But if you switch them around in this way, the stories we call "direct" causes (below) will become "reverse" causes and vice versa. Otherwise the pattern remains the same.

One story connecting them would be that the suspension part was badly fabricated and broke under the stress of racing, causing the driver to lose control of the car and clout the guardrail. This would be an example of direct cause. A → B, the broken part caused the crash. Another story would have the part perfectly sound right up to the guardrail. But because it was located at just the place the car made contact, it broke on impact. This would be reverse cause. B → A, the crash caused the part to break. Finally, it might be that another car collided with this one and the collision broke the suspension part, but the force of the collision was so great that nothing the driver did could have prevented impact with the guardrail. The broken suspension had nothing to do with it. This would be common cause. The collision caused both the crash and the broken piece, independently of each other.

We call these three kinds or categories "directions of causal influence" because this phrase captures our sense of the way the explanation flows or moves from one thing to another. The arrows represent that flow. There are, of course, many different stories in each direction. Others in the A → B direction would be (a) the broken piece was not enough to cause loss of control, but when it broke it flew up and blinded the driver, who then could not guide the car; (b) the same as (a) except it killed the driver; (c) the same as (a) except that the piece flew off and jammed in one of the brakes, locking the wheel and causing loss of control. Others in the B → A direction would be (a) the piece did not break on impact, but in the violent somersaulting after impact; (b) it broke when the engine broke loose from its mounts and slammed into that part of the suspension; (c) it broke in the ensuing fire. Other common causes are not very interesting, but easy to think of: other cars or even rolling boulders might have caused A and B independently.

Exercise 6.5

....

Give a *rival* story explaining the correlation between my flipping the switch and the light coming on that has the same direction as the obvious one. (Suggestions on p. 306.)

All this serves to divide up the "connected" (R_1) half of our possibilities balloon, as in Figure 6.2. One wedge has been left unnamed, to cover complicated stories that account for the correlation by a number of factors from more than one direction. Rivals such as this will sometimes be serious and we will say more about them shortly.

Using Correlations

The main reason to divide the balloon into these large wedges concerns the actions that we base on correlations. When correlations help us *do* something, we usually need to answer the general questions these superrivals answer. Are A and B connected? If so, in which direction does the causal influence run?

In a common application, for example, we use one correlate simply as *an indicator* of the other. To do this all we need is a yes answer for the first of these

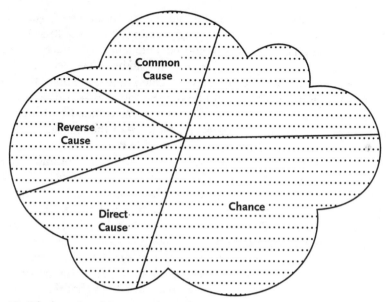

IQ: Why have A and B occurred together?

Figure 6.2. Stories grouped by direction of influence.

two questions: Are they connected? Eclipses correlate with unusually high tides, for instance, and a falling barometer correlates with bad weather. The main use of these correlations has been *prediction*. We know about one correlate and use it to forecast the other one. To do this all we need to know about the correlates is whether they are reliably connected. The particular connection, and even the direction of influence, does not matter. Long before humans knew enough celestial mechanics to figure out even roughly what was going on, they could use eclipses to forecast tides. They knew the correlation fell in the left half of Figure 6.1.

For much of what we do with correlations, however, we need more than just some connection. We need the direction of influence too. For we often wish to use one correlate to affect or influence the other. We quit smoking (or don't start) to avoid lung cancer. We raise interest rates to dampen inflation. We reduce fat intake to keep our hearts healthy. And if we do these things on the basis of correlations, they are reasonable only if the correlates are connected *in the right way*. A → B in each case. The connection between smoking and cancer must be "smoking → cancer," if quitting is to do any good, and the same for the others. Although we may be reasonably sure this is right for these cases, the matter is not always so clear.

When researchers first found the correlation between cholesterol and heart disease, for example, the initial reaction was to recommend that everybody reduce their cholesterol levels to keep their hearts healthy. This presumes that the cholesterol is somehow *causing* the heart disease. That is, the recommendation is reasonable only if the physiological story behind the correlation had the direction "cholesterol → heart disease," and many thoughtful people had reservations about this supposition. The human body is a very complicated mechanism. Without further information it might be that some common factor X was independently causing diseased hearts and high cholesterol, in which case reducing cholesterol would not directly help the heart. Or it could be reverse cause (B → A). The diseased hearts may have been causing the body to produce cholesterol, perhaps in an attempt to get better.[3] In this case reducing cholesterol would actually be harmful. So it was important to determine the direction of influence before making a recommendation. As we subsequently learned more about it, the connection turned out to be far more complicated than originally suspected and the initial recommendation was hasty in a number of ways. We will discuss this case a bit further in Chapter 7.

Completing the Argument

When we learn about a correlation, information available in the context may settle some questions about direction of influence without further investigation. That is, the circumstances may provide diagnostic resources adequate to eliminate one or another of the superwedges immediately, and perhaps enough to make one the strong favorite as the location of the underlying story. Because the direction is always useful and often all we need to know, let us look at the way diagnostic concepts systematize our understanding here. We will first explore the NTD characteristic of correlational arguments, then do the same for TD.

NTD

We often know enough about the kinds of things the correlates are, and how they work, to narrow the possible connections between them. We know enough about earthquakes and fallen overpasses, for example, to practically eliminate reverse cause and common cause in explaining a correlation between them. It's easy to see how an earthquake might knock down an overpass, but much harder to imagine the reverse. Since the causes of earthquakes are the titanic forces and features buried in the earth's crust, a common cause is equally hard to take seriously. So, from the outset, only direct cause and chance look like serious possibilities. This vastly simplifies investigation.

Exercise 6.6

Describe a common-cause story that would explain the correlation between an earthquake and a collapsed overpass. (An example is on p. 306.)

---

3. This is exactly the explanation of the correlation between infection in the body and high white blood cell count. The body reacts to the infection by sending white cells to fight it. This analogy was part of what prompted some to take seriously the reverse cause possibility for the cholesterol/heart disease correlation.

We are so familiar with the rudiments of earthquakes and bridges that we need not explicitly mention this understanding in an argument. We simply leave reverse and common cause stories off the serious list. When correlates are less familiar, however, we may have to include in the argument information about what might be going on behind the scenes. We often know something special about the sort of underlying story that might connect A with B and can add that to the support. This is a special kind of NTD known as **Modus Operandi** (literally: way of operating). It is information about how the correlates work, or about how *something* works that would connect them. The wilting-plant argument of Chapter 4 may serve as an illustration. Although we did not describe the case this way, what we had found there was a correlation between my watering the plant and its wilting, which we wanted to explain. But to explain it we needed some additional information, namely, that a local fungus thrives in wet soil and feeds on roots. This is a modus operandi (abbreviated MO) in our sense.[4] Adding this information to the argument supports a certain direction of influence.

S_1: Frequent watering/wilting plant.
S_2: Wet soil encourages a root-eating fungus. (MO)
———————————————————————— d
C: Watering → Wilting

Exercise 6.7

Schematize the argument for the obvious explanation of the earthquake/collapsed overpass correlation, explicitly adding to the argument the MO you take for granted in reaching this conclusion. (Answer on p. 307.)

Explicit or not, modus operandi considerations are almost always at work in our thinking about correlations. Earlier we mentioned the striking parallel between stock prices and sunspots at the beginning of the twentieth century. Everybody concerned with them knew enough about the correlates to rate coincidence a very good bet. But because the correlation went on so long people began speculating about just how these two phenomena might be connected, if it were not just chance. Knowing a little bit about sunspots makes it vastly more likely that they might influence terrestrial events, and hence maybe the stock market, than the reverse. Common causes seem unlikely for the same reason (the case is in a way just like earthquakes and overpasses). So just by thinking through possible connecting mechanisms (MOs), the serious possibilities were narrowed to two superwedges: chance and reverse cause (sunspots → share prices). Later events es-

---

4. There are two different ways to think about modus operandi, both of which fit in this case. You may think of the MO as belonging to one of the correlates (in this case, A). The MO explains how overwatering works. It encourages a fungus. Alternatively, you may think of it as belonging to the fungus itself. This is how the fungus works. It links overwatering with wilting. One or the other of these will fit most cases.

tablished that the correlation was merely a coincidence. But before that we had already ruled out much of the balloon.

Exercise 6.8

Leaving gravitational physics aside, the average educated person of the early twenty-first century knows enough about eclipses (i.e., the obscuring of the sun or moon by the moon or earth) to make a direct causal connection (in either direction) an implausible account of their correlation with high tides? Explain. (Answer on p. 307.)

One other kind of information that may be obvious as soon as we learn of an A/B correlation would be other things that *also* correlate with A and B (**Other Correlates**). These will be NTD, which, together with what we know about modus operandi, often favor common cause or chance explanations of the A/B correlation. For instance, if we know that two freeway overpasses, some distance apart, fell down at around the same time, that would count as a correlation: O_1/O_2. But if we also know they fell down during an earthquake (that is, they also correlated with an earthquake), that would make common cause the most likely account of the O_1/O_2 correlation.

Exercise 6.9

(a) What is the common cause account of O_1/O_2? (b) What modus operandi considerations make this more likely than the other directions? (Answers on p. 307.)

In another kind of case, suppose you forgot to put your name (or ID number) on one of the weekly quizzes in a certain course (A) and received an unusually low grade on that quiz (B). This would be a correlation, and you might speculate about how omitting your name might have affected the grade. However, if you also know that you skipped class and did not do the reading for the week, this would be something else that correlated with both A and B. In this context it would be NTD favoring a chance explanation of the correlation. For lack of preparation would be such a good explanation of the low grade that we need not try to construct weird stories involving your name.

Exercise 6.10

What is the most plausible story you can think of that would connect omitting your name to the grade in this case? What direction of influence does this story have? (Answers on p. 307.)

Perhaps the most important time to think of "other correlates" is in statistical studies: attempts to determine the causes and effects by looking at correlated properties within groups. Consider looking for effects. Suppose we study frequent flyers and find that traveling by air (A) correlates with something else, say hospital admissions (B): people who fly a lot spend more time in the hospital than other people. We may come away thinking that air travel is bad for your health and safety. But we should also suspect that frequent flyers have many other things in common besides airplanes and hospitals; and if they do, these other things may well explain the correlation better than any direct relation between flying and hospitalization. For instance, frequent flyers may have higher stress jobs than most of us. This might provide a common cause account of the correlation: increased hospitalization resulting not from the flying, which is a relatively safe and relaxing part of the job, but from illness traceable to stress-damaged immune systems. But you should suspect even more than this. Frequent flyers encounter a greater range of people and climates than the rest of us, keep less regular hours, and have less regular daily routines. All these things lead to lives that are systematically different from those of us who do not fly that much. The point is that the feature you use to identify a group (A) usually correlates with *many* other characteristics of that group. There may be a stable pattern connecting many different features of the group. Such a pattern holds endless opportunities for common causes such as the one singled out above. Many "other correlates" may provide rivals explaining B without going through A.

This is why researchers, when doing group studies such as this, will use what they call a "control group" to check direct causes and effects. That is, they will not, if investigating some effect of air travel, compare frequent flyers with all other people in general. They will select a control group that *matches* the flyers they've studied *on all other characteristics they think might matter* to the effect (B) in which they're interested. That way, the effect's common causes should show up in each group and eliminate misleading correlations. Of course the two groups cannot match on everything, but if B is hospitalization, they will match the two groups on other things that might explain differences in hospital admission rates. This means we must know a lot about modus operandi to hope to learn anything from such a study. We must have some understanding of what might cause and be caused by both flying and hospitalization. These are the connections that create stable patterns in our lives. But we often do know enough, which is why we can learn from group studies. Even when we do not, however, we can learn a lot about modus operandi from running group studies and noticing how they fail to meet our expectations.

Exercise 6.11

· · · · · · · · · · · · · · · · ·

The article below assumes you know there's a correlation between silicone breast implants and health problems. Use our discussion of "other correlates" to answer the following questions. (a) What commonly accepted connection are they raising doubts about? (b) What raises those doubts (give the *kind* of information, in our terms, and list the examples of it given in the article)? (c) Are these TD or NTD in the correlational argument? (d) What direction of influence do they make more serious? (e) Explain. (Answers on p. 307.)

> Women who have breast implants drink more alcohol, have children at a younger age, have more sexual partners and make other lifestyle choices that could account for some of the health troubles blamed on the implants, researchers from the Hutchinson Cancer Research Institute in Seattle, the National Cancer Institute and other organizations say. "We found that some demographic, life-style, reproductive, and medical characteristics of women with breast augmentations were notably different than those among women in general in our sample," said authors of the study of 3,750 women published in the current Journal of the American Medical Association.
>
> Women who got implants were more likely to dye their hair, for instance, and dyes are suspected to cause the kind of connective tissue disease sometimes attributed to implants. The point, the authors say, is that any studies that compare women with implants to those without must account for other differences between the women. Those differences might make women with implants more likely to have medical complications, although some could also make them healthier.
>
> (*The Associated Press*)

TRACE DATA

Easily available trace data may narrow down possibilities too. Sometimes a single trace will provide an explanatory hurdle for an entire segment of the possibilities balloon; and such hurdles can be insurmountable. The best example is **Temporal Order.** We often know which correlate occurred first in a single pair, or occurs first regularly in a sequence.[5] I know the hornet landed on my arm *before* I felt the pain. The flipping of the switch always *precedes* the light coming on. This virtually eliminates the reverse-cause direction. If A occurs before B, direct-cause and common-cause stories can usually be found that will explain this order. But reverse-cause stories (B → A) usually cannot. Philosophers have generated a whole literature discussing weird circumstances in which we might find it reasonable to think of causes coming after their effects. But as far as anyone knows, those weird conditions never occur. So in everyday cases we need not give them a second thought. Our normal experience tells us that causes *never* come after their effects. This is such familiar NTD that we do not even need to mention it in an argument. So when we know the order in which the correlates occurred, we can rule out one whole wedge of the balloon.

---

5. This can also be deceptively tricky. Sometimes it will depend on exactly how we formulate A and B, which in turn will depend on subtle details of context. We will treat this in some detail shortly in the section on *Refinements*.

Exercise 6.12
....

Explain how temporal order can effectively rule out any connection between the earthquake and the overpass collapse. (Answer on p. 307.)

Another trace that may be obvious or easily available is the **Length of a Sequence.** We may know at least roughly how many times A and B have occurred together. The longer the sequence, the less likely the correlation is just a coincidence. But just how unlikely it is depends on what we know about the correlates. If, like the sunspot/stockmarket correlation, the two are implausibly connected to begin with, a long sequence will simply allow us to take the correlation seriously. It's probably chance; but the long run makes it at least interesting and we may treat it as trace data. On the other hand, if a connection between A and B is plausible to begin with, as in the case of the grinding noise when you press the brake pedal, a long, reliable sequence will virtually establish that there is *some* connection between the two. It will virtually eliminate the possibility of pure chance (the null hypothesis). We will treat this sort of case further when we look at sample-to-population inferences later in the chapter.

Something else we may pick up along with the correlation are **Traces of a Modus Operandi.** That is, we know how certain kinds of causal factors work, and that allows us to recognize traces left by them, details they can easily explain. For instance, if we find in the debris of our racing car crash (B) that one of the tires is cut (A), we may suspect it caused the crash (A → B). But if it did, that may show up in the marks left on the track by the car as the driver struggled for control before impact. If there are three consistently dark black skidmarks and one that is light and irregular, that is reason to think the tire was flat before the crash and may have caused it. This works both ways, of course. If we find four identical dark black marks, that will be very hard for the A → B stories to explain. This would be an explanatory hurdle for that entire direction.

Exercise 6.13
....

What modus operandi NTD lie behind the trace data of this last example? (Answer on p. 307.)

Finally, a special case of this last kind of trace that is worth noting separately is **The Interval between A and B.** Some rivals explain short intervals easier than long ones, whereas others have trouble with short ones. So if, in addition to which came first, we also know the interval, we not only eliminate an entire superwedge (reverse cause), we can narrow down the list in the rest of the balloon as well. For instance, if a fungus accounts for my plant's wilting, the interval between watering and wilting will be a matter of days. For we know that a fungus takes a while to grow and do its damage (MO). So if the wilting occurred immediately, as I was pouring on the water, that would virtually eliminate the fungus explanation. We would have to look for something exotic that would have an immediate effect.

Exercise 6.14
....

What might have such an immediate effect? (Answer on p. 307.)

GENERAL CONSIDERATIONS OF BOTH KINDS

Occasionally our general understanding of how things work, together with obvious features of A and B, will make the *kind* of connection between them obvious. Nothing further will be required to place it in one superwedge of the balloon. The hornet/pain correlation is one of those: we know hornets sting, and how and where we feel the pain, and that not much else feels like that. So the general connection between the correlates is clear. More interesting, however, are the "correlations" we automatically (and correctly) attribute to chance. I had a flat tire the same day that the space shuttle *Challenger* exploded. But that provides no reason to suspect some kind of connection between them. If somebody asked me about them I would unhesitatingly attribute the "correlation" to chance. Normally we would not even consider these two events as correlated because an inexhaustible supply of pairs correlate as well as these two do, and are just as boring. The only reason to mention them is to show how obvious coincidence sometimes is.

Exercise 6.15
....

Give another example (from your own experience) of a correlation due obviously to mere chance.

Prodding Our Imagination

The main reason to look through all these possibilities in a reasoning text is to prod our imagination when thinking about correlational inferences. Tricky cases can deceive us about the connection (or lack of it) between correlates. So let us briefly summarize the points just examined:

1. When trying to explain a correlation, force yourself to try out rivals of more than one kind (in more than one superwedge). An explanation from one direction may seem more plausible than it is until you actually think through possibilities from the rest of the balloon.

2. Be alert for characteristic NTD, both General (MOs) and Specific (other correlates). These can narrow down the possibilities and even eliminate an entire wedge.

3. Be alert for obvious trace data. The temporal order of A and B, the interval between them, and traces of particular MOs will sometimes be easily available, and have a major impact on the kind of rivals that are plausible.

Exercise 6.16

a. The following article begins by suggesting one explanation of a correlation and ends by suggesting that a different direction of influence may be possible. (i) Give the correlates. (ii) Describe the correlation. (iii) What explanatory story does Dr. Gallerani think the correlation supports? (iv) What direction does it have? (v) What rival story do experts think also possible? (vi) What direction does it have? (Answer on p. 307.)

> An Italian study lends credence to speculation that low cholesterol may make people depressed. Researchers found that hospital patients who had attempted suicide had lower cholesterol levels than other patients. The findings "seem to support the hypotheses . . . that low cholesterol concentration could precede depression and consequently enhance the risk of parasuicide (suicide attempts)," concluded Dr. Massino Gallerani, one of the researchers at St. Anna Hospital in Ferrara, Italy. Other experts, however, say the study does not prove whether cholesterol altered moods or vice versa.
>
> *(The Associated Press)*

b. The following article argues against a certain connection between correlates. (i) What are the correlates? (ii) What correlation has been found between them (in earlier studies)? (iii) What connection (direction) does the article argue against? (iv) What two rudimentary stories from other directions does the article suggest? (v) Give the directions of these stories. (Answer on p. 308.)

> CHICAGO—The holiday season may bring visions of sugar plums to dance in kids' heads, but parents need not fear that candy-eating children will spin out of control, say researchers who analyzed 23 studies on sugar and behavior. Sugar consumption does not significantly affect the way most children act or think, researchers concluded after reviewing studies involving more than 500 youngsters, mostly younger than 15 years old. "The question remains as to why the results of controlled studies differ so much from the impression of parents," the researchers said in their report in the Journal of The American Medical Association.
>
> The answer may be in what parents expect, added researchers, led by Dr. Mark L. Wolraich of the pediatrics department at Vanderbilt University's Child Development Center in Nashville. Parents may remember reports of two studies from 1980 and 1986 that linked sugar intake and hyperactivity, the authors said. But the methods in those studies made it impossible to tell whether sugar caused the hyperactivity or whether the children's hyperactivity led to their eating sugar. Also, children get excited at parties and on holidays when large amounts of sugar are consumed. A variation in behavior related to events may be mistaken for a reaction to sugar, the researchers said.
>
> The new analysis involved 23 other studies, conducted between 1982 and 1994. All but one compared sugar and sugar substitutes given to children without anyone involved knowing whether the youngsters got the sugar or the substitute.
>
> *(The Associated Press)*

c. In the article below, two studies suggest an at least preliminary connection between two correlates. (i) Give the correlates. (ii) Describe the correlation. (iii) What preliminary connection is suggested (especially by LaCroix)? (iv) What other correlate has been ruled out (controlled for)? (v) What other correlates are mentioned as not having been ruled out? (vi) What kind of rival would these other correlates likely provide? (vii) Give an example (make up a story of this kind). (Answers on p. 308.)

> People who drink five or more cups of coffee a day are nearly three times more likely to develop coronary artery disease than non-drinkers, according to a newly published report from Johns Hopkins University Medical School. The heart troubles could be caused by eating foods high in cholesterol, not getting enough exercise or other bad habits that may be more pronounced among coffee drinkers, said Andrea Z. LaCroix, a disease specialist and one of the authors. But while studies continue, she advised people to assume the coffee is the culprit. "Individuals interested in acting prudently, based on questions we raised, should be discouraged from drinking large amounts of coffee," LaCroix, whose study appears in today's New England Journal of Medicine, said.
>
> Alan Dyer, author of another new study on coffee and heart disease, sounded a similar warning yesterday: "People should drink no more than three or four cups a day," said Dyer, acting chairman of community health programs at Northwestern University Medical School. However, Dr. Daniel Levy, director of cardiology at the Framingham (Mass.) Heart Study, cautioned against overreacting. Coffee "is not the smoking gun we have for cigarettes, cholesterol and high blood pressure, but it is at least prudent to cut back on extraordinary consumption."
>
> LaCroix's team followed 1,130 Johns Hopkins medical students for up to 35 years. Fifty-one suffered heart attacks, angina or sudden cardiac death; detailed comparisons were made between their coffee drinking habits and those of the rest of the group. The findings were dramatic: People drinking five or more cups a day were two to three times more likely to develop coronary artery disease than non-drinkers. Heavy coffee drinkers can substantially lower their risk by reducing their daily consumption.
>
> Dyers' study, presented last month at a meeting of the World conference of Cardiologists but not yet published, yielded similar findings. Men who drank six cups of coffee a day were nearly twice as likely to die from coronary artery disease than non-drinkers, based on a study of 1,910 workers at a Western Electric factory in Chicago. But while Johns Hopkins researchers found the risks of drinking coffee grew with each cup consumed, Dyer found troubles mainly in people who drank at least six cups. Both studies factored out the effects of cigarette smoking.
>
> (*KNT/Boston Globe*)

Refinements

In addition to the above reminders, the diagnostic model can refine our grasp of correlational arguments in three distinct ways.

SUPERWEDGES AS EXPLANATIONS

Sometimes a direction of influence (or chance) will count as a rival by itself and sometimes not. It all depends on what needs explaining. Usually the picture looks like this:

	RIVALS	PLOT
S_1 A/B		(SUPERWEDGE)
S_2 Other stuff	Story$_1$	
========= d	Story$_2$	$A \rightarrow B$
C: Story$_3$	Story$_3$	
	Story$_4$	$B \rightarrow A$
	Story$_5$	A
	Story$_6$	X
	Story$_7$	B
	Story$_8$	
	Story$_9$	Coincidence
	Story$_{10}$	

The rivals, normally, are *particular stories* connecting A and B—and these will be rather small slices of the balloon. When we group those rivals together in the superwedges called "direct cause," "reverse cause," "common cause," and "chance," we do so to point out an interesting feature those stories have in common. The direction of a story might be thought of as its "plot," in one sense. All the stories in a single superwedge of the balloon share a "plot" in this sense. So these general headings (directions) are often not themselves rivals, but simply a pattern that a number of the stories have in common.

But sometimes the plot itself is explanatory; and when this happens one of the superwedges may be treated as a rival (a superrival). In a standard context, for instance, one explanation of the smoking/cancer correlation is simply, "Smoking causes lung cancer." For some of our purposes this will adequately answer the question, "Why do these two things go together?" This is similar for the correlation between my flat tire and the *Challenger* disaster. In most contexts all that would be needed would be, "It was just a coincidence." The chance wedge is enough. We might go on to give a more detailed underlying story in each case, but that may be a waste of time. If the more general answer is right, it may resolve the puzzle if there was one.

Nevertheless, it is important to keep in mind that bare "plots" are explanatory only in special circumstances. Quite often none of the superwedge names will be explanatory all by itself; and even when one is, the others usually will not be. For instance, in the smoking/cancer case, the reverse-cause direction (cancer causes smoking) is not an explanation: as it stands it is just puzzling (how could cancer cause smoking?). So if you wish to include a rival from that direction, you will have to tell a story—say how something like that *could* explain the correlation. Similarly, if I tried to explain the flat/*Shuttle* disaster correlation by saying "The flat caused the disaster," it would only boggle minds. Before it can be a rival I will normally have to say a lot more about how the flat could cause the disaster. All this means is that you must pay attention to what is explanatory in a context. But we are all reasonably good at this when we put our minds to it, which is why diagnostic argument plays such a big role in our lives.

Exercise 6.17
....

Which plot is by itself explanatory of the overpass$_1$/overpass$_2$ correlation in normal circumstances? (Answer on p. 308.)

COINCIDENCE RIVALS

The "chance" superwedge is the one most commonly treated as a rival. For the role chance plays in these arguments is often purely negative. It is the "plot" that is left when nothing else looks very good. That is why it is called the "null hypothesis": frequently the only evidence we can get *for* it is simply evidence *against* all the others. If the best connections between A and B all look implausible, their correlation must have been a coincidence.

Nevertheless, there are genuine stories within the large chance wedge. They are stories about how A and B came about that show they had nothing to do with each other. Sometimes such stories will be on the list of serious rivals, offering better or worse explanations of some traces. I heard a gunshot just as an ugly fracture showed up in my windshield. But the gunshot clearly came from behind, where guns were being brandished in an intemperate dispute about driving style, whereas the fracture was only on the outside of the windshield. One serious story would be that the fracture came from an isolated piece of debris tossed up by a truck wholly unconnected to the menacing exchange to the rear, which was the source of the gunshot. Traces favoring the truck account of the windshield fracture would be the lack of holes in my other windows and that only the outside layer of windshield was cracked.

Exercise 6.18
....

Explain why the truck account of the fracture counts as a chance account of the correlation. (Answer on p. 308.)

This is of practical importance because sometimes the best we can do is find a *piece* of such a story. We may simply find some other factor D that caused one of the correlates and that looks unconnected to the other one, but not know enough detail to make it a complete story. By itself, however, such a piece will often be *very strong NTD favoring the chance superrival*. Consider an example. As I leave my office one evening I routinely flick off the light switch (A). Instead of the usual result, however, every light in the building, along the corridor and in other offices, goes out immediately (B). A → B is not very plausible, but the correlation is so impressive that, lacking any other account, I am inclined to accept it. On my way home, however, I hear on the car radio that the entire downtown area (where my office is located) has been plunged into darkness by a transformer that failed at the local substation (D). I heave a sigh of relief: the original correlation (A/B) was certainly just a coincidence. The reasoning is this: D most likely caused B, and D is certainly unconnected to A; so B is probably unconnected to A.

This is a powerful strategy, for which you will find many applications. But in trickier cases it holds some hazards that you must take care to avoid. For it is easy to overlook all the complicated ways in which correlates may connect with other factors and, hence, with each other. Consider the general case in which we have a correlation A/B and find that B was caused by D (D → B) This by itself does not show that B is not connected to A. For the following five arrangements are still possible:

1. $A \rightarrow D \rightarrow B$
2. $D \rightarrow A \rightarrow B$
3. $D \rightarrow B \rightarrow A$
4. $D \nearrow^{A} \searrow_{B}$
5. $X \nearrow^{A} \searrow_{D \searrow_{B}}$

Thus finding a D → B connection helps only under certain particular circumstances. That is, *when all three kinds of connection between A and D are implausible AND B → A is too.*

Exercise 6.19
....

Go through the five diagrams and note how meeting the four conditions in this last sentence does eliminate them all. (Answer on p. 308.)

Such circumstances nevertheless do occur, as in the "office switch" example. So with a little care this strategy can be immensely helpful in correlational arguments. Perhaps most useful are cases in which A occurs before B. That will eliminate B → A; so we can then concentrate on determining whether D can be plausibly linked to A. If it cannot, we have established that A/B was just a coincidence.

Exercise 6.20
....

Go through the "office switch" illustration above and sketch the most plausible stories you can think of connecting A with D in each direction and note their implausibility. Do we also have to worry about B → A? (Suggestions on p. 308.)

UNDERSTANDING A AND B

Another refinement concerns determining just how to think about the correlates themselves, that is, just what A and B are supposed to cover. For usually the terms we use for A and B will have a range of application and lean heavily on the context for their significance. For instance, if asked out of context what the word "smoking" means, we'd have to say something very general about visible fumes given off by combustion. But when talking about the correlation between smoking and cancer, we know the word means something much more specific. It doesn't cover just any smoke, nor just anything you might do with it. It means tobacco smoke, and it means inhaling it, and fairly frequently, certainly more than a couple of times a year.

With less familiar cases, however, we can often miss a subtlety about what a correlate is supposed to cover and misunderstand the entire argument. For instance, people not paying close attention to the original cholesterol/heart disease studies came away thinking they concerned the cholesterol in food. But they did not. They concerned cholesterol levels in the bloodstream. Heart disease was correlated with *serum* cholesterol, not dietary cholesterol. This is important because the relation between the two is very complicated. Some people can eat a lot of high cholesterol food and still have low levels in their blood. With others it is just the reverse. And it is often easier to change levels in the blood through drugs or exercise than it is through changing diet. So this relatively easy confusion about the trace data led to a serious misperception of the study's significance.

More important, if you misunderstand a correlate you will usually have trouble understanding the rivals. If someone proposed a reverse-cause account of the smoking/cancer correlation (cancer causes smoking), for example, we could make no sense of it on our normal picture of the correlates. For "cancer" (correlate B) ordinarily refers to the malignancies detected late in the life of a long-time smoker. This would make reverse-cause incoherent. So to even consider the reverse account requires that we radically revise our normal picture of the cancer correlate—of what counts as B. We would have to expand the notion of "having cancer" to include previously undetected early stages of pathological development that occur *before* a person starts smoking. Then we could have a story such as, lung cancer begins very early in life (may be genetic) and as it develops it produces a craving for smoky air, which is easily satisfied by lighting up, thus explaining the correlation.

A more plausible example occurred some years ago when a study by some Canadian physicians found a correlation between the fussiness of babies (A) and their intelligence (B). Fussy babies tended to be smarter. They thought the best account of this correlation was neurological stimulation. Parents interacted more with fussy babies (trying to quiet them down) and that interaction stimulated brain development. But to see how this could be a possible rival, you had to notice that the intelligence (B) in the correlation was measured some years after the fussiness occurred. For if intelligence and fussiness were measured at the same time, as you might naturally think, there would be no time for the stimulation to help IQ develop. So the physicians' favorite rival would not even be on the list.

One way to check your understanding of the correlates, therefore, is to see if they make sense in the explanations suggested by the author. More generally, you will want to think through stories from various directions that would explain the offered data, and note what plays the key causal roles in those stories. This will sometimes be a revelation.

Exercise 6.21
. . . .

Consider the following episode.

> Late for an appointment, Linda weaves her way through light, early evening traffic faster than she would usually drive, just making a couple of traffic lights that she normally finds herself stopped at when she takes this route. Up ahead the light is red. "Change, dammit," she yells to herself as she begins to slow. Obediently, the light flashes green and she continues without even having to downshift.

The word "obediently" suggests that her yelling actually caused the light to change, which we realize is preposterous, even though we could tell some fantastic stories linking the two things in that way. (i) What are the two things (the correlates) such stories would link? (ii) Give the best story you can think of linking them in the way "obediently" suggests. Far more plausible than this would be a *reverse*-cause story explaining the yell as a yip for joy upon realizing the light was about to change. (iii) Give this reverse story. Telling this reverse story doubtless required revising your picture of one of the correlates (changing what it covered). (iv) Which one and how? (Answer on p. 308.)

Finally, you have to be alert for tricky contrasts when the correlation is "comparative." In a comparative correlation, one or both of the correlates can vary continuously over a range. For instance to say that A correlates with B sometimes means that with A you get more of B than you do with not A, even though you get some B there too.[6] The obvious case again is smoking/cancer. There's a correlation because more smokers die of lung cancer than nonsmokers; but some nonsmokers die of it too. In any case, what we call the "contrast" in a case such as this is *nonsmokers*. To say there's a correlation between smoking and cancer is to say that smokers succumb to cancer *more than nonsmokers*. This is an easy case, but if you remember to keep the contrast in mind, you will avoid some serious misunderstandings. In the "fussy babies" example we just looked at, for instance, one way to see what's going on is to ask the comparative question: "these kids have a higher IQ than what?" And the answer, of course is, "higher than those kids who were *not* fussy when they were babies some years ago." As this case shows, asking for a contrast will often reveal the "control group" used in the group studies we discussed earlier under "other correlates" as NTD.

---

6. These include the cases we referred to earlier in which the correlation consists in a "differential frequency": Bs go with As more frequently than they go with not As.

Exercise 6.22
....

The following article infers a causal connection from a correlation. (a) What are the correlates? (b) What direction of influence does the article offer between them? (c) State the correlation in a way that makes its contrast clear. (d) Give a rival story with a different direction of influence (the contrast should help you do this.) (Answers on p. 309.)

> TOKYO—Take a dip in a hot spring everyday and you'll stay healthy, at least if you're a monkey living in botanical gardens on Japan's northern main is-land of Hokkaido. The 45 Japanese monkeys in the city Botanical Gardens at the Yukawa Hot Spring Spa in Hokkaido, about 500 miles north of Tokyo, make it a habit to take a hot bath each day, said one of the keepers recently. Monkeys kept in cages catch colds and are susceptible to serious diseases, but the botanical animals rarely do, the keeper said.
>
> *(United Press International)*

THE DIAGNOSTIC NATURE OF A CORRELATION

If the wind blows a door closed and five minutes later we hear a slamming noise, we don't even think of it as a correlation. Only in weird circumstances would we ask how the two events were connected. Correlations are not just any pair of events. They are ones that look like they might be connected, that look like they would be *interesting* to explain. **So Simply Identifying Something as a Correla-tion Automatically Picks It Out as Trace Data, as a Pair to Explain.** If asked to explain why we think something is a correlation, then, we would say of it just what we would say of any trace data: it needs explaining, or it suggests an ex-planation, or otherwise would be interesting to explain.

Our understanding of how things work (that is, of modus operandi) is thus in-volved in the very recognition of correlations. This is why traces such as interval and frequency are worth systematic attention. For no matter how implausible it might otherwise seem, one sign that A and B may be connected is that they occur at the very same time and place, or occur together frequently. If I spill my coffee just as someone comes into the room, that all by itself is reason to suspect some connection between the two events. And if the shower drain plugs up every time your cousin visits, that is something to explain. The explanation may be coincidence in either case; but the pairings were suspicious enough to be correlations.

Exercise 6.23
....

If nobody saw an overpass collapse, what about it might make it reasonable to think of it as correlating with an earthquake. Explain why in diagnostic terms. (Answer on p. 309.)

This of course allows for a whole range of borderline cases, pairings that may or may not be considered correlations. But, if suspicious, we can always take any pair to be a correlation, throw it in diagnostic form, and see how it checks out. This will guide us in looking around for characteristic traces and NTD. We know going in that chance is a good bet and we may simply confirm that by running through our checklist (p. 257). But diagnostic form will help us notice traces of a connection if there is one. If the matter is important enough, of course, we may do more than look around in the context. We may launch an investigation.

Correlational Investigation

As with any diagnostic question, correlational IQs naturally generate investigations. But we investigate correlations for two quite distinct purposes, one practical and the other theoretical, and that can affect the shape of inquiry. Our practical interest may lie in using one of the correlates to forecast or manipulate the other. We may care about the cholesterol/heart disease correlation, for instance, only to decide whether to adopt cholesterol-lowering life-style changes for the sake of health. We may care about the eclipse/tide correlation only to forecast tides. If we have such a practical interest, then the object of the investigation will be simply to place the connection between A and B in one of the superwedges of the possibilities balloon. Doing so may require discovering something about the underlying story, but that will be secondary. We will primarily want to know if the direction of influence is from cholesterol to heart disease or not, and whether the tides are actually connected to eclipses.

On the other hand, we may view the very same correlations not as something to exploit in our lives, but as a clue to a deeper phenomenon we would like to understand better. We may investigate the cholesterol/heart disease correlation to better understand the workings of the cardiovascular system, for instance. This may lead to remedies and recommendations about life-style; but the main aim would be to find the underlying story. This is similar for eclipses and tides. We may have no interest in forecasting tides, but nevertheless have some scientific curiosity about why they go with eclipses so regularly. In such cases we would need to know more than in which superwedge the explanation falls. We seek more of the explanatory story: details of the underlying mechanism.

Exercise 6.24

(a) Explain how it might be useful to discover that stock prices are connected to sunspot intensity even if we do not understand the underlying physical mechanism linking the two phenomena. (b) How might discovering the mechanism underlying this connection be relevant to that same utility? (Suggestions on p. 309.)

Some aspects of an investigation may be the same no matter which purpose is primary, however. For we will use clues about the general "plot" to reach an underlying explanation; and we will look at traces of the underlying mechanism to help us decide into which big wedge the connection falls. So research into correlations will in general look further into just those matters we have already used to help us form arguments. We will want to check out temporal order, interval, and other correlates; we should try to learn more about relevant modus operandi; and we should determine the length of a sequence, if there is one.

Exercise 6.25

In the fussiness/IQ correlation among Canadian infants (in the previous section), what other correlate or correlates might you check for to generate rivals competing with stimulation. (Suggestions on p. 309.)

Perhaps the most generally useful advice for investigating correlations is to *study the MOs of serious rivals to see what traces they might leave*. Then the investigation can look for those traces. In the correlation between the broken car part and its crash, for instance, the different rivals have the piece breaking in different ways. Determining just how it broke would help rank the rivals, and, fortunately, the different ways (MOs) all leave different traces. The three leading possibilities are (a) it broke on impact (with the barrier or another car), (b) it cracked from fatigue and broke in normal use, and (c) it was tampered with (weakened) and broke in normal use. A synopsis of the differentiating traces to look for goes something like this:

a. When metal breaks on impact it deforms at the rupture; so fit the two pieces back together and see if it looks bent. If not, that counts against impact.

b. When metal fatigues, a crack develops slowly at first and the piece breaks when the uncracked part is no longer able to do what's asked of it. So the surface of the break usually shows one part that is smooth and dirty (the "old" part) and another that is rougher and cleaner (fresh).

c. When a part has been partly cut through, it will look a bit like a fatigue failure (b), except that the old part of the break will have traces of the tool used to weaken it.

This is just a typical example; but it is a useful model of how to use MOs to organize a correlational investigation.

Exercise 6.26

You don't particularly like the meal you have at a restaurant and later that evening you get violently ill. What information would support the view that the meal and the vomiting were not connected? Would this be TD or NTD in the original argument? (Answers on p. 309.)

TESTIMONY

We constantly take people's word for things. The clerk at the airline counter says Flight 513 is overdue and has not yet landed. When you ask the time, the person next to you says it's 10:15. The voice on the telephone says the bank is open for business today until 6:30. The TV newsreader says an earthquake has closed Interstate 10. Your TA says the homework is number 13 on page 261. In countless cases such as these we commonly accept what someone says as true; and we are almost always right to do so. Moreover, what others tell us is hugely important to our lives. Much of what we do depends on information we derive from sources such as those listed above. Life would be unimaginably different if we could not count on it most of the time.

When we accept what others say in this way we are using them as instruments to tell us about the world. In this role other people function rather like the speedometer in a car or a thermometer outside a window. When the speedometer says I'm going 60 mph I can usually accept that as fact and base important decisions on it. The comparison is actually closer than it at first seems; for taking somebody's word covers more than actual speech. We accept written words, too, just as commonly and just as correctly in a huge range of circumstances. If the mechanics text tells us that $F = ma$, or the concert program says the first piece will be Beethoven's *Emperor Concerto,* or the sign at the curb says "Freeway Entrance," or the newspaper says trash collection will be on Wednesday because of the holiday, we simply accept it as information. Urban life and civilization itself are built on our ability to use such information immediately and confidently.

When we do use information in this way we are implicitly accepting a certain kind of argument. Somebody utters a sentence ("The flight is late") or that sentence occurs in a certain place (on a TV monitor in the waiting room) and we take that as *reason to think* that what the sentence tells us is true. So there's an argument going on. Using quotation marks to talk about the sentence itself (what's uttered or written), let us call the sentence in such an argument "P." Then we can use P (without quotes) to stand for what it tells us, and we can state the argument as follows: When somebody says "P," we take that as reason to think P (what it tells us) is true. In other words, we're using the *saying* of "P" as support in an argument for P. If we let X stand for the person or the sign or the program, or what have you, we may schematize the argument in this way[7]:

S: X says "P"

C: P

For example:

S: The attendant says, "The flight is late."

C: The flight will be late.

---

7. We can represent the information given by a speedometer in a similar argument:

S: The speedometer needle points to 60.

C: We are going 60 mph.

Because the speedometer does not give us a sentence (words), we will not think of this as a genuine testimony argument. It is so close in form, however, that we may think of the speedometer reading as figurative testimony. The analogy will help us again shortly.

Because of the way such arguments function in courtrooms, we will for convenience call these "testimony arguments" and refer to the characteristic support claim (X says "P") as testimony, even when it refers to signs and programs.

Obviously, not all testimony makes a good argument, just as speedometers and thermometers cannot always be trusted. We are all familiar with cases in which somebody (or a posted notice) has said something that you didn't believe for an instant. People sometimes lie, or don't know what they're talking about. You can get a copy of the wrong program; or the "Premium $1.54" sign may be displayed at a long-abandoned gas station. When we judge a bit of testimony we always take into account *its source*: who said it, how and where it was said, and many other features of the circumstances. Making these explicit will then give us the general form of testimony arguments:

S_1: X says "P"
S_2: How and where it was said (circumstances)
S_3: Who said it (background)

(T)   --

C: P (or not)

Because they appeal to the source in this way, arguments of this form are called "genetic" arguments: evidence for P depends on "where we heard it." We will stick with the term "testimony," however, which is why we've labeled the schema (T).

Exercise 6.27

Describe some circumstance in which you might find a freeway entrance sign that would make it obvious that it was not reliable information about a freeway entrance. (Suggestions on p. 309.)

The question for us then is *How should we think about these arguments?* What are we so good at that allows testimony to play such a big role in our lives? The diagnostic concepts of Chapter 5 can help us see how our understanding comes to grip with testimony in the clear and easy cases. That, in turn, should help us in tough ones, in which we get it wrong or find it difficult to judge.

Diagnosis

Consider Figures 6.3 and 6.4. Standing by a pond or quiet lake, you may occasionally see a fish leap from the surface, perhaps chasing an insect, and plop back into the water leaving characteristic ripples concentric on the spot of its return.

Had you not been watching as the fish executed its graceful acrobatics in Figure 6.3, you might well have turned, on hearing the "plop," to see the ripples in Figure 6.4. Had you done this (and not seen the jump itself), you would still have *evidence* that a fish had leaped out of the water: the "plop" and the ripples would be that evidence. Had no one been tossing rocks at the time, you would actually

Figure 6.3.   **Figure 6.4.**

have very strong reason to think the acrobatics in Figure 6.3 had taken place, even though you hadn't seen them. What else would explain the "plop" and ripples? We could schematize the reasoning like this:

S_1: There was a "plop" out on the water.
S_2: Concentric ripples disturb the placid surface.

== d

C: A fish just jumped out of the water.

This would of course be a diagnostic argument, with the conclusion and its rivals competing to explain both items of support.

Now consider the same fish and the same leap, except the water's too rough to see ripples and the wind is too noisy to hear the "plop." But this time a friend is looking out over the water and exclaims, "Look at that, a fish just jumped right out of the water." In the right circumstances, this would give you just as good reason to think a fish had jumped as hearing the "plop" and seeing the ripples, *and it will have the same* **diagnostic** *form.*

S_1: Your friend says, "A fish jumped out of the water."
S_2: The right circumstances (more on this shortly).

== d

C: A fish just jumped out of the water.

Here the conclusion would be offered as explaining S_1, and we would accept the testimony if no rival could explain it at all well.

In one way, this is a perfectly familiar kind of explanation and S_1 is a perfectly ordinary kind of TD: saying something is a kind of *behavior*, and behavior is the sort of thing we easily explain all the time. We explain the behavior of pets (Fido is standing by the door because he needs to go out) or humans (Dad's working on the roof because it has begun to leak). And we explain why someone said something (Tracy said "No thanks" because she's watching her diet). But saying something is a very special kind of behavior, because it has what we will call "content." If the agent says "The flight is late," the content is the late flight. In general, when somebody says "P," the content is P: it is a claim they're making that may be true or false (they're usually claiming it's true, of course). Ordinary behavior, such as brushing your teeth or working on the roof, doesn't have content like this; it doesn't make a claim that is true or false. But when we say something, what we do has content, we make a claim to truth.

The reason to dwell on this is that when we explain why somebody said something, the content of what they said will usually be a big part of the explanation. To explain why X said "P" usually involves P. For instance, if I asked you why you just said, "The White Sox beat the Athletics last night," you might say, "Because I thought you'd be interested." And of course *what* you thought I would be interested in is the *content* of what was said, namely, that the White Sox beat the Athletics. The explanation implicitly appeals to the content of what was said in explaining why you said it. Similarly, if I said to you, "Interstate 5 is all tied up because of an accident," and somebody asked why I said it, I might explain it thus: "I knew you were driving home after the party and might want to avoid the congestion." Here again, the content of what I said (the congestion on I-5) is crucial to explaining why I said it.

These explanations take for granted that the content is true, of course. But other explanations, equally dependent on the content, do not. The explanation of your saying "The White Sox beat the Athletics last night" might be that the newspaper mistakenly repeated the box score from the previous day. The explanation still involves the content (that's why I bothered to say it), but does not simply take it for granted. A big part of the explanation is that the content is unreliable; it may easily be false. This is similar for lying. If I said I-5 was congested (in spite of not having heard anything about it) in order to make you go home by another route, the explanation of my saying it still involves the content. I did not think that just any old lie would get you to take some other route. This *particular* lie (with this particular content) was important to my purpose. So the content was involved in explaining why I said what I did, even though it is not presumed to be true.[8]

Explanation and Reliability: The Speedometer Analogy

Because our interest in testimony is understanding *how we may rely on it*, we must find out how our diagnostic apparatus distinguishes between these two kinds of explanations. This will allow us to say diagnostically what makes a testimony argument a *good* argument. For help in doing this, let us return briefly to the speedometer analogy. A speedometer reading has content in something like the same way a sentence does: when the needle points at the "60" mark, that says we're going 60 mph. It makes a claim that may be true or false. So let's explore this case diagnostically. First, when the speedometer needle does point at 60 we may ask the diagnostic question, Why does the speedometer indicate 60? Obviously there are all sorts of different ways to account for this bit of trace data. Many different underlying stories all result in this reading. It could be that the car is on jacks and the wheels are spinning in air. Or the mechanism may be broken and the needle is stuck at 60. Or any number of malfunctions could have it reading 60 at many different speeds. Or it could be a painted mock-up, for a photo shoot, and it never was connected to anything.

Of course the usual explanation will not be any of these, but will have something to do with the fact that the car is actually going 60 mph. And this too may

8. Note that for it to be a lie it does not have to be false. Interstate 5 may well be congested when I say so, but it is still a lie if I thought it wasn't or didn't care.

involve any number of different stories. Let us assume the speedometer is a normal one connected to the spinning of the drive train (wheels, axles, crankshaft, bits of the transmission). In this case the explanation of the reading would be a story about why the drive train is spinning. It may be that the engine is driving it, pushing the car up a hill, for instance. Gasoline is exploding in the combustion chambers, which turn the crankshaft and everything else, pushing the car forward at 60 mph, and part of what gets turned in all this is the speedometer mechanism and the turning makes it read 60. But another equally common story would have the car coasting along without power, in which case the inertia of the car would be driving everything else, including the speedometer; or it could be coming down hill and gravity is doing all the work against brakes and engine compression, and this causes the speedometer to read 60. Furthermore, each of these rival stories will inevitably have different features at different times, so will actually represent a cluster of different stories. Different bits of pavement will take the thrust of different bits of tire and connect to components of slightly different dimension due to temperature and wear. But each story results in a reading of 60.

If we cared which particular story was right we would toss all the data we have into diagnostic form, use available NTD to help us think through the rival explanations, decide on seriousness, and rank on plausibility. But our interest here is not in details of particular explanations. We simply want to know whether we can use the reading as information. We want to know if the explanation is (a) one of those in which the car is actually going 60 or (b) one of the others. So, as we did with correlations, let us divide the possibilities balloon into two big segments, as in Figure 6.5. C_1 contains all the rivals that have the car actually going 60. C_2

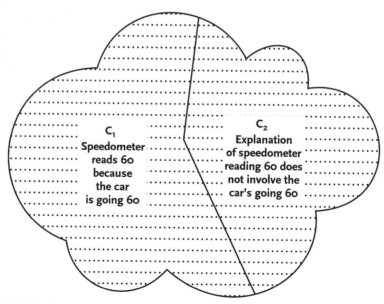

IQ: Why does the speedometer read 60 mph?

Figure 6.5. Possible explanations of the speedometer reading 60.

contains all the others.[9] From our point of view, then, C_1 rivals have one important thing in common: despite their differences, part of the explanation of the speedometer reading is that the car is actually going 60 mph. So if the best rival story falls in the left-hand superwedge, an argument that looks just like testimony form is sound:

$$S: \text{ The speedometer needle points to 60.}$$
$$\overline{\rule{6cm}{0pt}} = d$$
$$C_1: \text{ We are going 60 miles per hour.}$$

This says that the reading of 60 is TD explained by our actually *going* 60. In other words, the reading is explained by the *truth* of its content.

Exercise 6.28
....

(a) Schematize this argument: "The speedometer says we're going 60, but we seem to be virtually standing still, so the tires must be spinning on the ice." Label the TD and NTD and be sure to include the proper subscript on the conclusion. (b) The argument contains a hurdle for one entire superrival. What is it and what makes it a hurdle? (Answers on p. 309.)

This allows us to use all our diagnostic apparatus to articulate evaluation here. We may appeal to available TD and NTD to rank serious rivals. If the best account of what's going on falls in C_2 then the above argument is not sound. If *all* the serious rivals fall in C_1, it is not just sound but strong, and we can use the reading as information. If the case is mixed—C_1 is best but some C_2 rivals are serious—our confidence in the reading will depend on gaps in the ranking. When we trust our speedometer—as we usually do—it is because we know perfectly well that likely C_2 explanations are simply not possible. We have good reason to think the speedometer reading is explained by the truth of its content. *This is our criterion of reliability.*

Explaining Testimony

Genuine testimony, involving actual *sentences* instead of just pointer readings, may be analyzed in an exactly parallel way. Some explanations of why I said "P" depend on the truth of P in the same way that explaining a speedometer reading can depend on the car's going the speed it indicates. Suppose you ask me the time and I say it's ten o'clock. The explanation for my selecting this particular time may involve my checking an accurate clock and competently understanding the time. Or it could result from my hearing the time on a radio a few moments ago. Or the explanation might be that I have an uncanny ability to always know what time it is. In each of these cases, the fact that it's ten o'clock is part of the expla-

---

9. It's worth remembering that even if all the serious rivals fall in C_2, the car still may be going 60. But the car's speed will not explain the speedometer reading.

nation of my saying so. I said it was ten o'clock at least in part because it *is* ten o'clock. We will call these C_1 explanations because, just as in the speedometer example, these are the explanations that say we may rely on the testimony. In diagnostic terms, if any of these explanations are right, a testimony argument would be sound with "ten o'clock" substituted for "P."

$$S: \quad \text{I say "it is ten o'clock."}$$
$$=========d$$
$$C_1: \text{ It is ten o'clock.}$$

C_1 is the explanation of S: the statement is explained by the truth of its content.

On the other hand, this may not be what happened at all. The real explanation (of my saying "ten o'clock") might be that I wanted to leave, you were my ride, and knew you didn't want to stay past ten; so even though I had no idea what time it was, I said it was ten. Here its being ten o'clock is not part of the explanation of my saying so. The explanation appeals to my motivation to leave no matter what time it happens to be. This would be a C_2 explanation. My saying so was not connected to its actually being ten o'clock. Other kinds of C_2 explanation would be that I can't tell time, or misread the watch because it was upside down, or misunderstood the radio. In each of these cases the explanation of my saying it's ten o'clock would not involve its actually being ten o'clock.[10] So for the general testimony form, we may again divide the balloon into two big segments as in Figure 6.6. C_1 accounts are all those in which the truth of P is involved in explaining why X said "P"; C_2 covers all the rest.

Exercise 6.29

Suppose somebody advertises his car for sale in the newspaper and you go to look at it. While you are talking about it he says, "This car has fifty thousand trouble-free miles left in it." Give a C_2 account of his saying this. (Suggestions on p. 309.)

Actually determining whether an explanation falls in C_1 or C_2 generally requires knowing a lot about the "source" (who said "P" and where) as mentioned earlier. So the detailed testimony form we looked at earlier is also diagnostic.

$$S_1: \text{ X said "P"}$$
$$S_2: \text{ Circumstances}$$
$$S_3: \text{ Background on X}$$
(T) $$=========d$$
$$C: \text{ P or some } C_2 \text{ rival}$$

---

10. Again it is worth pointing out that in any C_2 account it may actually be ten o'clock when I say so. It's just that my saying so is not any reason to think so. If I'm right it is just an accident.

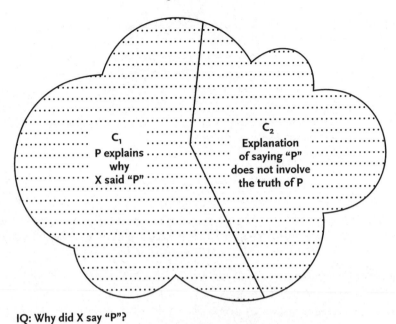

IQ: Why did X say "P"?

Figure 6.6. Possible explanations of why X said "P."

Circumstance would include how a spoken sentence was uttered (nervously, sarcastically), as well as anything bearing on the speaker's motivation and access to relevant information. For written sentences ("Freeway Entrance," "Flight 207 arrives at Gate 8") S_2 covers location and obvious clues to currency and appropriateness. If the "Freeway Entrance" sign is in the back of someone's garage, or "arrives at Gate 8" lingers in an abandoned air terminal, those circumstances count heavily in favor of C_2 explanations. S_2 thus may contain both TD and NTD. A C_2 rival would explain why "P" was said nervously, for instance; but it wouldn't explain the motivation responsible.

Background, on the other hand, is nearly exclusively NTD. It will include what we know about the character, training, and skills of an author, as well as the institutions surrounding the sentence in question. What we know about banks and telephones affects what we think about what the person at the bank says when we call for information. And a person's legendary commitment to honesty can do a lot to overcome circumstances that might otherwise support a C_2 account of what he says.

Exercise 6.30

Give some S_3 support (background/biography) that would favor a C_1 account in the used car example of Exercise 6.29. Is it TD or NTD? How can you tell? (Answer on p. 309.)

In simply learning to talk we naturally develop an understanding of why people say the things they do. In this way our diagnostic skill lies behind our use of language. We become expert at picking up contextual cues of substance and motivation that give words the significance they have for us. Testimony arguments exploit one aspect of this skill: the ability to tell when the truth of a sentence explains why it was said. When it does, we can use the sentence as information and, hence, add what others know to our understanding. This vastly increases the amount we can learn and the possibilities open to us.

Thinking about Testimony Rivals

Because "taking someone's word" for what they say is the normal case, C_1 explanations sound funny to the ear. Normally we don't explain why we *do* take someone's word; only refusing to accept someone's word requires a reason. So C_2 rivals are easier to understand. Familiar examples would be these:

> She was embarrassed to admit she saw you.
>   (That's why she said she didn't.)
>
> He was afraid he'd lose his job.
>   (That's why he said he didn't mind at all.)
>
> She can't read time.
>   (That's why she said it was ten o'clock.)
>
> He didn't hear what the announcer said.
>   (*See Exercise 6.31 below.*)
>
> I thought this was today's newspaper.
>
> They forgot to take the sign down.
>
> It was just a joke.

These are each C_2 accounts because they explain why "P" was said *without appealing to P*. They thus break the connection between P and saying "P." So if one of these is the right explanation, saying "P" can't be taken as evidence for P. P may still be true, we just can't come to know it in this way. By breaking that connection C_2 explanations destroy the testimony as evidence for what it says. We will call C_2 rivals "undermining accounts" of testimony.

Exercise 6.31
....

Fill in examples of what the last four C_2 accounts in the above list might be used to explain. (Suggestions on p. 310.)

C_1 rivals then are just those that do *not* break the connection between P and saying so: they are the explanations that presuppose P, take it for granted in accounting for the testimony. Sometimes, of course, the C_1 rival will simply be P:

he said it was two doors down on the right *because* it is two doors down on the right. But more usually, the presupposition will be implicit.

> I thought you'd be interested.
>   (That's why I said there's a party tonight.)

> She saw it happen.
>   (That's why she said you got a ticket.)

> He wanted to alert you to the congestion.

We call C_1 rivals "underwriting rivals" because they allow the testimony to count as evidence for the truth of its content. Just how much it counts depends on many things, which we will examine shortly. And of course the best testimony in the world may still turn out to be false through weird happenstance, no matter how sincere and competent it is. But if the best account of someone's saying "P" connects with P in this way, then their saying it counts as evidence for P.

Exercise 6.32

(a) Give two different C_1 accounts of the voice on the phone saying, "At the tone the time will be six forty one exactly." (b) Suppose a friend, who owes you money, says (on the phone) that she just sent you a check for the amount she owes you. (i) Describe circumstances (S_2) that would favor a C_1 account of her saying this. (ii) Describe circumstances favoring a C_2 account. (Suggestions on p. 310.)

Separating the Basic Issues

This simple picture captures much of what's interesting about testimony and articulates it adequately for many purposes.[11] Nevertheless, the way we've captured the positive value of testimony sounds a bit artificial in part because we're trying to do too much in a single explanation. So this section will complicate the picture somewhat to make the point sound a little better. In the process we will sharply distinguish two different *kinds* of doubt we may have about testimony: its sincerity, on the one hand, and its competence on the other. This will give us deeper insight into our use of what other people say.

Instead of asking directly about the relation between someone's saying "P" and P itself, let us first consider what that person *thinks* about P. We usually ask somebody for information (When does the bank close?) only because we take them to be in a position to know about it (they work at the bank). We try to learn what to think about P by finding out what somebody in a better position to know thinks about it. So testimony works as information only if they do tell us what they think.

---

11. The simple, single-step form is usually better than the more complicated one below in one kind of case: when the IQ is Why does it say "P" *there* (as in signs and programs), rather than Why did X say "P." The complication is valuable for dealing with what a person actually says, in conversation or in a letter or note.

This suggests a two-part strategy, which actually corresponds to what we do in many cases. When someone tells us something, we first ask ourselves whether he's sincere in what he says. That is, we want to know whether X said "P" *because he THINKS P is true.* If not, course, we need go no further, because the testimony cannot be information for us if X doesn't even believe it himself. But if he is being sincere and has said "P" with the conviction that it is true, we may then go on to consider (step two) whether the fact that X thinks P is true gives *us* any reason to think so.

To do this, we begin with the same balloon of possibilities (IQ: Why did X say "P"?) and again divide it into two large superwedges (Figure 6.7). But this time, instead of grouping explanations by how they depend on P itself, we will group them by what X *thinks* about P. So one superwedge will contain all the explanations holding that X said "P" because he thinks it is true (we will call these $C_{1'}$ explanations). These will include many of the C_1 explanations from the simpler picture:

> I said it because I thought you'd be interested.
>
>   or
>
> She said it to alert you to the congestion.

But it also includes some of the C_2 explanations:

> I said it because I thought this was today's paper.
>
>   or
>
> He said it because he misunderstood the announcer.

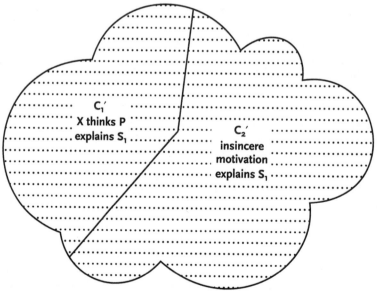

IQ: Why did X say "P"?

Figure 6.7. Step one division of possibilities.

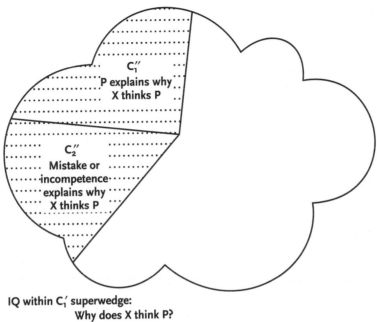

IQ within C_1' superwedge:
Why does X think P?

Figure 6.8. Step two division of possibilities.

In each case the person in question *thought* what they said was true, and that was part of the reason they said what they did.

The other superwedge will contain all the remaining explanations of why X said "P" that do not involve X thinking P is true (called C_2' accounts). These will typically appeal to things such as fear and embarrassment, which we have seen before, but here they explain why X would say "P" in *spite of not even thinking it is true*. For instance:

He said it because he thought he might otherwise lose his job.

She said it because she was embarrassed to admit she was there.

If the first argument tells us that the right explanation lies in the C_1' super-wedge, we may then look at the stories in that wedge to see if we can learn more about P. That is, we may treat the C_1' wedge as the whole balloon for the second step argument (Figure 6.8). What we would like to learn, of course, is why X thinks P (this is the IQ of the second step). In particular, we want to learn whether X thinks P at least in part *because P is true*. This is the second way in which the two-step schematization improves on the one-step form: it is more natural to explain my *thinking* P because P is true than to explain my *saying* P in that way. The reason I think it is ten o'clock may be simply that it is ten o'clock: I know how to read time, and I checked the right clock. That explains why I think it.[12] Similarly,

---

12. Note how much less contrived this sounds than the C_1 explanations of the single-step form with which we began.

the reason the dentist thinks your tooth is decayed usually is that your tooth is decayed. This is what we understand when we trust what someone thinks about something: its truth figured in their thinking it. So the second argument divides the C_1' superwedge into two smaller wedges, grouping those explanations by their connection with P itself. In one slice (C_1'') the explanations say that X thinks P because P is true; in the other (C_2'') X thinks P as the result of a mistake or some sort of incompetence. These will include explanations of why X *thinks* P that look a lot like some of the C_2 explanations of why X *said* "P" in the simpler form, namely, the ones that do not involve insincerity. C_2'' explanations would look like this:

> She thought it was 10 o'clock because she can't read time.
>
> He thought it would rain because he misunderstood the announcer.
>
> I thought last night's score was 5 to 2 because I took this to be today's paper (which it wasn't).

Let us use all this to flesh out the two-step schema and see how it helps our articulation. The package now looks like this:

STEP ONE	STEP TWO
S_1: X said "P"	S_4 X thinks P
S_2: Sincerity circ.	S_5 Access/competence circ.
S_3: Sincerity background	S_6 Competence background
===================d	================d
C_1': X thinks P	C_1'': P
C_2': X's motivation to say "P" insincerely.	C_2'': How X came to think P incompetently or mistakenly
IQ: Why did X say "P"?	IQ: Why does X think P?

Complete two-step schema.

The first step concerns only considerations of **Sincerity**: the first argument is good if it supports the conclusion that X sincerely thinks P. And we can go on to step two only if we have reason to believe that X does really think P. The second step then concerns the author's **Competence**, X's ability to judge whether P is true. This argument is good (supports P) if it gives reason to trust what X thinks here. As always in diagnostic argument, the rivals are trying to explain trace data. The central trace in Step One is S_1, whereas in Step Two it is S_4. Relevant circumstances (S_2 and S_5) may also contain TD, and we will look at that shortly; but the first step rivals are primarily trying to explain what X said and the second step rivals primarily what X thinks. Let us examine this in the steps individually.

STEP ONE

Arguments for C_1' are often negative. That is, to support the view that X thinks P, we often give reason *against* the likely C_2' rivals. So let us look at those first. Motivation to say "P" insincerely would fall into the familiar categories of fear of loss, hope of gain, embarrassment, and even simple amusement. A typical C_2' would be: I said I didn't see you at the party because I was embarrassed to admit I couldn't work myself up to come over and say hi. Another: the mechanic said I needed my valves ground because he desperately needs the work. We all know the kind of support we might find for such a rival: perhaps we discover that the mechanic is behind in his rent and his shop is empty. These would count as *circumstances* (S_2) relevant to sincerity. Background related to sincerity (S_3) would be things we could learn about the mechanic's character: that he has a reputation for doing unnecessary work, for instance. This would support the mentioned C_2' rival. On the other hand, if he had a reputation for extreme honesty that even the threat of bankruptcy could not override, this too would be relevant background here: it would count *against* the C_2' rival.

This is how C_1' gets negative support: details of circumstance or features of the source practically eliminate rivals from the other half of the balloon. Very often the simple observation that *conditions are normal* will be adequate to do this. If I say it's ten o'clock, and nothing in the context suggests that I might have motivation to lie or joke about it, that all by itself counts as support for the (modest) claim that I *think* it is ten o'clock. We know enough to know that in the run of contexts normal people are not motivated to misrepresent the time. But much of this depends on what you know about me (S_3). If I am famous for joking around, saying things just to get a reaction, that automatically undermines much that I say in casual social conversation. You always have to worry that I've said something for effect rather than because I think it true. To summarize:

S_2: Circumstances that would motivate X to say something he didn't think, and also those that would motivate honesty.

S_3: Relevant background on the author's character.

Exercise 6.33

The guy you've asked to look at your disabled computer says it is not worth fixing. Describe circumstances (S_2) that would favor a C_2' rival in Step One. Describe circumstances favoring a $C_{1'}$ rival. (Suggestions on p. 310.)

STEP TWO

When Step One clearly supports C_1' (X thinks P), we may then go on to ask whether this gives *us* any reason to think P. To do this, we take Step One's conclusion (X thinks P) as trace data (S_4 in the general schema) and ask the diagnostic question of it: Why does X think P? This gives us Step Two, as illustrated in Figure 6.8. We have called the evidence relevant to the second step "competence" considerations, and this is a useful shorthand. But step two covers everything except sincerity. So S_5 and S_6 will include information that might reveal a simple mistake or misunderstanding too, no matter how excusable that is in the context. Let us agree to let the word "competence" cover all these considerations.

To accept the testimony as information, of course, we want P to be the explanation of why X thinks P. And on everyday matters, in which competence is not very important, evidence that the account falls in the C_1'' part of the balloon will again usually be negative, just as in Step One. If a normal adult checks a clock and comes to think it is ten o'clock (or looks outside and comes to think it is raining) that by itself is good reason to think it is ten o'clock (or raining) unless something unusual can be produced under S_5 or S_6. Ordinary competence in these matters allows P to make us think P in normal circumstances. So for my thinking it's ten o'clock to *not* be good reason for you to think so we would have to discover that my watch had been tampered with or that I was too drunk to tell time, or something else out of the ordinary.

Exercise 6.34

Suppose you ask a friend to check the schedule to find the time and day of the final exam in a sociology course you both are taking. She looks in the schedule and says, sincerely, that the final is at three o'clock on Monday. Say something about why you would accept her judgment here. (Answer on p. 310.)

But Step Two allows far greater range for positive considerations than Step One. For when a competence is unusual or exotic, we can (and usually must) get direct support for it of many different kinds. If a dentist thinks my tooth is decayed, I can appeal to training, experience, and reputation to support my conviction that decay explains his thinking so (C_1''). And if a stock expert thinks General Motors stock will rise in value, I should at least check her track record before acting on the forecast (which presumes the C_1'' rival). To summarize:

S_5: Circumstances relevant to the application of X's competence.
S_6: Background testifying for or against X's competence to judge the matter in question.

As in the simpler version, we may refer to the C_1 rivals in each step as "underwriting" and the C_2 rivals as "undermining"; the significance of these characterizations is the same as before except for C_1'. Both C_2s undermine the testimony in something like the same way as did the C_2 in the earlier single-step form. And C_1'' underwrites it in the same way as the earlier C_1. But if we get C_1' in the Step One, that only goes part way toward underwriting the testimony: it licenses our proceeding to Step Two; but there is more to be done in that step before we may use the testimony as information. So what C_1' underwrites is not the testimony itself, but just continuing the analysis.

Illustration

Consider the following conversation between Rob Farnsworth and his father:

MR. FARNSWORTH: Rob, would you drop the car off at Turner's sometime this morning? I'm having him overhaul the engine. He said he'd get you a ride home if you got there before noon.

ROB: Overhaul the engine!? Why do you want to do that?

MR. FARNSWORTH: Fred said it needs an overhaul, and he'll do it for me if I can leave the car all week.

ROB: Gee, Dad, I know Mr. Turner's an old friend, very honest and all that, but this is way out of his league. He runs a good gas station, but changing oil and fan belts is about as complicated as it ever gets there. I doubt he owns a compression gauge. You really should check with somebody more experienced in automotive diagnosis before tearing into the engine.

Here Rob and his father disagree about whether to take Fred Turner's word for something. Rob's argument against illustrates the value of the expanded, two-step schema. He agrees that everything is fine in Step One, but problems arise in Step Two: Fred says what he does because he believes it, but his believing it is not well explained by its truth.

S_1: Fred says the engine needs an overhaul.
S_2: Fred runs a gas station.
S_3: Fred is a long-time family friend with a reputation for honesty.
$$=== \text{d}$$
   Fred thinks the engine needs an overhaul (C_1').

S_4: Fred thinks the engine needs an overhaul.
S_5: Fred's shop is not well equipped for engine work.
S_6: Fred has had little experience rebuilding engines.
$$=== \text{d}$$
   Whatever made Fred think the engine needed an overhaul, it was probably not the truth of that diagnosis (C_2'').

Two-Step Summary

We may often articulate our evaluation of testimony adequately in simple one-step form; this is especially so for formal announcements, programs, and highway signs. The two-step complication helps when we wish to treat motivation and competence separately, which we often will when we're concerned with someone's conversation or personal communication. Motivational matters tend to be relevant mostly to an author's sincerity, helping us decide whether he has represented his understanding accurately. Competence considerations help us decide whether that understanding, once discovered, is of value to us. This means, of course, that the word "competence" here covers not just what skills an author has but also aspects of the circumstances that affect their application. So if we know of deceptive features of a situation that the author does not, that may undermine the value of his testimony as much as lacking skill in perception or judgment.

One reason to distinguish motivation from competence is that they frequently pull in opposite directions. People who know the most about a subject may also have the greatest motivation to misrepresent that knowledge. The guy selling you his used car, the company executive testifying before a federal committee, and the attorney talking to the press about an upcoming trial all illustrate this tension. If we accept what they say, it will be in spite of what may be strong reason to shade the truth in their favor; if we don't, that will be despite their comprehensive familiarity with the topic. Separating those two matters into different arguments improves clarity of thought about them.

Two final observations: First, we can never keep motivational considerations completely out of the second step. For motivation can affect our competence. If we strongly wish something to be true (or false) that will sometimes affect our judgment about it. This is why we usually do not place too much weight on a mother's movingly sincere testimony that her little Johnny simply could not have killed all those people he is accused of killing. So although deception, as an undermining consideration, goes in Step One, *self*-deception goes in Step Two. The second observation, which is obvious as soon as you think about it, is that testimony may be true even though the fact that a person said it gives us no reason whatever to believe it. Even pathological liars occasionally tell the truth. So it's worth remembering that even when the fact that X said "P" gives us no reason to think P, it still may be true. We would have to find out in some other way. It may, after all, turn out that little Johnny didn't kill all those people.

Checklist for Two-Step Schema

STEP ONE RIVALS

C_1' Statement made, at least in part, because its author thinks it is true. May use this fact as TD for Step Two.

C_2' Statement explained by motivational factors independent of belief in P. No support for key Step Two TD (S_4).

STEP TWO RIVALS

C_1'' Author thinks P because P.

C_2'' Author's confidence in P due either to incompetence, simple mistake, or self-deception.

Relation of Testimony to Other Kinds of Evidence

No matter how good the credentials of a source (X), the weight we place on a bit of testimony (X says "P") always depends on what else we know about P (the content of the testimony). If P is plausible to begin with, we require very little of the testimony to accept it. If it's not, we require much more—and may not take it seriously at all. If, right after Christmas, we ask someone what the date is, and they say December 28, that would normally be good reason to accept the answer. But if they say it's April 15, that by itself would be enough to reject the testimony. We would react similarly had we asked for the temperature outside on a beautiful spring day and someone said it was just thirty-two degrees Fahrenheit. No matter how reliable and competent they were, we would look for a C_2 account of what they said. Did they misunderstand the question? Are they having a daydream? Under the influence of something? Perhaps joking?

This is just to say that as important as it is, testimony is only one kind of evidence among many, and we do and should take it all seriously. Any given bit of evidence—no matter what its kind—must be weighed against everything else relevant. We may occasionally prefer some kind of C_2 account of somebody's saying (or thinking) something based *not* on their character or competence or even their personal circumstances, but simply on our having independent good reason to think what they said is false. Sometimes the best reason to think someone is insincere is that you know they are competent to make a judgment, and you know they had access to the relevant data, and you know that what they said is not true.

Exercise 6.37
....

If you're timing some runners and your watch says they just completed a mile in three minutes flat, what are some plausible explanations of the watch's reading? (Answers on p. 310.)

SAMPLING

Our third kind of trace data will be the *sample*. The word "sample" may convey a picture of complicated statistical analysis, since we most often hear about samples in discussions of election forecasts or health and safety studies. These usually do require special training and mathematical techniques. But sampling, as we will think of it here, is far more common and useful than you might imagine. We sample the soup as we cook it to see if it needs more salt, or examine a sample of the material (cloth, wood) we're having something made from. You are sampling when you feel around in the dryer to see if the clothes are dry, or when you test-drive a car.

The motivation for sampling is pretty obvious from these examples. We wish to know about something and, for one reason or another, can *examine only a small part of it*. Sometimes what limits our examination is simply time: we don't have the time to ask *all* likely voters who they prefer in the election or we can't take time to feel every inch of everything in the dryer. Elsewhere it is expense: Consumers' Union can't afford to buy *all* the Toyota Camrys to test for their report. Closely related to these are cases in which accident or good luck reveals a bit of something we'd have no idea how to reach on our own. Volcanoes, for instance, give us samples of the earth's mantle, access to which would be simply beyond us otherwise.

The problem is deeper, however, when the test is destructive. If I tasted *all* of the soup, or the government crashed *all* of the cars in their safety trials, there would be no point in the tests. And autopsies provide invaluable information about everything from the effects of disease and injury on vital organs to the general health of a population; but a civilized culture reserves autopsies for people who die of other things (a small sample). Of course, more than one of these restrictions may limit a single case, as in my tasting the wine suggested by a waiter in a restaurant.

Exercise 6.38
....

List the restrictions that apply in this last case (wine tasting). (Answer on p. 310.)

Representativeness

The principle behind sampling is this: we may use a sample of something to tell us about the whole thing *if the sample resembles the whole thing* in the right way; that is, if the sample is *typical*. We may use a spoonful of soup to judge the saltiness of the whole pot, if it is enough like the rest of the soup. Consumers' Union may use a single Toyota to judge others we might buy or rent, if the one they get is typical of Camrys generally. So the question we must ask in this section is, "How do we determine that a sample is typical?" How do we support that conclusion? It should be no surprise that the answer is diagnostic, but to spell out the details it will be useful to introduce some jargon.

The "big thing" that we want to investigate (pot of soup, all voters or Camrys) is usually referred to as the *population*: we sample a certain population. This terminology works best for countable things such as voters or cars, but we will use the term generally to cover soup and the earth's mantle too. The spoonful of soup is a sample, the whole pot is the population we've sampled. There is also a jargon term for the resemblance at the center of our interest. When a sample resembles, or is typical of a population in the right way, we will call it *representative*. We may use a sample to tell us about a population if it represents the population accurately. The task of this section is to say something systematic about the evidence we might have that a sample is representative of a certain population: the population from which it was taken. How do we support the conclusion that the soup in the spoon is enough like that in the pot that we may judge the saltiness of the pot from the saltiness of the spoonful?

The main reason this question arises, of course, is that a sample is *Always Unrepresentative* in one respect at least: it, unlike the rest of the population, is what we ended up with. The rest escaped our grasp. The soup in the spoon is unlike all the rest of the soup in that it was where it had to be to end up in the spoon. Consumers' Union's Camry is unlike all the other Camrys in that it was the one they drove off the lot. The voters in our sample were the ones we happened to encounter when we followed a certain interview routine. And although this difference may not matter to us, it may be linked to *other* differences that do.

So we can approach our problem armed with two observations. First, a sample can *never* be representative of a population in every possible respect. What we need to know in order to use a sample to reveal something about a population is whether it is representative *in the respect that matters to us*. The second observation follows easily from this one: to do this we must make sure that the atypicality of the sample resulting from how it was selected does not also make it atypical in a respect that matters to us.

To prepare us for the diagnostic treatment of this issue, note that in an enormous range of cases our understanding of a sample, a population, and a selection procedure is perfectly adequate for us to make this judgment. We know that if we stir the soup and take a sip from the top, that will likely be representative of saltiness, but not of the amount of rice or barley or other heavy things that settle quickly to the bottom. We know that any reasonably normal new Camry will be representative in an enormous number of large-scale ways: significant dimensions (length, wheelbase, shoulder room, gas tank capacity, and so on), location of major controls and gauges, ease of entry, and much else. We also know that the bugs on the windshield and the gravel in the tire tread will almost certainly *not* be representative of Camrys in general. We know what to watch out for too. If the Camry was flattened by a truck on the way home from the store, we will no longer count on the representativeness of major controls and dimensions. And we would rightly reject a sample of voter sentiment taken at a Republican Party function.

Trace and Explanation

What we understand that underwrites our judgment is something about how the sample *came to have the characteristic* we care about in each case. This means we must understand something about the population itself *and* the procedure we used to come up with the sample. But when we do, we may then form the relevant diagnostic argument in the following way. Call the characteristic we care about *property P*. P will stand for the saltiness of the soup that we care about, or the pref-

erence of voters for Al Gore, or the wind noise around the windshield of Camrys. Suppose that we have examined our sample and found that it has property
P. To articulate the support this provides for the conclusion that the population
also has property P, we simply take **the Sample Property as Trace Data** and ask
the IQ, "Why does the sample have property P?" We then add to the argument
what we know about the selection procedure and the nature of the population.
This will often support a surmise about how the sample came to have property
P.

S_1: Sample has property P
S_2: Nature of selection
S_3: Background on population
=================================d
?

IQ: Why does the sample have property P?

This IQ, of course, leads us to the balloon of possibilities containing all the rival explanations of how the sample came to have property P (Figure 6.9). As before the trick is to group the rivals by their relevance to the issue of our concern:
whether the population has P. In some of those explanations the sample will have
P *because the population itself does*. The spoonful of soup may be salty simply because the soup itself is; the sample of voters may prefer Gore because the whole
electorate does; the Camry may have wind noise because that's just how Camrys
are. These we will group together in the C_1 superwedge. In other explanations
(call them C_2 rivals), the sample has P not because the population does, but be-

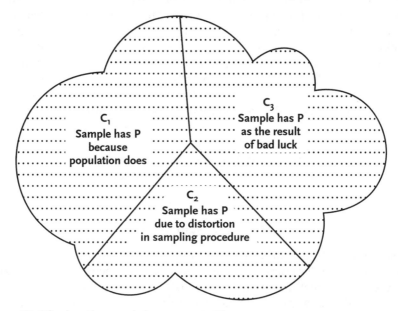

IQ: Why does the sample have property P?

Figure 6.9. Three ways the sample could get property P.

cause of some feature of the sampling procedure. The spoonful of soup has no barley in it *not* because the soup itself doesn't, but because it was taken from the very top (where it is hard to find barley). The sample may prefer Gore because we unknowingly sampled people at a Democratic rally, not because the electorate as a whole favors him. The sample Camry may have a wind whistle around the A-pillar not because all of them do, but because something in the Consumers' Union's treatment of it loosened the windshield. Finally, a third superwedge of the balloon contains explanations in which the sample came to have P not because the population did, nor due to some distorting feature of the sampling process, but simply through bad luck. The survey team did everything right and still ended up interviewing only Democrats; there was no salt in the sampled part of the soup through some statistical freak in the random motion of molecules; this Camry just happened to be the only one in the country with a badly installed windshield.

Exercise 6.39

An instructor wishes to know how well a large class has understood a difficult homework assignment. He samples by asking three volunteers to write out their solution on the board (without looking at each other's). All three get it right. What's the most likely explanation of the sample's having this property? In what superwedge does this account fall? (Answers on p. 310.)

Evidence of Representativeness

If all the serious rivals fall in C_1, of course, then we have good reason to think the population has property P: P in the population is what explains P in the sample. So if the support yields this result, it is evidence for the representativeness of the sample. And as before, we often reach this result *negatively*: by directly noting the *im*plausibility of rivals from C_2 and C_3. We think the spoonful representative of the soup's saltiness because, in the circumstances, we think dipping the spoon in the soup is unlikely to distort the saltiness, and we comfortably discount statistical freaks in the motion of molecules. In other words, reason to *worry* about the representativeness of a sample will always be in the form of a plausible account of its properties from the C_2 or C_3 superwedges.

S_1 Sample has property P.
S_2 Circumstances surrounding sampling.
S_3 Background on nature of population.
$$\overline{\phantom{S_3 \text{ Background on nature of population.}}}=d$$
C_1 versus $(C_2 + C_3)$

This articulation helps us most when sampling is a form of investigation, which it often is. For then we have some control over the circumstances surrounding the sampling and can use our understanding of the population to manipulate those circumstances to get rid of serious rivals from C_2 and C_3. Other cases may be evaluated by how close they come to the investigative ideal. That is, when we read about sampling already completed, we must determine how well the circumstances reduce the plausibility of C_2 and C_3 rivals. In the next few pages we will explore the diagnostic foundation of these judgments.

Exercise 6.40

Suppose you're experimenting with a new rinse in an automatic dishwasher to see if it eliminates water spots, which have been a problem. After a wash using this rinse you carefully examine one perfectly clear glass and a knife, find them spotless, and conclude the rinse works. (a) What about the property and the population gives us reason to think this sample is representative? (b) What else (besides likely representativeness) about the sample makes it a good sample to use? (Answers on p. 310.)

THINKING ABOUT C_2 RIVALS

Rivals in the C_2 wedge say that there's some *connection* between P and the sampling procedure; and that this connection, not the population, explains why the sample has property P. For instance, there's a connection between being at a Democratic Party fund raiser and preferring a Democratic candidate. This connection would explain why the sample you took at the fund raiser preferred a Democrat, even if the electorate as a whole did not. So to avoid C_2 rivals (reduce their likelihood), we try to *break these connections* between P and the procedure.

We can gain some clarity in dealing with such connections if we think of them as coming in essentially two different kinds: "where" connections and "how" connections. The properties of a sample may not be representative because of *where* in the population we found it; or they may not be representative because of *how* we treated the sample in our examination of it. Of course it may be distorted in both ways at once; and sometimes the distortion will be on the how/where borderline. The distinction will nevertheless assist our articulation of this tricky matter.

Let us first look at where considerations. If we stir the soup, the salt will distribute itself fairly uniformly around in the pot. It will then not matter *where* we sample, *if what we care about is saltiness*. Any spoonful will be pretty much like any other in this regard: they will all be equally representative. We call such a population "homogeneous" with respect to saltiness. In a homogeneous population we may choose a sample on convenience alone. Barley and rice, however, are another matter altogether. They settle to the bottom and it is nearly impossible to get them homogeneously distributed in the pot. So in this case, *where* you sample matters a lot. If you sample from the top, or too close to the surface, you know the sample will not be representative: the lack of barley will be explained by where you sampled, not by how much is in the soup.

Something similar holds for the Camrys tested by Consumers' Union. We're adequately familiar with cars to know that their major features and dimensions are uniform in the population (wheelbase, location of headlights and speedometer, and the like). To learn about these properties Consumers' Union may simply choose one from a nearby dealer. You can see from these examples that some properties are easier to learn about through sampling than others. If a property is uniformly distributed throughout a population—or if we can do something to make it so—we have a big advantage at the beginning. We do not have to worry about one sort of C_2 account of the sample property ("where" connections). For other properties, such as the amount of barley in soup or preference for political candidates, uniformity cannot be practically achieved, however. We may still be able to get a representative sample, but it will be far more complicated. We will deal with such cases shortly.

It's good to keep in mind that, as always in reasoning, our judgment in all these matters depends heavily on our general understanding of things. To competently test cars we must know something of the uniformities of mass production as well as the vagaries of distribution networks and the motivation of dealers. For soup we must know a good deal about the ingredients, the nature of liquids, and heat. Otherwise we would have no idea how different "places" in the population might explain various properties of a sample, or how to increase homogeneity.

"How" connections require even broader understanding. To see that *how* we deal with the spoonful of soup might affect what we find, we must know a lot about spoons and tasting. To see that how we test a Camry might change what we learn about it, we must understand what abuse will change a car's properties. Being too rough on a car during testing can degrade its performance and even change its dimensions. So even if our Camry is perfectly representative, the test results may not be. The same applies to soup. If our spoon is made of something that tastes salty, that might explain why the sample tastes salty (C_2) better than the soup itself.

Exercise 6.41

Give other ways in which how you sample may affect the results of the soup testing. (Answer on p. 311.)

Illustrations

The usefulness of distinguishing between "how" we sample and "where" we sample perhaps shows up best in the familiar activity of investigating voter sentiment. We all know that political opinions are not uniformly distributed in the population. Voting trends are different in different neighborhoods, age groups, ethnicities, genders, incomes, and much else. And the variations are different for different issues and candidates. Just "where" in the population we sample—just *who* we interview—will be very important. We should worry if our sample contains a disproportionate number of retired people or men or farmers or welfare recipients or civil service workers. For each might distort the sentiment you find in the sample. Each may be a good C_2 account of what we find.

We will shortly discuss different ways to reduce the plausibility of such C_2 explanations. But we need to notice that even if we do, that eliminates only half the C_2 problem. For even when we end up with a sample that perfectly mirrors the sentiment of the population, we can still ruin the result by interviewing badly. For what we want to know is what voters would choose in the isolation of a voting booth. But whether the voters respond to an interview in the same way they would in a voting booth depends on just how the questions are worded, what order they come in, whether they are asked in private or before an audience, and whether the interviewer is pleasant, aggressive, partisan, condescending, or otherwise offensive. This is what we called the "how" part of the sampling procedure. How we sample matters as much as where we sample in cases such as this.

Exercise 6.42

Because swimmers have complained about irritated eyes and green hair, the swimming coach uses a coffee cup to collect a sample of pool water to check the chlorine level. He leaves it on his desk and the lab sends somebody out four days later to retrieve it. They find it has no chlorine at all. This is certainly unrepresentative. Is the problem more likely "where" or "how"? Explain. (Answer on p. 311.)

Another reason to distinguish between how and where we sample is that we may say far more systematic things about where than about how. The manner of sampling (how) simply requires a lot of common sense understanding of the population that allows us to anticipate what would abuse a sample. The part of the population we examine, on the other hand, usually relates to the circumstances, and to P, in ways we may say something more general about. The following illustration will exploit this systematicity, and diagnostic form, to say something about how we deal with inhomogeneous populations.

To present the systematic understanding professional pollsters exploit to competently sample public opinion would be a curriculum all by itself, far beyond anything we can attempt here. But we may illustrate its diagnostic nature using a simpler example in a more familiar context. We all know enough about the conditions and institutions surrounding a kitchen cookie jar to make reasonably informed judgments about samples drawn from it in various circumstances. The thing to notice is how background and circumstance change what we can infer from the sample by changing the serious explanations of its properties. As ever, whether it is representative will depend generally on three matters: the nature of the population, the sampling procedure, and the property, P, we care about.

Let us begin with some circumstances. The jar is opaque and I cannot see into it, but it seems to be full of something (heavier than it should be when empty, and my hand touches something close to the top). Now suppose that I sample the contents by drawing out the first thing I touch, which turns out to be a chocolate chip cookie. What does this tell me about the contents of the jar (the population)? Without knowing more about how things go in this particular kitchen, we cannot say much, but perhaps we're justified in thinking we've found the cookie jar. Why? Because of our general understanding of human life: it's unlikely that a jar of tea bags or jelly beans would have a cookie on top. If this is right, then one property of the sample is very likely representative: that it's a cookie jar. What about chocolate chip? That's harder to say.

It would definitely be easier to rank explanations of that sample if we knew something about what goes on in that particular kitchen. So let's assume some "background on the population" and note how this kind of non-trace data helps judge representativeness. Suppose we know that the person who fills the jar buys (or makes) only one kind of cookie at a time and, further, fills the jar only when the last batch is gone. This is something like stirring the soup: we may presume homogeneity. So *any* sample will be representative as to kind. If we get a chocolate chip cookie off the top, that's almost certainly because the jar is filled with chocolate chip cookies. Given the background, that property of the population is by far the most plausible explanation of the sample.

S_1: Sample property: 100% chocolate chip cookies.
S_2: Circumstances as described, in particular: sample taken from top of jar.
S_3: Background on population: ordinary kitchen and jar filled only when empty, with a single kind of cookie.

$$=== d$$

C_1: Population has same property: 100% chocolate chip.

Let us complicate S_3 a little and explore its ramifications. Suppose the jar is filled only when empty, but it is filled *either* with a single kind of cookie *or* with a random assortment (the two kinds of packages available at the local grocery). If we keep everything else the same, the C_1 account gains a plausible C_2 rival: You got a single chocolate chip because it was what was on top of the assortment in the jar. The sampling procedure (C_2) explains the nature of the sample, just as well as a chocolate chip population (C_1) would. To tell what's in the jar we now need a better sample.

For a new sample, I take four more cookies off the top and, let us suppose, they too are chocolate chip (c.c.) cookies. The sample property, then, remains the same (100% c.c.), but the procedure has changed (five off the top). Does this help? Yes, certainly. For now the C_2 rival is not nearly as plausible. Recall that C_1 reads, "You got five chocolate chip cookies because the jar is filled with chocolate chip cookies." Whereas, given our presumptions about what goes on in the kitchen, the most plausible C_2 now reads, "You got that sample because there just happened to be five chocolate chip cookies on top of a random assortment." Given what we know, this is not likely. So you have good reason to think the sample is representative: you've found a jar of chocolate chip cookies.

Let us try one more change. If we make the filler less fastidious and say that the jar gets filled whenever we happen to have cookies, perhaps with several different kinds at a time, or with assortments that are not completely random, then *layers* are a real possibility. In this case one explanation of our sample property (100% c.c.) would be that our procedure is just working its way through a layer of similar cookies in a jar filled in different ways with many kinds. This, of course, is a C_2 account of the sample property: we got the sample property (100% c.c.) because of *where* we sampled, not because the population has that property. So again, to tell what's in the jar we need a different sample, a new procedure. What should we do?

What we would like is a procedure that would raise hurdles for a layer-type C_2 account of the sample property. To do this we boorishly reach around in the jar, drawing cookies from several levels, even one from the very bottom. If we get the same sample (100% c.c.) that would be a hurdle for the layer rival and make representativeness much more likely. But it would not be as good a bet as it was earlier. For our new background allows all sorts of C_2 possibilities not available before. Suppose the jar contains just three or four sugar cookies, for instance, the rest being chocolate chip? How likely are we to miss all the mavericks just reaching around? There is a good chance, actually. Determining just how likely begins to involve mathematical analysis beyond anything we can do here. But you can see that that analysis will depend on the general diagnostic structure we've been fleshing out in this section: we must determine the relative plausibility of various explanations of the sample property.

Exercise 6.43
....

In the homework investigation of Exercise 6.39 the sampling procedure made a certain C_2 rival very plausible. (a) What change in the sampling procedure would essentially eliminate that rival? (b) In that case what background on the class would make the original sample more likely to be representative? (Answers on p. 311.)

Randomness

The less we know about how properties are distributed in a population, the less certain we can be about how the properties of a sample might be affected by *where* we sample in a population. So when we know little, it is hard to have confidence that the selection procedure will not influence the results. One recourse, when we are thus uncertain, is to overwhelm our ignorance by breaking as many where connections as we can between the selection procedure and P. This is sometimes very useful.

As we have already noted, simply selecting a sample *always* distorts something: we can never break every connection between procedure and sample. And there's always the chance that the uneliminated connections affect P. But our ignorance is never complete. We usually understand P and the population and how the world works well enough to at least describe a sampling procedure that breaks all *plausible* connection to P. We call such a sample "random." Choosing lottery numbers by putting (otherwise) identical numbered balls in a barrel, spinning it around, and choosing from anywhere is random in this way. No plausible connection exists between the numbers and the selection.

The lottery barrel is typical of how this problem is solved in more complicated cases. To take a random sample of registered voters, for example, it would not be enough to wander (even randomly!) through neighborhoods knocking on doors. People who happen to be home, or accessible, or cooperative may not be representative: being home or accessible or cooperative may correlate with having particular opinions. If we don't know, those connections would be a worry, so the selection would be insufficiently random. But we could make the selection like the lottery by writing every voter's name on a ball—or just a slip of paper—putting them all in a barrel, spinning it to mix them up, and choosing our sample from many different places. We know enough to know that the opinion of a voter can hardly affect the way a ball with her name on it bounces around. So this would break all plausible connections between the selection and the opinions in which we are interested.

Exercise 6.44

Suppose a disk jockey is interested in voter opinion on a certain topic. What would be wrong with his taking a poll by simply asking his listeners to call in with their opinion? List at least four connections we should worry about. (Answer on p. 311.)

Many problems remain, of course. Randomizing can actually increase the risk of bad luck (discussed shortly), and in any case solves only the where questions: all the how questions remain. We must interview the chosen voters in a way that does not distort the results; and we must make sure we interview all (and only) the voters chosen from the barrel. Randomizing is merely a useful device for using meager information to draw an unbiased sample. But sometimes this is immensely valuable.

As a practical matter, however, randomizing is often pointless or impossible due to the nature of the population or aspects of the circumstances. Numbering the cookies in our cookie jar and then tossing slips of paper in the air would be a waste of time, for instance. The only reasonable way to number them would be to take them out of the jar, which would tell us everything we'd want to know about them before sampling. We could shake the jar, of course, but if it's nearly full, as we're presuming, the cookies would not move around very much. So that wouldn't randomize them. We might be able to break up layers and sequences by shaking very hard, but that would likely break up the cookies too. Crumbs and powder would defeat the purpose of the survey. Often enough a nonrandom sample is all we can get and, as we have seen, it may be just right for our purposes.

C₂ SUMMARY

When you cannot presume a homogeneous population, you still can sample representatively. But to do so you must either (a) know a great deal about the connections among properties in the population (e.g., know what the "layers" look like), or (b) be able to adequately randomize (which is sometimes impractical).

Exercise 6.45
....

Suppose the disk jockey in Exercise 6.44 wants the opinion of his *listeners* (not a larger group) on some topic. A call-in selection procedure would still have most of the problems you found in Exercise 6.44, so he might want to randomize. (a) What's the major obstacle preventing him from getting a random sample of his listeners (this has two distinct aspects)? (b) Opinions on some topics would be far less affected than others by the connection you listed in Exercise 6.44. Give an example of something objectively useful the disk jockey might discover from a call-in survey: something we should expect a random survey to agree with were we able to get it. (Answer on p. 311.)

Thinking about Bad Luck (C_3)

Sometimes you can do everything right and still end up with an unrepresentative sample. Reaching around you may get the only five chocolate chip cookies in the jar. Just as with everything else in life, you can never completely eliminate the possibility of getting it wrong. But risk may be minimized by two different stratagems, and we can deal reasonably with what's left by being aware of its magnitude.

The first and easiest trick is to keep an eye out for implausible sample properties. If we know enough to sample we have a good idea of the range within which P will fall with any plausibility. So if the Camry shows up missing its windshield, we don't simply record that Camrys don't have windshields and go on with the test. We know enough about things to realize we've gotten an unrepresentative one just by luck and send it back. Similarly, if we survey voters and 100% favor Gore for president, we know that's extremely unlikely to be representative and try again with a different procedure. Given a couple of centuries of experience with elections, we would accept 100% only after trying many different ways to get a more plausible sample property. In general, the more spectacular (and newsworthy) the result, the more you should suspect something's gone wrong in sampling, at least at first.

Exercise 6.46
....

Give an example of a survey in which 100% would not be suspicious. (Suggestions on p. 311.)

The other obvious way to reduce the risk of bad luck is to increase sample size. If the second Camry shows up without a windshield we begin to suspect the first one wasn't just bad luck. We certainly won't infer representativeness just yet; but we may suspect a C_2 account: something in the sampling procedure. (This is usually an improvement because, unlike bad luck, we learn something about the population from sampling failures.) But the point is to notice that increasing the sample size always reduces the risk of simple bad luck. With voters, we reduce the chance that 100% for Gore is just luck of the draw by, say, doubling the sample. Again, if P remains 100% Gore as the sample gets large, that may signal a C_2 problem with the procedure, but it definitely reduces the chance that it is mere luck.

Exercise 6.47

(a) If we infer a C_2 problem from the uniform sample in the last paragraph, schematize the argument, including our historical experience with elections, and articulate the conclusion. Label the TD and NTD. (b) Suppose you're impressed by the number of pickups and SUVs you see with campus parking permits and want to do a survey to check your perception. Somebody gives you a list of phone numbers from the campus vehicle registration logs and the first three students you call own motorcycles, not cars of any kind. So you skip around on the list and the next 10 own motorcycles too. What should you suspect? (Answers on p. 311.)

More interesting is the case in which we really know what we're doing and have C_2 considerations well under control (for instance, when we've properly randomized). For when we can neglect C_2 rivals, we can then say that a sample's properties become more and more certainly representative with increasing sample size. The principle is this: as sample size increases, *the chance that a population without P produced a sample with P* decreases. Consider the case in which P is the percentage of the population favoring Gore, for instance. No matter how weirdly preference for Gore is distributed in the population, if our procedure is not connected to that weirdness (C_2), then every addition to the sample improves our chances of revealing it. For a finite population (eligible voters, for example), as sample size approaches the entire population it has no choice but to mirror the population more and more exactly.

Mathematical statisticians have worked out ways to state exactly how the risk of bad luck varies with sample size for any given population. To do this, they think of all the ways that different populations could have produced the sample we have and estimate the likelihood of each.[13] Then see how the combined likelihoods of populations having P stack up against those not having it. A general reasoning text cannot describe this in any detail: a statistics course would be required to adequately introduce you to this and other related mathematics. If you'd like to know the risk in a certain case without taking the course, you may always take your data to a statistician to calculate the size sample you need for the risk you can tolerate.

---

13. If you've randomized, this is easier: each "way" is equally likely, so you may simply count the ways.

Exercise 6.48
....

Suppose you've sampled more than half of the eligible voters and the property is still 100% for Gore. (a) What may you conclude absolutely? (b) If you've made a reasonable attempt to break obvious connections, what may you safely conclude? (Answers on p. 311.)

Summary

The point of this section is to show that using samples as evidence is both widespread and diagnostic in nature. When we take a sample of something and find that it has a certain property, P, and we wish to know whether the thing we sampled also has it, the strategy is to treat the sample's property as trace data and construct a diagnostic argument. We use what we know of the circumstances of the sampling and our understanding of the population to sort through various explanations of the trace. Then we group those explanations into three kinds by what they tell us about the source of P: namely, whether the source is the population itself (C_1), the sampling procedure (C_2), or bad luck (C_3). If a single explanation or kind of explanation stands out, we may say yes (C_1) or no (C_2 or C_3) to the inference. Otherwise the matter is indeterminate.

As usual in diagnostic reasoning, how well you can do depends on how much you understand about the matter in question. If you know very little about the population or the sampling procedure or the property P, sampling will not be of much value.

COUNTING CASES: INDUCTION BY ENUMERATION

The last kind of trace data we will examine is the simple *list* of similar cases. Suppose I had studied crows for years and had concluded from my experience that all crows are black. If I had a record of that experience, I might set it out in the following way as evidence, that is, as an argument for my conclusion.

S_1 Crow #1 is black.
S_2 Crow #2 is black.
S_3 Crow #3 is black.
   .

   .

   .
S_{296} Crow #296 is black.

C All crows are black.

The simple counting of cases such as this sometimes strikes us as a purer, less hazardous form of reasoning than the complicatedly human, diagnostic arguments we have been examining. Some thinkers have argued that the enumeration of cases such as this is actually the basic form of evidence (or inductive argument), underpinning the more elaborate forms we have been examining. Attempts to show how such underpinning might work have not met with any success, however. For even the purest cases of enumeration seem to presuppose the general understanding of things that complicates the diagnostic model of evidence. Enumerative arguments, it turns out, are diagnostic arguments in disguise.

This does not mean that lists of cases never support generalizations. But when they do, it is never the list itself, in isolation, that does the work. It provides support only against the background of everything we know about the items on the list and the circumstances of their collection. In other words, enumerations turn out to be complicatedly human too. And as always, the best way to deal with the complexity is to look at how we came up with the list. That is, we treat the list as trace data and ask for its explanation. Sometimes the best account of the list will be a generalization such as "all crows are black," and sometimes not, depending on much outside the list.

Note that many lists, schematizable in the same way as our list of crows, lead to just the opposite conclusion, because of what we know of the items. In California, or any other seismically unstable region, we may seek to reassure ourselves by reflecting on a recent string of earthquake-free days:

S_1 Day 1: no earthquake.
S_2 Day 2: no earthquake.
S_3 Day 3: no earthquake

.

.

.

S_{296} Day 296: no earthquake

C We will never have another earthquake.

This argument has the same enumerative form as the one about crows. But geologists tell us that in such parts of the earth's crust, the best account of a long string of earthquake-free days does not look anything like C here. A far better explanation is that local faults are locked together so as not to allow the release of subterranean stress in small, frequent quakes; they are therefore building up for a much more dramatic fracture. A long string of quiet days is a bad sign not a good one. Similarly, the evidence of our daily lives would, by enumeration, yield immortality:

S_1 Day 1: I did not die.
S_2 Day 2: I did not die.
S_3 Day 3: I did not die.
And so on.

But we know full well that with each passing day death is closer, not more remote.

The point to notice is simply that sometimes lists of similar cases support generalizations and sometimes not. And when they do, they support them because the generalization is the best account of the list, given our general understanding of how these things work. It may be that the best account of the fact that all 296 crows I've seen have been black is that all crows everywhere are black. But if it is, it is not a matter of merely counting cases.

CIRCUMSTANTIAL EVIDENCE

We are now in a position to throw some light on the common but misunderstood notion of *circumstantial evidence*. Evidence from the "surrounding circumstances" has obviously played a major role in out diagnostic articulations. Many of our schemata have places explicitly reserved for something called "circumstances." Sometimes the circumstances contain trace data (a speaker's nervousness) and sometimes essential NTD (how the sample was selected). Often they are all we have (in the racing car crash, for example), and they can constitute very strong support for a conclusion (the tires were intact when control was lost).

Nevertheless, the term "circumstantial evidence" is commonly used derogatorily, as a way of criticizing evidence. We say that "The suspect was acquitted because the case against him was merely circumstantial." This suggests the evidence is not very good, and not very good *because* it is circumstantial. There is something right about this. But it is a subtle point and we must be careful to see how it fits with everything we have learned so far.

When we speak of "merely circumstantial" evidence in a criminal case, the problem is usually that nobody (still living) saw the defendant commit the crime. No one saw him kill the service station attendant, for instance, or could even place him near the scene of the holdup on the evening in question. There were no witnesses. The evidence we do have in such a case may include reliable testimony that a car just like the suspect's was in the neighborhood of the service station immediately before the crime and perhaps that he suddenly seemed to have more money than usual shortly afterward.

But even if we add that the suspect had no alibi, the case for conviction of this particular crime is rather weak because it lacks, quite specifically, evidence that is not circumstantial: direct identification of the suspect at the scene of the crime. So we can begin to see the point of calling evidence "merely circumstantial." If the question concerns identifying an individual—especially one who does not want to be identified—recognition by a reliable witness is an ideal kind of evidence. Our ability to recognize people, to discriminate among other human beings, is one of our best, most well-developed perceptual skills. In the right circumstances, a personal recognition can be irreplaceably valuable evidence.

By contrast, circumstances of the kind mentioned in this case are too crude to implicate a particular individual. They do not have the right kind of detail to provide a confident identification. Too many rival accounts of them are possible. The suspect's car is usually not unique; even if it is, he may not have been driving it, or he may have been on his way elsewhere; everybody has times for which no alibi could be given; sudden wealth can have many sources. So when "circumstantial evidence" refers to circumstances such as these, and a personal identification is in question, we can see that "merely" might easily fit. This is the way in which circumstances can provide intrinsically weak evidence.

But the lesson to be learned from this is a narrow, practical one about a certain kind of case, not a general one about the basic nature of evidence. For as soon as we look at other kinds of conclusions or a broader range of circumstances, the contrast vanishes. When they don't involve personal identification, we have already seen how strong diagnostic arguments can be that simply marshal circumstances in the support. Inferring that the earthquake knocked down the overpass is just one example. But even in criminal identifications, we might make a case from the circumstances every bit as strong as a direct observation of the crime, simply by allowing more finely detailed circumstances.

Fingerprints are as unique as faces; ballistic markings are nearly so. But, in contrasting with an eyewitness account of a crime, they will all be part of the circumstances. So if we find that the fresh fingerprints on the empty cash drawer belong to the suspect, that the bullet taken from the attendant's body is from the suspect's gun, which he was known to never let out of his sight, and that the bills he spent the evening of the crime were ones marked by the service station owner in anticipation of a robbery, such a case would be circumstantial. But it is easily as strong as an isolated eyewitness's identification. And we can always make it stronger still simply by accumulating more (circumstantial) detail.

So we might think of the basic distinction as between (a) the direct observation of something and (b) all the other evidence for it, which we might call "indirect" by contrast. Much indirect evidence would be from the surrounding circumstances, as we have been using the term. But they would not be "circumstantial" in the derogatory sense. We reserve the expression "merely circumstantial evidence" for the crude but common kind of indirect evidence mentioned above, which is of limited value, especially in personal identification. Considered generally, however, there is no categorical difference between direct and indirect evidence.

In fact, indirect evidence can be so strong that we will quite properly reject eyewitness accounts conflicting with it. Spectators testify that the victim was standing when the fatal shot was fired, but the path of the bullet through the body makes that simply inconceivable. We may reject the observers' descriptions because it is easier to explain the descriptions away as deceived or dishonest than to make them compatible with the pathologist's examination.

It's also worth keeping in mind that there's nothing magic about direct observations. They may be undermined in all sorts of ways, and can be absolutely worthless. Sometimes observation reports will conflict: one witness says the victim was standing when shot and another says he was already on the ground. The lack of agreement suggests that circumstances have undermined perceptual competence. Perhaps both observations are suspect. All the considerations relevant to the competence of testimony bear on these cases. If there is much excitement and we are scared out of our wits, our reliability as observers will decrease. It will also be affected if we have a deep emotional commitment to something or someone in the events unfolding in front of us. We may let our hopes guide our eyes and see what we wish had happened rather than what did.

In short, the reliability of our perceptions *depends on* the circumstances. Even our best direct observations may be undermined by circumstance. A perfectly normal, competent personal identification may be demolished by the existence of an identical twin. So in general, the only rule is to set out all the relevant data—direct and indirect—and find the best account of it all. Sometimes eyewitness testimony may be discounted and sometimes it will be impossible to explain away.

SUPPLEMENTAL EXERCISES

A. Review Questions

1. A correlation becomes trace data when it _____.

2. When X is a common cause of A and B it causes both A and B, but causes them _____ of each other.

3. In a correlational argument, what is a modus operandi? How is it relevant? Does this make it TD or NTD?

4. What about an argument identifies it as a testimony argument?

5. What is wrong with saying that in a testimony argument the rivals explain what the person said?

6. Testimony may be undermined in two very different ways. What are they?

7. In diagnostic terms, explain how testimony can be both worthless and true?

8. The following questions concern the two-step testimony form.
a. What is the central trace data in Step One? What makes it trace data?
b. What result of Step One is required for Step Two? Is it trace data? Explain.
c. Give one version of the underwriting rival in Step One.
d. Give an example of an undermining rival in Step One.
e. Motivation may be relevant to both steps, but differently. Explain the difference.

9. What two general sorts of reason are there for sampling (that is, for investigating something by taking a sample of it)?

10. Explain why a sample is always unrepresentative in some way.

11. Because samples are inevitably unrepresentative in some way or other, how can we use a sample to learn about a population?

12. Reread Supplemental Exercise B.1 at the end of Chapter 5. This passage contains an argument for the conclusion that a certain pin had jammed the scoop arm of Viking I during earlier operations. The evidence offered is all circumstantial: nobody actually saw the pin jam the arm. (a) Explain why this does not seriously challenge the strength of the argument offered. (b) Explain why it would take a very special observer to give eyewitness testimony that could compete with the circumstantial evidence we have.

B. Passages for Analysis

1. Consider the following inference from a correlation to a cause and answer the questions below.

> The mean income of Yale graduates is three times the national average. So apparently going to Yale substantially increases the amount of money you can expect to make.

a. What are the correlates?
b. What is the conclusion's direction of influence?
c. Provide a rival conclusion with a different direction of influence.
d. What direction does your rival have? Briefly explain.

2. Because people using stronger sunscreens don't feel the effects of sunburn as quickly, they spend more time outside and increase their risk of skin cancer, according to a study that finds even the best prevention isn't foolproof. The European researchers concluded that "sunscreens may encourage prolonged sun exposure because they delay sunburn," results they say help explain previous studies linking sunscreen use with higher skin cancer rates. "It's not due to the fact that sunscreens are bad. It's because people have a bad attitude, using sunscreens to increase the amount of time they spend in the sun," said Dr. Ferdy Lejeune, an author of the study being published today in the Journal of the National Cancer Institute.

(*The Associated Press*)

a. What correlation does Dr. Lejeune's study think it can explain?
b. What direction of influence does the study's explanation have?
c. Give a rival with a different direction. What direction does it have?

3. Soccer players who repeatedly hit the ball with their head suffer a mild form of the same mental impairment that afflicts boxers who have received multiple concussions, according to a new report presented Saturday in New York. Skilled soccer players who head the ball at least 10 times a game score an average of nine points lower on a standard IQ test than do their peers who head the ball infrequently, psychologist Adrienne Witol of the Medical College of Virginia told a meeting of the American Psychological Assn. And 10 of the 17 players in this highest heading category scored among the bottom 5% of all Americans in a frequently used test of concentration and attention, she said, suggesting that years of having a 13-ounce ball hit their heads at 60 m.p.h. have produced significant damage. "Blows to the head damage the brain, and it doesn't make much difference what causes the blow," said Dr. George Lundberg, editor of the Journal of the American Medical Assn., who has long campaigned against the more obvious brain damage caused by boxing.

The current study by Witol and psychologist Frank M. Webbe of the Florida Institute of Technology appears to be the first scientific investigation of the problem. Witol and Webbe studied 60 skilled male soccer players over the age of 14 and compared them to each other and to a control group of 12 males of comparable age and educational attainment. They then administered an IQ test and a variety of other tests that measure mental agility and concentration. The only significant differences appeared on the IQ test and on two different forms of the so-called trail making tests—which are, in effect, sophisticated versions of the connect-the-numbers games popular with children. On the IQ test, the average in the group that did not head the ball was 112, compared to 103 for the group that headed it most frequently. Score differences were similar for the trail making tests, indicating that those who headed the ball frequently had much more difficulty maintaining concentration.

(Thomas H. Maugh II, *Los Angeles Times* medical writer, abridged)

a. This article offers an argument from a correlation to a cause. Schematize the argument and label the correlates A and B.
b. What direction of causal influence does the conclusion have?
c. Give a rival with the opposite direction.
d. What non-trace data are offered in the article in support of its conclusion?

4. Researchers at Boston University have found that younger men with bald spots on the top of their heads have an increased risk of heart attacks. They studied men under 55 with vertex baldness, as such baldness is called, and found that the larger the bald spot the higher the risk. Men with mild vertex baldness were about forty percent more likely to suffer heart attacks than men with a full head of hair, while for those with severe

vertex baldness the risk rose to three hundred forty percent. The correlation did not hold for hair loss from other areas of the scalp.

This is not to suggest that baldness causes heart attacks. In an article published in the Journal of the American Medical Association, the authors of the study suggested that the culprit may be the male sex hormone dihydrotestosterone. Research elsewhere has identified this hormone as a principal factor responsible for male baldness. It has also been offered as possibly explaining the dramatically greater heart attack rate among younger men as compared with premenopausal women.

a. What correlation has the Boston University study found?
b. What explanatory story does the article begin to develop?
c. What causal-influence pattern does it represent?
d. Give a different (better developed) story with the same direction of causal influence.
e. Give a rival story with a different direction of influence.

5. STATE COLLEGE, Pa.—College grades will suffer more from cutting classes than from cutting study time to a minimum, according to researchers. The researchers, writing in the June issue of Social Forces, said they found little correlation between the amount of time spent studying and a student's grade point average. "I guess I really don't want to believe that studying doesn't pay off," said Edward Walsh, associate professor of sociology at Pennsylvania State University, who assisted in the series of studies conducted by University of Michigan sociologist Howard Schuman. Schuman was on sabbatical and could not be reached, his secretary said.

In the first study . . . , researchers interviewed 424 students in Literature, Science, and Arts College about their study habits and grade point averages. Students who reported studying less than two hours each weekday had an overall grade point average of 2.94. The average grade point was 2.91 for students studying two to three hours a day, 2.97 for those studying three to four hours, and 2.86 for students hitting the books four to five hours a day. The grade average jumped to 3.25 for students studying five to six hours a day, but dropped to 3.18 for those going at it six or more hours.

Several subsequent studies yielded similar results, the researchers said. The first study also found that grades went up steadily with the percentage of classes attended regularly by students. That finding was supported in a later study, the researchers said.

(The Associated Press)

a. This article finds *no* significant correlation between study time (A) and grade point average (B) and reluctantly infers that study time does not improve grades. The reluctance is due to the plausibility of supposing at least *some* A → B connection; that is, it is reasonable to think study time improves grades at least a little. Assuming that there is no correlation between A and B, there are variations in people and courses that might explain this result even though studying *does* improve grades. Give two such explanations, one involving differences among students and the other differences among classes. In other words, explain how variations in people or variations in courses might prevent the benefit of study time from showing up in these statistics.

b. Another possibility is that there actually is a distinct overall correlation between study time and grades, but that students systematically misreport their study time in a way that yields no correlation in the data. Give two rival accounts of this form, one involving dishonesty and the other not.

6. Suppose a coach, just before the first game of the season, says to her team, "This team has the ability to go undefeated this year." Consider this as testimony to be evaluated in our two-step form.

a. Make up circumstances and background that would support C_1 rivals at each step.

b. Change things so that $C_{2''}$ would be better for Step Two.

c. Change things again so that $C_{2'}$ would be better for Step One.

7. CARLSBAD, N.M.—A hiker rescued from the desert back country of Carlsbad Caverns National Park says he killed his companion to put him out of his misery when the pair became lost and were dying of thirst, authorities said. Raffi Kodikian, 26, of Boston was arraigned Monday on an open murder charge, which authorities said means investigators have not determined how serious the charge should be. An autopsy Tuesday showed 26-year-old David Coughlin of Millis, Mass., had been stabbed twice in the chest.

   Park rangers on Sunday found Kodikian camped next to Coughlin's shallow grave. Kodikian was suffering from dehydration and exposure when rangers found him about a mile from the nearest road and about two miles from the park's visitors center, the sheriff said Tuesday. Rangers launched a search Sunday, two days after the pair were supposed to return.

(The Associated Press)

a. Here Kodikian makes a claim about the circumstances of Coughlin's death. If we use the two-step form for assessing testimony, in which step would the most serious difficulties arise for accepting Kodikian's description? Explain.

b. What considerations might be relevant from the other step?

c. What might we discover about Kodikian, or the circumstances relevant to testimony form, that would allay the reservations you raised in (a)?

d. What relevant evidence might we find that is *not* part of testimony form? How would it affect your evaluation of Kodikian's testimony. Why?

8. Just over four thousand students have taken professor Ogden's introductory course for credit during the ten years it's been offered. During that time 284 students have come in during office hours to discuss a quiz. Of these, 279 (an overwhelming majority) thought their quiz had been graded too harshly: that the grade was unfairly low. From this we can conclude that an overwhelming majority of professor Ogden's students think their quizzes have been graded too harshly.

a. What C_2 rival probably accounts for the sample property?

b. What does this say about the inference?

c. Describe a sampling procedure that would better underwrite this inference.

9. Suppose I would like to know what sort of thing is in a medium-sized cardboard box, into which I can neither see nor reach my hand. To investigate, I tie a small magnet on a string, drop it into the box, and record the things clinging to it when I pull it back up. I drop the magnet in several times and each time various small metal objects cling to it. I describe each as well as I can on a list. I infer from my accumulated sample that the box contains small metal objects.

a. In diagnostic terms, explain why the sampling procedure undermines my inference.

b. The sample might have many other properties besides small and metallic. Give an example of a property it might have that would not be affected by the sampling procedure and so be representative of the population of the box.

c. Describe a selection procedure that, if it yielded the same sample, would be more likely representative of what's in the box. That is, the sample would be reason to think the box contained only small metal objects. Explain.

10. Police officers occasionally become deeply pessimistic about the human condition: they come to think badly of the general level of civility, motivation, and self-control in the community. Describe the likely experience behind this perception in a way that shows how the perception might be a bad sample-to-population inference. In other words, explain how a police officer's experience with people might be unrepresentative in a way that would tempt such an inference even if the perception is too pessimistic. More than one thing is worth mentioning.

11. While researching human longevity (how long people live), the Guinness organization found that birth and death records have been kept so badly in most parts of the world that claims to great age are both generally suspect and wholly unverifiable. In the passage below, they describe an exception to this melancholy rule that they then argue they cannot use because of its unrepresentativeness.

> The most reliably pedigreed large group of people in the world, the British peerage, has, after ten centuries, produced only two peers who reached their 100th birthdays, and only one reached his 101st. However, this is perhaps not unconnected with the extreme draftiness of many of their residences and the amount of lead in the game they consume.

    a. What is the population about which they obviously wish to get information?
    b. What is the sample they consider in this passage?
    c. What property do they care about?
    d. What C_2 rival do they think undermines an inference from this sample?

ANSWERS

6.1 The first would be: whenever Charlie has a pain in his elbow, we have bad weather. The second would be: Whenever we have eclipses, we have high tides.

6.2 **a.** A = the phone rings; B = somebody responds when I answer.
    b. Whenever the phone rings, somebody responds when I answer
    c. The phone rings *because* somebody is there to talk.

6.3 **a.** **i.** The meteorite impact and the extinction seem to have occurred at about the same time.
      ii. Both (broken latch and vanished equipment) happened while you were away.
    b. Plausible connection: the person who took the equipment broke the latch to get in.

6.4 **a.** A = not completing high school; B = dying earlier.
    b. People who fail to finish high school have a 30% higher rate of death before age 64 than those who graduate.
    c. Dropping out of school is hazardous to your health.

6.5 Instead of physically completing an electrical circuit (the obvious rival) the switch could emit a high-frequency sound or a burst of infrared radiation and that turns the light on in the same way that a TV remote changes channels. Or the switch could pull a string that drops a piece of cheese attracting a mouse living in the light, and the motion of the mouse triggers a motion detector, turning on the light.

6.6 As suggested, such a story would have to be fantastic, because the sorts of things that cause a fault to slip are not easily brought to bear on a freeway bridge. But we might imagine that the stress on the fault in question was so high that it would take very little to break it loose. Then terrorists overdid it and used vastly too much explosive to blow up the overpass. The shockwave from the explosion was then just enough to fracture the last bit of rock holding the fault, unleashing the earthquake. The explosion would then be a common cause.

6.7 S_1 The overpass fell down during the earthquake.

S_2 Ground motion generated by an earthquake can be strong enough to move an overpass off its supports.

== d

C The earthquake caused the overpass to fall.

6.8 First, we know that eclipses are just shadows: the shadow of the earth on the moon or of the moon on the earth when one of them gets between the sun and the other. Hence, for there to be any sort of direct cause, the shadows would have to affect tides, or the tides would have to push the earth and moon into each other's shadow. Neither seems very plausible. Furthermore, solar eclipses never affect more than a tiny stripe across the earth a few hundred miles wide, but the higher tides that go with eclipses are global in extent. So we not only have to have a shadow affect the oceans, but we have to have a sometimes relatively tiny shadow, mostly on land, affect tides all over the earth. This seems even less plausible.

6.9 **a.** The earthquake.
b. We know that a falling overpass will not normally have consequences (e.g., produce shock waves) that would endanger distant structures. But we know that earthquakes produce ground motion across a wide area and hence may affect structures far apart.

6.10 It depends on your personality. But for most people, perhaps most plausible, would be that you realized you were unprepared and the anxiety or panic or fretting caused you to omit your name. This would be a common cause: being unprepared caused both the bad grade and the omitted name, independently.

6.11 **a.** The connection they're raising questions with is "implants cause the health problems." "Blamed on" just means "caused by" here.
b. What raises the doubts are what we've called "other correlates" above. The specific ones offered are earlier childbirth, more sexual partners, and using hair dye.
c. Other correlates are NTD, helping rival accounts of the correlation.
d and e. They make common cause more serious by suggesting that there is a stable life-style pattern that includes all these possible causal factors, and these other factors may cause health problems independently of the implants.

6.12 If the overpass collapsed before the earthquake, that effectively rules out any connection between the two. For it leaves only two possibilities: overpass collapse caused the earthquake and common cause. And, as we noted earlier, neither of these is plausible in ordinary circumstances.

6.13 It's the way tires work: if one is flat it will not grip the road in the nice, smooth, regular way it does when properly inflated. And hard braking or sliding puts forces on a tire that would make this even more obvious.

6.14 This would require something truly bizarre that would essentially take the roots right off the plant. Perhaps the soil contained a corrosive chemical that needed only water to be released in active form, immediately dissolving the roots.

6.16 **a.** **i.** A = suicide attempts; B = low cholesterol.
ii. Correlation: patients who attempted suicide had lower cholesterol than other patients.
iii. Lower cholesterol causes depression, which inclines people to suicide.
iv. B → A.
v. Depression (mood) causes both suicide attempts and lower cholesterol. (If this is puzzling, look back at A and B.)
vi. Common cause.

b. **i.** A = kid's sugar consumption; B = (their) hyperactivity.
  ii. Sugar consumption is accompanied by hyperactivity.
  iii. They argue against A → B.
  iv. 1: Hyperactivity leads to (lots of things including) increased sugar consumption.
  2: Parties and holidays excite hyperactivity and happen also to include more than normal sugary confections.
  v. 1 is B → A; 2 is common cause.

c. **i.** A = drinking a lot of coffee; B = heart disease.
  ii. People who drink a lot of coffee develop coronary artery disease far more than those who do not.
  iii. Excessive coffee drinking causes coronary artery disease.
  iv. Cigarette smoking has been controlled for.
  v. Unhealthy diet and lack of exercise have not been ruled out.
  vi. Common cause.
  vii. People inclined to drink a lot of coffee are also, as a matter of their make-up, more than ordinarily inclined to other indulgences such as fatty foods and rich desserts.

6.17 Common cause: for example, an earthquake caused both.

6.18 The correlation is between gunshot and windshield crack. The truck account explains the crack as having occurred in a way wholly unrelated to the gunshot. If that account is right, the correlation was mere coincidence.

6.19 If we eliminate A → D, that eliminates 1. If we eliminate D → A, that eliminates 2 and 4. If we eliminate an A → D common cause, that eliminates 5. And eliminating B → A eliminates 3.

6.20 Because the example assumes I'm innocently involved in this, only fantastic stories may be marshalled for D → A and common cause: something would have to cause my flipping the switch. In direct cause the substation failure would have to do it, and before the lights went out. Perhaps this: early stages of substation failure caused static on my radio, annoying me, which caused me to leave early and hence throw the switch just as the substation went off line. Common cause might exploit the same device: deterioration of a transformer caused the static and independently caused the substation failure. A → D would be less fantastic, but still implausible: my office switch was rigged through a relay to short out something essential in the substation. Finally, we may ignore reverse cause (B → A) since A happened before B.

6.21 **a.** **i.** A = Linda's yelling; B = the light's changing.
  ii. Linda might, for instance, have a voice-activated transmitter on her dashboard that sends signals to tiny receivers in traffic lights, making them change.
  iii. Linda might be able to anticipate the light's flashing green in a number of ways: she might see that the light in the other direction is already amber, or she might notice the smooth flow of cross-traffic suddenly beginning to slow at the intersection.
  iv. For the first story B might simply be taken to be "the light's flashing green." But for the reverse cause, it cannot be read this way, because what caused her to yell would not be the green flash, but the fact that the light had begun the process of changing to green in her direction. So what counts as "changing" would have to be expanded a bit if it was interpreted narrowly at first.

6.22 **a.** A = daily dip in a hot spring; B = good health.

b. A → B.

c. Monkeys in a botanical garden that bathe daily in a hot spring are healthier than those caged elsewhere.

d. Simply being free to roam the gardens might be a common cause: this could be what keeps them healthier than the caged monkeys, and, independently allows them their hot baths, which don't have any affect on health.

6.23 If it had been first noticed just after the quake, or we knew it happened on the same evening as the quake, that would make it reasonable to think we had a pairing to explain. Overpasses very seldom simply collapse on their own, and earthquakes are one of the few plausible explanations of such a collapse.

6.24 **a.** Because physics of sunspots is so far removed from economics, a sunspot/market connection would allow the possibility of radically new information to be used in the understanding of markets and hence economic forecasting.

b. If we understood just how the connection worked, that might enable us to refine our understanding and forecasts by taking other factors into account. For example, if it worked by influencing the weather or by directly damaging crops, we could trace that particular influence and note its ramifications in detail.

6.25 You might check to see if the fussy infants received more or different nourishment to keep them quiet, which would yield a rival in the same direction. Or you might look for early signs of intelligence, to make a reverse-cause story serious. Or, for a subtler rival in the same direction, you might check to see whether something systematic happened to the quieter infants that could actually damage their intellectual development.

6.26 Information favoring the chance rival would be (a) others ate the same thing and did not get sick, (b) you have all the symptoms of a flu virus that typically causes vomiting, and (c) one common early symptom of that flu is being repelled by food. The original argument consisted in correlational TD (not liking meal/vomiting) in support of a food poisoning rival. (b) is a gesture at TD explained by the flu rival, whereas (a) and (c) are NTD, the former hurting the poisoning rival and the latter helping the flu rival explain the correlation.

6.27 One set of circumstances: the sign is on the top of a pile of similar signs in the back of a highway maintenance truck. Another: it is mounted on the wall of a friend's bedroom.

6.28 **a.**

S_1 The speedometer reads 60 mph.	TD
S_2 We seem not to be moving.	TD
S_3 The road is icy.	NTD

$$============================ d$$

C_2 The wheels are spinning.

b. S_2 is an explanatory hurdle for all C_1 rivals: it is difficult for them to explain.

6.29 C_2: He said it because he wants you to buy the car.

6.30 Background on the car seller favorable to a C_1 account of his positive assessment of the car would be that he has a reputation for being painfully honest. This would be NTD because in answering the IQ we would not be trying to explain his honesty. (Alternatively: his honesty is relevant only in helping C_1 explain his saying what he did.)

6.31 He didn't hear what the announcer said.
(That's why he said the runner was out.)
I thought this was today's newspaper.
(That's why she said the bombing had restarted.)
They forgot to take the sign down.
(That's why it still says "be back in five minutes.")
It was just a joke.
(That's why she said you couldn't come with us.)

6.32 a. One C_1 account would be: she said it because it will be six forty one at the tone. Another would be: because they finally got the tape synchronized with a good clock.

    b. i. Circumstances favoring C_1: Your friend called; she knows there is no hurry to get the money back; you have a history of relying on each other that you know she values; and you've lent her money before and she's always returned it as soon as she could afford to.

      ii. Circumstances favoring C_2: You've been trying to get the money back for weeks; you've left message several places and she's not returned them; and you've finally tracked her down at a friend's, when the friend inadvertently reveals that she's there.

6.33 Circumstances favoring C_2': The guy's been trying to sell you his old computer for weeks and is now desperate to get rid of it because his new one has arrived. Circumstances favoring C_1': The guy would make a lot of money repairing it, knows you can afford it, and does not have anything to sell you in its place.

6.34 This question is difficult for a reason: it's so hard to say anything. To be competent, all such a judgment requires is a fairly modest level of reading skill and memory. If your friend does not have any special problems on either score, that (negative consideration) would be adequate to accept her judgment of the time and day.

6.35 a. S_5.

    b. This would not be acceptable because people ordinarily need to check a clock to know what time it is. That's why the world is filled with clocks and watches. The special information that would get around this objection would be evidence of my unusual ability to tell time without the help of a clock (tests passed or feats recorded).

6.36 S_5: Fred's shop is reasonably well equipped for engine diagnosis.
S_6: Fred has recently taken a dealer-sponsored training course on cars like the Farnsworth's.

6.37 Plausible accounts of the watch's reading three minutes: (a) It's running down. (b) You stopped it as the runners passed the wrong marker. (c) It's running erratically.

6.38 Tasting wine is restricted by both expense and point: if you "tasted" the whole bottle, tasting could not be free, and there would be no wine left for others or to drink with the meal.

6.39 The best explanation of every member of the sample's getting it right is called "self-selection": only those reasonably sure of their understanding would likely volunteer. Most who did not understand, or who were uncertain, would be anxious to avoid displaying that fact. This explanation falls in C_2: influence of the sampling procedure.

6.40 (a) We know that water splashes everything in a dishwasher thoroughly, and hence leaves whatever residue it leaves more or less uniformly. So anything you inspect should have the same residue. (b) This is a good sample because a clear glass and a (smooth) knife will reveal water spots more easily than other surfaces.

6.41 If you (the taster) have been eating something very salty or with any very distinctive taste, that could affect how the spoonful of soup tastes quite independently of how much salt it contains.

6.42 The problem is certainly in how the sample was treated. We may presume that the chlorination in a well-used pool is reasonably uniform. But leaving a sample out on a desk may affect the chlorine level either through natural processes (evaporation, sunlight) or adulteration. Somebody might even have drunk or discarded the original and replaced it with water from the cooler.

6.43 **a.** Self-selection may be eliminated by avoiding volunteers. This could be done by having the instructor choose the students to write out their assignments.

   b. To encourage participation by those who need it most, the instructor awards points for working out misunderstandings on the board. Suppose the rule for awarding homework points was that you got a certain number of points for getting it right. But if your solution was flawed in some way, you could get additional points by volunteering, up to the maximum for getting it right to begin with. (So no extra points for volunteering if the solution is correct.) This would make the original sample more likely to be representative by motivating the confused and uncertain to volunteer.

6.44 (a) There might well be a connection between listening to his show and the opinion in question. So even if the result were representative of his listeners it might not be of voters. But the callers may not even represent his listeners, because (b) most radio listeners are in cars; responding would require a cellular telephone, and there might be a connection between owning one and the opinion in question. (c) and (d) There is also a "self-selection" problem like that in the homework example: those who have the time and motivation to call in may not even be representative of audience members who own a cell phone.

6.45 **a.** To get names to put in the barrel to randomize we'd have to identify all the listeners and there's no way to do this. There are two aspects of the problem: (i) we cannot even identify all the radios tuned to the disk jockey's station at a given time. But even if we could, (ii) it's probably harder to decide who within earshot of a radio to count as a "listener." Many are not responsible for the dial's being set to this station and perhaps most are not paying any attention.

   b. The sort of opinion that might be representative would be the weather. If all the callers said it was raining, we might well get the same opinion from a random survey.

6.46 If you randomly asked people on a hot, humid day if they're looking forward to cooler weather, for example. Or if you wanted to know how many people at Yankee Stadium during the playoffs considered themselves baseball fans.

6.47 **a.** (TD) S_1 In our large sample, 100% favor Gore.
   (NTD) S_2 In centuries of experience, national candidates seldom receive more than 60% of the vote, virtually never more than 70%.
   $$\overline{}\text{d}$$
   C   We have been sampling a Gore stronghold.

   b. You should suspect the list you've been given is from the motorcycle registrations logs.

6.48 (a) You may conclude absolutely that a majority of voters favor Gore. (b) You may safely conclude that a vast majority of voters prefer Gore.

CHAPTER 7

FURTHER APPLICATIONS

Prediction and Recommendation

.... Diagnostic argument is important even when it is not the whole
OVERVIEW story. Predictions and recommendations go beyond diagnosis, but
.... often rely on it. In this chapter we examine diagnostic elements in
arguments involving these two notions.

INTRODUCTION

Much reasoning that is not simply diagnostic may involve diagnosis in many different ways. Arguments for conclusions that are not diagnostic may have diagnostic support, for instance, and hence allow diagnostic tributaries. Some nondiagnostic arguments provide frameworks that organize diagnostic investigations. Examining these arguments will show us how to extend the skills and apparatus developed in the last two chapters to another large group of important arguments.

Recall that an argument is not diagnostic when it contains no trace data, when its conclusion does not explain any of the support. This can happen in any argument, of course, even one with a diagnostic IQ, if the support happens to contain no trace data. Such arguments may become diagnostic if we simply find some relevant TD. More interesting for us, however, will be arguments that are *inherently* nondiagnostic: ones whose conclusions are not even offered in explanation of anything. Both predictions and recommendations, for instance, concern things that have not yet occurred and may never occur. Predictions concern what *will* happen; recommendations concern what *ought to* happen. So if they are the conclusions of arguments, they will have left no traces to explain. An argument supporting a weather forecast, or one urging that the Federal Reserve lower interest rates, plainly cannot be diagnostic. Conclusions in the future tense (this will happen) and normative conclusions (this ought to happen) do not attempt simply to explain what's going on. They go beyond simple diagnosis.[1]

In analyzing arguments for predictions and recommendations we naturally fall back on the more general apparatus of Chapter 4. We may still talk of IQ and rivals, relevance and ranking. We just cannot appeal to explanation, trace data, and non-trace data; the relevance of our understanding of things is less direct. This of course applies only to the main or overall argument for a prediction or recommendation. Diagnosis may still be *indirectly* involved in the support of either kind of conclusion, however, when something in the main argument is itself the conclusion of another argument. That is, the main argument may have a diagnostic tributary.

DIAGNOSTIC TRIBUTARY

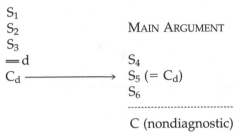

S_1
S_2 MAIN ARGUMENT
S_3
$= d$ S_4
$C_d \longrightarrow S_5 \; (= C_d)$
           S_6

C (nondiagnostic)

This will allow the rich apparatus of Chapter 5 to play a role—sometimes the crucial role—in nondiagnostic arguments too. For when much rides on the diagnosis—when it is unclear or controversial—a diagnostic tributary becomes central to the reasoning. It often turns out that a future-tense conclusion or a normative conclusion will hang on explaining trace data, just as much as ordinary diagnostic ones do.

PREDICTION

Reasonable forecasts, like inferences generally, rely on our understanding of how the world works. Unlike other inferences, however, predictions simply *extrapolate* that understanding: they extend into the future our understanding of how things have been up to now. When we construct an argument for a prediction, the support will often contain an explanation of how the bit of the world works that we're interested in forecasting. The explanation gives the understanding we wish to extrapolate.

We have already noted this characteristic relation between prediction and explanation in Chapters 2 and 3. Meteorologists and other scientists commonly base forecasts on phenomena that would explain them if the forecasts turn out to be right. To illustrate complex structure in Chapter 3, for example, we schematized a weather forecast in which rain was predicted from the position of a storm (p.

---

1. A proviso: any statement may be the conclusion of a testimony argument, of course, and hence the result of diagnostic reasoning. This may be profoundly important philosophically, but we will ignore it in this chapter. Here we will be concerned directly with the *substance* of conclusions, not other people's understanding of that substance.

121). That storm, of course, accounted for the rain when it fell the next day. In Chapter 2 this pattern shows up in one kind of systematic double subordination, [e$_c$]/[s] (p. 76), to which we devoted an entire section. You might review those two sections before going on: it will help you see how the following discussion ties together parts of Chapters 2, 3, and 5.

Traces of Something

Predictions commonly arise, in everyday life as well as in science, because of something we've noticed in our surroundings. We see a flash outside during a rainstorm and predict a thunderclap; we read of a candidate's sagging poll results and forecast his defeat. Meteorologists observe a distant cold front and predict rain; astronomers pick up a tiny speck in their photographs and predict that a comet will be visible in the nighttime sky; pilots smell smoke in the cockpit and predict a crisis. In each case we might say that *support* for the prediction—reasons to think it true—simply are these data from our surroundings. The flash is reason to think there will be a thunderclap; the speck on the photograph is reason to expect a comet. Because the forecast is not the right sort of thing to explain data such as this, such an argument will be essentially nondiagnostic:

S_1
S_2 Data (from the past or present)
S_3

Prediction (conclusion about the future)

For example,

S_1: It's raining and windy outside.
S_2: A very bright flash occurs.

C: We'll soon hear an explosion.

It is also quite clear in each case, however, that what connects the data to the prediction is a diagnosis that we simply take for granted. The flash, we think, is lightning nearby. That is our diagnosis and that's why we expect a crash of thunder. The speck, we're sure, is a ball of ice on a certain trajectory through the solar system. That is our diagnosis and that's why we expect the dazzling display. What we extrapolate into the future is a *diagnosis lying behind the data*. The data include **Traces of Something**: traces, we think, of a particular diagnosis. So sometimes, especially when the prediction is controversial, we will find it useful to complicate the schematization by articulating this diagnostic step as a tributary:

S_1: It's raining and windy outside.
S_2: A very bright flash occurs.

===============================d

C_{d1}: Lightning has just struck nearby. → S_3: Lightning nearby.

C: Loud noise soon.

So the general picture is as follows:

DIAGNOSTIC TRIBUTARY

S_1 Data

S_2 (including traces   MAIN ARGUMENT

S_3 of something)

$===============================$ d

C_{d1}: Diagnosis (account of data)   → S_4: Diagnosis

                                                C: Prediction

---

Exercise 7.1

Identify the TD and NTD in the lightning argument. Explain what makes it TD and NTD. (Answer on p. 348.)

Of course you will not always need this complex structure. Often the diagnosis may simply be taken for granted and the earlier, one-step schematization will adequately articulate the reasoning. But remembering that this tributary is possible can help us think about predictions in a number of ways. When a forecast is controversial, for instance, the entire disagreement may rest on different understandings of the data, that is, on different diagnoses. The data themselves may be beyond dispute; the difficulty arises only in judging what explains them. To continue our illustration, suppose that someone thinks the flash outside is not lightning, but rather two sagging power conduits touching in the wind. This will produce a zap that is audible nearby, but nothing dramatic. Their prediction will thus be very different from the one schematized above:

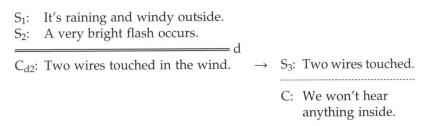

S_1:   It's raining and windy outside.

S_2:   A very bright flash occurs.

$=============================$ d

C_{d2}: Two wires touched in the wind.   → S_3: Two wires touched.

                                                C: We won't hear
                                                   anything inside.

We call such a diagnostic rival an *undermining* rival, because if it is true, it undermines our evidence for the prediction.[2] But as soon as we notice this, we

---

2. The reason to use "undermining" here is the same as in testimony arguments. Such a diagnosis, even if true, would not rule out the prediction absolutely: we still might hear an explosion at the proper time, it just would have to come from elsewhere. All the undermining diagnosis does is rule out the flash as a reason to expect the explosion. It doesn't say there can't be one.

can see that a diagnostic rival may be *underwriting* too. Many different diagnoses may license the same forecast. Many sources of a flash are noisy, for example, bombs. If the flash were not lightning but rather an atomic bomb going off down the street, we'd get an explosion just as startling, even though the original diagnosis turned out to be wrong. For this diagnosis to be reasonable, of course, we would need different NTD in the diagnostic tributary. Something like this:

S_1:   We are at war with a nuclear power.
S_2:   A very bright flash occurs.
─────────────────────────────────── d
C_{d3}: An atom bomb has exploded nearby.   → S_3: Atom bomb nearby.

                                                        C: Loud noise soon.

Exercise 7.2
....

(a) Give another (rival) underwriting explanation of the flash; (b) Give another undermining one. (Suggestions on p. 348.)

Extrapolating Understandings

We may develop a handy, graphic picture of this process by considering a quantitative but homely example. Suppose I grow suspicious of one of my car's tires and begin regularly checking its pressure. I check it for 4 days and find the pressure one pound lower each time I check. I then predict that tomorrow it will be another pound lower. Schematically it would look like this:

S_1: Day 1, 29 pounds
S_2: Day 2, 28 pounds
S_3: Day 3, 27 pounds
S_4: Day 4, 26 pounds

C: Day 5, 25 pounds

Graphically, it would look like this:

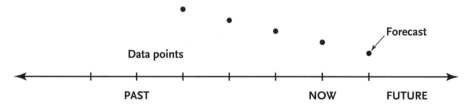

My prediction, of course, is based on the plausible diagnosis that the tire has a slow leak.

S_1:   Day 1, 29 pounds
S_2:   Day 2, 28 pounds
S_3:   Day 3, 27 pounds
S_4:   Day 4, 26 pounds
═══════════════════════ d
C_{d1}: Tire has a slow leak.   → S_5: Tire has slow leak.

                                 C: Day 5, 25 pounds

This explanation may be represented on the graph as a line connecting the points: it is the understanding I am extrapolating into the future:

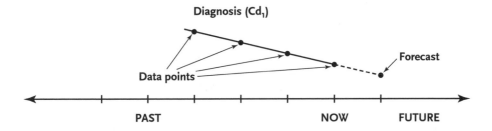

Quite obviously, C_{d1} has rivals: we may be able to explain these data points in ways other than a slow leak. And some explanations (understandings) will lead from these very same points to a *different* prediction. What would an undermining rival look like? Well, the temperature of the tire will vary during the course of a day due to just driving around as well as the heat of the day. This will affect the pressure: higher hot, lower cold. So what might be going on is that the tire does not have a leak, but I just happen to measure the pressure at a different point of the up and down variation each day. Let us suppose that variation looks like this:

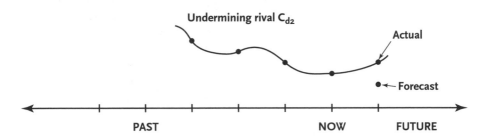

If this is the right explanation of the data, we get a different prediction for to-morrow. So this is an undermining rival.

Under*writing* rivals, then, would include other pressure variations that happen to go through the same future point. In this case, a slightly different daily variation in air pressure would do:

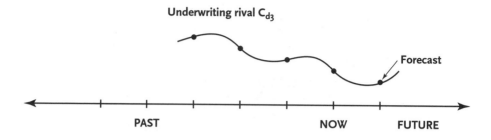

Underwriting rival C_{d_3}

Forecast

PAST   NOW   FUTURE

Exercise 7.3
....

Draw in and label other undermining and underwriting rivals. (Suggestions on p. 348.)

Checks on Our Understanding

Because predictions extend our understanding into the uncharted future, they play a central and irreplaceable role in *testing* that understanding. In other words, we learn a lot from the successes and failures of our predictions. If a prediction turns out to be wrong, that could point to a flaw in the understanding on which it depends. Conversely, if it turns out to be right, we may take that to confirm the understanding in question. This observation is absolutely crucial to science, because scientists are always working at the boundary of our understanding of things. But it plays a role in everyday life as well.

The reason, of course, is that a failed prediction is an *explanatory hurdle* for the extrapolated understanding: it is new trace data our diagnosis has difficulty explaining. A successful prediction, on the other hand, is easy to explain and hence counts to some degree as support in a new argument for the old understanding. Suppose my tire's air pressure on the fifth day turns out to be 29 pounds. If nothing relevant has changed much in the interim,[3] that pressure reading counts heavily against the slow-leak rival: a hurdle. I should probably look around for some other explanation of the 4 days of declining pressure. My understanding has been shaken. I may find that the real story involves weird daily temperature variations of the kind sketched above. But if I cannot think of a rival to take the place of the old one, I may have to do some investigating to come to some understanding of what's going on.

We might sketch the basic picture of testing our understanding by prediction in two steps:

---

3. We will shortly look into this interesting assumption (see the section "Complicating the Picture," p. 323).

STEP ONE: SCHEMATIZE PREDICTIVE ARGUMENT:

S_1
S_2 Data
S_3
================================ d
C_{d1}: Diagnosis (account of data) $\rightarrow$ S_4: Diagnosis
                                                ----
                                                C: Prediction

STEP TWO:

  a. Wait
  b. Observe success or failure of the prediction
  c. Construct one of these ex post facto arguments:

POSITIVE   NEGATIVE

S_1 S_1
S_2 Original data S_2 Original data
S_3 S_3
S_5 Success $S_{5'}$ Failure
=========================== d   =========================== d
Original diagnosis confirmed   Original diagnosis now less plausible
(But see next section)   ($S_{5'}$ is a hurdle for original diagnosis)

We construct one or the other of these arguments "after the fact" simply by adding the new data point to the support and noting how it affects the serious rivals. In the first (successful) case, the original diagnosis easily explains the new data (S_5), which never hurts and can help it in the ranking. This is all it means to say it is "confirmed" by S_5. In the second (unsuccessful) argument, the original diagnosis has difficulty explaining the new data point ($S_{5'}$) and that drops it down in the ranking.

Exercise 7.4

....

(a) In the "bright flash" example we've been following, schematize the Step Two diagnostic argument that would result from a failed prediction of thunder. (b) Is the failure TD or not? Explain why. (Answers on p. 348.)

A common and useful application of this form, both in science and in everyday life, involves predicting an *observation* of something that may have happened in the past. That is, our understanding of something suggests that *if we look in a certain place* we should find something in particular. The success or failure of this sort of forecast affects our understanding in exactly the same way; we just don't have to wait for the predicted event to occur. Suppose, for instance, that I hear and feel in my feet a "thump" that rattles the windows. I think we've had an earthquake; my wife offers a rival account: a sonic boom. If I'm right there are other signs I might check, that is, predictions I can make from my diagnosis, that would confirm it.

For instance, if we've suffered an earthquake, local seismographs should have some record of ground movement. If I investigate and find a seismographic record of ground movement at the proper time, that confirms my diagnosis. An earthquake would then look far more plausible than a sonic boom as an account of all the data, original and predicted. But if my prediction does not check out, that presents a nearly insuperable hurdle for my account of the thump and rattling. A sonic boom would then be the better account of the data. Schematically:

STEP ONE:

S_1: Thump heard
S_2: Thump felt
S_3: Windows rattle
================================d

C_{d1}: Earthquake. C_{d2} Sonic boom.
(Not clear which is more plausible.)

Test C_{d1} by prediction: → S_4: We've had an earthquake.

C: Trace on local seismograph.

STEP TWO:

a. Check seismograph
b. Observe success or failure of the prediction
c. Construct one of these ex post facto arguments:

POSITIVE   NEGATIVE

S_1: Thump heard S_1: Thump heard
S_2: Thump felt S_2: Thump felt
S_3: Windows rattle S_3: Windows rattle
S_5: Trace on seismograph $S_{5'}$: No trace
==========================d   ================d

RANKING: RANKING:

C_{d1}: Earthquake C_{d2}: Sonic boom
C_{d2}: Sonic boom
                                          .

                                          .

                                          .

                                       C_{d1}: Earthquake

The gap in the negative ranking (indicated by dots) displays the fact that finding a seismograph trace has smaller impact than not finding one. For when we do find one, the thump and rattling could still be due to a sonic boom, if the earthquake was small and the boom occurred at the same time, whereas the lack of a trace practically rules out an earthquake. This asymmetry is typical.

Exercise 7.5
······················

Suppose my car sputters to a stop on my way home from work and, before turning off the ignition, I notice the fuel gauge reads "empty." I infer (diagnose) that the car is out of gas. [Rivals: plugged fuel line; electrical failure.] (a) Give an easy prediction I could make from this diagnosis, the success or failure of which would affect my understanding of this case. (b) Schematize the Step Two diagnostic argument that would result from a successful prediction and another that would result from an unsuccessful one. Be sure to give the different plausibility rankings. (Answers on p. 348.)

What We Learn from Experience (Simple Version)

This basic picture of how we test our understanding oversimplifies the process in one important respect. It treats the diagnostic tributary as the only place doubt can arise. It simply assumes we understand perfectly everything else related to the forecast. We will shortly relax this assumption and make the picture more realistic. But before we do, we can use it to display some basic features of learning from experience. Seeing them in oversimple form will make it easier to grasp the more complicated, realistic versions we will then go on to develop.

We learn from experience by having our expectations met or defeated, and then adjusting our understanding accordingly. This is what the simple testing picture begins to articulate. And ordinarily we're pretty good at this adjustment. Nevertheless, sometimes people disagree: they come away from the same experience learning incompatible things. I may think the explosion shows that the flash was lightning; you may think it is a bomb. So it will be worth saying a bit more about the diagnostic nature of our learning, to help us see how we might approach the tough cases.

First note that the asymmetry we found in the earthquake example is built into the basic picture of testing by prediction. A feature of that picture is that we learn more easily from failure than from success. For when a forecast *fails*, that always counts against our understanding: it is a hurdle that, without anything further, reduces the plausibility of our diagnosis. No thunder counts strongly against lightning in the case we've been following. No trace on the seismograph indicates that the earthquake is no longer a good bet. We may not know what it was, but our original understanding has been shaken.

On the other hand, if the forecast turns out to be right, that may not confirm any particular understanding *at all*. Whether it does, and if so, how much, depends on an additional element: the plausibility of underwriting rivals. You can do everything right and still not confirm your diagnosis if underwriting rivals are a good bet to begin with. A dramatic burst of noise following a flash does not confirm the diagnosis of lightning everywhere. It's not even a serious rival if it happens on a clear day while you're hunkered down in a foxhole on the front lines of a raging battle: only bombs and artillery shells are plausible. For a successful prediction to count in favor of a diagnosis, as an unsuccessful one counts against it, we must know more than just the result of the forecast. We must also have some sense of how plausibly underwriting diagnoses would explain the original data.

Exercise 7.6

In the original lightning example, successful prediction in normal circumstances really does confirm our diagnosis. Explain why. (Answer on p. 349.)

When we predict from correlations, for example, the "common causes" and "reverse causes" of Chapter 6 often provide troublesome underwriting rivals that, if we're alert, prevent our taking much comfort in successful predictions. An ancient seafarer, noting a correlation between eclipses and unusually high tides, may suspect that one causes the other. To test his suspicion, he forecasts an extraordinary tide during the next eclipse and of course turns out to be right. Does this confirm his suspicion? No, it does not: it confirms common and reverse-cause rivals just as much. We of course know, as he could not, that the right story is a common cause: the celestial alignment that produces eclipses also exaggerates tides. But even without access to planetary dynamics, the ancient mariner should be able to see that stories from all three directions would account for all the data points, including the prediction. So just what the prediction confirms will depend on which direction is most plausible to begin with. A successful forecast such as this cannot by itself promote a previously inferior rival.

The major application of this precaution is to cases, such as that of the ancient mariner, in which our understanding of some data is not very good. When we're working on something unfamiliar, and don't yet have a confident grasp of rival possibilities, we may think we understand it and make a prediction on that basis. We need to remember the success/failure asymmetry at that point. For if the prediction fails, that counts strongly against the understanding. If it succeeds, however, our weak grasp of what else might be going on prevents us from taking much reassurance from that fact alone. This is a circumstance in which scientists constantly find themselves as they push our understanding into new regions.

Exercise 7.7

When California passed a law requiring motorcyclists to wear helmets, proponents of the law predicted that motorcycle fatalities would drop sharply. When statistics showed that motorcycle fatalities had dropped by an enormous 36% in the first year, sponsors proudly proclaimed that they had made motorcycle riding safer. Opponents of the law had always argued that helmets actually made riding more dangerous by interfering with vision and hearing and increasing neck loads in a crash. They of course had a radically different explanation of the 36% drop that is not wholly implausible. Try to guess what is was. (Answer on p. 349.)

Complicating the Picture

We are now ready to relax the oversimple assumption behind the basic picture we've been using. To display the basic diagnostic features of learning from experience, we've been assuming that the sole source of risk in making a forecast lies in the diagnosis behind some raw data. This will seldom be so, of course: usually our grasp of other aspects of the case will also be imperfect. When my tire produced a 29-pound reading on the fifth day, for example, that made me rethink the leak diagnosis. But I could blame my diagnosis only if I assumed that "nothing relevant has changed much in the interim." For if something, or someone, had intervened in the normal course of events, that could change everything. A failed prediction may not affect my original diagnosis, if some external interference can easily explain why it failed.

The point to notice is that forecasts normally depend on many aspects of our understanding besides the main diagnosis with which we are concerned. To extrapolate any given diagnosis, we must know a lot about its environment. In particular, we must know which things don't change much and which ones do and how fast and in response to what. In the simple cases, we may reasonably take all these things for granted: normally nothing interferes with the noise made by nearby lightning; seismographs seldom ignore earthquakes. But when we cannot take the circumstances for granted like this, we must complicate the picture to include them.

Consider some plausible interference in the tire case: suppose somebody, without my knowledge, added air late on day 4. That would change everything: 29 pounds would be just what to expect on the slow-leak rival if somebody stole into the garage and brought the tire up to 30 pounds after the fourth measurement.

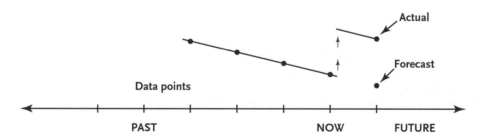

Here my forecast turns out to be wrong even though my diagnosis is fine: the tire does have a slow leak. What ruined the forecast was to be found in the circumstances I depended on to *connect* my diagnosis to the future pressure reading.

When aspects of the circumstances are uncertain, and cannot reasonably be taken for granted, we should make a place for them in our argument form. We should do this not just to draw attention to a risk, but also to be clear about the diagnostic aftermath of the forecast. For noting the role of "connecting circumstances" can help organize our thinking after we find out whether the forecast was right or wrong. So the more complete general picture would look like this:

DIAGNOSTIC TRIBUTARY

S_1 Initial data
S_2 (including traces   MAIN ARGUMENT
S_3 of something)
$$=========================d$$
C_{d1}: Diagnosis (account of traces) $\rightarrow$ S_4: Diagnosis
                                            S_5: Connecting
                                                 conditions

                                         C: Prediction

Complete prediction form.

Of course saying something about the connecting conditions may make the reasoning *clearer* even when those conditions are not in question. Sometimes a reminder is useful. For instance, we may expand the lightning example to include a bit of linkage that is not in doubt:

S_1:   It's raining and windy outside.
S_2:   A very bright flash occurs.
$$=========================d$$
C_{d1}: Lightning has just struck nearby.

                                  $\rightarrow$ S_3: Lightning nearby.
                                       S_4: Normally, the closer the
                                           lightning, the sooner and
                                           louder the thunder.

                                    C: Loud noise soon.

The inference clearly takes something like S_4 for granted; and mentioning it may help someone from a storm-free climate better understand the argument. But a failed forecast here would not raise problems in the main argument: we'd simply revise the diagnosis and give up on lightning.

Exercise 7.8

Describe the prediction failure in this last case and explain why we'd give up on the diagnosis rather than question the connecting conditions. (Answer on p. 349.)

Connecting conditions do play an especially important role in our reasoning, however, when they locate genuine sources of risk. We may expand the tire pressure illustration to make that risk explicit:

S_1:   Day 1, 29 pounds
S_2:   Day 2, 28 pounds
S_3:   Day 3, 27 pounds
S_4:   Day 4, 26 pounds
==============================d
C_{d1}: Tire has a slow leak.   → S_5: Tire has slow leak.
                                         S_6: Slow leaks stay slow.
                                         S_7: Nobody will add air or repair the tire
                                             or otherwise interfere

----

C: Day 5, 25 pounds

Given how little we know about the circumstances, the connecting conditions are in this case easily as uncertain as the diagnosis. We cannot neglect the risk added in the main argument. If the fifth day reading is 29 pounds, for instance, explanations questioning these assumptions in the main argument would be serious diagnostic reading. In other words, the list of rival accounts of the five readings would include not just undermining rivals of C_{d1}, such as the one graphed previously, it would also include accounts that keep C_{d1} but explain the readings as violations of the connecting conditions we have assumed in making the forecast.

EX POST FACTO ARGUMENT

S_1: Day 1, 29 pounds
S_2: Day 2, 28 pounds
S_3: Day 3, 27 pounds
S_4: Day 4, 26 pounds   SERIOUS RIVALS
S_8: Day 5, 29 pounds
==============================d
          ? $C_1 = C_{d2}$: Undermining cycle
                                       $C_2 = C_{d4}$: Different undermining rival
                                       $C_3 = C_{d1}$ + somebody added air
                                       $C_4 = C_{d1}$ + other interference
                                                And so on

Exercise 7.9
....

Describe a rival that would count as C_4. (Suggestion on p. 349.)

Organizing the Aftermath

WHEN A FORECAST FAILS

Recall that on the simpler picture, a failed prediction had clear significance for us: it damaged the original diagnosis. When we add the failure to the ex post facto argument it becomes trace data that the original diagnosis cannot easily explain. This is obviously no longer true on the more complicated picture: a change in the connecting conditions can allow the original diagnosis to easily explain failure. The diagnosis may be completely innocent. Nevertheless, the complicated picture does organize our thinking about this case by dividing our worries into the two categories, diagnosis and connecting conditions. A failed forecast is still trace data in the ex post facto argument, but it may be explained in three significantly different ways. The failure may be due to a mistaken diagnosis, or to misunderstood conditions, or both. So to learn something from a failed prediction, we can group the rivals into—and organize an investigation around—these three general possibilities.

This is valuable because we can usually discover vastly more about the connecting circumstances *after* the prediction has failed than we could prior to the event. So we can learn something from a prediction even when it is made in chancy conditions. In the tire example, even though the likelihood of external interference may be impossible to estimate beforehand, we may, after the failed prediction, find evidence that somebody did add air (fingerprints, disturbed items, surveillance video). In the same way we could find evidence that nobody interfered. And whatever evidence of that sort we find may be included in the ex post facto argument to help us rank rivals after the fact. This may allow us to eliminate one whole category, diagnosis or circumstances, and hence locate the source of the failure quite precisely: in the diagnosis, in the connecting conditions, or even in a particular aspect of the conditions. We may even find, again quite precisely, that there were several problems, each of which would have defeated the prediction.

Therefore, the general picture of learning from a failed prediction looks like this:

Ex Post Facto Diagnosis	Kinds of Rivals to Consider
S_1	1. Diagnosis wrong and
S_2 Original Data	connecting conditions right.
S_3	(Standard undermining rival)
S_5 Failure	2. Diagnosis right,
S_6 Circumstances	connecting conditions wrong.
===========d	(Conditions explain failure)
?	3. Diagnosis wrong,
	connecting conditions wrong.

If we care specifically about the original diagnosis, we may say that a failed prediction counts against it only when the best account of the trace data in this argument falls in rival category 1 or 3. And that may depend heavily on just what TD and NTD we find in the circumstances afterward.

Exercise 7.10

In the earthquake example we've been using, what would be an example of a category 2 rival? What might we find in the circumstances that would support that rival? Would it be TD or NTD? (Answer on p. 349.)

WHEN A FORECAST SUCCEEDS

Allowing risk in the connecting conditions complicates learning from successful predictions even more than from unsuccessful ones. But the complexity is manageable if we keep in mind that a successful prediction is simply trace data for the ex post facto argument: it helps whatever rival explains it most easily. Then, adding connecting conditions to the simple picture requires us just to expand slightly the rival categories we had before and add two new ones.

Recall that on the simple picture, because we assumed well-understood circumstances, getting the forecast right could be accounted for in only two different ways. Either the original diagnosis was correct, or it was wrong and some underwriting diagnosis lay behind the original data. We must now expand these two possibilities to explicitly note the connecting conditions, which we had previously taken for granted. So the first becomes: we predicted correctly because we had the correct diagnosis together with a proper understanding of the connecting conditions. The second expands into: we got the prediction right, in spite of the wrong diagnosis, because the actual diagnosis gives the same result in the assumed conditions.

If we now allow that the connecting conditions may also be suspect, two further kinds of rival might explain the ex post facto data. In the first of these (now the third kind of rival) the prediction turns out to be true even though we're wrong about *both* the diagnosis *and* the conditions. We got it right through sheer luck: the actual diagnosis, which would not have given the right result in the conditions we thought we had, did give it because of what those conditions actually were. Suppose that what's going on with my car is that one of my co-workers, just to annoy me, lets a pound of air out of my tire every day while I'm parked at work. Day 5 is Saturday and I think the car is securely locked in the garage. On this rival the pressure should not drop on Saturday: it should stay at 26 pounds for the fifth reading in the circumstances as I understand them. But suppose I'm mistaken about the conditions: my annoying colleague has a key and gets into the garage to continue the prank. The fifth reading will then be 25 pounds. So my prediction is right, but only because I'm mistaken about both the diagnosis (I think it's a leak) *and* the conditions (I think the garage is secure).

The fourth kind of rival would explain the predicted result as wholly unrelated to the original data: it was brought about by something in the circumstances unconnected to any diagnosis underlying the data. My wife may have had the winter tires installed without telling me. I didn't notice the change in the darkened garage and the winter tires just happened to be set at 25 pounds. This, however, is one of those times in which our understanding of the case changes so much that it undermines the IQ with which we've been working. So far we've not had to mention the IQ because it's been so obvious: "What's causing the pressure drop?" This naturally takes for granted that a single explanation lies behind all the data points. And to this point that assumption has been reasonable. But, as we've seen before, any diagnostic investigation can come up with data that radically alter our sense of a case. And if we have reason to take this fourth kind of rival seriously, that would radically alter our sense of this case.

We could of course keep the IQ and give a complicated answer: the first data points were due to one thing, which we're still not sure of, and the last one was due to something completely different. But since we're trying to develop a *systematic* way to talk about learning from predictions, it would be better to revise the IQ so that it works systematically with all these different arguments. So the best IQ would be, "What explains getting the prediction right?"[4] In this case: "Why was the fifth reading 25 pounds?" All the different rivals answer this question; and the only real structural change is that the first four readings become peripheral TD rather than central TD.

Exercise 7.11
....

(a) Go back and check to see that rivals of categories 1, 2, and 3 also answer this IQ. (b) Explain why the earlier data would now be peripheral TD. (Answers on p. 349.)

As the third and fourth cases illustrate once again, we have many opportunities to gain information on the circumstances *after* the fact: after the prediction has succeeded or failed. And the ex post facto rivals would have to account for the traces in the circumstances, as well as everything else. So the general picture of learning from a successful prediction looks like this:

Ex Post Facto Diagnosis	Kinds of Rivals to Consider
S_1	1. Diagnosis right and
S_2 Original Data	connecting conditions right.
S_3	2. Diagnosis wrong, connecting
S_5 Success	conditions right.
S_6 Circumstances	(Standard underwriting rival)
========= d	3. Both wrong.
?	(Wrong conditions compensate for undermining diagnosis)
IQ: What explains S_5?	4. Result not related to
	original data.
	(Brought about by circumstances alone)

It will sometimes be difficult to say whether a rival falls in category 2 or 3, but the distinction is still useful as a guide.

Exercise 7.12
....

Describe rivals under each heading for the lightning example we've been using. (Answer on p. 349.)

---

4. We could of course make the IQ in each of the ex post facto arguments concern only the forecast, failed or successful, and it would merely have this same structural consequence. But it is not really necessary in the earlier cases.

As before, if we care specifically about the diagnosis underlying the original data, we may say that a successful prediction confirms that diagnosis only when the best account of the ex post facto trace data is category 1. For in the other three categories, the diagnosis is not involved in explaining the successful result and hence does not gain anything from that success. So something of the asymmetry we found in the simple case survives here too: we learn more easily from failure than success.

Exercise 7.13
....

(a) Explain why rivals from categories 2, 3, and 4 do not allow a successful forecast to support the original diagnosis. You may paraphrase the text, but do so in very different words. (b) Schematize the successful ex post facto argument as it applies to the tire pressure case we've been using. Sketch the four rivals we've used to illustrate the four different types. (Answers on p. 350.)

Illustration

An election forecast can be used to illustrate all of this. Suppose we hire a competent pollster to take a survey of voters and find that a week before the election, substantially more than half of the sample favors Smith. We predict Smith's victory on the basis of these data, generating a diagnostic tributary from the sample/population section of Chapter 6. The two major connecting conditions required for the forecast are (a) that support for Smith not decline much during the intervening week and (b) that Smith supporters vote in representative numbers. This would schematize thus:

S_1: Sample of voters favors Smith.
S_2: Sample taken by competent pollsters.

$$========================= \text{d}$$

C_{d1}: Voters favor Smith. $\rightarrow$ S_3: Voters favor Smith.
                                                S_4: Enthusiasm for Smith will not decline much in a week.
                                                S_5: A representative number of Smith supporters will vote.

                                                C: Smith will win.

If Smith loses, this schematization locates three possible things we might learn. The loss may be due to bad polling, or to a decline in enthusiasm for Smith, or to overconfidence, sloth, or something else preventing Smith voters getting to the voting booths. Just which was the case will depend on what we are able to discover afterward.

Exercise 7.14

Construct ex post facto diagnostic arguments (3) that would favor each of these. (Take as the central TD that Smith lost in spite of leading in the polls a week ago.) (Suggestions on p. 350.)

If Smith wins, that may be due to our getting everything right in the main argument. But it could also be due to an underwriting rival, a bad poll compensated that demoralized Smith's opponents, or stuffing the ballot boxes.

Exercise 7.15

What would an underwriting rival look like in this case? (Answer on p. 350.)

RECOMMENDATION

The other major class of inherently nondiagnostic conclusions is normative: conclusions about what *should* be done, about what's *right or wrong*. Our earlier paraphrases contained many points of this form, such as "The Federal Reserve should lower interest rates," "I ought to lose some weight," and "It would be wrong for Congress to reward China for its human rights violations." Declarations such as these don't explain data, but, as we noticed in Chapter 2, they usually have arguments offered for them. And as with predictive conclusions, our general understanding, and hence diagnostic form, may relate indirectly to such arguments through diagnostic tributaries.

Any normative argument may of course be analyzed using the apparatus of Chapter 4: IQ, rivals, relevance, ranking, investigation, and ways to deal with disagreement. Sometimes that will be adequate and often, even when inadequate, it will be the best we can do. Normative concerns arise from so many different and profound aspects of our lives that they frequently test and often exceed our ability to think and reason at all. When we suffer doubt or encounter disagreement about them, the best we can do is take seriously the guidance offered in Chapter 4 for allaying doubt and dealing with disagreement. Learning anything from disagreement may, as suggested at the end of Chapter 1, require great patience with and generosity toward the person with whom you disagree. The depth of our normative commitments often makes this the hardest thing to do.

Appeal to Consequences

So we should welcome any opportunity we can find to apply our diagnostic apparatus to normative questions. In the remainder of this chapter we will deal with a variety of such applications. Conveniently, they may all be found within a single kind of argument that we commonly employ in dealing with public policy:

the appeal to good (or bad) consequences. For example, the argument usually given for lowering interest rates is a good consequence: it will stimulate the economy; similarly, an argument for more teachers is that it will improve education; an argument for losing weight is that it will make me feel better and/or live longer. Conversely, we may argue *against* free use of certain chemicals because they cause cancer, or against computers in elementary schools because they undermine the learning of important basic skills.

The basic form of such arguments is obviously this:

[A]
S_1: X would have Y as a consequence.
S_2: Y is good.

C: We should do X.

For example:

S_1: Lowering interest rates would stimulate the economy.
S_2: Stimulation would be good right now.

C: We should lower interest rates.

For a more homely example, consider my neighbor's recommendation that I move the time I water my lawn from the evening to early in the day. This, he says, would improve the lawn's appearance. The argument would be as follows:

S_1: Watering early would make my lawn look better.
S_2: I like a good-looking lawn.

C: I should water earlier.

There will of course be the parallel negative form to remember:

[B]
S_1: X would have Y as a consequence.
S_2: Y is bad.

C: We should not do X.

But this form is so easily derived from the positive one we will not keep mentioning it explicitly.

Just as with predictions, one particular aspect of our understanding does such crucial work in these arguments that it will be worth making explicit in the schematic form itself. For predictions, "connecting conditions" introduced systematic risk that was worth keeping an attentive eye on. For normative arguments of this form it is "other consequences" we need to watch. Moving my watering to earlier in the day will not just affect the health of the lawn. It will increase the watering bill a bit, because I'll have to water more to compensate for daytime evaporation. It will also get my shoes wet as I leave for work and sometimes douse the newspaper. And so on. To judge an action (or policy) by pointing to a good (or bad) consequence always takes for granted that all the other consequences do not matter for the calculation: they're neutral or balance out or are otherwise irrelevant.

Since this is not always so, and is sometimes so difficult to determine, let us reserve a special line in the schematic form just to remind us of what we take for granted in these arguments.

[A]
S_1: X would have Y as a consequence.
S_2: Y is good.
S_3: Other consequences of X don't matter.

C: We should do X.

Even before we get to diagnosis, this general form can be useful in structuring disagreement about the appeal to consequences. In particular, just flagging the possibility that Y may not be good in some circumstances, or that other consequences may matter, will sometimes be enough to get antagonists into productive conversation. But our main interest in [A] is that it helps us see several different ways in which our diagnostic apparatus may bear on normative conclusions.

Unfortunately, in what follows we will not be able to address the quantitative issues obviously relevant to these arguments. For in many cases, whether we should do X will depend on *just how much* good Y will do, and *just how bad* the other consequences of S_3 turn out to be. Treating these explicitly would add another layer of complexity to the already complicated forms we'll examine. So although we will occasionally mention an implied calculation (this good more than compensates for that bad), you will for the most part have to take your own account of them when they matter.

Exercise 7.16
·····················

Suppose a friend considers replacing his old computer with an expensive new one, because the new one is faster and has dazzling new features. Take speeding things up and having new features to exploit as consequences recommending the purchase. What cautions might you raise under S_2 and S_3 that might be worth considering before the purchase? (Answer on p. 351.)

Diagnostic Possibilities

Our ability to explain trace data can be relevant to each of the three lines of support in [A]. We will treat each in turn, taking the other two lines for granted while we treat the third. So, for example, as we examine diagnostic possibilities in S_1, we will assume that S_2 and S_3 are uncontroversial for the time being. This is not pure idealization: we often find actual cases in which only one of the three categories is at issue. After developing an understanding of the diagnostic elements in each, we may then go on to consider arguments in which everything needs diagnostic support. The first of these examinations is most complex: under S_1 we consider three distinct issues: correlational support, noncorrelational diagnostic support, and a commonly misleading variant.

S_1: WOULD X BRING ABOUT Y?

Controversy (doubt, disagreement) about a recommendation often centers on *whether* doing X actually would bring about Y. What reason do I have to think changing the watering schedule will help the lawn? Why does the Federal Reserve think lowering interest rates will stimulate the economy? And because the question concerns causes, and statements such as "X causes Y" occur prominently in Chapters 5 and 6, we reasonably expect diagnostic reasoning to address this question—to be offered in support of S_1. Furthermore, because both X and Y lie in the future, we should expect that much of what we discussed earlier under "prediction" will fit here too. And so it does.

Recall that to use normal evidence (data) to support a claim about the future we had to first find an underlying account of the data (diagnosis) to extrapolate into the future, and then take note of the connecting conditions allowing the extrapolation. The picture looked like this:

DIAGNOSTIC TRIBUTARY

S_{t1} Initial data
S_{t2} (including traces   MAIN ARGUMENT
S_{t3} of something)
═══════════════════════════════d
C_d: Diagnosis (account of traces) → S_{m1}: Diagnosis
                                          S_{m2}: Connecting
                                                  conditions

                                          C: Prediction

To use this in support of S_1 we must modify it to accommodate the fact that S_1 is a *conditional* prediction (Y would occur *if* we did X) and make sure the conditions are those in which we would interfere by doing X. So the general picture would be this:

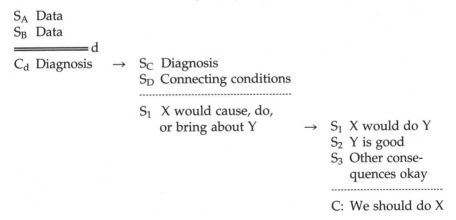

S_A Data
S_B Data
══════════d
C_d Diagnosis   → S_C Diagnosis
                       S_D Connecting conditions

                       S_1 X would cause, do,
                              or bring about Y   → S_1 X would do Y
                                                          S_2 Y is good
                                                          S_3 Other conse-
                                                                 quences okay
                                                          ----
                                                          C: We should do X

This general form can organize our thinking about recommendations in all sorts of different ways. We will illustrate three.

CORRELATIONAL SUPPORT

One kind of diagnostic argument commonly relevant to recommendations is correlational. Much of my reason to change my watering schedule may be that other lawns in the area have responded well to this change: watering earlier seems to correlate with healthier grass. In addition I may learn something that counts as modus operandi NTD: that a fungus common in this climate thrives on lawns left wet at night. So evaluating a purely diagnostic argument will allow us to say whether earlier watering caused better health in those cases. Then, all I need to support the (conditional) forecast in *my* case is that the connecting conditions are right: namely, like those in my neighbor's yards. So the tributary on S_1 would look like this:

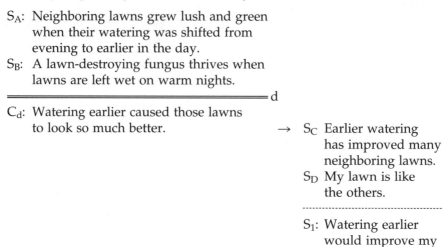

S_A: Neighboring lawns grew lush and green
        when their watering was shifted from
        evening to earlier in the day.
S_B: A lawn-destroying fungus thrives when
        lawns are left wet on warm nights.
──────────────────────────── d
C_d: Watering earlier caused those lawns
        to look so much better.   → S_C Earlier watering
                                                 has improved many
                                                 neighboring lawns.
                                           S_D My lawn is like
                                                 the others.

                                           S_1: Watering earlier
                                                 would improve my
                                                 lawn.

The general form of correlational support would be as follows:

S_A: X/Y (in certain conditions)
S_B: Relevant NTD
──────────────────────────── d
C_d: X → Y (in those conditions)   → S_C: X → Y
                                         S_D: Current conditions
                                               are similar.
                                         ----
                                         s_1: X would cause Y
                                               in this case.   → S_1
                                                                       S_2
                                                                       S_3

                                                                       C: We
                                                                          should
                                                                          do X.

The important thing to note here is that controversy about the recommendation C may be diagnostic. Someone may think a rival account of the correlation, from a different direction of influence, is a more plausible account of the observed correlation. A common cause, for instance, would undermine the recommendation. Consider the following story. People who naturally water early are also those who lavish attention on their yard. Because it's important to water before weeding and spraying, early watering is just part of a fastidious gardener's routine. But it is the fastidiousness (weeding, spraying, feeding), not the early watering, that makes the lawns look so good. In some circumstances this would be plausible and would destroy this reason to water early. So an argument about a recommendation would rest on judging the plausibility of various explanations of trace data.

Exercise 7.17
....

a. Suppose I had been doing badly in a course until I accidentally left my name off a quiz and got an A. I then use this correlation to support the recommendation that I leave my name off future quizzes. (i) Structure the predictive part of my argument, modeled on the one above, using "my TA hates me" as the diagnostic NTD. [*Hint*: just copy the above form and fill in the blanks to fit this case.] (ii) Be sure to make explicit a connecting condition you're counting on. (iii) Provide an undermining rival.

b. Suppose I discover that people who exercise are healthier than those who do not. I then use this correlation as reason to start exercising myself. (i) Schematize the predictive part of my argument modeled on the one above. (ii) Think of a reverse-cause undermining rival. (Answers on p. 351.)

NONCORRELATIONAL DIAGNOSTIC SUPPORT

Although very common, diagnostic tributaries need not be correlational. They may appeal directly to an underlying understanding of what's going on, as they did in the prediction section. An argument from the plant sciences about my lawn in particular could support S_1 without adding anything about other lawns. The diagnostic argument would then be botanical: the TD would be the results of experiments on my lawn, the NTD would be disciplinary background. The connecting conditions would be what we learned during the investigation about the role of moisture in the life of the fungus. This too can have direct diagnostic support, which is flagged by the little argument off to the right in the diagram below.

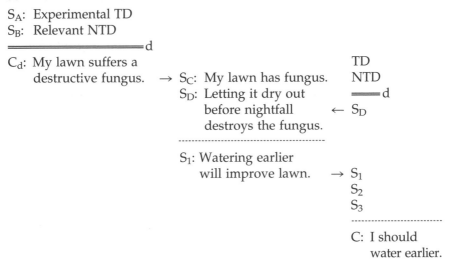

S_A: Experimental TD
S_B: Relevant NTD
$=\!=\!=\!=\!=\!=\!=\!=\!=\!=\!=\!=$d
C_d: My lawn suffers a   TD
destructive fungus.   → S_C: My lawn has fungus.   NTD
S_D: Letting it dry out $=\!=\!=$d
before nightfall   ← S_D
destroys the fungus.
- -
S_1: Watering earlier
will improve lawn.   → S_1
S_2
S_3
- - - - - - - - - - - - - - - - - -
C: I should
water earlier.

Exercise 7.18

Even if I had not read studies correlating exercise with health, I might still be able to construct an argument similar to the one above recommending that I exercise more. The key elements of this argument would be (a) I get winded easily, (b) I'm sure being in bad shape increases the risk of disease and injury, and (c) our common experience with exercise suggests (diagnostically) that it improves physical condition. Fill out the rest of the above form around these key elements. (Answer on p. 352.)

A COMMONLY MISLEADING VARIANT

Sometimes, of course, we may appeal to bad consequences as reasons *not* to do something, and then the [B] variant of recommendation form will be easier to use (see p. 331). You shouldn't eat old leftovers that smell bad, because of the risk of food poisoning, for example. This would schematize as follows:

S_1: Eating bad-smelling leftovers can make anybody very sick.
S_2: This is bad.
S_3: Nothing compensates in the circumstances.

C: We shouldn't eat bad-smelling leftovers.

Diagnosis will be relevant to S_1 here in exactly the same way it is to the [A] form: if we have evidence that ugly smelling food poisoned people in the past, we may extrapolate this by assuming similar conditions still exist.

Exercise 7.19

Fill out the predictive tributary on S_1 in this case, using a simple correlation as TD. (Answer on p. 352.)

We are sometimes mislead, however, by a very common appeal to bad consequences that *looks* like this one, but is actually very different. For instance, I should start smoking again because giving it up caused me to immediately gain 12 pounds. This looks like it should be parallel to the [B] example above:

S_{1x}: Giving up smoking caused me to gain weight.
S_{2x}: This is bad.
S_{3x}: Nothing compensates in the circumstances.

C_x: I should start smoking again.

In looking at this argument we may be distracted by S_{3x}: the world is abuzz with the bad consequences of taking up smoking. But here we're concerned only with S_1 and take the other two for granted. So ignore S_{3x} for the moment. The point of looking at this case is to note a problem with S_{1x}: despite appearances, it does not fit the [B] schematic form. Recall that form:

[B]
S_1: X would have Y as a consequence.
S_2: Y is bad.
S_3: Other consequences of X don't matter.

C: We should not do X.

The big problem with S_{1x} is that it talks about the past rather than the future, as required by [B]. This is not trivial. For the whole point of this section is to note that facts from the past can bear on conditional predictions like S_1 only in fairly complicated tributaries. Simply trotting out a past fact as though it were a prediction ignores all the hard lessons we've learned so far.

As soon as we realize that S_{1x} must be a (conditional) prediction, we look to the conclusion to see what the prediction should be about. For C_x it is "I should take up smoking again." What conditional prediction would support this here? It must be that I think I will lose weight if I smoke again. This reveals two things. First, the form of the argument is not [B], but rather [A]. I'm offering a good consequence as reason for doing something, not a bad one as a reason for not doing something:

S_{1x}: Smoking would cause me to lose weight.
S_{2x}: This is good.
S_{3x}: Nothing compensates in the circumstances.

C_x: I should start smoking again.

Second, the 12 pounds I gained on quitting fits into the reasoning only as support for the conditional prediction (S_{1x}). And because I'm offering a correlation (stopped/gained) as evidence for a causal connection, it might seem at first that it fits exactly into the earlier correlational form:

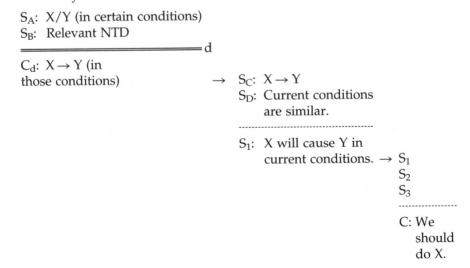

But there's a crucial difference: in this case, S_1 deals with the *reversal* of X, not X itself. This argument form schematizes my very good reason to think *quitting caused the gain*. But we're not trying to support the prediction that quitting will cause weight gain in the future. We're trying to support the reverse: that *smoking again will take off the weight*. This is far more complex and requires more than just "conditions are similar." It's quite common for processes such as this to not be easily reversible. Just because falling off the horse broke your arm, that is no reason to think climbing back on will heal the break. Similarly with smoking: the eating habits developed during tobacco withdrawal may not simply vanish upon reacquiring the addiction. So the middle step of this three-part argument will take some special care to make work. Y must be the sort of thing that may be undone by simply reversing whatever brought it about; in particular, it (Y) cannot be being sustained by other things. S_D below attempts to capture this:

S_A: X/Y (in certain conditions)
S_B: Relevant NTD
$$\overline{\qquad\qquad\qquad\qquad\qquad}d$$
C_d: X → Y (in
those conditions)   → S_C: X → Y
                          S_D: In these conditions, all
                                 that keeps Y going is
                                 whatever brought it about.

                          S_1: Reversing X will undo Y in
                                 current conditions.   → S_1
                                                          S_2 Undoing Y is good.
                                                          S_3 Ceteris paribus.

                                                          C: We should reverse
                                                             X.

In general, arguments of this form will not be as strong as the simple version, in which we do not simply reverse the cause.[5]

SUMMARY OF THIS IMPORTANT POINT

When an argument appeals to a bad consequence of something already done as a reason to do the *reverse*, the argument should be schematized by appeal to the *good consequences of doing the reverse*, in form [A]. The past bad consequences, then,

---

5. Note that all these problems arise because we are concerned with a recommendation. If the conclusion is "I should not have stopped," the argument will be very close to [B], except that it offers a regret about the past instead of a proposal for action:

S_1: Giving up smoking caused me to gain weight.
S_2: That was bad.
S_3: Other consequences don't compensate.

C: I should not have stopped smoking.

may be used in a diagnostic tributary on S_1, but will require special circumstances to make the reversal work.

Exercise 7.20
....

(a) Schematize: we should lower the interstate speed limit because the highway fatality rate went up when it was increased (taking S_2 and S_3 for granted). (b) Comment on what might be problematic about S_D (connecting conditions). (Answer on p. 352.)

S_2: Is Y Good?

Whether something (Y) is good, as required in these arguments, will often depend on things too deep to easily articulate. It is here that reasoning often reaches its limit, and the only recourse, if a disagreement is important, is to work on increased understanding of the matter in question, sometimes perhaps through patient conversation. Normative arguments usually work only when we already share enough to agree on S_2, or can easily accept it for the sake of the discussion. Occasionally, however, whether something is good, in certain circumstances, will depend directly on diagnostic reasoning, which is such a happy circumstance as to be worth brief treatment and illustration.

We already have one example of this: S_2 in the recommendation that the Federal Reserve lower interest rates. The good this is supposed to do is stimulating the economy. Schematically:

> S_1: Lowering rates would stimulate the economy.
> S_2: Stimulation would be good right now.
> S_3: Lower rates wouldn't have bad consequences worth noting.
> --
> C: The Federal Reserve should lower interest rates.

But whether S_2 is true depends on what the economy is doing at the time. If it is in recession, or in clear danger of it, stimulation would be just the thing to make things better. If the economy is already growing at a healthy pace, however, and unemployment is low, stimulation would be destabilizing (bad). It would likely lead quickly to inflation and increase the chances of a severe recession and perhaps social chaos later on. So *whether* stimulation is good depends on the state of the economy and this is something that will leave traces all over the place that we may explain to support or undermine S_2. Schematically, in this case:

S_A: Various economic indicators.
S_B: Economic background.
$$==================================d$$
C_d: The economy has stopped growing. $\rightarrow$ S_C: The economy's stagnant.
                                                                        S_D: Stimulation would get it
                                                                        growing again.

                                               C (= S_2): Simulation would be
                                                             good right now.

As indicated, this is a tributary offered in support of S_2 in the broader argument of form [A] schematized above. You may note that it also appeals to good consequences in a way very similar to the broader argument. This will be typical of diagnostic S_2 tributaries: if the question were different ("Should we stimulate?" instead of "Should we lower rates?"), this simply would be the [A]-form argument of our interest. There's nothing mysterious in this. It merely serves to point out the complex way that diagnostic arguments can be relevant to normative ones. The understanding relevant to a complex normative issue such as this will usually include a nest of interrelated issues of cause and consequence.

Exercise 7.21

(a) Use our general recommendation form [A] to schematize the following: We should reduce global CO_2 emissions because that would reduce the amount of the sun's heat trapped by the atmosphere (the greenhouse effect). (b) Then construct a tributary on S_2, similar to the one above, showing how it depends on a diagnostic argument. (c) Explain how a diagnostic rival could be undermining (destroy support for S_2). (Answer on p. 353.)

Keep in mind that our interest in complicated economic or political issues may give rise to many different doubts and disagreements. Just how we structure an argument for a recommendation will depend on what is controversial in a given context and what may reasonably be taken for granted. In some circumstances the argument to the Federal Reserve might be: We should lower interest rates because that will speed recovery from the current recession. This would simply take for granted the issues raised in the tributary just constructed and move them all to S_1. The causal question would then be: Will lowering interest rates speed recovery? The new S_2 would then be "Speeding recovery is good," which is less controversial. Schematically:

> S_1: Lowering rates would speed recovery.
> S_2: It's good to shorten recessions if possible.
> S_3: Lower rates wouldn't have bad consequences worth noting.
> --
> C: The Federal Reserve should lower interest rates.

But this would be an acceptable way to frame the argument only if the state of the economy were not in question. So if it *is*, the earlier schematization would better address our concerns. In general, these schematic forms will be helpful only if you exploit them imaginatively: experiment with them until they display actual points of contention.

S_3: Do Other Consequences Matter?

If S_3 is controversial, that controversy will involve all the considerations we looked at under S_1 and S_2, for other consequences of X. So diagnostic reasoning will be relevant to S_3 in exactly the ways sketched above. If somebody objects to a recommendation by appeal to other consequences of X, they will need to show both *that* X has those consequences *and* that they are bad. Both of these may involve the diagnostic tributaries spelled out under S_1 and S_2, respectively. Conversely, to show that other consequences do *not* matter, the author of a recommendation must show either that X doesn't have the consequence in question, or, if it does, that it is not bad or, at least, not bad enough to compensate for Y. These may involve variations on the same tributaries. This last matter, deciding on the balance of consequences, depends on all those deep and intractable differences among us that can make S_2 so contentious. Nevertheless, we often do share enough to make such comparisons: examples of S_3 arguments abound in legislative debate and are sometimes decisive.

For instance, the argument for lowering trade barriers between different countries is normally that doing so will boost both economies. Opponents sometimes agree both that lowering barriers will have this consequence (S_1) and that it is good (S_2). But they argue that it will also be very hard on certain *particular* industries in one country or both, causing pockets of unemployment and damaging some communities (which would fall under S_3). The pain of this, they contend, more than offsets the virtue of the general economic boost and so barriers should not be lowered. Setting the matter out in this way may not settle it immediately, but it does tell us what sort of investigation would be relevant.

Exercise 7.22
....

Describe the investigation that would be relevant in this last case. (Answer on p. 353.)

A very general application of the S_3 objection might be called the "zero-sum" objection. In such a case, opponents of a policy, X, again allow that it has good consequences (that is, accept S_1 and S_2), but argue that it is too expensive. That is, it uses resources that would be better used elsewhere. Such an objection falls under S_3, since it is offering the neglect of other things for which the resources might be used as a bad consequence overwhelming the good X does. We call this the "zero-sum" objection because it assumes that we cannot do X and the other things too, that is, there's only so much money (or other resource) to go around. Sometimes this is obviously true; other times it too will be controversial and become part of the argument.

A standard application of this kind of argument does not actually point out other uses of the resources, but merely points out terrific expense and suggests that certainly *some* better use of such enormous resources could be found. This kind of argument defeated the giant "supercollider" installation in Texas, which would have enabled physicists to conduct some microphysical experiments impossible in current laboratories. It was also used, unsuccessfully, against the installation of airbags in automobiles as a safety measure.

Exercise 7.23
....

The following passage recommends cancelling the International Space Station. Using basic form [A], schematize the argument two ways. First (a), as an argument *for* the space station that fails because of considerations falling under S_3. Then (b) as an argument directly recommending cancellation because of its good consequences. (Answer on p. 353.)

It has taken 14 years to move from drawing board to launch-pad. Along the way, supporters of the International Space Station have tried and discarded various justifications: an orbiting factory, a demonstration of American technological supremacy, a staging-post on the way to Mars and, most recently, an exemplar of international co-operation in space. With Russia's contribution to the project fast dwindling to nothing, the station is now losing even symbolic value. Since it has never had much scientific value, should it be going ahead at all?

The answer is no. Almost the only reason for building the space station now is to keep America's astronauts busy . . . (yet) . . . designing, building and operating the international space station is likely to cost more than the current best guess of $100 billion in all. And even that figure is based on the assumption that none of the 75 launches required for its construction goes wrong—something that is, statistically, extremely unlikely. . . . By draining funds from other programmes, and tying up shuttle capacity, the space station is impeding research. . . . Abandoning the space station now would save at least $30 billion, and probably more. And it would complete NASA's transformation into a leaner and more responsive organisation, better able to concentrate on its main objectives of research and helping to catalyze the gradual privatisation of the space industry.

(From *The Economist*)

Illustration: Structuring Controversy

Let us use the argument patterns we've developed here to structure and articulate an actual controversy. The central concern of the following article involves a dispute between two physicians over the sport of boxing.

CHICAGO—Boxing is "an obscenity" that should be banned in civilized countries because it causes brain damage to thousands of fighters, the editor of a medical journal says.

2. "Some have argued that boxing has a redeeming social value in that it allows a few disadvantaged or minority individuals an opportunity to rise to spectacular wealth and fame," Dr. George D. Lundberg said in an editorial in today's issue of the Journal of the American Medical Association.

3. "This does occur, but at what price? The price in this country includes chronic brain damage for them and the thousands of others who do not achieve wealth, fame or even a decent living from the ring."

4. The editorial accompanied a report by medical researchers who examined 40 former boxers and concluded that all fighters—not just battle-hardened professionals—risk debilitating brain atrophy, or deterioration.

5. The study recommended active boxers get regular neurological examinations, including CT scans, which are computer-enhanced X-ray pictures of the brain.

6. But Dr. Edwin A. Campbell, medical director for the New York State Athletic Commission, disputed both the editorial and the usefulness of such tests.

7. "I've been a party to [brain damage research]. . . . But frankly it doesn't conform to reality," Campbell said by telephone from New York, where boxing safety standards are among the strictest in the nation.

8. Campbell argued that boxing provides thousands of young men with a way to develop themselves physically, intellectually and psychologically. He said it seldom produces the punch-drunk stereotype.

9. But Lundberg disagreed. "No prudent physician could have watched the most recent debacle mis-match between Larry Holmes and Randall "Tex" Cobb and believe that the current boxing control system is functioning," Lundberg said.

10. A professional boxer, 23-year-old South Korean Kim Duk-koo, died Nov. 17 of brain damage after being knocked out five days earlier by Ray "Boom-boom" Mancini.

11. "Boxing is wrong at its base," Lundberg said. "In contrast to boxing, in all other recognized sports, injury is an undesired by-product of activity."

12. "Boxing seems to me to be less a sport than is cockfighting; boxing is an obscenity. Uncivilized men may have been blood-thirsty. Boxing, as a throwback to uncivilized men, should not be sanctioned by any civilized society."

13. Dr. Ronald J. Ross, one of the study's authors, recommends a boxer be required to have a medical "passport" showing when the boxer last fought, whether he was knocked out, and the date of his last medical exam and CT scan.

14. Last summer, the American Medical Association issued several recommendations. They included creating a national computer registry of boxers to keep track of injuries and won-lost records, giving ring physicians authorization to stop bouts in progress, restricting fight sites to those with neurosurgical facilities nearby and requiring advanced life-support systems at ringside.

(Brenda C. Coleman, *The Associated Press*)

Perhaps the most important function of our model schematizations is to help us see that a number of distinct things are going on in a complex article such as this, and to let us coherently extract the ones containing reasoning. To this end, first note that the article contains several recommendations that are not directly part of the Lundberg/Campbell argument. Those of Dr. Ross and the American Medical Association in the last two paragraphs, for instance, are not made by either Lundberg or Campbell and are at odds with each in one way or another. The recommendation at the center of the controversy is Lundberg's suggestion in the first paragraph *that boxing be banned altogether*. So our interest in the article will be limited to its first 12 paragraphs. Let us look through them one at a time and note how they fit together with the models of this section.

The first paragraph gives Lundberg's argument for his recommendation by appeal to a consequence. Because the appeal is to a *bad* consequence, the form is (B):

S_1: Boxing causes brain damage.
S_2: This is bad.

C: Boxing should be banned.

In the next two paragraphs (2 and 3) Lundberg goes on to raise the issue that made us expand the form to include S_3. He agrees that boxing does have other consequences that are by themselves good, but they are not good enough to compensate for the bad of S_1.

> S_1: Boxing causes brain damage.
> S_2: This is bad.
> S_3: The virtues of boxing do not compensate.
> --
> C: Boxing should be banned.

The fourth paragraph provides a diagnostic argument, from a correlation, in support of S_1. Lundberg does not cite it explicitly, but it's clear from the context that this study occasioned his editorial. We may add some obvious NTD not mentioned in the article to display the strength of the diagnosis.

> S_A: A study of 40 boxers found extensive brain damage.
> S_B: In boxing your head gets pounded a lot.
> ===d
> S_1: Boxing causes brain damage.

The fifth paragraph contains recommendations made by the study's authors that are irrelevant to our controversy: they're incompatible with Lundberg's recommendation and disowned by Campbell in the following paragraph.

In that paragraph (6), Campbell first hints at his argument against Lundberg, though he offers no substance. The substance lies in paragraph 7, but it is so cryptic that we can't say exactly what part of Lundberg's argument he's attacking. All he says is "this doesn't conform to reality." If we then look for help in paragraph 8, we see that there are actually just two possibilities, and that does help our thinking about the case. In paragraph 8 he appeals to his extensive experience to allege that boxing "seldom produces the punch-drunk stereotype." This might be attacking either S_1 or S_2. He might be simply denying the diagnostic conclusion, suggesting that S_1 is not the best account of S_A in the circumstances. To pursue this we'd have to show that there is some better account of S_A than S_1, taking Campbell's experience into account. On the other hand, he may agree that boxing has caused the brain damage found in the study, but disagree that it is all that bad (denying S_2). This he would base on his observation that few boxers in his experience show outward signs of damage. Even if there is damage, it's not frequent enough to condemn an entire sport. To argue against this, Lundberg must either question the accuracy of Campbell's observation or show that brain damage with no obvious early manifestations is nevertheless very serious. Either of these would require some investigation, but our schematic form helps us understand how to proceed if we wanted to, which is all it can be expected to do.

The controversy has another aspect too, however. Campbell probably also disagrees with Lundberg on S_3. For when he offers in paragraph 8 "that boxing provides thousands of young men with a way to develop themselves physically, intellectually and psychologically," he suggests the benefits of boxing extend to more than the few "spectacular" cases Lundberg concedes. So Campbell might concede that boxing does cause some serious brain injury—occasionally does result in the punch-drunk stereotype—and still have reason to think it should not be banned. Again we would have some work to do if we wished to settle the matter. But, again, we see where the investigation must be pursued: we would have to find a way to actually estimate the amount of good boxing does for its many participants.

Paragraph 9 illustrates one of Lundberg's particular concerns, but does not clearly add much to the argument we have found. It describes a fight that Lundberg thinks should have been stopped or perhaps never scheduled because of the potential for injury to an outclassed underdog. But we'd need to have more information to know whether this adds anything to the fact that people get beat up in boxing, which has already been taken into account in the argument.

The next paragraph (10) points out that people occasionally die from their boxing injuries. This serves to show that boxing's damage is sometimes very great indeed and hence cannot simply be dismissed. But Campbell essentially concedes this and makes the argument hang on the preponderance of reward over risk. For this kind of point to count here we would need to discover just how high the risk of death is, which would naturally be part of the investigation mentioned above into the reliability of Campbell's observations.

The last two paragraphs we must examine (11 and 12) are actually quite revealing. For here we get a completely different argument, one suggesting that Campbell may be wasting his time if he thinks he can advance the case for boxing by pointing out niceties of risk and reward. For what Lundberg says in these two paragraphs is that boxing is *intrinsically* bad ("wrong at its base"), not something a civilized society should tolerate, not even a sport. This is no longer our form [B]. He's not saying that boxing has a certain consequence Y and that Y is bad. What he's saying is simply "boxing is bad," by its very nature. This allegation has nothing to do with any particular consequence it has. Here, of course, the disagreement may become intractable; but it has in any case moved away from the forms examined in this chapter. Those forms are valuable primarily because they help us see what is going on in the first part of this article. But in doing that they *also* allow us to see a complexity we may not have noticed without them: that Lundberg offers two very different arguments against boxing that must be thought about and responded to in very different ways.

SUPPLEMENTAL EXERCISES

A. Review Questions

1. In a standard, two-step argument for a prediction, what is an underwriting diagnostic rival?

2. Why can't arguments for recommendations or predictions be diagnostic? Why might you expect to find diagnostic steps relevant anyway?

3. Explain why, when we learn from experience, either the success or the failure of a prediction would provide trace data.

4. When we support a prediction with some simple data, why is it useful to interpose a diagnosis between the two?

5. How can a diagnosis be relevant to whether a consequence is good or bad?

B. Passages for Analysis

1. As you drive along a city street at night you approach a traffic signal that is red in your direction. You begin to slow, but then notice the light in the other direction has changed to amber. Anticipating the green, you take your foot off the brake and begin to accelerate. In doing this, you have made a predictive inference from a bit of data.

    a. Schematize the inference as a simple one-step argument.

    b. Then schematize it in compound, predictive form, interposing a diagnosis.

    c. Give an undermining diagnostic rival.

    d. What non-trace data would support your undermining rival in (c)?

    2. Southern California has not had a very large earthquake in more than a century. It is therefore likely that it will have one in the near future.

    a. Structure this inference in standard two-step predictive form, supplying an underlying diagnosis.

    b. How does this structure help you explain why you cannot make the same inference from the same data in other parts of the country, such as Indiana.

    3. Eleanor Langen paused briefly on her walk from the bus stop to gaze sadly at the majestic shade trees she had known since her youth—or what was left of them. Soon none would remain to shade her walk on hot summer days or cast stark silhouettes against a gray winter sky. Six or eight had died each summer for the past few years, and now nearly half of the original stand was gone. Eleanor was convinced the mysterious disease could be stopped if the city would just take the problem seriously. But she was sure it wouldn't: She had already wasted hundreds of hours chasing through the municipal bureaucracy, trying to find a responsive agency.

    a. Schematize Eleanor's argument for her prediction in standard compound predictive form.

    b. Describe the connecting conditions she offers in the main argument.

    c. Give an undermining rival for Eleanor's diagnostic conclusion.

    d. Give a diagnostic rival that might be underwriting.

4. The argument in Supplemental Exercise B3 at the end of Chapter 6 has been used to recommend that soccer players avoid hitting the ball with their heads.

    a. Reread the article in that exercise and schematize such an argument, using the correlation-form tributary on S_1 (see p. 303).

    b. Describe an undermining diagnostic rival.

    c. What objections might be raised under S_3?

    5. In the middle of a writing exercise with her fifth-grade class, Mrs. Lippencott hears a strange roar and the windows begin to rattle. Ever since coming to California she had worried about how she would react when this happened; now she would get the chance to find out. "It's an earthquake, children," she said with only a touch of panic. "We all had better get under our desks until it is over."

    a. Mrs. Lippencott is offering diagnostic support for S_2 in an argument of form [A] for her recommendation. Use the form offered in our discussion of S_2 to help schematize her argument.

    b. Give an undermining diagnostic rival.

    c. Provide some support (in the spirit of an investigation) that would make your undermining rival serious.

    6. The government warned consumers that some chopped garlic-and-oil mixes may pose a risk for potentially fatal botulism food poisoning if not refrigerated. Citing a recent incident in New York in which three people got botulism from eating garlic bread, the

Food and Drug Administration emphasized garlic-and-oil mixes containing little or no acidifying agent, such as cotric or phosphoric acid, should be kept in the refrigerator. Two men and a woman from Kingston, N.Y. were hospitalized Feb. 19 with botulism after eating bread spread with a garlic-and-oil mix. A preliminary investigation by state officials implicated "Colavita Chopped Garlic in Extra Virgin Olive Oil," which investigators say may have been stored at room temperature even though it was labeled "Keep Refrigerated." Colavita Pasta & Oil Co., of Newark, N.J., has recalled the product, even though distribution of the line has been discontinued, officials said.

(The Los Angeles Times)

In this article you may find a recommendation based on the following diagnostic argument.

S$_1$ Three people were hospitalized with botulism after eating bread spread with Colavita Chopped Garlic in Extra Virgin Olive Oil.

S$_1$' Garlic-and-oil mixes that have little on no acidifying agents and are not refrigerated can cause botulism.

=== d

C$_d$ Eating Colavita Chopped Garlic in Extra Virgin Olive Oil caused the three people who ate it to get botulism.

A simple intermediate argument connects this one to the following standard recommendation argument of form [A] (see p. 332).

S$_1$?

S$_2$ Decreasing the chances of getting botulism is good.

S$_3$?

C Colavita Chopped Garlic in Extra Virgin Olive Oil should be taken off the shelves.

a. Write out S$_1$.

b. Write out a simple argument connecting the diagnostic one to S$_1$ (use the general form at the beginning of the S$_1$ section, p. 333).

c. Write out S$_3$.

d. If we discovered that the Colavita olive oil mix eaten by the victims mentioned in the article had been refrigerated, where would this information fit in the schematization? Would it be trace data? Why? What effect would it have?

e. Suppose we discovered that the three victims had all eaten sushi on the day they became ill, at the restaurant where several dozen others had contracted botulism from eating sushi. Where would this fit in the schematization? Would it be trace data? Why? What rival would benefit most from this new information? What kind of rival would it be? Explain.

f. Suppose somebody said, "I think you have to be irresponsible to buy something labeled Keep Refrigerated and then not keep it refrigerated. Anybody who does that deserves to get botulism." What item in the schematization would this challenge? Briefly explain.

7. SMITH: I'm going down to the post office to pick up a package they couldn't deliver on Friday. Keep an ear out for my phone.

WILLIAMS: You can't get your package today; the post office is closed.

SMITH: How do you know, were you there today already?

WILLIAMS: No, I wasn't there, but the Social Security office was closed when I tried to stop by this morning; and if they're closed on Monday, it must be a federal holiday.

Although not strictly a prediction, Williams' argument that the post office is closed has the same form as the predictive arguments we looked at in this chapter.

    a. Schematize her argument.

    b. Give an undermining diagnostic rival.

ANSWERS

7.1 C_{d1} offers an explanation of the bright flash, so S_2 is TD. The wind and rain are relevant because they make that account of the flash more plausible (not because they're being explained in this argument). So S_1 is NTD.

7.2 **a.** A bright flash might be fireworks or a nearby chemical plant exploding. Each would soon be followed by a loud noise and so would underwrite the prediction.

    b. A bright flash also might be a meteorite or a police helicopter, neither of which need be followed by a bang. So they would be undermining.

7.3

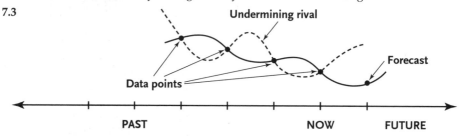

7.4 **a.** S_1: It's raining and windy outside.

      S_2: A very bright flash occurs.

      $S_{5'}$ No loud noise after a long wait.

$$\overline{\hspace{6cm}}\text{d}$$

      C: ? Some undermining rival.

    b. The failure ($S_{5'}$) would be a hurdle for the lightning rival and better explained by an undermining rival, so it is TD.

7.5 **a.** The easy prediction is that the tank will take a lot of gasoline (more than any normal fill up) if towed to a filling station.

    b.

POSITIVE	NEGATIVE
S_1: Car sputters and stops	S_1: Car sputters and stops
S_2: Fuel gauge reads empty	S_2: Fuel gauge reads empty
S_5: Tank takes a lot of gas	$S_{5'}$: Takes only a little

$$\overline{\hspace{3cm}}\text{d} \qquad\qquad \overline{\hspace{3cm}}\text{d}$$

RANKING: RANKING:

C_{d1}: Out of gas C_{d2}: Electrical failure

.   .

. C_{d3}: Plugged fuel line

.   .

C_{d2}: Electrical failure   .

.   .

C_{d3}: Plugged fuel line C_{d1}: Out of gas

Some Remarks on This Case: First, other predictions would work as well (hear sloshing in the tank, won't run even when fuel and electrical system completely replaced), just not as dramatically as this one. Second, electrical failure is the better of the rivals because it would explain the empty reading, which the plugged line would not. Third, "plugged" is a stand-in for all sorts of fuel problems, such as water in the gas, which you might prefer to taking "plugged" literally. Fourth, in the second argument (Failure) electrical failure (C_{d2}) would not be nearly as strong a conclusion as out of gas (C_{d1}) was in the first, so its position is a little misleading. It is just at the top of a weaker bunch after the prediction fails.

7.6 A bang in normal circumstances would make lightning an overwhelmingly good bet because battle rivals (and any other underwriting rivals) would be very long shots, normally, and the wind and rain help the lightning rival quite a lot.

7.7 Motorcyclists argued that the helmet law made motorcycling so unpleasant that it reduced riding enough to completely account for the drop as resulting from fewer miles ridden. They also noted that California had been unusually wet because of an El Niño condition that year, which further reduced motorcycling. Given this, they argued, fatalities should have fallen much farther without the law, supporting their view that the law made cycling more dangerous.

7.8 As before, the prediction fails if we wait a reasonable time and hear no thunder. If this happened after a very bright flash, that would not show we were wrong to think closer meant louder: it would show the flash wasn't lightning. The only ways to make nearby lightning quiet are exceedingly implausible (e.g., we're enclosed in a transparent, sound-absorbing dome).

7.9 Conditions accounting for 29 pounds in spite of a slow leak would be things such as a very high temperature. If somebody drove the car at high speed on a hot day just before the pressure measurement, that would heat it up and raise the pressure reading. Or it might be that the garage was very hot that day. More bizarre possibilities include a gas-producing chemical reaction inside the tire.

7.10 The rivals here are all trying to explain a failed prediction, which means no seismograph trace in the earthquake case. Category 2 rivals must explain this with a *correct* diagnosis (there was an earthquake), by appeal to something in the conditions connecting the quake to the forecast. Here, the easiest account of this kind would be that the seismograph was down during the quake: that would explain the lack of a trace. Support for this could be that the neighborhood around the laboratory suffered a power failure just before the earthquake. This would of course be NTD.

7.11 **a.** Because each of the other three kinds of rival explains the successful prediction, the rivals must answer the IQ, "What explains getting the prediction right?"

b. The earlier points would be TD, because they'd boost some rivals by being explained by them. But central TD is something all the rivals must explain to be serious; and the fourth kind of rival would not even be trying to explain them. So they'd be peripheral. In this case, for instance, my wife's having the tires changed might obviously be the right account of the fifth reading though it has nothing whatever to say about the other four.

7.12 *Four Ways of Accounting for a Successful Prediction:* In the lightning case, the prediction is a loud "bang." So the category 1 rival would just be that the flash was lightning—we were right. Category 2 would be that our diagnosis was wrong (in an underwriting way), but we understood everything else. So examples of category 2 would be atomic bombs and fireworks. In category 3 the flash was from a quiet source, but we get a bang anyway through surprising conditions. An example would be a flash due to wires quietly touching, but the contact causes a current surge that explodes something in the garage. In category 4 we get a bang unrelated to the flash, for example, a cement truck skids in the rain and thunders through the bedroom wall.

7.13 a. In each case (rivals from categories 2, 3, and 4) the forecast does not support the original diagnosis because it is not the best explanation of the forecast, even though it gets it right. In diagnostic arguments, data collectively support what explain them *best*, not any old explanation of them.

b.

SUCCESSFUL EX POST FACTO ARGUMENT	RIVALS
S_1: Day 1, 29 pounds	C_1: Slow leak
S_2: Day 2, 28 pounds	C_2: Temperature cycles
S_3: Day 3, 27 pounds	C_3: Co worker prank
S_4: Day 4, 26 pounds	C_4: Tires replaced
S_8: Day 5, 25 pounds	

$$\overline{} \, d$$

?

7.14 Argument 1:

S_1 Smith lost, even though favored by polls a week ago.

S_2 Turnout was high in areas the polls said favored Smith.

S_3 Smith's opponent was out of money, so only Smith campaigned during the final week.

S_4 A postelection survey indicated that many who favored Smith's opponent were embarrassed to admit it publicly.

$$\overline{} \, d$$

C The pre-election poll results were inaccurate.

Argument 2:

S_1 Smith lost, even though favored by polls a week ago.

S_2 Turnout was high in areas that favored Smith in the polls

S_3 Smith's opponent waged an intense negative ad campaign the last few days before the election.

S_4 Smith ran out of money and couldn't counter the negative ads.

$$\overline{} \, d$$

C Voter sentiment turned against Smith in the last week.

Argument 3:

S_1 Smith lost, even though favored by polls a week ago.

S_2 Turnout was remarkably low in areas favoring Smith in the polls.

S_3 Smith's opponent was underfunded and nearly invisible in the campaign.

S_4 In a postelection poll, many Smith supporters said they thought he was unopposed.

$$\overline{} \, d$$

C Smith supporters disproportionately failed to vote due to overconfidence.

7.15 An underwriting rival would have to imply that the diagnosis was wrong, but in a way that gives the right prediction. So perhaps the most plausible one would be a rival that states that the poll was not representative of all registered voters as it claims (so the diagnosis is wrong), but it just happened to represent voters who actually planned to vote. We could then say that we'd predict Smith's victory even if we'd discovered ahead of time that our original diagnosis was wrong. So it is an under-writing diagnosis.

7.16 S_2 The question of whether these are *good* consequences will depend on whether the speed and features will actually be useful. We all occasionally talk ourselves into getting things, especially computers, because we're dazzled by something we will never use. So it would be important to be clear about the actual difference these things would make in your friend's life.

S_3 Obviously having less money (or being in debt) is one downside to the new computer. But even if your friend's reflections under S_2 show that the speed and features are clearly worth the money, there are still other negatives to consider: time spent setting it up and learning new skills, for instance, and the risk of crashing at inopportune times until you've got the bugs worked out. This says something about the good you find in S_2: to license the inference (purchase, in this case) the good must be more than trivial: it must be adequate to compensate for these negatives.

7.17 a.

    i.

S_A: I got my first good quiz
grade when I omitted my name.
S_B: My TA hates me.
$$========================= d$$
C_d: I got the good grade
because I omitted my name. $\longrightarrow$ S_C: Omission caused grade
    ii. $\rightarrow$ S_D: The TA won't catch on.

S_1: Omitting my name will
improve my grade.

    iii. Undermining rival (common cause): I was so excited that I finally understood something in the course that I got rattled and omitted my name. The grade was (also, independently) due to understanding the stuff.

b.

    i.

S_A: People who exercise are
healthier than those who don't.
$$========================= d$$
C_d: Exercising makes you
healthier. $\longrightarrow$ S_C: Exercise $\rightarrow$ health.
S_D: I don't exercise now.

S_1: Exercising will make me healthier.

    ii. Reverse-cause rival: The exercise/health correlation is more than accounted for by the fact that really sick people can't exercise. Further, it turns out that being healthy makes you want to do physically exerting things that actually damage your health (so those exercising would actually be healthier if they exercised less).

7.18

S_A: I get winded easily.
S_B: I live at sea level.

══════════════════ d

C_d: I'm out of shape. → S_C: I'm out of shape. S_F: Our common
                         S_D: This makes me more   experience with
                               prone to illness   exercise.
                               and injury.   ══════════════ d
                       S_E: Exercise improves   ← S_E Exercise
                            physical condition.   improves condition.

                     S_1: Exercise will improve
                        my health. ──────────→ S_1
                                              S_2
                                              S_3

                                   C: I should exercise.

7.19

S_A: Healthy people often get very
      sick right after eating stinky food.

══════════════════ d

C_d: Stinky food has made
     made people sick. → S_C: Stinky food has made people sick.
                              S_D: Everybody's digestive system
                                   is the same in this respect.

                     S_1: Eating stinky leftovers can
                        make anybody sick. → S_1
                                          S_2
                                          S_3

                                   C: We should avoid
                                       stinky leftovers.

7.20 a.

S_A: Fatalities increased
      when speed limit raised.
S_B: Higher velocity impacts
      are more likely fatal.

══════════════════ d

C_d: The higher limit
     caused the increase. → S_C: Higher limit increased fatalities.
                             S_D: Lowering the limit will return us to
                                   the earlier driving conditions.

                     S_1: Lowering limit would decrease
                        fatalities.   → S_1
                                            S_2
                                            S_3

                                   C: We should lower the
                                       speed limit.

b. The safe flow of traffic is a complicated thing, so we know that S_D is uncertain. Lowering the limit by itself could actually make things worse, for example, if some drivers found it harder than others to change habits, creating greater speed variation in the flow of traffic. And if drivers generally feel a particular limit is unreasonable, that may lead to less respect for limits in general.

7.21 **a.** S_1 Lowering CO_2 emissions would reduce greenhouse effect.
S_2 It would be good to reduce the greenhouse effect.
S_3 Other consequences of CO_2 reduction don't matter.

C We should lower CO_2 emissions.

b. Diagnostic Tributary on S_2:

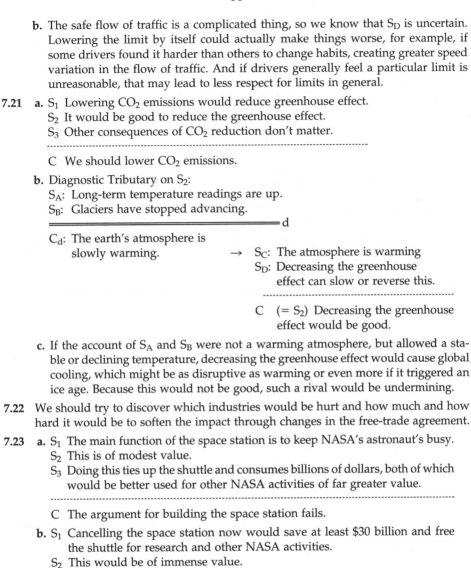

S_A: Long-term temperature readings are up.
S_B: Glaciers have stopped advancing.
==d

C_d: The earth's atmosphere is
    slowly warming.   → S_C: The atmosphere is warming
                                 S_D: Decreasing the greenhouse
                                     effect can slow or reverse this.

                                 C (= S_2) Decreasing the greenhouse
                                     effect would be good.

c. If the account of S_A and S_B were not a warming atmosphere, but allowed a stable or declining temperature, decreasing the greenhouse effect would cause global cooling, which might be as disruptive as warming or even more if it triggered an ice age. Because this would not be good, such a rival would be undermining.

7.22 We should try to discover which industries would be hurt and how much and how hard it would be to soften the impact through changes in the free-trade agreement.

7.23 **a.** S_1 The main function of the space station is to keep NASA's astronaut's busy.
S_2 This is of modest value.
S_3 Doing this ties up the shuttle and consumes billions of dollars, both of which would be better used for other NASA activities of far greater value.

C The argument for building the space station fails.

b. S_1 Cancelling the space station now would save at least \$30 billion and free the shuttle for research and other NASA activities.
S_2 This would be of immense value.
S_3 The downside would be laying off some astronauts, which is a relatively small price to pay.

C We should cancel the space station.

CHAPTER 8

FALLACIES

······················ When reasoning is not effortless, we fall prey to certain temptations
so systematically that they deserve special names to remind us of
OVERVIEW their hazard. In this chapter we catalog some of the more common
······················ of these temptations.

INTRODUCTION

With the analytical apparatus in this text we have tried to codify patterns in our most competent reasoning for use when the going gets rough. The most important function of that apparatus is simply to remind us of what to do when we're stuck or in doubt, when our reasoning is not effortlessly intersubjective. The fallacy categories we will examine in this chapter have something like the opposite aim. Properly understood, they serve as reminders of the limits of our competence. They codify not things to *do* but temptations to *avoid*, temptations that arise precisely because our competence normally is so effortless.

We may of course run past the limits of our reasoning skill in either of the two contexts: inquiry or controversy. In the first, where we're just trying to figure out something difficult, we may think we understand the topic better than we do and deceive ourselves about the strength of our reasons. In the second, what we easily misunderstand is *somebody else*: their competence or their perception of something. We may then fail completely to grasp an argument they've advanced or, equally, fail to see that they could not possibly appreciate one of our own.

Our look at fallacies will come primarily from this second, interpersonal, set of concerns. Because the dialectical nature of controversy offers such rich possibilities for describing our limits and temptations, we will derive a fallacy vocabulary from the context of *disagreement*. This allows us to group fallacies under two large headings. The first involves *constructing* arguments and the second involves *criticizing* them. The aim of our study will be to avoid squandering time and effort on giving reasons and offering criticism that our audience cannot (and usually should not) appreciate. The source of the temptation is in every case our (often forgivable) failure to see how much understandings can differ on matters of controversy. On basic matters and easy cases we find our understanding of things so broadly shared that we easily miss the point at which perceptions begin to diverge. The vocabulary of this chapter provides both a tool for detecting this point and some guidance in reestablishing the conversation. Lessons for the context of inquiry will be implicit in this guidance.

As a final introductory note, a chapter on fallacies falls at the end of this text for two reasons. First, the issues we grapple with here are very subtle and benefit enormously from the sophistication acquired in thinking through the issues raised in the first seven chapters. Second, and relatedly, we will use some of the analytical apparatus developed in these earlier chapters to help us see the point of having various fallacy categories. Some of them are difficult to grasp without that preparation.

FALLACIES OF CONSTRUCTION

We naturally try to resolve disagreement by reasoning—by giving reasons. And on everyday matters, where disagreement is not deep, we are reasonably successful in doing this.

A: I can make it from here to Nashville in fifteen minutes on my new bike.

B: Not a chance. The frost heaves along Wolf's Hollow will put you right in the stream bed if you even approach the speed limit through there. You'd be lucky to be out of Green county in fifteen minutes.

A: Hey, you're right. I forgot about that bad stretch of road.

Easy resolution of differences is possible when both parties understand the topic well and differ only about some matter of detail such as this. But as we noted in Chapter 4, deeper, more serious disagreements arise when people do not share the same understanding of a matter. Controversy becomes heated because what one person takes to be a good reason to think something, another rejects as silly or irrelevant. And sometimes, as we saw in our discussion of General Support (see p. 176), this means that a disagreement cannot be resolved by argument— by simply giving reasons. The difference between my understanding and yours may be so great that no simple list of supporting statements could be adequate to recommend your conclusion to me, even if you are right about the matter. My understanding may be inadequate to appreciate your reasoning without a large supplement of further education or experience.

The point to recognize, then, is that for a disagreement between us to be resolved by giving reasons, those reasons must be sensitive to the actual understanding we bring to the dispute. If you are to convince me *through argument* that you are right and I am wrong, you must produce support that recommends your conclusion to someone with *my* understanding of things. So in matters of great controversy, when understandings greatly diverge, this will always mean working with an understanding that differs from your own in some important and immediate way. We find ourselves tempted by the following fallacies mostly because of the special care required to give reasons for an understanding very different from our own. It's not something we naturally do very well. So the most important function of the fallacy headings we are about to treat is to remind us of the attention we must pay to our *audience* when constructing arguments.

Begging the Question

Even though recent journalism has found many different things for the expression "beg the question" to do, it has a long tradition of describing a particular objection to an argument. Perhaps the most common formulation of the objection is this: I have begged the question in offering an argument if in that argument I simply presuppose that its conclusion is true. And although this does give you some sense of the problem, it's not much of a guide to application. For on the one hand, many arguments presuppose the conclusion in a way that's perfectly fine. Diagnostic arguments presuppose a conclusion to see what it will explain, for instance, and normative ones may presuppose one to trace its consequences. On the other hand, what many traditionally question-begging arguments objectionably presuppose is not quite the conclusion itself but something related to it in a certain way. So the formulation needs refinement.

Let us look at an example to develop a better sense of this fallacy.

Editor,
There seems to be decreasing respect for religion and faith in Almighty God in our country today. Those who shirk religion and deny God's very existence will surely regret that choice when they face their Creator on Judgment Day.

This is a representative paraphrase of letters that have appeared in many local newspapers over the years. It is reasonable to read this as offering an argument directed at unbelievers.

S_1 Unbelievers will face bad consequences on Judgment Day.

C They should believe in God.

This, of course, is a simple version of the recommendation-form argument we examined in Chapter 7, and we all know the sort of context in which such an argument will arise. More importantly, in such contexts this argument fails to work in an obvious way. And it is this way of failing that has come to be called "begging the question."

What's gone wrong here is that the support offered for this conclusion is something nobody would accept unless they already accepted the conclusion itself. This is a better formulation of what it is to beg a question. You can see what somebody would mean by objecting here, "you're simply presupposing the conclusion in the argument you offer." But the presupposing here is a very *special kind* of presupposing, not the benign sort of presupposing for the sake of argument mentioned above; and furthermore, what's presupposed is not precisely the conclusion, but rather some larger picture that somehow "includes" the conclusion. Nevertheless, we can see what's going on, and it won't work; and it's a common enough failure to deserve its own name. So we call it "begging the question." The value of having this fallacy on our list is that it directs attention to the human context surrounding an argument, and to the sort of thing that would reasonably recommend a conclusion *to a certain audience*. So a better way to express it is this: I have begged the question if I support a conclusion with reasons that would not be accepted in the context by anyone who did not already accept the conclusion. With a little reminding, this is a judgment we can often make.

Loaded Descriptions

The main reason to begin with the heading of "question begging" is that all the other fallacies of construction are variations on this theme. From the example above you may not think that you yourself would ever be guilty of such a crude misunderstanding; but frustration can run deep when our frail articulation skills face the chasm that sometimes separates different understandings. It is here that our natural generosity often runs out and we stop thinking of our audience as an interlocutor and begin thinking of it as an opponent, even an obstacle. The work required to grasp a different perception presumes a *respect* for your adversary that you no longer can muster. It is here that all of us begin to sound like the author of the above letter. The minimal preconditions of reasoning with one another have then vanished.

A symptom of this you can watch for is the insistence on descriptions of key elements of a case that are not equally acceptable to both sides of a disagreement. Descriptions can be so "loaded" in favor of one side of a dispute that simply accepting the terminology begs the question for the other side. A standard example from a current controversy would be this:

> S Abortion kills innocent children.
>
> --
>
> C Abortionists should be prosecuted as murderers.

This argument would of course be perfectly worthless to anyone who favors legal abortion: they simply wouldn't concede that description of abortion. Calling it "killing innocent children" here begs the central question. If the disagreement is to be *reasoned*, it will have to be couched in different terms.

Loaded terms are often even easier to recognize than this because they are so transparently evaluative: their whole point is to carry a judgment. I think I have a nice house and you condemn it as a hovel. Where you see a decent used car, the salesman sees a golden opportunity. "Hovel" and "golden opportunity" are pointedly not neutral descriptions. Part of their function is to judge. And of course judgments such as this may be objective and agreed on by all concerned. I may live in a hovel and the car may be an unbelievably good deal. But when they are the focus of a disagreement—when opposing parties do *not* accept the same judgment as descriptive—these terms count as loaded: they beg questions that cannot be begged if we wish to reason together.

When embroiled in controversy, however, we naturally see only the other side's descriptions as loaded. Ours seem just good sense. This is why the "sides" in great controversy tend to be marked by matched pairs of question-begging descriptions. What one side sees as a justified reprisal for some great evil, the other sees as simple terrorism. One side sees prudent defense and the other sees nuclear blackmail. One sees a homeless victim of social inequity and the other sees a welfare loafer. One sees the minimum requirements for essential services and the other sees confiscatory taxation. Motivating profit versus corporate greed. Exploiting resources versus destroying the planet. The list extends indefinitely.

These terms not only alert us to the fact that questions are being begged, but also manifest the difficulty human beings have in maintaining even the façade of reasonableness when disagreement is great. For the generosity required to even comprehend a view very different from your own requires a certain respect for its holder that we have trouble sustaining when the difference is very important to us. With even modest good will we would not insist on terms our interlocutor could not accept. This is the challenge of reasoning together.

Exercise 8.1
....

(a) Identify the loaded term in the following quote and (b) rewrite the argument in a way an opponent might be able to appreciate. (Answers on p. 369.)

> Long distance freight shipment should always be by rail where possible because trucks and airplanes irresponsibly squander our natural resources.

False Dilemmas

One way loaded descriptions beg questions is to misrepresent available options and oversimplify choice. When we have strong opinions on a topic, we naturally want to make the virtues of our own view clear. One convenient expository device for doing this is to simply lump all alternative views under a description we may easily discount.

> Are we going to offer a solid, traditional education or run slavishly after every curricular fad that comes along?

If these are the choices it seems clear that a solid, traditional education is to be preferred. Such an argument is called dilemma form: we have only two choices; one is obviously bad and so the other wins. But on complex matters such as curriculum, alternatives are never so clear and choice is never this easy. This bit of diatribe dismisses all innovation as fad, for instance, and that is surely unreflective. It may be that a traditional education is better than a faddish one, but those are clearly not the only options. The alternatives are too boldly drawn with heavily loaded terms. The dilemma is a false one.

Another common variation on this form would be this:

> Do you realize that you spend the first 2 days of every week working for the government? You don't start working for yourself until sometime Wednesday morning.

This is a cute way to dramatize the amount of your pay that goes for various taxes, and sometimes it is simply this. But taken literally, it insists that the time you spend "working for the government" is not time spent "working for yourself," which suggests that this fraction of your pay is simply lost and wasted. So it implies a recommendation-form argument:

S_1 You spend 40% of the week working for the government instead of yourself.

S_2 This is an intolerably high percentage of your pay to simply throw away.

C Taxes should be substantially reduced.

But the contrast between "government" and "yourself" on which this argument is based is a false one: it is too sharply drawn. For much that is financed with tax revenue is of great value to us all: social security, national defense, schools, roads, and fire protection, to name a few. So whether reducing taxes would be in your or my interest is a very complicated business. It depends on what particular changes would result and on the indirect economic consequences of the reduction. The "government versus yourself" oversimplification obscures all this. You may not like all of the things government does with your money, but some of them are things you would pay for if they weren't provided through taxes. So, again, the contrast is more complicated than the terms suggest. The dilemma is a false one.

Exercise 8.2

(a) Explain why the following quotation offers a false dilemma and (b) rephrase it as an argument that does not depend on a false dilemma. (Suggestions on p. 369.)

> The pendulum has swung too far in the direction of protecting the environment and away from providing a decent life for people.

Appeal to Ignorance

Suppose I left my car in the garage last night and as I head out to work in the morning a member of my family asks, "Why do you think the car's still in the garage where you left it?" I might in turn ask them if there's something special about today, some special reason to think the car's not where it usually is in the morning. Suppose there isn't: the question was idle curiosity. "No, I just wondered whether you had good reason to think it's there." In such a case I might reply that the fact that there isn't any special reason for concern is itself good reason to think the car is in the garage where I left it.

This is actually a fairly common circumstance. In familiar surroundings, a perfectly good reason to think something is that you see no reason not to. Perhaps the most familiar examples are again normative. "I don't see why I can't turn left here," or "there's no reason to keep these old gloves." When these are good reasons, which they often are, it is because we're in familiar circumstances in which we have an objective competence. Because I've been driving for years and am familiar with downtown Oak Falls, I *would* naturally notice anything that would be a reason not to turn left here. Because I've been moving these tattered gloves around for years, I certainly *would* by now have found any use for them that would make them worth saving. These may of course not be conclusive reasons—good reasons seldom are. But they are often as good as reasons get: we successfully operate this way in much of our life. This was the point of our discussion of the credentials of our understanding in Chapter 4 (p. 189). Recognizing our competences has great utility and survival value.

We may extend this to point to other contexts as well. If pressed for my reason to think many things that I rightly think, my reason will be negative in this same way. Why do I think a third world war has not been declared? I've heard nothing of it. I read newspapers and listen to the radio; certainly I *would* have heard of it. These things are hard to keep quiet. Why do I think my daughter still lives in London? I've heard nothing to the contrary. I surely would have heard had she left.

As good as these arguments are, however, they must usually be foregone in matters of controversy. For when you disagree sharply with someone, the issue is precisely the adequacy of your understanding of the matter. As we saw in Chapter 4, a disagreement persists only because someone will not grant this. So you can't simply appeal to the competence of your judgment on the topic as a reason. If I disagree with someone about farm subsidies I can't offer *as an argument* "I don't see why we should keep them in business if they can't make it on their own." In a controversy about drug laws, I can't offer as a reason for legalization, "I don't see why I shouldn't be allowed to smoke or inject or snort anything I like." These may be perfectly good conversational gambits, requests for further explanation, perhaps, but they cannot here function as arguments in the way they can in situations in which the competence of my judgment is uncontroversial. Offering such negative arguments in matters of controversy is the *illicit appeal to ignorance*.

The point is, of course, that if you and I are trying to address a disagreement by giving reasons, then the understanding that determines the adequacy of a reason belongs to the *other* person. I don't need a reason to think what I think: I already do. You are the one who needs a reason to think what I think; so if I am to reason with you about it I must find a reason that works for your understanding, not mine. And vice versa. The often frustrating difficulty of doing this explains why even minor disagreements can become heated.[1] For even if you are right, and your understanding is adequate, it can still be very hard to figure out what to say that would work for me. And again, as we saw in our discussion of General Support in Chapter 4, there may be nothing you can *say* that would work as a reason for me. What I lack may require more than can be accomplished by simple argument. But even when there is something to say, figuring out what and

---

1. The heat of controversy can also weld other fallacies to this one. So we get illicit appeals to ignorance in loaded terms, for instance. "I don't see why I should have to pay for other people's stupid mistakes." This has been offered as an "argument" against everything from smog regulations (where the mistake is choosing to live downwind of a lot of driving) to welfare for unwed mothers.

how to say it usually takes care, skill, and generosity. These are often the first casualties of controversy.

To sum up, because negative arguments of the "I don't see why" sort work only when my judgment on the question is uncontroversial, such arguments cannot be used to address disagreements in which my judgment is precisely what's in question.

The Relevance of Construction Fallacies to Inquiry

These four headings can serve as useful reminders when we reason alone as well. When there's nobody else involved and I'm reasoning to allay my own doubts or to figure something out, I may fall prey to each of these temptations and thus misunderstand the value of my reasons. We may beg a question in any of the three ways discussed by fixing on a misleading characterization of something that obscures things we should distinguish. I may actually think "working for the government" is a good way to describe the first 40% of my week. If this misleads me about the complexity of taxation, it could result in my investing time and effort in something counter to my own clear interests.

Similar remarks apply to understanding my skills. I may feel comfortable with a decision because I don't see anything that would trouble it, but fail to see that my comfort is a bad guide due to unfamiliar circumstances. If I'm driving in a strange country and turn left because "I don't see any reason not to," I'm doing something far more risky that I am in familiar Oak Falls. It's both important and difficult to spot the limits of our own competence. So these reminders work for inquiry as well as controversy.

CRITICAL FALLACIES

Critical fallacies concern temptations to avoid in criticizing arguments rather than in making them. Because the source of temptation is the same, namely, the mysterious workings of human understanding, you will see parallels between these and the construction fallacies just covered. The activity of criticism is sufficiently distinct to make a second perspective valuable, however.

Attacking Straw Men

A straw-man argument is what you get when you use the principle of charity but turn it upside down. Instead of making an argument as strong as possible before criticizing it, you render it artificially weak and easy to make fun of. The weakened form then does all the critical work, because the resulting argument is so obviously silly it falls of its own weight, requiring no further attack. In a way, straw-man criticism is simply uncharitable paraphrase at work. The generous reading of an argument is A, but you represent it as B, which is substantially weaker, and this destroys the value of the criticism. It's as simple as this, but we all fall into the trap occasionally.

The uncharitable readings of Chapter 1 would illustrate this fallacy, but for exercise let us try a new example. A bit of family conversation might run as follows. Preparing to leave on vacation, dad says, "It might be good to try the scenic route along the coast because the snow level is low, making mountain driving risky." One of the kids responds, "Who's afraid of a little snow?" We might look at this as a bit of conversational repartee, but if we take it seriously, as a criticism of dad's argument, it fits in the straw-man category. A generous rendering of that argument would be something like this:

[A]

S_1 The snow will make mountain driving unpleasant and perhaps risky.
S_2 The coastal route is snow free and has some beautiful scenery.

C We should take the coastal route.

The criticism, however, represents it thus:

[B]

S_1 There's a little snow in the mountains, nothing to be afraid of.

C We should take the coastal route.

The criticism here simply consists in substituting weak argument B for the stronger one A. It's a fallacy because if you're interested in the reasoning—how good dad's reasons are in this case—it's a waste of time and energy to simply misrepresent them.[2] (In conversation, dad might respond, "That's not what I said and you know it.")

The flaw in this criticism lies in its contriving to weaken the support offered. More common, perhaps, is creating a straw man by strengthening an argument's conclusion, which has the same effect. The standard way to do this is through overgeneralizing. Recall Harriet Markman's argument against a recycling proposition in Chapter 3 (p. 107). Her argument consisted partly in laying out the burden it would place on small retailers like her. So an unsympathetic reader might characterize her position as "being opposed to burdening small retailers with the details of recycling programs." But this is far broader than her actual conclusion, and far more difficult to support. She may be opposed to all involvement by small businesses in such programs, but that doesn't matter for the task of examining the argument she actually makes. Her letter argues for a far more modest and easily defended position. It opposes one particular proposal, with one particular set of burdens and consequences. Criticizing this argument by pretending it has the more general conclusion is attacking a straw man.

Testimony arguments are particularly sensitive to this maneuver. Recall that the support offered for a statement can sometimes simply be that somebody believes it: she offers her judgment on P based on her understanding of things. As we saw in Chapter 6, this can be strong support indeed. But it is also quite vul-

----

2. There are of course all sorts of circumstances in which you may gain social or political advantage by publicly beating up on a straw man. That is not the issue here.

nerable to straw man formulations. For a slight change in our understanding of a statement can make a big difference to the competence necessary to underwrite it. When a meteorologist forecasts snow down to the 3500-foot level, for instance, anything within a few hundred feet either way counts as getting it right. That degree of accuracy is both very useful and a sign of great skill. So if I criticize the forecast as badly supported by noting (rightly) than nobody can get it right to exactly 3500 feet, I'm attacking a straw-man version of the testimony argument. I'm invoking a standard that is neither intended nor useful.

Though it does not involve testimony, the kind of straw man most commonly heard in public argument is rather like this in exploiting aspects of the understood context that are hard to articulate. Somebody in the legislature might argue, for instance, that a particular statute—a traffic regulation, say or a fine point of the municipal code—should be repealed because it is routinely ignored. Quite commonly opponents will counter by characterizing the legislator as saying, "Whenever a law is violated, it should be repealed." This is of course such a laughable position it needs no refutation. But it is also a straw man. For everything depends on what "routinely ignored" comes to in the context, which will depend on details of the statute and its application.

A wave of murders or burglaries may count as the "increasingly routine" ignoring of laws against those crimes, but nobody would be tempted to use that fact as a reason for scrapping the laws. But compare a highway speed limit, for instance. Choosing an exact velocity to impose on highway traffic involves striking a balance among safety, convenience, energy consumption, noise, and the like. It also involves a kind of arbitrariness unlike anything in the laws against murder and burglary. The last 5 or 10 miles per hour are nearly impossible to justify objectively by explicitly balancing considerations. So a venerable procedure has been relatively subjective: Let the traffic set its own speed. In the absence of special hazards, the speed at which the average driver feels comfortable is an important consideration; so the limit is often set at the speed only a small percentage (e.g., 20%) of the traffic exceeds. The point is just that different laws deal with such distinct problems that radically different considerations may be relevant to each.

Not only is the laughable generalization above a straw-man conclusion, many others more carefully phrased would be too. "He thinks that whenever a law is routinely violated by a majority of those having an opportunity to do so, it should be repealed." No, this too would be too general and much harder to defend than the proposition the legislator has advanced. Sticking him with a conclusion that is not sensitive to relevant details of the context would be making a straw-man criticism. It might make good press, and hence good politics, but it makes bad reasoning.

Demanding Proof

The notion of proof is probably too slippery to find a useful role in public debate. It mainly does harm to reasoning. We abuse it most commonly by demanding proof when all we need is good reason.

What proof do you have that welfare reform will increase (or decrease, or do anything related to) poverty?

Here proof is just a straw man to attack. Complex policy decisions always involve some gamble on consequences. The best we ever get in advance are good reasons one way or the other. So the unanswerable demand for proof is irrelevant to our reasoning. Decisions rest on the best reason we can find.

This doesn't mean that we never can prove anything in everyday reasoning.[3] We prove Maggie is taller than I am by having us stand back to back in our bare feet. We prove the battery is not discharged by turning the key and starting the car. It's just that proof is a very strong kind of reason reserved for and only possible in very special contexts such as these. The standards our reasons must meet—how good is good enough—will always depend on our purposes and on what's possible. If we set our standards too low we risk avoidable mistakes, if we set them too high we paralyze ourselves into inaction. So it's important to be sensitive to all the practical details that determine these limits. The facile demand for proof tends to obscure the practical complexity of these details and thereby damage our reasoning.

Accordingly, on most matters complex enough to be the subject of public debate, beware of the demand for proof. It's usually in the service of a forensic straw man.

The Charge of No Evidence

The concept of evidence is very closely related to the diagnostic notion of trace data. The broken latch and missing stereo are evidence of a burglary; oildrops on the pavement provide evidence that Emily has parked her incontinent Volvo in the driveway again. These things are evidence for those things because those things explain them. We have traces of a burglary and traces left by the Volvo. In some circumstance such evidence is strong, but it need not be strong to be evidence.

In general when we say we have some evidence for P, what we mean is that we have something that is best explained by it. Call the evidence E. Then E is evidence for P if, when we ask the question "How come E?," P is the best available answer in the context. Schematically:

$$\text{RANKING OF RIVALS}$$

$$
\begin{array}{ll}
S_1\ E & \\
S_2\ \text{Relevant NTD} & \quad P \\
\rule{4cm}{0.4pt}\ d & \quad Q \\
P & \quad R \\
IQ = \text{How come E?} &
\end{array}
$$

E may not be *much* evidence for P, that is, this may not be a very *strong* argument. But given the ranking it is a *sound* argument; and that is all it takes for there to be *some* evidence for P.

---

3. We may be tempted to think that the notion of proof belongs only to logic and mathematics, where the conditions for accomplishing it are formally specified with some precision. But this is only one special kind of proof.

Consider our familiar Baker Lake example. If we know a satellite's orbit is sinking dangerously close to the atmosphere and the satellite is due to pass over northern Canada tonight, then this evening's widespread reports of a fireball over Baker Lake constitute evidence that the satellite has fallen back to earth. The evidence is far from conclusive, of course; given the little we know the fireball still could be a meteorite or perhaps some other satellite. But the best bet is that it was the satellite everybody's been worrying about. That is why we call the fireball evidence of the satellite rather than of something else. If we did not have all the background NTD on the satellite, the fireball would quite reasonably be taken to be (evidence of) a meteorite. *That* would then be the best account of it. But as things stand, the streak in the sky is evidence of a falling satellite—and a specific one at that.

We belabor the semantics of "evidence" here to help us see a hazard in its abuse. The problem arises most frequently when public officials or corporate officers issue statements designed to avert responsibility for something or allay public fears. During the swine-flu vaccination program in the 1980s, for example, there was a well-publicized incident in which three elderly patients died shortly after being vaccinated at one clinic in Pennsylvania. The deaths raised some general fears about the safety of the program, which the officials involved were understandably anxious to quell. Unfortunately, what the officials said was that there was *no evidence that the deaths were linked to the vaccination program*. Given our common understanding of evidence talk, which we sketched above, this is a confusing—nearly incomprehensible—thing to say in the circumstances. The whole reason for the announcement was the publication of something reasonably taken to be evidence of that causal connection. Given our understanding of vaccination, it would not be surprising to find that frail, older people sometimes reacted badly to it. Against normal background, the best account of the striking correlation between vaccinations and death in this incident seems clearly to be some causal connection. In short, the published correlation simply is (some) evidence of a causal link between the two.

The most generous way to read what the officials meant by saying there is no evidence is that they knew something about the case that was not common knowledge and that this private information promoted some other account (some form of the chance rival) to the top of the ranking. But if this *is* what they were trying to say, they did it in a spectacularly inept and misleading way. For what they said made them appear foolish or deceitful. To avoid that appearance all they would have had to do was to tell us what they knew that changed the ranking so significantly. Or, if something prevented revealing the secret, they might at least have told us that they knew something important that we did not, and assure us that we would certainly change our judgment of the matter if we knew it. Given what they said, however, they should forgive us if we suspect that they were trying to get away with something, distracting us with an incoherent bit of PR, hoping the whole thing would blow over before anybody caught on.

Sometimes, perhaps in this case, when someone charges that there is no evidence for something they mean to say *there is no reason to think it*. This is a far more general claim and even more difficult to defend. For in saying there is no evidence for (or of) P, you have to worry only about trace data P might explain. Saying there's no reason to think P opens up all other considerations as well, in particular NTD. So, for example, before the Ballard expedition, we might have said we had no evidence the Titanic lay on the floor of the Atlantic Ocean. We had no trace data to be explained by that conclusion. But we had plenty of *reason* to think it was there, just from our general understanding of water and metal and where it was and what it was doing the last time anybody had seen it.

The point of this section is in some ways the obverse of the previous one. When somebody charges that you haven't given proof, they're almost always right, and it almost never matters. When somebody charges that you have no evidence for something, or worse, no reason at all to think it, it does almost always matter. But in normal circumstances it is almost always wrong: what you think is some evidence usually is, even if not much. The burden of this section has been to help you see the temptation to and the remedy for the charge of no evidence.

Exercise 8.3
. . . .

Consider again the motel explosion argument as set out in Exercise 5.2e on p. 205. Comment on the claim by the maintenance worker's attorney that "There is no evidence that the maintenance worker set off the explosion." (Answer on p. 369.)

The Charge of Circularity

One way to accuse an argument of begging the question is to call it "circular." The circle metaphor is applied to an argument that ends up in the same place it started out: with the conclusion. We saw in the discussion of question begging that indeed some arguments do this in an objectionable way. They are "viciously" circular, and not so much because they "start out with" the conclusion, but because the *support* with which they start out is too closely tied to the conclusion. We can tell from the context—and from the conclusion—that *this* support is not the way to start. And the circle metaphor does capture the feeling of this kind of mistake. This metaphor is easily misapplied, however. In particular, perfectly good diagnostic arguments strike the unwary as falling under this heading. So we will close our discussion of fallacies with a little guidance on how not to use the charge of circularity.

First, note that many things we might call "starting out with the conclusion" do not beg the question and may be perfectly legitimate ways to start. Entertaining a conclusion, for instance, can begin an inquiry, which results in an argument for that conclusion. Or you may begin with C to discover whether you have any interest in pursuing the argument. Or, in constructing an argument, you may begin with C to make sure it is carefully formulated for its purpose. And when you *present* an argument, good practice recommends that you present C first just to let everybody know where you are headed. None of these beginnings fallaciously *presupposes* the conclusion. Each uses it in a wholly unobjectionable way.

Moreover, we may even *presuppose* a conclusion without begging the question—and without reasoning badly in any other way either. It all depends on how we go about it, what we're up to. A perfectly proper technique, we've noted before, is to presuppose a conclusion *for the sake of argument*. We may assume it is true in order to see where it leads or where it leaves you: to think through its consequences, for instance. Something like this happens in all diagnostic arguments. Before we can decide on the sound conclusion, we must generate a plausibility ranking. To do this generally requires trying out each rival on the trace data to see which one best handles the entire collection. In a way, we assume a rival is true to see how it fits, how easily it explains things.

In criticism, this ordinary diagnostic procedure is sometimes mistaken for the question-begging kind of presupposing a conclusion: it strikes some as circular. With your background in diagnosis from Chapter 5, and the above reminder, you should have no trouble recognizing this as a mistake, nor even explaining it to someone unfamiliar with diagnostic reasoning patterns. Nevertheless, one kind of diagnostic reasoning contains some special hazards both for our articulation and our judgment. This is the very common case in which the reasoning is so clear that we end up entertaining only a single rival. We will close this chapter with a look at that case.

While working in my garage one afternoon I notice an arc of red drips characteristic of automatic transmission fluid on the otherwise clean floor. Thinking about how the drips might have gotten there (IQ: How'd they get there?), I recall that I had replaced a worn part on an automatic transmission just this morning, and it was a part that typically does contain a small amount of fluid that may splash out after it is disconnected. I figure that must be it: I dripped some on the floor as I carried it to the trash. To check, I pull the old part from the trash and as I do a few drops of reddish fluid drip out. Case closed. That's the source of the drips. No other explanations are worth considering. Much of our diagnostic reasoning is like this. Only one suspect, one rival, comes close to accommodating all the data. We may know the subject and circumstances well enough to know that the next best bet is some outrageous conspiracy theory, or *any* conspiracy theory. All the other rivals are so bad as to not be worth formulating.

Because we try out only a single rival in a case such as this, it is more easily confused with question begging, more easily thought viciously circular: I assumed *the* conclusion, if only to try it out on the traces. Of course, finding only a single rival worth consideration does not make the procedure wrong or the resulting argument fallacious. This case is a picture of our diagnostic reasoning at it best: the clearest sort of example of our diagnostic competence at work. But the simplicity of the reasoning does make it harder to explain to someone unfamiliar with the rudiments of inferring explanations. If you find yourself having to do this, and something like the above paragraph proves inadequate, you will probably have to expand on the role of our general understanding in reasoning and how it manifests itself in plausibility judgments. You may end up teaching the skeptic much of Chapter 5. But that is the problem that originally set us out on the project of this text. Articulating our reasoning is far harder than the reasoning itself in the best and strongest cases. Any explanation will require mastering at least part of our new vocabulary.

Finally, these (single-rival) cases do have a certain danger about which we should be clear. When a single rival overwhelms the data, we don't then engage in the typical diagnostic activity of explicitly comparing rival explanations. We place all of the weight of our reasoning on our general understanding of topic and circumstance. We dismiss all other rivals at once with a general judgment. And, again, this is often just the right thing to do. But we must bear in mind that the explicit comparison of rivals is what we do best. So if there is any uncertainty, *that* is how to address it: we must use our imagination to fashion the most serious rivals we can, if only to dismiss them. This danger is easier to keep in mind, however—and easier to treat intelligently—if we do not confuse it with question begging.

SUPPLEMENTAL EXERCISES

A. Review Questions

1. Explain why "presupposing the conclusion" is a misleading characterization of the fallacy of begging the question.

2. In what circumstances can "I don't see why" introduce a perfectly good argument (reason)? Why is controversy (disagreement) not one of those circumstances? What perfectly legitimate and helpful role might "I don't see why?" play in controversy?

3. List pairs of terms with roughly the same descriptive content but that differ evaluatively. Use the example of house/hovel in the text as a model.

4. Suppose San Francisco is flattened by a terrific shaking of the ground that surviving residents all describe as a great earthquake. Comment on the following quote by a geologist in the newspaper the next morning: "There is no evidence of seismic activity in the San Francisco area yesterday."

5. Comment on the fallacies illustrated by the following (that is: name them and try to rephrase the sentiment in a way sympathetic to *both* sides of the dispute).

    a. It is one thing for the municipal police to go on strike for higher pay. It is quite another for them to mug a city into submission.

    b. The criminal justice pendulum has swung too far in the direction of protecting the criminal and away from protecting the victims of crime.

B. Passages for Analysis

[*Note*: Genuine applications of the fallacy vocabulary presented here must be in the context of extended conversation or rumination of far greater length than can be accommodated here. The following exercises are meant to be suggestive.]

1. Background: In a recent Venezuelan election, a retired military man who had earlier attempted to overthrow the previous government by force was elected president by a landslide. The following exchange concerned that landslide victory:

    A: "In giving an Army Colonel such an overwhelming mandate, Venezuela's voters were simultaneously frustrated with corruption and beguiled by a populist demagogue."

    B: "You can't write the country's voters off as hopelessly manipulated simpletons."

    a. What terms are loaded (unlikely to be simply accepted by the other side).

    b. What proposition (conclusion) do the two sides likely disagree about.

    c. Recharacterize what A and B said to support their different conclusions in a way not dependent on the loaded terms.

    d. Why does B's reply to A count as a straw-man criticism?

    2. Some years ago a professor of oral diagnosis ran some experiments on rats. In two separate studies, rats given saccharin were found to suffer substantially less tooth decay than rats on an ordinary rat diet. Although obviously excited by the finding, he went on to self-deprecatingly add, "there is no data suggesting that the decline in tooth decay is more than coincidentally related to the increased use of saccharin. I can only raise the question."

    a. Why is the professor's own description of the results of his study puzzling?

    b. Reading generously, what might the professor know that we do not that would make his description less puzzling?

ANSWERS

8.1   **a.** The loaded term is the phrase "irresponsibly squanders." An opponent would be somebody who thought trucks and planes were at least sometimes okay, and so could not agree with this as a simple description of their use.

      b. Long distance freight shipment should always be by rail where possible because trains use far less energy per unit of cargo than do trucks and planes.

8.2   **a.** The pendulum image creates a false dilemma by suggesting that protecting the environment is always at the expense of a decent life for people. Environmentalists of course would contend that one main reason to protect the environment is to keep life from becoming worse *for people*. So the characterization begs this question without argument.

      b. [The sentiment behind the pendulum metaphor might be rendered in many ways without the offending oversimplification. One would be this:] In their enthusiasm for the environment, environmentalists pay too little heed to the problems involved in making life tolerably decent for people.

8.3   The fact that the explosion occurred while the maintenance worker was investigating a problem with a propane heating system is evidence that he caused it. Given what we know, that's a very serious rival, and no others seem better. Perhaps the attorney knows something about the case that he's not revealing, which would make another rival a clear favorite; but until we know what that is we have evidence it was the maintenance worker.

APPENDIX

DEDUCTION

INTRODUCTION

The key to our evaluating an argument is comparing and ranking its rival conclusions. This is why the notion of an implicit question is so important to our analysis: it organizes the rivals into a coherent list. The crucial *practical* element in any evaluation is making sure we've thought of all the serious rivals, so that we may derive an evaluation from their comparison. If we are careful in this aspect of our analysis, however, we may treat *un*serious rivals in a number of different ways. Often we may simply ignore them. Fantastic answers to the IQ will fall in areas of the possibilities balloon that we do not even bother to name. In the argument about how to get home after work (p. 180), we simply ignored all helicopter rivals; in the Baker Lake argument (p. 226) we ignored orbiting satellites other than the specific Soviet one, as well as alien attacks and outsized fireworks displays. When an IQ is very general, as in the hung jury argument (p. 160), we may ignore *most* of the balloon, concentrating on a small corner of it in which the conclusion's contrast is interesting. (See Figure 4.7 on p. 162, for a graphic picture of this.)

We usually ignore certain regions of the balloon simply because we understand enough to know rivals in them cannot be serious (helicopters, fireworks). Sometimes, however, the way the support is stated actually *guarantees* that the IQ's answer does not lie in a certain part of the balloon: that this region is empty of serious possibilities. To see how this works, consider a slightly artificial version of an argument summarizing the investigation into the assassination of President Kennedy. The IQ would be "Who killed Kennedy?" Let us suppose we have narrowed the list of suspects to Lee Harvey Oswald, a few others, and a friend of mine I will call "Pete." Further imagine the support to be just those well-known aspects of the Warren Commission report. The picture, then, would look something like this:

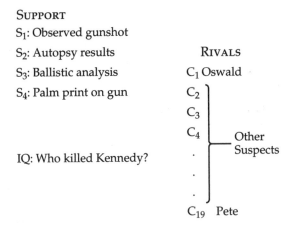

Support

S_1: Observed gunshot

S_2: Autopsy results   Rivals

S_3: Ballistic analysis C_1 Oswald

S_4: Palm print on gun C_2

                                            C_3

                                            C_4 Other
                                                         Suspects
        IQ: Who killed Kennedy?   .

                                          .

                                          .

                                        C_{19} Pete

Given the little we know, we may wonder whether Pete is a suspect—a serious rival—in the investigation. Now suppose we discover, and add to the support, the fact that Pete was not in Dallas on the date of the assassination (call this S_5). This would, for practical purposes, eliminate Pete as a suspect; it would drop him off the list along with the billions of others alive on that date who are also not under suspicion. But the point to notice is that what eliminates Pete is simply his *implausibility* as a suspect, given that he was out of town. We can easily imagine bizarre ways in which he still *could* have done it. He might, for instance, have set up the rifle on a mount in the book depository, aimed it at a certain spot, and fired it by remote control while watching the procession on television in New York. Pete is implausible precisely because we would have to resort to such weird stories to have him on the suspect list.

On the other hand, the fact that we can tell such stories shows that C_{19} is *compatible* with the support even with S_5 included. The support does not *contradict* C_{19}. This is interesting because we sometimes state the support in an argument in such a way that it *does* contradict one or another of the rivals; that is, the support sometimes will explicitly rule out all the ways one rival might be true, including bizarre ones. This opens some interesting possibilities and creates a hazard too. Exploring these is the purpose of this Appendix.

SEMANTIC CONFLICT

Incompatibilities of this kind often arise when, in thinking through a case, we make explicit a small part of what we take for granted.[1] So we might say something like "look, we may safely assume the killer was in Dallas on the day of the assassination." And if we add this "safe assumption" to the support in the argument above, we achieve incompatibility in this case.

---

1. Recall from our discussion of relevance in Chapter 4 that most of our relevant understanding *must* go without saying or we could not give reasons at all; for there is no end to it. But it is sometimes helpful to articulate a bit of it for a specific purpose.

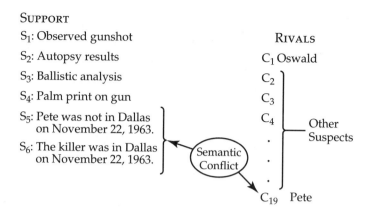

Support

S_1: Observed gunshot

S_2: Autopsy results

S_3: Ballistic analysis

S_4: Palm print on gun

S_5: Pete was not in Dallas on November 22, 1963.

S_6: The killer was in Dallas on November 22, 1963.

Rivals

C_1 Oswald

C_2
C_3
C_4 Other Suspects
.
.
.

C_{19} Pete

Semantic Conflict

Adding S_6 to the support rules out even fantastic stories of remote control, and does so as a *matter of semantics*. If we accept that the killer was in Dallas and we accept that Pete was not, then we have thereby accepted that Pete could not be the killer. S_5 and S_6 together are *incompatible with any story naming Pete as the perpetrator*. We will say in a case such as this that by including S_5 and S_6, the support *conflicts semantically* with C_{19}. As long as those two claims are part of the support, Pete has been *semantically eliminated* from the list of suspects. This is what was intended in saying that the way the support is stated *guarantees* a part of the balloon is empty.

Such elimination depends on details—often accidents—of the way we characterize IQ, support, and rivals. So we must take care that such accidents do not exclude any serious rivals. But we usually do this quite naturally. Such conflicts as do exist normally involve rivals we would not take seriously anyway, and are therefore harmless. In Joyce Karlin's argument (on p. 160), for instance, we used the IQ "What caused the mistrial?"; and one answer to this question would be (C_8): "Two jurors refused to vote for conviction." Two jurors refusing to join the others in this way *would* cause a mistrial, so that's one answer to this IQ. But because the 11–1 vote of the jury would naturally be part of the support, this rival would be semantically eliminated. This elimination raises no problems, however, because C_8 is not a rival we need to consider seriously. It is only a possibility because the IQ is stated so generally.

The point to notice is that in any argument, the balloon of possibilities may have certain areas that are not open possibilities (shaded in Figure A.1), simply as a result of the way the support is stated. Unless we've characterized the support badly, however, the serious rivals will be found among the possibilities still open, and our analysis may proceed as usual.

We should, nevertheless, register a pair of cautions. If in thinking about an argument we find reason to take seriously a rival in an eliminated (shaded) wedge, we must revise our characterization of the support to allow it on the list. Accidents of terminology must not affect our evaluation. Investigations invite this kind of revision constantly, for instance. Matters thought settled—things we naturally take for granted—come into question as new information appears. We may discover a remote control apparatus in the book depository, for example, and suddenly S_6 (Killer was in Dallas) is no longer a safe assumption. If that happens, we must drop

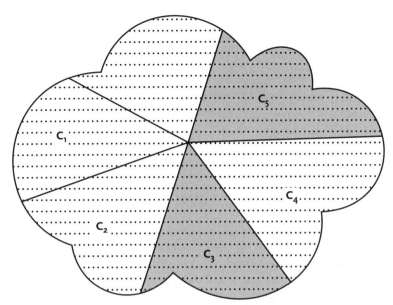

Figure A.1. Rivals that are incompatible with support.

S_6 from the support, or soften its formulation, to allow the possibility of a distant assassin, at least until another discovery drops it off the serious list again.

This is what's behind the admonition in Chapter 4 (p. 180) that you keep data gathering "in the spirit of investigation." If you characterize a discovery too generally, you may accidentally exclude—just by the characterization—rivals you have not thought about enough to simply eliminate. In the Flight 800 case, if we found no blast damage on the engines, that might drop the missile rival from serious consideration. That would be accomplished by simply adding "engines show no blast damage" to the support. But if, recognizing this impact, you instead characterized the discovery as "it couldn't have been a missile" and added *that* to the support, in just those words, that would *semantically* eliminate the missile rival. As long as it remained part of the support, missiles could never return to the serious list, no matter what we discovered. This would usually be incautious. But more important, if the point of setting out the argument is to examine or publicize our *reasoning*, we should record the evidence rather than its impact. Giving the impact is valuable only as a summary of reasoning done elsewhere.

A second caution concerns the implicit question itself. Because the IQ determines the balloon of possibilities, accidental features of how we state *it* may have the same kind of consequence: a possibility may be excluded from the list of rivals because it isn't even in the balloon. Often, especially if the IQ is very general (What caused the mistrial? What's going on here?), this is not a problem. But when we try to make an IQ helpfully specific (Why did Danny Hamilton abandon his rig on Highway 86?) we may draw the balloon so tightly as to exclude reasonable possibilities. In the Baker Lake example in Chapter 5 (p. 226) for instance, the IQ we assumed was What caused the fireball? So if, in thinking about the case, we come to wonder whether the whole thing is a hoax—a ruse designed to divert local residents from the boredom of an Arctic winter—that possibility will not be in the balloon defined by the IQ. It is not a possible answer to "What caused the fireball?" because part of its point is to say there *was* no fireball. So if we wish to take the hoax rival seriously, we will have to change the IQ—expand the balloon. Something like "What provoked all those fireball reports?" would do nicely: it would still have all the old answers (meteorites and falling satellites could provoke such reports) but would allow entertainment as well.

The point of these cautions is simply to note that our vocabulary and apparatus must be in the service of our understanding of a case: we should never let convenient expression preclude consideration of live possibilities.

SEMANTIC EVALUATION

We may nevertheless consider the possibility, infrequent in practice, that the entire evaluation of an argument may proceed semantically. For this, we must first manage to achieve a *complete* list of rival conclusions. That is, *every* dot in the balloon must be covered by a rival on our list. This is, as noted, normally not important to our reasoning: we simply ignore irrelevant and fantastic possibilities. But we may always achieve a complete list simply by giving a name to the ignored part of the balloon. A general name that usually works is "something else." Using the balloon in Figure A.1 we may say the IQ's answer is C_1, C_2, C_3, C_4, C_5, or "Something else," which we would simply call C_6. In other words, we may achieve a complete list by letting the part of the balloon not covered by serious rivals be a rival of its own. To take a real case, the NTSB offered four initially serious rivals in the crash of TWA Flight 800: the cause was a bomb, a collision, a missile, or a mechanical failure. This list of rivals could be completed merely by adding C_5: it was something else. C_5 would cover all the rest of the dots in the balloon, from various kinds of bad weather and pilot errors to weird interference by Martians.

In any case, when we have a complete list of rivals, we may then imagine support that, through accident or contrivance, manages to conflict semantically with *all but one* of the rivals. Only one rival would then remain compatible with the support, as illustrated in Figure A.2. When this happens, the uneliminated rival (C_6 in this case) will be the only possible sound conclusion. Again, most practical reasoning will not look at all like this. Such a picture will be useful only in special circumstances, in which the reasoning behind the elimination of the excluded rivals is not important. In some contexts, all we might need is to summarize or be reminded of reasoning that took place elsewhere.

DEDUCTIVE ARGUMENTS

The kind of semantic argument most commonly discussed is the *deductive* argument.[2] The support in a deductive argument semantically eliminates all rivals to

---

2. What we will call "deductive arguments" here are often referred to as "deductively valid arguments" in the literature primarily concerned with them. The reason for the more elaborate expression is irrelevant here, so we will simply call arguments "deductive" that meet the criteria about to be given.

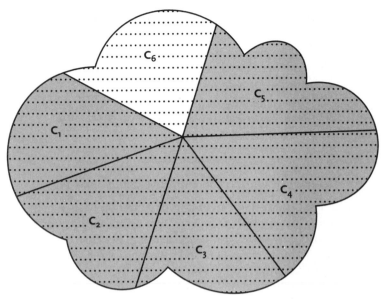

Figure A.2. Only one rival is consistent with support.

their conclusions, but it also does a bit more than this. If the support in a deductive argument is true, it semantically guarantees the *truth* of its conclusion. To do this, the support must contain, in addition to items incompatible with all the other answers to its implicit question, something guaranteeing that *one* of the answers to this question is true. Otherwise you could eliminate all but one of an IQ's answers and still say that even *it* is not true, because *none* of that question's answers is true. This might happen, for instance, because that was the *wrong question* to ask in the first place.

The most natural IQ in the Kennedy assassination case, for example, would be "Who shot President Kennedy?" So the rivals would be all the individual suspects, and also perhaps teams of suspects acting in concert. But, given the data offered above, nothing would rule out the possibility that what actually happened on that melancholy afternoon was that the vibrations of the cheering crowd jarred loose a precariously placed rifle that had been left long ago in the Dallas book depository, which discharged when it fell, killing the President by a freak of trajectory. In this case none of the suspects or teams would have done it. So we might eliminate every suspect but X and still the conclusion "X shot President Kennedy" would not be true, because nobody did.

So to guarantee the truth of its conclusion semantically, the support in a deductive argument must also guarantee that what we seek lies in the balloon we have: that some answer to the IQ is true. So, to construct a deductive argument for Oswald's guilt, using the natural IQ, *something* must tell us that somebody or other shot the president. Because this is a reasonable assumption, let us explicitly include among the support the statement "Somebody shot President Kennedy." Then, if the rest of the support is incompatible with everybody but Oswald, we could say we had a semantic guarantee that

Oswald shot the President. This would give us a *deductive argument* for that conclusion.

S₁ Somebody shot President Kennedy

$$S_2$$
$$S_3$$

Support conflicting
semantically with every
suspect or group except
Lee Harvey Oswald.

$$S_n$$

—————————————————————————

C Lee Harvey Oswald shot President Kennedy.

Here we have adopted the usual convention of signaling that an argument is deductive by separating the support from the conclusion with a single solid line.

This schematization is actually a bit misleading, because it seems to depend on the substantial evidence collected in the investigation. But the semantic guarantee does not depend so much on the *substance* of the support as it does on the precise formulation of what we have learned from it. So a better, more candid schematization of that deductive argument would look like this:

MODEL DEDUCTIVE ARGUMENT

S_1 Somebody shot President Kennedy.
S_2 Lee Harvey Oswald could have done it.
S_3 Nobody else could have done it (alone
    or in concert).

—————————————————————————

C Lee Harvey Oswald shot President Kennedy

In ordinary (nondeductive) reasoning we would simply let the data suggest these three things. But to semantically guarantee the conclusion, the support must be explicitly stated in this very general way. The word "categorical" is often used to represent the sweeping generality that support must have to semantically guarantee the truth of substantive conclusions in this way. We must assert *categorically* that somebody did it, that nothing rules out Oswald, and that something or other *does* rule out everybody else. These three together place the conclusion in the Oswald wedge of the balloon.

STRUCTURE

This categorical nature explains why deductive arguments, like semantic arguments more generally, typically play a secondary, structural role in our reasoning. That is, they are better for summarizing, or reminding ourselves of substantive reasoning done elsewhere, than actually capturing that reasoning. This last argument about the Kennedy assassination is structural in this sense. The hard work of reasoning (done elsewhere) involved actually looking over the evidence that Oswald could have done it and that other suspects were implausible and thinking through the various live possibilities. The deductive argument then presents, in simplest terms, the bare outlines of what we learned there, omitting the subtle qualifications implicit in our diagnostic judgments. A deductive argument provides the structure of our reasoning in something like the way an outline provides the structure of an essay.

To see the structure/substance point more clearly, let us look again at the truck crash argument we used in Chapters 3 and 4. The initial data, that the tire marks went straight off the road and showed no signs of braking, left us with only four even remotely serious rivals:

C_1: Driver fell asleep.
C_2: Driver died at the wheel.
C_3: He crashed on purpose.
C_4: Steering and brakes failed simultaneously.

Suppose the investigation turns up the following support: (a) the driver had been driving all night after a long day loading the truck; (b) he was young and healthy; (c) he had a happy life and no known emotional problems; (d) inspection of the truck found the steering and brakes in working order. Thinking about how this support would affect the rivals' ability to explain the central trace data would yield the following ranking:

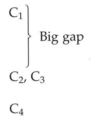

$$C_1$$

Big gap

$$C_2, C_3$$

$$C_4$$

If somebody did not immediately see how we reached this result, we might summarize our reasoning by exaggerating the impact of the various bits of support in categorical form. This would yield a deductive argument:

S_{d1}: He could have fallen asleep.
S_{d2}: He couldn't have died at the wheel.
S_{d3}: He wouldn't have crashed on purpose.
S_{d4}: There was nothing wrong with the steering or brakes.
S_{d5}: These are the only possibilities.

C: He fell asleep at the wheel.

The more complicated the reasoning, the more valuable such a structural sketch will be. You might try this out on some of the more complicated forms of Chapter 7.

We must nevertheless bear in mind that our substantive reasoning about what's going on in the world is never categorical like this. Our skill in judging what supports what in such cases requires us to actually examine the substantive differences among serious rivals and generate a ranking. Even when only one rival remains serious, that fact is made clear by the failure of a search for actual competition. So categorical support, which sweepingly dismisses whole ranges of the possibility balloon, is useful only after the serious work of looking through the live possibilities and evaluating their virtues and liabilities is done.

This is much like the point we made about two-answer IQs in Chapter 4. IQs with two answers (C and not C) were sometimes useful *after* we had done the hard work of comparing the best rivals we could think of, as a way of simply registering the fact that we had found no serious competition for C. And, it turns out, many standard examples of deductive arguments have this characteristic too.

S_1 All men are mortal.
S_2 Socrates is a man.

C Socrates is mortal.

For this argument, it is hard to think of an IQ other than "Is Socrates Mortal?" This is another reason deductive arguments are better at representing the structure of our reasoning than its substance.

TESTS AND CRITERIA

The standard characterization of a deductive argument is that it is an argument in which you would contradict yourself if you accept all the support and still deny the conclusion. This is the criterion an argument must meet to be deductive. Sometimes this feature of an argument will be obvious, as it is in the Socrates argument above. If I agree that all men are mortal, and that Socrates is a man, and at the same time deny that Socrates is mortal, I contradict myself. That is, I deny in the second part of what I say something I have already asserted in the first part. This is just a particularly helpful way to express a semantic guarantee: if the support in a deductive argument is true, that semantically guarantees its conclusion is true, on pain of contradiction.

If the semantic guarantee is not obvious, as it is in the Socrates argument, there are various tricks and devices you might use to make it so. These are studied in courses on formal or deductive logic and are beyond the scope of our interest in this text. Because the value of a deductive argument in everyday, practical reasoning is almost exclusively *structural*, its deductiveness will be obvious when it is helpful at all.

We will nevertheless find it useful to look at the way our analytical apparatus allows us to articulate the distinction between deductive arguments and others, and to comment directly on some misunderstandings that sometimes haunt this distinction. First let us give a name to the others: we will call arguments that do not meet the contradiction criterion *inductive arguments*. The word "inductive" is used in a number of different ways in the literature on argument, but this is a typical use. On this terminology all arguments are either deductive or inductive, and no argument is both. If an argument meets the contradiction criterion, it is deductive; if it fails, it is inductive. Of course, if it is unclear, then so is the status of the argument as inductive or deductive.

Although we can say little in general about how to show that a deductive argument meets the contradiction test for deduction, we may use the vocabulary of this chapter to show that an inductive argument does *not* pass this test. That is, we may use our analytical apparatus both to discover that an argument is inductive (not deductive), and to explain why when required. An argument fails the contradiction test if you can deny its conclusion without contradicting its support. In other words, the denial (falsehood) of an inductive argument's conclusion does *not* conflict semantically with its support. This fact about an argument may be articulated using our familiar notion of rival conclusions. Recall that C's rivals are all *incompatible* with C: if one of them is true, C is then automatically false. So an easy way to show that we may deny C without contradicting the support is to show that one of C's rivals is consistent with that support. And this means that in our balloon of possibilities, at least one segment other than C has not been semantically eliminated by the support. This is illustrated by the unshaded C_{r2} in Figure A.3. Such a rival is called a "counterexample": an example that "counters" the claim that the argument is deductive.

Sometimes counterexamples also are obvious. The original version of the truck-crash argument schematized like this.

> S_1: A truck drove straight off the road into a barrier.
> S_2: Tire marks revealed no attempt to brake or steer before impact.
>
> ---
>
> C: The driver fell asleep at the wheel.

Here a number of counterexamples are obvious. The support given is obviously compatible with the driver's dying before impact rather than merely falling asleep. It is also compatible with a suicide attempt and with generally malfunctioning controls. So the balloon for this argument will look like Figure A.1, with lots of unshaded areas besides its conclusion. The argument is plainly inductive (i.e., not deductive), and these counterexamples articulate that fact. They explain *what the*

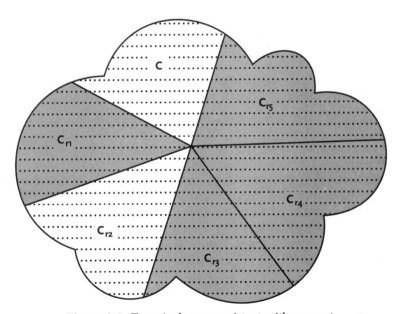

Figure A.3. Two rivals are consistent with support.

argument lacks that it must have to be deductive, namely, conflict between the support and *all* of C's rivals.

Often enough, however, it will not be obvious that a rival is a counterexample, that is, it will not be clear whether it semantically conflicts with the support. In such a case we can sometimes *show* that it is a counterexample. We can *demonstrate* its compatibility with the support, by telling a story. This exploits our narrative skill to make clear how a certain rival could be true without giving up anything in the support. We have already seen this device in action in the Kennedy assassination example. Let us try it on a slightly different argument arising from that case.

S_1: One of four suspects shot President Kennedy
S_2: Oswald is one of the suspects
S_3: The other three were not in Dallas on the day of the shooting.

C_1 Oswald shot President Kennedy

This argument is inductive, and we have indicated this by adopting the usual convention of separating support from conclusion with a double line instead of a single one. If its inductiveness is not obvious, or if it is and we wished simply to explain why, we could do so by showing that some rival conclusion is a counterexample.

Let us choose rival C_3 (suspect number 3) as the counterexample, just because it may at first not be obviously consistent with the support. (We may at first think that the fact that C_3 was not in Dallas rules him out absolutely.) To make it obvious that C_3 is a counterexample, we could simply retell the story we told before, showing how C_3 might be true along with everything else above the line. The story, recall, goes something like this: suspect 3 set up a rifle in the Dallas book depository, aimed it at a certain spot on the presidential parade route, and left town. When the President's car reached the targeted spot, he fired the rifle by remote control from New York, inflicting the fatal wounds described in the autopsy report. This shows that suspect 3 could have done it consistently with everything in the support. So C_3 is a counterexample; and that shows the argument to be inductive.

RELATIVE STRENGTH

Note that showing an argument to be inductive does *not* show that it is a bad or weak argument. How strong an argument is has nothing in particular to do with its form (whether it is inductive or deductive). The strongest arguments you will ever encounter will be inductive: they are the strong arguments we've used for illustration in this text, for instance. On the other hand, we can manufacture bad deductive arguments endlessly. Consider the following:

S_1 All pet frogs are named Oscar.
S_2 I have a pet frog.

C My frog is named Oscar.

This argument is perfectly deductive, yet it is a lousy argument. That is, it provides practically no support for its conclusion because its deductiveness depends on a crazy bit of support, namely S_1. Deductive arguments typically depend on great generality for their deductiveness (to semantically eliminate all rivals), and only occasionally will such great generality provide reasonable support for a conclusion. In arguments, as in everything: garbage in, garbage out.

Misunderstanding this can damage our reasoning. For we can easily turn a good argument into a bad one by trying to "improve" its form—trying to "improve" an inductive argument by converting it into a deductive one. For the generality we must add to do so almost invariably degrades the argument in practical circumstances. Consider this diagnostic argument that appears twice in exercises:

S_1: Driving along, my car sputters to a stop.
S_2: The fuel gauge reads "empty."
$$=====================================\text{d}$$
C: I'm out of gas.

This is a reasonably good argument. Without anything further, no rivals are very serious and certainly none is better. If we try to "make" this argument deductive, however, say by adding a minimal generalization ruling out the not-very-serious rivals, we actually weaken it:

S_1: Driving along, my car sputters to a stop.
S_2: The fuel gauge reads "empty."
S_3: Whenever a car sputters to a stop and the fuel gauge reads empty, it is out of gas.

C: I'm out of gas.

Exactly what to say about S_3 here is complicated in a way we can't go into. It is enough to note that this very general claim takes us far beyond anything we might know, and beyond anything we would have to know to reason about this diagnosis. If we make our evaluation dependent on S_3, it suddenly becomes very shaky: surely other possibilities crop up now and then. All it would take is one to make the generalization false; and then the argument would provide *no support at all* for C. For a deductive argument says something about the truth of its conclusion *only* if all the support is true.

Such attempts to "strengthen" inductive arguments are usually misbegotten in this way. When reasons are strong, that strength—very great strength—may easily be represented inductively. For instance, I once walked to the board in a classroom and tapped it lightly with a piece of chalk. A white dot appeared just where I tapped the board. From this we may derive the following argument:

S_1 I tapped the board with a piece of chalk.
S_2 A white spot appeared just where I tapped.

C The chalk made the mark when I touched the board.

This is a very strong argument—about as strong as you will every find in practical circumstances. But it is also obviously inductive, since the support does not semantically eliminate all sorts of weird possibilities. For instance it does not rule out the possibility that the chalk had a hard spot at the end, preventing it from leaving a mark, and the board spontaneously produced the white dot coincidentally with the tap. So the rival C_n: "The white spot came from inside the board" is a counterexample.

This of course is not at all plausible; but to demonstrate inductiveness a counterexample need not be plausible, just consistent with the support. On the other hand, the strength of the argument *is* connected to our having to reach for such an implausible counterexample. For this counterexample is one of the rival answers to this argument's natural IQ ("What caused the spot?"). If it represents C's most plausible competition, then the argument is virtually conclusive: C has no serious rivals. Judging the strength of an argument will usually require thinking about the substantive virtues of the most serious rivals. When we represent *this* reasoning schematically, the argument will generally be inductive in form.

SUMMARY

Deductive arguments categorically summarize enough of the substantive reasoning to guarantee their conclusion's truth. This is a very useful thing to do sometimes, especially when reasoning is at all complicated. It may help us see more clearly just what we have achieved, or point out overlooked issues that need to be addressed. But we must always be wary, when we represent reasoning in this way, that we do not mislead ourselves about the force of the arguments we construct, or the source of our inferential competence. For in practical arguments we almost never categorically reject all rivals, nor is the operative IQ ever beyond revision come what may. To understand the confidence we may place in a conclusion (such as "Oswald shot Kennedy") we must always return to the substantive judgments we made in thinking the matter through, especially those that recommend the IQ and those that count against rejected rivals. We judge the security of a conclusion in that context.

The force of everyday reasoning does not derive from and cannot be found in the categorical semantics of deductive arguments. The relation is actually just the reverse. The characterizations that make an argument deductive are themselves valuable in this function only to the extent that they offer just the right oversimplification of the substantive reasoning, categorically misrepresenting what went on in just the right way. The categorical support of a deductive argument is valuable just to the extent that it allows us to see clearly the pattern in a cluster of noncategorical judgments made in contexts flattering our competence. If that pattern is already clear, we have no need for the oversimplification.

GLOSSARY OF IMPORTANT TERMS

Argument: An argument is one or more statements offered in support of another statement. The statement being supported is conventionally called the *conclusion* of the argument.

Bare-bones paraphrase: A bare-bones paraphrase is the shortest summary of a passage that adequately captures its substance. (Compare *Headline*)

Causal connection: Two correlates (A/B) are causally connected if their occurrence together is not a *coincidence*. So the causal connection between two correlates is whatever explains why their correlation is not mere chance.

Causal influence: See *Direction of causal influence*

Chance rival: A chance rival is any story that explains a correlation (A/B) as a mere coincidence. It says that A and B are not connected in a way that can explain why they occurred together. (See also *Causal connection*)

Charity: See *Principle of charity*

Common cause: A common cause is a kind of (rival) explanation of a correlation (A/B). A common cause rival explains that the two correlates are *causally connected* to each other, but indirectly. A direct connection would have A causing B (A → B) or vice versa (B → A). A common cause is some third factor (C) that causes A and causes B, but independently of each other.

Compatible: Two statements are compatible if they do not contradict each other, that is, if they can both be true.

Competence step (testimony argument): The competence step is the second part of a testimony argument when it is cast in standard, two-step diagnostic form. This part concerns the speaker's competence to judge the matter in question (whether the speaker is a reliable judge of the matter or has access to relevant data, for instance).

Compound argument: An argument is compound if a conclusion of one part is offered as support in another. In other words, a compound argument is an argument with tributaries. [See also *Tributary (argument)*]

Conclusion: The conclusion is the statement in an argument for which the other statements are offered as support.

Conclusion flag: See *Indirectness flag*

Correlation: Two things (A and B) form a correlation if they occur together in such a way as to suggest a causal connection between them. A correlation may be a single occurrence of A and B, but it may also be a sequence in which A and B occur together regularly. In either case the correlation is abbreviated A/B. Correlations are trace data for diagnostic arguments in which the rival conclusions include various possible causal connections between the correlates.

Diagnostic (argument): Diagnostic arguments are arguments in which the rival conclusions explain some of the support. The support thus explained (by one, several, or all of the rivals) is *trace data*. Such arguments will have for an implicit question something like "What's going on?" or "What happened?" or "How come THIS happened?" or "What was that?" An argument may, of course, have an implicit question of this kind but no trace data. Such arguments may be thought of as potential or borderline diagnostic arguments.

Direction of causal influence: Different directions of causal influence are different ways in which correlates (A/B) may be causally connected. The occurrence of A may explain B (A → B), or vice versa (B → A), or some third factor may explain them independently (common cause). These are the three directions of causal influence.

Explanation (rival): Rival explanations are simply the rival conclusions of a diagnostic argument. Diagnostic conclusions answer implicit questions such as "What was that?" or "How come this happened?" and hence must explain what happened or why. They are essentially stories designed to make the traces intelligible.

Explanatory hurdle: An explanatory hurdle is an item of trace data in a diagnostic argument that is difficult for a particular rival to explain (hurdles are always hurdles *for* a particular conclusion). A single bit of data may be a hurdle for more than one rival, of course.

Flag term: A flag term is a word or phrase that characteristically indicates one of our distinct kinds of secondary point (one kind of dependent subordination). Various subordination flags are listed and described in Chapter 2. (See also *Reasoning flag*)

Headline: A headline is a first attempt to capture the main point of a passage in a few words. This will usually not be a complete sentence and will resemble the headline that might appear above the piece were it to appear in a newspaper.

Hurdle: See *Explanatory hurdle*

Implicit question: An argument's motivation may be captured in a question that it is being used to answer. We call this the argument's *implicit question* because it is usually unstated and only implicit in the surrounding context. The argument's conclusion is the answer it offers to this question. *Rival conclusions* are other (different, incompatible) answers to the same question.

Incompatible: Two statements are incompatible if they contradict each other, that is, if it is inconceivable that they both are true. An argument's rival conclusions must be incompatible with each other. (See also *Mutually exclusive*)

Indirectness: One common indicator of reasoning is that we know one thing *indirectly* through another. When we know (can tell) that A is true only as a result of knowing that B is true, we are *inferring* A from B; alternatively, B is our reason to think A.

Indirectness flag: Certain words tip us off that we know one thing only indirectly *through* another, that is, we infer the second from the first. These are indirectness flags. Basic indirectness flags are words such as *must, may, probably,* and *doubtless;* they locate the conclusion of an argument (It must be raining, because the sidewalk's wet). Certain "mental" terms form another class of indirectness flags: words such as *thinks, believes, speculates,* and *surmises* often simply mean *concludes* and hence also locate the conclusion of *somebody's* argument (He thinks it's raining, because the sidewalk's wet).

Infer: To infer is to conclude, to draw a conclusion from some evidence; so, to infer is to offer an argument. If I infer A from B, I have constructed an argument with A as its conclusion and B as its support.

Inference: In most contexts *inference* is simply another word for argument. (See also *Argument* and *Infer*)

Link flag: A link flag is a word such as *so, hence,* or *therefore* that comes between the support and conclusion of an argument, when it is written out in exposition. A link flag indicates that the support of an argument has just been given and the conclusion is about to be stated.

Main point: The main point (MP) in a passage is its most important information, the main thing the author is trying to say. In a short piece, everything else will be there in the service of the MP: dependent on the main point for its role in the passage. In a bare-bones paraphrase, the MP is stated first.

Modus operandi: This Latin phrase literally means manner of operating; so when we talk of a causal factor's modus operandi we are referring to how that factor normally works, and hence what sort of traces it might leave. Information about a causal factor's modus operandi may be *relevant* to an argument by helping or hurting that factor's ability to explain available traces.

Mutually exclusive: Two statements are mutually exclusive if they are incompatible, if they cannot conceivably both be true (literally: the truth of one excludes the truth of the other). An argument's rival conclusions are mutually exclusive: only one can be true.

Natural rivals: A conclusion's natural rivals spell out its *contrast* in the context. They will be the one the argument's author is clearly rejecting in choosing the conclusion offered. The conclusion together with its natural rivals represent the list from which the argument's support is being asked to choose.

Non-trace data: "Non-trace data" is the name we give to all items of support in a diagnostic argument that are not trace data; that is, they are not there to be explained, better or worse, by the rivals. Such information gains *relevance* (affects the serious rivals) by pointing out what needs explaining, or by providing explanatory resources (i.e., by helping or hurting rivals in their attempt to explain trace data).

Overlap (of conclusions): In proposing possible conclusions (IQ answers) for an argument, you may write down two that are not mutually exclusive, that is, two that might *both* be true. We say these conclusions "overlap" because the wedges representing them in the possibility balloon would overlap. Overlapping conclusions cannot be *rival* conclusions, that is, they cannot both be on the same list of rivals.

Padding: Padding is the metaphor for everything in a passage omitted from a bare-bones paraphrase of it—everything but main and secondary points. This will include introductory stage setting, other useful background, helpful explanations and definitions of terms, restatements of the main and secondary points, as well as digressions and pure irrelevancies.

Paraphrase: (*verb*) To paraphrase a passage is to say the same thing in different words.
(*noun*) A paraphrase (of a passage) is another passage that says the same thing in different words. Different paraphrases of a passage will differ in length and emphasis depending on the purpose of the paraphrase. (See also *Bare-bones paraphrase*)

Plausibility ranking: A plausibility ranking is the list of a diagnostic argument's rival conclusions in an order determined by how easily they explain the argument's trace data, given its non-trace data. (See also *Ranking*)

Population: A population is a mass or group of things from which we wish to make an inference based on a sample selected from it.

Principle of charity: The principle of charity is the requirement that you make the most plausible sense of a passage in your summary of it (which includes your schematic summary of an argument it contains). This is called "charity" because a sensible paraphrase is often just a sympathetic one, and being sympathetic may require effort and generosity. We may have to go out of our way to view things from an author's point of view, when it is a view we do not share and may not even like.

Priority (of substance in a passage or paraphrase): Priority refers to the relative importance of the various items of substance in a passage. One function of a bare-bones paraphrase is to display this priority, that is, to show which items are of first importance (MP) and which are subordinate (SPs).

Ranking (of serious rivals): The ranking of serious rivals is simply a list of them in order of how good they are as answers to the argument's IQ: better ones are first and lesser ones are lower in the ranking.

Reasoning flag: A reasoning flag is a word or phrase indicating that an argument is being given, and, sometimes, what part of the argument is coming up. Words that indicate structural parts of arguments are called *structure flags,* because they tell you where you are in the argument at the time. (See also *Structure flag*)

Relevant (relevance): Information is relevant to an argument—that is, belongs in the support—if it has a detectable impact on the serious rivals. Explaining the relevance of information consists in describing its impact on the serious rivals.

Rival conclusion (a rival): A rival conclusion is an answer to an argument's implicit question that is different from and incompatible with the original one.

Rival conclusions (the rivals): An argument's rival conclusions are all the different, mutually exclusive answers to its implicit question that we wish to consider.

Sample: A sample is a relatively small selection of items from a group or mass (the population), which we may try to use to diagnose properties of that group.

Schematize (an argument): To schematize an argument you first list its supporting statements (paraphrased succinctly), then draw a line, and then write the conclusion (again stated economically) at the bottom, under the line.

Secondary point: A secondary point (SP) is information in a passage that needs to be mentioned in its bare-bones paraphrase, but is subordinate to (less important than) another point in the passage we call the *main point* (MP). In a complicated passage, an SP may be directly subordinate to a more important SP instead of the MP.

Serious rivals: An argument's serious rival conclusions are the ones reasonably included in the ranking that determines the relevance of support. Serious rivals normally include all of the argument's *natural rivals,* and perhaps others the author has overlooked. Crucially, to be serious, a rival would have to have a level of detail sensitive to the argument's support.

Sincerity step: When a *testimony argument* is put in two-step diagnostic form, the first step is called "the sincerity step" because it concerns whether the speaker believes what she says. The second part of a standard two-step argument is possible only if the first part concludes that the speaker was sincere in what she said.

Structure flag: A structure flag (or inference-structure flag) is a word or phrase that indicates where you are in an argument when it is written out in prose.

They come in three kinds: (a) *support flags*, such as "because" and "since," tell you that the support is about to be stated; (b) *link flags*, such as "so" and "therefore," come between support and conclusion; and (c) *conclusion flags* (or *indirectness flags*), such as "must," "probably," and "seem," tell you the conclusion is about to be given. When schematizing arguments, the location of the statements in the schematization takes the place of all structure flags; so structure flags should not appear in a schematic argument. (For more see *Indirectness flag*)

Support: See *Supporting statements*

Support flag: A support flag is a word or phrase that indicates the support in an argument is about to be stated. Examples are "because," "since," and "after all."

Supporting statements: The supporting statements of an argument are those statements that the argument offers as recommending its conclusion as the answer to its implicit question.

Testimony: Testimony is any statement used as trace data in a diagnostic argument about whether the statement itself is true. We try to explain why the statement was made by appeal to its truth or, alternatively, to ulterior motivation or incompetence.

Trace data: Trace data are the items of support in a diagnostic argument that the rival conclusions explain, or must explain, or try to explain. They are in some way or other *objects of explanation* by the rival conclusions. Trace data affect plausibility, and hence gain relevance, by being either easy or hard for various rivals to explain.

Tributary (argument): If the conclusion of one argument is offered as support in another, then the first argument is called a tributary of the second. A tributary argument provides support for a statement that, in turn, is offered in support of a further conclusion. Both arguments together form a compound argument.

Undermining rival: In a compound argument, the conclusion of a tributary argument functions as support in the main argument. That tributary will, of course, have rival conclusions, and some of those will, if substituted for the original conclusion, hurt the conclusion of the main argument (make the support weaker). These are called undermining rivals.

Underwriting rival: In a compound argument, the conclusion of a tributary argument functions as support in the main argument. That tributary will, of course, have rival conclusions, and some of those will, if substituted for the original conclusion, support the conclusion of the main argument just as well as (or even better than) the original. These are called underwriting rivals.

INDEX